THE ANCHOR BIBLE is a fresh approach to the world's greatest classic. Its object is to make the Bible accessible to the modern reader; its method is to arrive at the meaning of biblical literature through exact translation and extended exposition, and to reconstruct the ancient setting of the biblical story, as well as the circumstances of its transcription and the characteristics of its transcribers.

THE ANCHOR BIBLE is a project of international and interfaith scope: Protestant, Catholic, and Jewish scholars from many countries contribute individual volumes. The project is not sponsored by any ecclesiastical organization and is not intended to reflect any particular theological doctrine. Prepared under our joint supervision, THE ANCHOR BIBLE is an effort to make available all the significant historical and linguistic knowledge which bears on the interpretation of the biblical record.

THE ANCHOR BIBLE is aimed at the general reader with no special formal training in biblical studies; yet, it is written with the most exacting standards of scholarship, reflecting the highest technical accomplishment.

This project marks the beginning of a new era of co-operation among scholars in biblical research, thus forming a common body of knowledge to be shared by all.

William Foxwell Albright
David Noel Freedman
GENERAL EDITORS

THE ANCHOR BIBLE

GENESIS

INTRODUCTION, TRANSLATION, AND NOTES

BY

E. A. SPEISER

THE ANCHOR BIBLE
DOUBLEDAY
NEW YORK   LONDON   TORONTO   SYDNEY   AUCKLAND

THE ANCHOR BIBLE
Published by Doubleday, a division of
Bantam Doubleday Dell Publishing Group, Inc.,
666 Fifth Avenue, New York, New York 10103

THE ANCHOR BIBLE, DOUBLEDAY and the portrayal of an anchor
with the letters AB are trademarks of Doubleday, a division of
Bantam Doubleday Dell Publishing Group, Inc.

PREFACE

As the foundation for a rising biblical structure, Genesis began to be quoted and discussed even before the Old Testament as a whole had been completed; and it remains to this day one of the most intensively cultivated books of the Bible. Volumes have been written about single chapters, and monographs about individual verses and clauses. Any comprehensive treatment of Genesis must, therefore, be highly selective, if it is to be at all suitable for the layman while not ignoring the scholar's needs. Accordingly, the present work devotes only as much space to matters that have already been covered elsewhere as is necessary for clarity and continuity; a minimal bibliography of the excellent works that are available is provided in the section on Genesis Exegesis (pp. LX f.). By the same token, greater emphasis has been placed on questions about which there is as yet no definite consensus, and on points that remain to be adduced.

The introductory essay deals with critical approaches to the Bible, the nature of the biblical process, the contents of Genesis, and the general problem of Bible translations. The body of the work has been divided into sections that follow the exact order of the original, but do not necessarily coincide with the customary division into chapters. Each section contains a translation of the text, some textual notes, more extensive annotations, and an appended commentary. The NOTES are addressed to specific verses, whereas the COMMENT is directed to the given section as a whole and is concerned with literary treatment, cultural and historical background, and problems of authorship. The study follows in the main the moderate school of documentary criticism, and the presumed sources have been indicated at the head of each section. But the sequence of the original remains undisturbed, so that any reader may ignore, if he so chooses, both the markers and the reasons behind them.

The transliteration of Hebrew terms has had to be simplified for typographic reasons. With personal and place names, the traditional spelling has been retained in order to avoid confusion. Further details are given in the brief Note on Transliteration.

In the preparation of this book I enjoyed the privilege of thoughtful editorial advice from Professor William F. Albright and Professor David Noel Freedman, who contributed many comments and suggestions, without ever interfering with the writer's freedom of decision.

It is a genuine pleasure to express thanks to the editorial and technical staffs of *Anchor Books* for their understanding and resoluteness in facing many novel problems that this volume posed, especially since some of the decisions could not but set precedents for the rest of the Series. For this author the "front office" proved to be a friendly refuge.

The full extent of my indebtedness to the ever expanding literature on Genesis could not possibly be acknowledged within the space available to me; the general tenor of the present work was an added bar to a detailed literary apparatus. The credits that are explicitly indicated are but a small measure of what I owe to uncounted predecessors.

There is, however, one acknowledgment that I have left for the end in order to give it special prominence. The present translation bears frequent and close resemblance to the version of Genesis that is contained in the new rendition of the Torah brought out by the Jewish Publication Society of America (1962). The resemblance is not coincidental. As a member of the small committee that had been entrusted with the task, I had a share in that translation from the start. And because of my preoccupation with Genesis, that particular share was correspondingly larger. My own results were available to the committee and were frequently utilized by it. In turn, I had the benefit of my colleagues' contributions. But I owe more to my fellow members than the sundry words or phrases which I elected to appropriate. The over-all gain from constant written interchanges of views, and daylong sessions every other week over a period of years, cannot be reduced to statistics. I take this opportunity, therefore, to express my deep appreciation to my six co-workers on the committee and to the Society which originated the project.

E.A.S.

August 25, 1962

CONTENTS

JOSEPH AND HIS BROTHERS

PRINCIPAL ABBREVIATIONS

1. PUBLICATIONS

AASOR	Annual of the American Schools of Oriental Research
AfO	Archiv für Orientforschung
AJA	American Journal of Archaeology
AJSL	American Journal of Semitic Languages and Literatures
ANET	Ancient Near Eastern Texts Relating to the Old Testament, ed. J. B. Pritchard, 2d ed., 1955
AOS	American Oriental Society: Monograph Series
ARM	Archives royales de Mari
BA	The Biblical Archaeologist
BASOR	Bulletin of the American Schools of Oriental Research
CAD	The Assyrian Dictionary, Oriental Institute of the University of Chicago
CBQ	Catholic Biblical Quarterly
CT	Cuneiform Texts . . . in the British Museum
Dr.	S. R. Driver, *The Book of Genesis.* 12th ed., 1926, reprinted 1954
Ehrl.	A. B. Ehrlich, *Randglossen zur hebräischen Bibel,* Vol. I, 1908
Gen. Apocr.	N. Avigad and Y. Yadin, *Genesis Apocryphon,* 1956
Gilg.	The Epic of Gilgamesh
HSS	Harvard Semitic Series
JAOS	Journal of the American Oriental Society
JBL	Journal of Biblical Literature and Exegesis
JCS	Journal of Cuneiform Studies
JEN	Joint Expedition . . . at Nuzi
JNES	Journal of Near Eastern Studies
JQR	Jewish Quarterly Review
KB	L. Koehler and W. Baumgartner, *Lexicon in Veteris Testamenti Libros,* 1953
MSL	Materialen zum sumerischen Lexikon
OTS	Oudtestamentische Studiën

SB   R. de Vaux, *La Genèse*, in La Sainte Bible, 1953
Vergote   J. Vergote, *Joseph en Egypte*, 1959
von Rad   G. von Rad, *Das erste Buch Mose*, 1953
VT   Vetus Testamentum
ZA   Zeitschrift für Assyriologie und ver wandte Gebiete

2. VERSIONS

AT   An American Translation: The Old Testament, 1931
JPS   Jewish Publication Society of America: The Holy Scrip-
            tures, 1917; new ed., The Torah, 1962
KJ   The Authorized Version of 1611, or the King James Bible
LXX   The Septuagint
MT   Masoretic Text
RSV   The Revised Standard Version, 1952
Sam.   The Samaritan Pentateuch
Syr.   Syriac version, the Peshitta
TJ   Targum of (Pseudo-) Jonathan
TO   Targum Onkelos
TP   Palestinian Targum
Vulg.   The Vulgate

3. OTHER ABBREVIATIONS

Akk.   Akkadian.
Ar.   Arabic.
Aram.   Aramaic.
Eg.   Egyptian.
Gr.   Greek.
Heb.   Hebrew.
OT.   Old Testament.
Sem.   Semitic.
Sum.   Sumerian.
"T."   Predocumentary traditions.
cons.   The unvocalized, consonantal form.
cun.   Cuneiform.
hend.   Hendiadys.
trad.   Tradition(al).

NOTE ON TRANSLITERATION

The reduced Hebrew vowel known as *Shewa* is represented by an ᵉ. No distinction is made between the Hebrew stops *b, g, d, k, p, t* and their respective postvocalic variants, which are technically spirants. While it would be simple enough to alternate *b:v, p:f,* and *t:th,* there are no convenient counterparts for *g, d, k.* More important, the spirant forms are relatively late developments within Hebrew itself, certainly later than the time of Moses; hence a more precise transcription might do justice to the dialect of Ezra, but would be an anachronism in the speech of Abraham.

The vowel sign *Segol* is transcribed as *e* and *Sere* appears as *ẹ*. Each carries the macron wherever the quantity is demonstrably long.

There is no satisfactory solution to the problem of adequate transcription of personal and place names in the Old Testament. Our *Isaac* is a far cry indeed from Heb. *Yiṣḥāq.* But as long as we retain some of the traditional spellings, we might as well keep all the others rather than cause still greater confusion. There is the added complication of foreign names in the Bible. Traditional Haran represents Heb. *Ḥārān,* which in turn reflects cun. *Ḥarrānu(m).* In such instances it seemed advisable to write *Har(r)an,* except in actual translation. For analogous reasons, the name *Asshur* has been retained in direct quotations from the text, but the simplified *Ashur* has been substituted in the NOTES and COMMENTS.

INTRODUCTION

THE BIBLICAL PROCESS

WHAT'S IN A NAME?

Genesis is a book of beginnings in more ways than one. It starts out with an account of the origin of the world, hence the name, introduced in the third century B.C. by the Greek translators to whom we owe the so-called Septuagint (or LXX) version. Then, too, Genesis is the initial portion in the first of the three major subdivisions of the Old Testament, and hence the first book of the Bible. But Genesis also marks a beginning from within as well as from without. It is not only the starting point of a long series; beyond and above that, Genesis is our main clue to the process which ultimately produced the Bible, as a witness to one of the profoundest experiences of mankind. The Book of Genesis is thus, among other things, the key to the genesis of the Bible as a whole.

In the Hebrew, Genesis bears the (normalized) title of *Bereshit*. By sheer coincidence, this name, too, applies to beginnings. The first word in the original happens to be *berēšīt;* and it was standard practice in the ancient Near East to call a literary work by its initial word or phrase. For this reason, for example, the Hebrew name for the third book of the Bible is *Wayyiqrā*, although all it means is "and he called"; the more pertinent term Leviticus has been adapted from the Greek version. Similarly, the Babylonians called their own Genesis, or Poem of Creation, *Enūma eliš* "when on high," and the Epic of Gilgamesh *Ša nagba īmuru* "he who experienced all." It was mere chance that placed the word *berēšīt* "in the beginning (of)" at the head of the Hebrew Bible. As it turned out, it is indeed an appropriate opening for the Scriptures as a unit.

When it comes, however, to the collective section which the Book of Genesis heads, it is the secondary term *Pentateuch,* from the Greek for "five-volume (work)," that deals with an external detail, whereas the Hebrew title *Torah* addresses itself to the content. Yet for all its basic merit, the latter designation was to be, paradoxically enough, a hindrance rather than a help. For one thing, this name (technically *tōrā*) is invariably translated "Law," thus giving the impression that the work is devoted in the main to legal questions. And for another thing—and far more important—the title *Torah* was to lead very early to a mistaken notion about the authorship of the first five books of the Bible. The matter is of sufficient consequence to warrant a brief statement about some of the details involved.

It goes without saying that the Pentateuch does not confine itself to laws either in the secular or in the ritual sense of the term. The outstanding feature of this part of the Bible is its narrative content, and it is surely to its narrative material that the Pentateuch owes its universal appeal. The mechanical equation of Torah with law does little justice to the work as a whole; nor is it an accurate rendering of the name itself.

What is fundamental, however, is the fact that nowhere does the Pentateuch speak of itself as the Torah. To be sure, the noun is often used throughout the work; but it has numerous connotations, none of which can be mistaken in the context for the title of the work as a whole. The nominal form *tōrā* is based on a verbal stem signifying "to teach, guide," and the like; cf. Exod xxiv 12 "and the Torah and the Instruction which I have written for their guidance." The derived noun can carry a variety of meanings, which range in the Pentateuch from specific rituals for so-called leprosy (Lev xiii 59; xiv 2, 54, 57) to general precepts and sayings (as in the Exod passage just cited). In Deut xxxi 26 *tōrā* refers to the long hortatory poem that follows. And when the same term is applied to the Deity, its connotation is broadened to embrace a cherished way of life (Exod xiii 9). Thus the stereotyped rendering "law" can be justified neither as an exclusive juridical term nor as a distinctive literary title.

There are occasions when the Pentateuch speaks explicitly of a written *tōrā*. Yet this usage does not of itself narrow down the meaning of the word; each occurrence has to be judged from its own context. In Exod xxiv 12, for example, the document in question turns out to be the Covenant Code (xxi–xxiii), which was inscribed on two stone tablets (cf. Exod xxxiv 1) and was thus automatically restricted in length. In Deut xxix 20, on the other hand, the writing concerned specified sanctions in an entirely different covenant; and Deut xvii 18 and xxx 10 allude only to general instructions and provisions. The only Pentateuchal passage that refers comprehensively to a written *tōrā* is Deut xxxi 9, where we are told that "Moses wrote down this *tōrā*." This particular statement points either to the portions of Deuteronomy that precede, as most moderns assume, or to the poetic sections which follow, as some scholars believe. In neither event could the Pentateuch as a whole be at issue. Yet it is this one ambiguous reference, more than anything else, that eventually gave rise to the doctrine of the Mosaic authorship of the entire Pentateuch.

It is not too hazardous to trace back the steps whereby such a belief attained the status of an article of faith. The Pentateuch was the first portion of the Old Testament to be accepted as sacred and canonical. This meant that the work was ultimately attributed to God and emerged thus as a body of teachings comprising the one Torah above all others. Thus it was this particular connotation of the term that would occur most readily to the reverent mind. In these circumstances, there could be but one answer to the question as to what it was that Deut xxxi 9 records as having been written by Moses: the Torah proper, of course, that is, the Pentateuch.

The devout students of the Bible who first perpetrated this semantic anachronism—in all innocence—could scarcely have anticipated the ironic consequences of their interpretation. So far from enhancing the status of the Torah, the axiom that Moses was the author of the Pentateuch has often tended to lower the work in the opinion of independent investigators. For objective inquiry must soon turn up various flaws in a Pentateuch that is attributed to a single author, whereas no such defects would be found in the composite product of various writers. The five books as we now have them contain many instances of duplication, inconsistencies, and mutual contradictions, aside from manifest stylistic disparities. In a collective work, however, all such irregularities become self-explanatory, once they are viewed as the natural result of various traditions and different individual styles and approaches. Nor does uncommitted analysis undermine the credibility of the Bible, as has often been feared and alleged. The ensuing pages should make it abundantly clear that in Genesis in particular, and in other biblical books by extension, independent study helps to increase one's respect for the received material beyond the fondest expectations of the confirmed traditionalists.

To sum up, Torah is not strictly law, and there is no warrant in the Pentateuch itself—as opposed to sundry echoes in later books of the Bible—for ascribing the authorship of the work as a whole to Moses. Modern biblical criticism has established this last point on the strength of massive internal evidence. The grounds on which that conclusion was arrived at will now be sketched in barest outline, before we probe further into the Book of Genesis for clues to biblical origins.

BIBLICAL CRITICISM

The first signs of a critical approach to the Old Testament reach back as far as the second century of the present era.[1] In the Middle Ages, the distinguished Jewish commentator Abraham Ibn Ezra (twelfth century) managed to suggest his acute awareness of the problems implicit in the assumption of the Mosaic authorship of the Torah. Although he couched his hints on the subject in guarded language, Ibn Ezra was able, nevertheless, to intimate to his readers that certain passages in the Pentateuch must be post-Mosaic, and that the statement in Deut xxxi 9 cannot be construed in the traditional manner.[2]

It required, however, the penetrating probing of Spinoza (seventeenth century) to launch "higher" biblical criticism—that is, internal analysis as opposed to textual or "lower" criticism—on a truly productive course. Steady subsequent progress left little doubt that instead of being the work of Moses in its entirety, the Pentateuch was actually the product of a number of writers. In time, the critics were able to draw a sharp line between Deuteronomy (D), on the one hand, and the four preceding books—or the Tetrateuch—on the other. Within the Tetrateuch, a cleavage soon became apparent between the so-called Priestly source (P) and the outright narrative material; and the narratives, in turn, eventually

[1] See R. H. Pfeiffer, *Introduction to the Old Testament*, 1941, p. 43.
[2] Cf. I. Husik, JAOS 55 (1935), Suppl., 31 f.

yielded two main strands which came to be designated as *J* (Yahwist) and *E* (Elohist).

To state the findings in this summary fashion is to give only such end results as have won qualified acceptance from the great majority of biblical scholars. Actually, the course of Pentateuchal criticism has been exceedingly tortuous, and an immense amount of effort and ingenuity has been invested in the process over a period of some two hundred years. The fact is that the Pentateuch, with a long history of growth, compilation, and transmission behind it, cannot be dissected at this late date with the confident assurance that all its original components have been duly isolated and identified. We are as yet a long way from being able to attribute every passage to its ultimate source. The critics of the nineteenth century may have felt that they had all the answers that really mattered. But fresh discoveries and more refined tools of analysis have made twentieth-century students at once more sophisticated and less sanguine. This is perhaps one reason why some scholars would today substitute for the "documentary" solution with its emphasis on individual authors, the so-called "form" hypothesis, which lays stress on literary categories rooted in separate oral traditions. Nor have attempts been lacking to experiment with still other modes of approach.

The all-important point, at any rate, the conclusion which virtually all modern scholars are willing to accept, is that the Pentateuch was in reality a composite work, the product of many hands and periods. This is the fundamental fact behind all recent progress in biblical study, as it has opened the way to a solution of many difficulties that would otherwise remain unresolved. The result is a working hypothesis which should be judged solely by how well it does its work. The documentary theory in its classic form (*J, E, P,* and *D,* as well as *R* for redactors or compilers) has proved to be a master key which has opened many doors; and with each such success, the hypothesis has become that much less tentative. The thing to bear in mind, however, is that, where so many unknowns are involved, a reasonable margin of error must be allowed. While the vast majority of passages can now be ascribed to one source or another with considerable confidence, there is still a residue that leaves room for doubt. Some of these marginal portions may have to be reallocated after further study; others are now so fused that they may never be pried apart; and still others appear never to have had any connection with the relatively tangible sources before us, and may have been independent from the start.

The Book of Genesis provides clearer examples of each of the types just mentioned than is the case with any other part of the Pentateuch.

THE DOCUMENTARY SOURCES OF GENESIS

As the earliest book in the Pentateuch, Genesis is not affected by the special problems that beset the Book of Deuteronomy: it shows no trace whatever of source *D*. But precisely because it deals with the earliest stage, Genesis also raises certain questions that do not arise elsewhere in the Pentateuch. One such question concerns the content of the first eleven chapters, which involve the prehistory of the world as contrasted with the story of the patriarchs of Israel. If the latter story was based on native traditions, what material did the writers utilize for the former? Or how is one to account for the unique character of a chapter like xiv? But before these and similar problems can be isolated and examined, it is necessary to indicate what it is that makes a given passage fall under one of three relatively well-defined rubrics, namely, *J, E,* and *P.* In other words, the first task that faces a modern student of Genesis is literary analysis of the book. It is the one area in which documentary criticism has scored truly impressive gains.

A significant milestone in the literary criticism of Genesis was the observation published in 1753 by the French physician Jean Astruc that, when referring to the Deity, some narratives in this book use the personal name Yahweh ("Jehovah"), while other and apparently parallel accounts employ Elohim, the generic Hebrew term for "divine being." It would thus seem to follow, Astruc argued, that Genesis was made up of two originally independent sources.

As matters turned out, the criterion which Astruc introduced was useful principally as a point of departure. There are many sections in Genesis, and elsewhere in the Pentateuch, which do not mention the Deity. Nor is the mere occurrence of Elohim decisive in itself, since the term can also be used, by virtue of its general connotation, not only for alien gods and idols but also in the broader sense of our "Providence, Heaven, Fate," and is actually so attested in the

J source, among others. The evidence remains significant, but one-sided: Elohim could well appear in any document, as is only natural in the circumstances; on the other hand, Yahweh is in Genesis the exclusive companion of *J* (barring occasional lapses in the composite text under the influence of an adjacent passage from another source). To be established, therefore, as homogeneous, a document has to exhibit a combination of distinctive features harmoniously blended; it should stand out by reason of its style, content, and concepts, not to mention the cumulative evidence of the vocabulary. When enough such details have been found to configurate time and again, they yield a pattern that is typical of a particular source; at times they may even afford a glimpse of the person behind the written record.

It was on just such collective evidence that the term Elohim, when not paralleled by Yahweh, proved to signal not merely one source, as had been originally assumed, but two otherwise unrelated documents. These came to be labeled respectively as *E* (from the initial letter) and *P* (for Priestly document); the use of Yahweh, on the other hand, remained the hallmark, as was just indicated, of a single author, whose anonymity continues inviolate under the code-letter *J* (from "Jehovah"). The Pentateuch itself lends a measure of credibility to this argument from divine appellations. For Exod vi 3 (*P*) states explicitly, and Exod iii 14 (*E*) indirectly, that the personal name Yahweh was not employed prior to the time of Moses; what this adds up to is that the use of the name Yahweh had been unfamiliar to these two sources until then.[3] This lends circumstantial confirmation to the hypothesis of the composite character of the Pentateuch, since the frequent occurrence of the term Yahweh in Genesis would otherwise involve the two passages in Exodus in outright contradiction of inescapable facts. On various other counts, however, *E* sides with *J*, and the two diverge jointly from *P*. All such divergencies are self-explanatory in material that is related but has come down through more than one channel; they could not be explained away in a composition by a single author.

What are, then, the salient characteristics of the several components of Genesis which modern scholarship has been able to isolate? The scope of the present work permits only a sketchy treat-

[3] See COMMENT on Sec. 5.

ternal evidence—in favor of dating various portions of *P* to pre-Exilic times, and in some cases to the premonarchic period. This evidence embraces even certain passages in the ritualistic Book of Leviticus. A careful new look at the *P* material in Genesis is therefore definitely in order.

When we re-examine, for instance, the genealogies of the patriarchs before the Flood (cf. v), the style and approach are unmistakably *P*'s, yet the material has to be derived from ancient data. The same applies to the Edomite lists in ch. xxxvi. Just so—to stray for a moment from the Book of Genesis—the census records in Num xxvi, although again set down by *P,* deal with names and situations (notably the distribution of land holdings by lot) that go back of necessity to the early stages of the Israelite settlement in Canaan. At the same time, there are other passages throughout the Tetrateuch that are undoubtedly much later. All this testifies to a wide coverage by *P,* ranging over many centuries. The conclusion that is usually drawn from these facts is that we have before us a series of separate *P* documents, as many as ten according to some critics. But such solutions fail to account for the prevailing uniformity in outlook and phraseology which typifies *P* as a whole.

The assumption that commends itself in these circumstances is that *P* was not an individual, or even a group of like-minded contemporaries, but a school with an unbroken history reaching back to early Israelite times, and continuing until the Exile and beyond. Such a hypothesis would readily account for the essential homogeneity of the underlying traditions, while not precluding such occasional discrepancies as, for example, in the lists of Esau's wives (cf. xxvi 34, xxviii 9, xxxvi 2–3); such differences might easily develop over a long period of time even among custodians of the same type of traditions. The generally stilted language and the circumscribed range of interests would be similarly explained. The end result would thus represent the carefully nurtured product of a standing scholastic committee, so to speak, in regular session since the inchoate beginnings of ethnic consciousness in Israel.

(2) J

Aside from the exclusive use of the name Yahweh, there are in Genesis few words or phrases that immediately betray the hand of *J;* and even such exceptions are all but confined to the Joseph ternal evidence—in favor of dating various portions of *P* to pre-Exilic times, and in some cases to the premonarchic period. This evidence embraces even certain passages in the ritualistic Book of Leviticus. A careful new look at the *P* material in Genesis is therefore definitely in order.

When we re-examine, for instance, the genealogies of the patriarchs before the Flood (cf. v), the style and approach are unmistakably *P*'s, yet the material has to be derived from ancient data. The same applies to the Edomite lists in ch. xxxvi. Just so—to stray for a moment from the Book of Genesis—the census records in Num xxvi, although again set down by *P*, deal with names and situations (notably the distribution of land holdings by lot) that go back of necessity to the early stages of the Israelite settlement in Canaan. At the same time, there are other passages throughout the Tetrateuch that are undoubtedly much later. All this testifies to a wide coverage by *P*, ranging over many centuries. The conclusion that is usually drawn from these facts is that we have before us a series of separate *P* documents, as many as ten according to some critics. But such solutions fail to account for the prevailing uniformity in outlook and phraseology which typifies *P* as a whole.

The assumption that commends itself in these circumstances is that *P* was not an individual, or even a group of like-minded contemporaries, but a school with an unbroken history reaching back to early Israelite times, and continuing until the Exile and beyond. Such a hypothesis would readily account for the essential homogeneity of the underlying traditions, while not precluding such occasional discrepancies as, for example, in the lists of Esau's wives (cf. xxvi 34, xxviii 9, xxxvi 2–3); such differences might easily develop over a long period of time even among custodians of the same type of traditions. The generally stilted language and the circumscribed range of interests would be similarly explained. The end result would thus represent the carefully nurtured product of a standing scholastic committee, so to speak, in regular session since the inchoate beginnings of ethnic consciousness in Israel.

(2) *J*

Aside from the exclusive use of the name Yahweh, there are in Genesis few words or phrases that immediately betray the hand of *J;* and even such exceptions are all but confined to the Joseph birth of his oldest son (e.g., ch. v), the names of other members of the family, and the like.

P's constant preoccupation with the purity of the line through which God's purpose has been implemented leads at times to motivations that are not found in the parallel versions. For instance, according to *J* (xxvii 41–45), Rebekah told Jacob to flee to her relatives in Haran in order to escape the revenge of his brother Esau. In *P*, however (xxvii 46–xxviii 7), the motive for Jacob's journey to Central Mesopotamia is no more than matrimonial, the search for an acceptable wife: his mother had become disenchanted with Esau's "Hittite" wives, and was determined that her younger son marry within her own class and clan. More surprising still, Rebekah's scheme has the full approval of Isaac, who gives Jacob his warm blessing, although a few verses earlier—this time, however, from another source (xxvii 33–37: *J*)—Isaac was driven to rage and despair by the discovery of Jacob's hoax. *P* is either unaware of, or unmoved by, the drama and pathos of that encounter. What matters to him solely is that Jacob's line be maintained through a worthy wife.

The horizons of *P* are thus sharply circumscribed. His world is not only directed from heaven but heaven-centered. To be sure, it is natural enough that in the majestic account of Creation man's role should be a passive one. Yet elsewhere, too, mortals are conceded little if any individuality. For one aberrant moment Abraham lapses into incredulity when told by God that he is to have a son by Sarah (xvii 17); but his record of absolute obedience is never marred again. The eventful history of Joseph's stay in Egypt is reduced in this source to an exchange of amenities between Jacob and Pharaoh (xlvii 7–10) and the symbolic adoption by Jacob of his grandsons Manasseh and Ephraim (xlviii 3–7). Where history is predetermined in every detail, personalities recede into the background, while the formal relations between God and society become the central theme. There are thus ample grounds—theological as well as ritualistic—for ascribing the *P* document to priestly inspiration.

The question of *P*'s date is difficult to solve for several reasons. Numerous sections, especially in the other books of the Tetrateuch, have long been relegated by the critics to a relatively late age, after the Babylonian Exile in many instances. Of late, however, there has been a growing sentiment—backed by a substantial amount of in-ment, yet this should suffice to illustrate both the method and the results. The comments that follow pertain primarily to *P, J,* and *E* —to adopt the order in which these sources first turn up in Genesis. The survey will conclude with a few remarks on passages that are as yet difficult to classify, as well as on the process whereby the separate strands were combined into the unit that now constitutes the received Book of Genesis.

(1) P

To begin with vocabulary, *P* employs for the Deity, in addition to Elohim (Gen i 1 ff.), the term *El Shaddai* (cf. xvii 1), which is usually translated "God Almighty."[4] The sole occurrence of Yahweh in xvii 1 is apparently a scribal error induced by the similar opening sentence in xviii 1 (*J*), which also records a theophany.

The term that is most typical of this source—one might call it *P*'s signature—is *tōlᵉdōt,* etymologically "begettings," and hence also genealogy, line, family tree (v 1, vi 9, x 1, etc.), and by extension also story, history; in the latter sense we find this term used in ii 4, and perhaps also in xxxvii 2. Another telltale expression is "to be fertile and increase" (e.g., i 22, 28, viii 17, ix 1, 7). For the homeland of the partriarchs, *P* uses *Paddan-aram* (cf. xxv 20, xxviii 2, 5, 6, 7); *J* calls the same region *Aram-naharaim* (xxiv 10).

For other words and phrases to which *P* is partial, cf. the long list given by Dr. (pp. vii–ix). This vocabulary is not limited, of course, to Genesis, but carries over to other books; it is absent, however, from the parallel documents. Consistency and cumulative impact enhance the total effect of this type of evidence.

P's frequent recourse to the term *tōlᵉdōt* (the traditional rendering "generations" is now obsolete in the sense required) is a correct reflection of the writer's abiding interest in genealogical detail. There must be no break in the chain of transmission through which God's dispensation has been handed down; hence it is essential to trace the pertinent line all the way back to Creation. For related reasons, *P* is forever concerned with such other statistics as the total life span of the given individual, the age of a father at the

---

[4] The exact meaning, however, remains uncertain.

J source, among others. The evidence remains significant, but one-sided: Elohim could well appear in any document, as is only natural in the circumstances; on the other hand, Yahweh is in Genesis the exclusive companion of *J* (barring occasional lapses in the composite text under the influence of an adjacent passage from another source). To be established, therefore, as homogeneous, a document has to exhibit a combination of distinctive features harmoniously blended; it should stand out by reason of its style, content, and concepts, not to mention the cumulative evidence of the vocabulary. When enough such details have been found to configurate time and again, they yield a pattern that is typical of a particular source; at times they may even afford a glimpse of the person behind the written record.

It was on just such collective evidence that the term Elohim, when not paralleled by Yahweh, proved to signal not merely one source, as had been originally assumed, but two otherwise unrelated documents. These came to be labeled respectively as *E* (from the initial letter) and *P* (for Priestly document); the use of Yahweh, on the other hand, remained the hallmark, as was just indicated, of a single author, whose anonymity continues inviolate under the code-letter *J* (from "Jehovah"). The Pentateuch itself lends a measure of credibility to this argument from divine appellations. For Exod vi 3 (*P*) states explicitly, and Exod iii 14 (*E*) indirectly, that the personal name Yahweh was not employed prior to the time of Moses; what this adds up to is that the use of the name Yahweh had been unfamiliar to these two sources until then.[8] This lends circumstantial confirmation to the hypothesis of the composite character of the Pentateuch, since the frequent occurrence of the term Yahweh in Genesis would otherwise involve the two passages in Exodus in outright contradiction of inescapable facts. On various other counts, however, *E* sides with *J*, and the two diverge jointly from *P*. All such divergencies are self-explanatory in material that is related but has come down through more than one channel; they could not be explained away in a composition by a single author.

What are, then, the salient characteristics of the several components of Genesis which modern scholarship has been able to isolate? The scope of the present work permits only a sketchy treat-

[8] See COMMENT on Sec. 5.

story. There we find the name *Israel* as against *Jacob* in the other sources; the geographic term *Goshen;* and the noun *'amtaḥat* "bag" for the otherwise familiar *śaq* "sack." On further analysis, the relative scarcity of such shibboleths is not at all surprising. For *J* is not given to stereotypes, in vocabulary or in other respects. What is truly distinctive about this writer is his incisive style, his economy and boldness of presentation, his insight into human nature, and the recognition that a higher order and purpose may lie behind seemingly incomprehensible human events. There is common agreement that we have in *J*—or alternatively, in those portions of Genesis that critical consensus attributes to *J*—not only the most gifted biblical writer, but one of the greatest figures in world literature. If so much in the Book of Genesis remains vivid and memorable to this day, the reason is not merely the content of the tales but, in large measure as well, the matchless way in which *J* has told them.

J's style is clear and direct, but its simplicity is that of consummate art. An unobtrusive word or phrase may become the means for the unfolding of character, a single sentence can evoke a whole picture. The leading actors on *J*'s stage are realized in depth. It is their inner life that invariably attracts the author's attention; yet he manages to show it in action, not through description; and the reader is thus made a participant in the unfolding drama. *J*'s world, moreover, in diametric contrast to *P*'s, is emphatically earth-centered. And his earth is peopled with actors so natural and candid that even their relations with Yahweh are reduced to human scale, so that God himself becomes anthropomorphic.

In the Eden prelude, Adam is portrayed as a lost and confused child, and is so treated by Yahweh (iii 9). Later, in the more sophisticated context of the patriarchal age, human problems gain in complexity. The acute domestic crisis that is brought on by Sarah's childlessness (xvi 1–6) leaves Abraham irresolute in the clash between two headstrong women. Later on (xviii 12), Sarah is impulsive enough to respond with derision to the promise of a child in her waning years. Nor does *J* hesitate to betray his own feelings concerning Jacob's behavior toward Isaac and Esau. Every detail in that intensely stirring account (xxvii 1–40) shows that, although the outcome favored Jacob, the author's personal sympathies lay with the victims of the ruse.

J's art rises perhaps to greatest heights in the handling of the real climax of the Joseph story (xliv) The author is not concerned in the main with the poetic justice of Joseph's triumph over his brothers, or his magnanimity in forgiving his onetime tormentors. J's interest reaches much deeper His protagonist himself had been plagued by gnawing doubts which he could not banish from his mind: Had his brothers been morally regenerated in the intervening years? To find the answer, Joseph was forced to resort to an elaborate test, using his full brother Benjamin to bait the trap When Judah offered himself as substitute for the innocent boy, Joseph had his answer at long last; the brothers had indeed reformed. After the unbearable suspense of this episode, the actual self-disclosure could be no more than an anticlimax

In J's world view, then, man is not a mere marionette, as he is in P's scheme of things. Rather, the individual is allowed considerable freedom of action, and it is this margin of independence that brings out both his strengths and his weaknesses At the same time, however, no mortal should make the mistake of assuming that he is in complete control of his destiny. Ultimately, man is but the unwary and unwitting tool in the hands of the Supreme Power who charts the course of the universe. On rare occasions, to be sure, an Abraham may be favored with a fleeting glimpse of the divine purpose. But no one may grasp the complete design, which remains reasonable and just no matter who the chosen agent may be at any given point. This would seem to be the meaning of the unintentional blessing of Jacob by Isaac (xxvii), or the eerie encounter at Penuel (xxxii 23–33) There are more things in heaven and on earth, J appears to be implying, than a mortal's wisdom can encompass. In this regard man remains irredeemably human.

It goes without saying that a work with such distinctive personal traits could stem only from an individual author. When it comes, however, to J's date, the indications are not nearly so compelling The prevailing tendency today is to put J in the tenth century B.C., or about a hundred years earlier than was estimated a few decades ago. If the current view is right, J may well have been a contemporary of that other outstanding writer to whom we are indebted for the court history of David and his immediate successors (especially II Sam ix–xx). Did the two, then, know each other personally? And if so, what were the relations between them? It would require a latter-day J to do justice to a situation of this sort.

It may be of interest to note, in passing, how J and P compare in the few instances in which their accounts coincide. Their respective approaches to the story of Joseph have already been touched upon. Otherwise, significant contacts between these two sources are confined to Primeval History (i–xi), and there primarily to the subjects of Creation and the Flood. In the former instance, each version has come down to us as a unit, and basically intact: *P*'s in i 1–ii 4a, and *J*'s in ii 4b–25. The far-reaching differences between these parallel accounts are immediately apparent (cf. the remarks on Secs. 1 and 2) and require no special comment at this time.

The account of the Flood, on the other hand, was fused in the compilation to such a degree that it can no longer be reassembled without surgery at a number of joints. Nevertheless, there is enough internal evidence for a dependable analysis, aside from the external factors of vocabulary and style. Thus the reason for the Flood is cited twice, first by *J* in vi 5–8, and next by *P* in vi 13: in the one instance, Yahweh "regrets" that man has not been able to master his evil impulses, and there is "sorrow in his heart"; in the other formulation, the world is lawless and hence it must be destroyed. In regard to other details, the differences between the two versions are more specific. *J* records that the ark accommodated seven pairs of each kind of bird and clean animal, but only one pair of the unclean species (vii 2–3), whereas *P* knows only of a single pair in each case (vi 19–20, vii 15). There are differences also in connection with the chronology of the Flood. According to *J* (vii 4, 12, viii 6, 10, 12), the rains came down forty days and nights, and the waters disappeared after three times seven days, the whole deluge lasting thus sixty-one days. But in *P*, whose calendar is typically detailed down to the exact day of the given month, the waters held their crest for one hundred and fifty days (vii 24), and they remained on the earth one year and eleven days (vii 11, viii 14). Both the repetitions and the contradictions are accounted for automatically, here as elsewhere, by the presence of two independent sources, each consistent within itself though at variance with the other.

One may ask why such obvious discrepancies were not eliminated by the redactor or compiler to whom we owe the composite version. The answer is significant, for it has a decisive bearing, as we shall see later on, on the whole issue of editorial authority in piecing the pertinent documents together. It is, in sum, this: such authority was exercised, if at all, only with utmost hesitancy and with the barest minimum of substantive change.

(3) E

In form and subject matter E is closely related to J. Together, these two sources stand apart from P with its dominant genealogical content. Hence, J and E are at times difficult, and in some instances impossible, to distinguish from each other. Closer probing, however, has by and large yielded ample evidence for isolating the two documents. The major question on which many critics are as yet undecided concerns the extent of the interrelationship between J and E. Did either of these sources actually utilize the other, and if so, which had that advantage?[5] Assuming that E came later—which is the prevailing view among the critics—was it E's purpose from the start merely to supplement and correct J, or was the former's work entirely independent? It is the view of the present study that the extant material from E represents indeed a separate source. But before this position can be defended, it will be necessary to summarize the reasons for assuming the presence of an E source in the first place.

When the terms Yahweh and Elohim occur in otherwise duplicate narratives, and the presence of P is ruled out on other grounds, there is the inherent probability that the passages with Elohim point to a source that is neither J nor P. In ch. xxviii, for example, two accounts about Jacob's first stay at Bethel have been blended into a single sequence. One of these components used Elohim (vss. 12, 17), while the other spoke of Yahweh (13, 16). Taken as a unit, the fused version is repetitious; but separately, each strand represents an independent tradition. Similarly, in xxx 25–43, where Jacob's wealth is attributed to his own shrewdness, the patriarch himself refers to Yahweh by name (30). In the next account, however, the success of the scheme is credited to the advice of an angel who conveyed it to Jacob in a dream; and there, significantly enough, the Deity is called Elohim (xxxi 9, 11). The same pattern, in which Elohim or an angel occurs together with dreams, is found in other passages where J must be ruled out as the author (notably in xx).

In general, E lacks the directness of J where man's relations with God are concerned. This is precisely why E is led to interpose angels or dreams, or both, the Deity being regarded, it would seem, as too

---

[5] Although it is customary to date J about a century earlier than E, the evidence is so ambiguous that the reverse is by no means ruled out; cf. M. Noth, *Überlieferungsgeschichte des Pentateuch*, 2d ed., 1948, p. 40, n. 143.

remote for direct personal intervention. The center of *E*'s world has not shifted all the way to heaven, as it has with *P;* neither is it earth-bound, on the other hand, as in the case of *J.*

E has a tendency, furthermore, to justify and explain rather than let actions speak for themselves. This is true, for example, of the account about Laban's flocks, as has just been indicated; and the same applies to the encounter between Abraham and Abimelech of Gerar (xx). One thus misses in *E* the bold touches that make *J*'s narratives so vivid and memorable. Yet it would be grossly unjust to *E* to dismiss him as a wordy and pedestrian writer. Abraham's ordeal with Isaac (xxii), an account in which *E* certainly had a prominent hand, is a masterpiece of poignant presentation. Basically, however, *E* is interested in events, whereas *J* is concerned with people. This alone would be enough to make a great deal of difference.

Yet all such departures from *J* might conceivably be found in an annotator, and do not of themselves presuppose the existence of a separate and independent *E* source. There are, however, other points that cannot be explained away in like manner. Among the strongest of these are two sets of parallel narratives which differ much too sharply for direct mutual correlation. These examples merit a close look.

The first illustration is based on three intimately related accounts, each of which revolves about the wife-sister motif. The pertinent passages are: (a) xii 10–20; (b) xx 1–18; and (c) xxvi 6–11. The sociological significance of these narratives is discussed in Section 15; it does not concern us here. The documentary bearing of the same cycle is reviewed in Section 25; but since the results are germane to the present context, they may be restated here in brief.

In each instance, a patriarch on a visit to a foreign land pretends to his royal host that his wife is only a sister; he feels that his wife's beauty might be a danger to the husband but not to a brother. In case (a) the encounter involves Abraham and Sarah with the ruler of Egypt; in (b) the same couple confronts Abimelech of Gerar; and in (c) Abimelech is similarly embarrassed by Isaac and Rebekah. In a work by a single author, these three cases taken together would present serious contradictions: Abraham learned nothing from his narrow escape in Egypt, and so tried the same ruse in Gerar; and Abimelech, for his part, was so little sobered by his perilous experience with the first couple as to fall into the identical trap with the next pair. What immediately rules out any such construction is the fact that Abimelech is depicted as both upright and wise; and after his first attempt misfired, Abraham would not be likely to make the same mistake again. No competent writer would be guilty of such glaring faults in characterization.

But we can dispense with idle conjectures. Incidents (a) and (c) prove to stem from *J*, while (b) goes back to *E*—on independent grounds in each case. And as soon as the two documents come into view, the duplications and contradictions vanish. *J* knew only of two wife-sister episodes (a and c), one featuring Abraham-Sarah-Pharaoh-Egypt, and the other Isaac-Rebekah-Abimelech-Gerar. Each case involves different principals, centers, and generations. In *E*, however, these two episodes became telescoped, thus juxtaposing Abraham and Sarah with Abimelech (b). But while each source remains thus self-consistent, two original incidents branched out into three.

What matters for the moment is whether such a result could have been obtained if *E* was merely an annotator of *J*. Since *E*'s Abimelech was neither a fool nor a knave, but a man of whom the author clearly approves (cf. xx), *E* could scarcely have depicted the king as he does had he been familiar with *J*'s narrative in xxvi. The only reasonable conclusion, therefore, that one can draw from the joint evidence of all three narratives is that *J* and *E* worked independently. Each was acquainted with the wife-sister motif in patriarchal times, but the respective details had come down through different channels and developed some variations in the course of transmission.

Another compelling argument for viewing *E* as a separate rather than supplementary source is provided by the Joseph story. In spite of its surface unity, this celebrated narrative yields, on closer scrutiny, two parallel strands which are similar in general outline, yet markedly different in detail. Since a comprehensive discussion is included with the running commentary on the pertinent sections, a schematic recapitulation should suffice at this point.

In the *J* version, which continues to employ the divine name Yahweh, Judah persuades his brothers not to kill Joseph but sell him instead to Ishmaelites, who dispose of him in Egypt to an unnamed official. Joseph's new master soon promotes him to the position of chief retainer. But the lies of the master's faithless wife land the boy in jail. Still, Joseph's fortunes again take a favorable turn. . . . When the brothers are on their way home from their first mission to

Egypt with a supply of precious grain, they open their bags at a
night stop and are shocked to find in them the full payment for
their purchases. . . . In due time, Judah prevails on his father to
let Benjamin accompany them on a second journey to Egypt, in re-
luctant compliance with the Vizier's demand. . . . Judah finally
convinces Joseph that the brothers have really reformed. Joseph invites Israel—the name Jacob does not appear in this version—to
settle with his family in the district of Goshen.

E's parallel account is marked on the surface by the consistent
use of Elohim and Jacob, as opposed to Yahweh and Israel. But
the differences from J reach much deeper. Joseph is saved from his
brothers by Reuben, not Judah; the boy is left in an empty cistern,
where he is picked up, unbeknown to the brothers, by Midianites; it
is they, and not the Ishmaelites, who sell the boy as a slave to an
Egyptian by the name of Potiphar. In that lowly position, Joseph
must serve, not supervise, the prisoners in his owner's charge. . . .
The brothers open their sacks (not bags) upon their return home
(not at an encampment along the way). Reuben (not Judah) gives
Jacob (not Israel) his personal guarantee of Benjamin's safe return.
. . . Pharaoh (not Joseph) invites Jacob and his family to settle in
Egypt (not just Goshen).

From all this, it must be obvious to the unbiased observer that
the Joseph story is composed of two once separate, though now intertwined, accounts. One of these is manifestly J's, not only because
of the divine name that it employs but also because of a full complement of other characteristics that have elsewhere been established
for that source. On analogous grounds, the parallel version aligns itself with E. But E is here much more than a mere annotator or an
occasional dissenter; the dichotomy is much too sharp and sustained
for such an interpretation. E tells a complete and essentially independent story of his own. If he knew J's version at all, there was
very little in it with which he agreed. In all probability, however, he
was unaware of the other tradition, with its consistently different pattern of details.

For reasons that are no longer apparent, E has no part in the
Primeval History (i–xi), unlike both J and P; his work may never
have reached back beyond Abraham. Actually, the first substantial
contribution by E is not in evidence until ch. xx, well past the middle
of the Abraham story. It is improbable that this is where it started
originally. An initial section could well have been lost in the early

stages of transmission. In any event, fragmentary preservation of a
work cannot be used as an argument about its original scope.

There are no reliable data for fixing the time of the composition
of the *E* source with any degree of accuracy. Most critics are inclined to place the date of *E* in the ninth century or later, that is, at
least a century after the date assigned to *J*. It should be stressed
in passing, however, that *E*, no less than *J*, had access to authentic
ancient traditions, a fact that is particularly noticeable in the accounts about Jacob (cf. COMMENT on xxxi) and Joseph (see xli).

(4) *The Residue*

After the three major sources of Genesis have thus reclaimed all
the material that could be plausibly assigned to them, there still remain some sections which have proved elusive for one reason or
another. Two of these (30 and 61) were actually considered by the
older critics as more or less safely identified, but recent students
have shown greater diffidence in the matter. A third passage (Sec.
17), however, has always been viewed as unique and without documentary mates anywhere in the Bible. A brief analysis of these passages will be followed by a few remarks about the work of *R*—the
redactor or redactors of Genesis.

Section 30: The Machpelah Purchase (xxiii). Certain portions of
this chapter appear to support the older view, which regards the
narrative as part of the *P* document. It is a fact, moreover, that *P*
refers to the Machpelah purchase more than once (xxv 9 f., xlix
29 f., l 13). Nevertheless, the opposing argument would seem to
carry greater weight. The account is not only narrative in character,
but is marked by a mock solemnity that is totally out of keeping
with the sober manner of *P*. Besides, the repeated description of
members of the local council as "those who came in at the gate of
his city" (vss. 10, 18) has its idiomatic complement in the phrase
"those who went out by the gate of his city," which occurs twice in
xxxiv (24), a narrative that stems from *J*.[6] What this adds up to is
that *P* appropriated and introduced the account in question because
legal title to the Machpelah burial ground was considered vital by
that source; but the secular overtones of the story did not suffer

---

[6] On these two idioms, see BASOR 144 (1956), 20 ff.

in the process. The end result was an excerpt from *J* in a framework by *P,* a unique blend in itself.

Section 61: The Testament of Jacob (xlix 1–27). On the mislead-ing title "Blessing of Jacob," see COMMENT *ad loc.* This poem has long been recognized as a product of the premonarchic age in Israel. The composition must, therefore, antedate all of the standard documentary sources. To be sure, verse 18 contains a reference to Yahweh, but the brief sentence in which it occurs is evidently a marginal gloss. It is possible, however, that *J* incorporated this collection of poetic sayings about the tribal eponyms as a fitting pronouncement by Jacob on the eve of his death. In any event, the authorship of the poem has to be designated by an "X," at least for the time being.

Section 17: Invasion from the East. Abraham and Melchizedek (xiv). This unique account has always been a question mark to the critics. The entire chapter departs from the rest of the book in subject matter, approach, emphasis, and phraseology. There are indications that the narrative may have been assimilated from a non-Israelite source. Chief among these is the fact that Abraham is referred to as "the Hebrew" (vs. 13); elsewhere, this description is applied to Israelites only by outsiders or for the benefit of outsiders; the Israelites did not use it among themselves in an ethnic sense. Incidentally, if the extra-Israelite origin of this chapter is borne out, the above reference would go a long way toward establishing the historicity of "Abram"—for an outside source would hardly be likely to make a central figure of a foreign legendary hero. Significantly enough, the Abram in question is depicted as a powerful chieftain, a far cry from the patriarch whom we know from the other traditions.

R. Lastly, a brief comment is appropriate about the joining of the several sources under review into one integrated unit. For this particular process critics are generally inclined to posit two separate redactional (*R*) stages: an earlier one, which combined *J* and *E* (*R*JE); and a much later stage, which linked the work of *P* with the already merged *JE.* The alternative would be to assume a single redactorial effort, after *P* had taken definite shape.

We know that the original material from *J* and *E* was left substantially intact through the simple device of treating parallel accounts as consecutive—most notably so in the Joseph story. This holds true, to a considerable degree, even of shorter passages, for example, xxviii 10–22, where separate verses, rather than paragraphs or chapters, were excerpted and rearranged to yield a consecutive text. No concerted attempt was made to harmonize the composite version by ridding it of duplications and inconsistencies, although at least some of these flaws (e.g., xxxvii 28) must have been apparent at the outset. It follows that the person or persons responsible for the compilation pursued a policy of minimal editorial interference. And this, in turn, could only mean that the respective constituents had already attained a measure of canonical status. Thus *R*'s approach was one of utmost reverence for his—or their—sources. Indeed, if it had not been so, modern recovery of the underlying documents would have been seriously impeded, if not blocked altogether.

Because of such self-effacement, however, there is next to nothing that can be gathered today about the personal traits of *R*. Even the number of stages involved in the process remains in doubt, as was indicated above. The only thing that may safely be assumed is that, if *R*JE was distinct from *R*P, both had nevertheless the same conception of their function and authority.

If the entire compilation, however, was accomplished in a single stage, one further deduction should be permitted. It was suggested earlier that *P* was, in all probability, not an individual writer but an established school in continuous operation over a long period of time. In that case, the activities of such an academy would not have come to a halt after the document that we now attribute to *P* had assumed definitive shape. The next logical step would be precisely the kind of compilation that was ultimately to result in the present Book of Genesis, and the rest of the Pentateuch; and in that case, *R* would be a late product of the *P* school. It should be borne in mind that, analogously, the eventual adoption of a formal Pentateuchal canon, followed by the canons of the Prophets and the Writings, and finally by the complete canon of the Hebrew Bible, was a work based on prolonged study and deliberation of a continuous synod. To be sure, there is no concrete evidence to support such a conjecture; but neither are there any compelling arguments against it.

It should be emphasized, in passing, that the position advocated in the foregoing survey is based throughout on the methods of documentary criticism, and that it reduces the latest results to bare fundamentals. Departures from older views are relatively few and slight. Some readers might raise the valid objection that the whole presentation is oversimplified; the alternative, however, would have been a detailed technical analysis far beyond the scope of the present work. On the other hand, failure to mention other conjectured sources and sub-sources should be ascribed not to lack of space but to lack of confidence in the reasoning behind such proposals. The fragmentation and proliferation of documents in which some authorities have indulged appears to this writer to be a self-defeating procedure. The suitability of a working hypothesis must be judged ultimately by how well the scheme works.

If the preceding section has thus been a restatement by and large, the two sections that follow venture into territory that has been little explored so far. It is only fair to warn the reader in advance.

The Tradition behind the Documents

Disclosure of the documentary sources of the Pentateuch cannot in itself be the end of the trail; it is but a means to further and more productive ends. Literary criticism, for all its labors and accomplishments to date, cannot as yet rest on its laurels. And as it pushes ahead, past its onetime objectives, it is bound to run into other lines of inquiry which start out from extra-biblical records. The chronological level at which these investigations converge is known to biblical students as the patriarchal age. And the book that is most intimately affected is Genesis.

The foregoing analysis of the sources of Genesis could not but show that the three principal documents—*J, E,* and *P*—exhibit far-reaching agreements as well as marked disagreements. The differences affect a large body of detail. The agreements, on the other hand, pertain to the general content and the central theme of the work. Thus both *J* and *P* follow similar outlines of Primeval History; and all three sources reflect the same basic data in regard to the patriarchs: family tree, migration from Mesopotamia, settlement in Canaan, beginning of the sojourn in Egypt. The common themes continue in the subsequent books of the Pentateuch, and comprise the oppression in Egypt, the Exodus, and the wanderings in the desert. Now both these aspects of the biblical sources—their mutual agreements as well as their disagreements—prove to be important guides to further study.

Since it is evident on a number of counts that the documents before us are basically independent, in spite of the common subject

matter, it follows that all three must have drawn on the same prototype. This point has already been made for *J* and *E* by several
scholars, notably Martin Noth, who designates the assumed predecessor by the symbol *G,* abstracted from "gemeinsame Grundlage"
(common base).[7] But this symbol and the reasoning behind it run
into a serious methodological objection: the underlying term *Grundlage* implies a written source; but any such implication should be
scrupulously avoided, at least for the time being.

It is not improbable, to be sure, that some of the original data
were preserved and transmitted in written form. The very circumstance, however, that our sources exhibit so many mutual disagreements should be enough to suggest that the channels through
which much of the material has been handed down were fluid rather
than fixed. And this implies, in turn, a predominantly oral mode of
transmission; a written source would scarcely have given rise to so
large a number of deviations. It should be remembered, moreover,
that *J* and *E* were not the only recipients of traditional material. *P,*
too, was a prominent beneficiary; note, for example, his accounts of
Creation and the Flood. The one thing that can be safely inferred at
this stage is that none of the standard sources of Genesis—and the
same applies also to the rest of the Tetrateuch—improvised its subject matter as it went along. In these circumstances, the logical symbol for our hypothetical antecedent would seem to be "T,"[8] for Tradition, a term that has the added advantage of enjoying international
currency.

As a bridge between the Pentateuchal sources and the past that
these documents record, "T" unblocks the path to further study. The
subject can now be viewed in truer perspective. One can understand, for example, why none of the writers who drew on "T" was
free with his subject matter—a point that was by no means self-
evident to the early critics: each author was bound by the data that
had come down to him. It is all the more remarkable, therefore, that
J and *E* were able to achieve literary masterpieces despite such
curbs.

What was it, then, that made the received material normative and
impelled gifted writers to hold their imagination in check? The an-

---

[7] Cf. Noth, *Überlieferungsgeschichte* . . . , pp. 40 ff.

[8] In quotation marks, so as to distinguish this assumed source from extant
documents designated by simple initials.

swer is not far to seek. *J,* and *E,* and *P* as well, were writing, each in his way, not stories, but history. The data were not to be tampered with because tradition had stamped them as inviolable; and they had acquired an aura of sanctity because the subject matter was not secular but spiritual history, history a writer might recount, but could not color to his own liking. The retelling, in short, was the Bible in the making.

That the unfolding story was selective rather than comprehensive is attested in the Bible itself; not just in the Pentateuch but also in other historical books. The writers remind us time and again that theirs is a special theme. The reader who may be interested in other aspects is told explicitly where he can find them: in *The Book of the Wars of Yahweh* (Num xxi 14); the *Chronicle of Solomon* (I Kings xi 41); *The Chronicles of the Kings of Israel* (I Kings xiv 19, xv 31, xvi 5); or *The Chronicles of the Kings of Judah* (I Kings xiv 29, xv 7, xxii 46). The first of these references is especially instructive, for it occurs in an archaic passage which antedates the monarchic age, and hence also any of the standard documentary sources. Its date falls, accordingly, within the period of "T." In other words, criteria for distinguishing between "biblical" and secular themes had already been evolved by that time.[9]

At this point it may be advisable to pause and take stock. A selective medium like "T" presupposes the existence of some screening canon. This is not to be confused, of course, with the final Old Testament canon, which was not brought to a close until the beginning of the present era. Yet the basic concept and the guiding criteria would have to be much the same in all such instances. Is it not hazardous, then, to assume canonical standards for pre-Davidic times, solely on the basis of the circumstantial evidence that has been cited so far? The answer is that the whole story has not yet been told. More evidence does in fact exist, but it is based on the combined yield of biblical and extra-biblical sources. The pertinent material must now be sampled.

Among the various patriarchal themes in Genesis, there are three in particular that exhibit the same blend of uncommon features: each theme appears to involve some form of deception; each has proved to be an obstinate puzzle to countless generations of students, ancient and modern; and at the same time, each was seemingly just

[9] Cf. my paper on "Three Thousand Years of Bible Study," *Centennial Review* (Michigan State University) 4 (1960), 206–22.

as much of an enigma to the biblical writers themselves. In all three cases, unexpected help has recently come from the same outside quarter.

(1) The first case in point is itself compounded of three closely related passages (xii 10–20, xx 1–18, xxvi 6–11) which have already been discussed in another connection. The joint theme here is the wife-sister motif: a patriarch's wife is introduced as his sister. The subject was recorded by both *J* (xii, xxvi) and *E* (xx), which implies prior, and presumably oral, handling by "T." At all events, there are enough differences in detail to presuppose a long period of antecedent transmission; besides, *E*'s involved explanation of the incident, and his endeavor to exonerate the persons concerned, would seem to betray an element of uncertainty, not to say embarrassment, on the part of the author.

Today, however, there can be no longer any serious doubt as to what was really at issue (see the detailed COMMENT on Sec. 15). In Hurrian society a wife enjoyed special standing and protection when the law recognized her simultaneously as her husband's sister, regardless of actual blood ties. Such cases are attested by two separate legal documents, one dealing with the marriage and the other with the woman's adoption as sister. This dual role conferred on the wife a superior position in society.

As a onetime inhabitant of Haran—an old Hurrian center—Abraham was necessarily familiar with Hurrian social practices. Hence when he and his son, on visits to foreign lands, spoke of their wives as sisters, they were apparently intent not so much on improving their own prospects as on extolling and protecting their wives. But this is not the explanation that is given in the accounts of the incidents; there the motive is definitely selfish. Of the two interpretations, one based on original and contemporary records of a society that is closely involved, and the other found in much later literary narratives, the first is obviously to be preferred. Egypt[10] and Gerar were hundreds of miles away from Haran. And by the time of *J* and *E* there had developed the further gap of hundreds of years. The import of so specialized a practice would scarcely be retained over such distances. Another explanation would be substi-

[10] The brother-sister marriages in Egypt are of an entirely different type; nor would this superficial parallel apply to Gerar. For the subject as a whole see the writer's essay "The Wife-Sister Motif in the Patriarchal Narratives," *Biblical and Other Studies*, Harvard University Press, 1963, pp. 15–28.

tuted in course of time, one more in keeping with local conditions and universal human failings.

Our main concern for the present, however, is neither with the sociological nor the moral aspects of the incidents under discussion. What we are concerned with is, first, why tradition insisted on recording these episodes; and second, why both *J* and *E* included them in their histories even though they could not be altogether clear about the meaning. The answer to the first question is tied up with the established superior status of the wife-sister. Sarah and Rebekah were vital links in the chain through which the biblical way of life was being transmitted; and the purity of the line had a bearing on the quality of the content. Thus any detail that pointed up the privileged position of the patriarchs' wives was bound to be cherished by tradition.

The second question, namely, why *J* and *E* were obliged to record these episodes, whether or not they understood their significance, goes to the heart of the matter. They had to do so, because they were not free to choose. Nothing that tradition had nurtured could be ignored by its eventual literary executors. And this is but another way of saying that the transmitted material had already acquired a measure of canonical status.

(2) The next illustration pertains to the transfer of birthright and paternal blessing from Esau to Jacob (Sec. 35 [xxvii 1–45: *J*]). Once again, the incident involves deception, this time of a singularly heartless sort. Biblical tradition itself accepted the whole episode at face value, inasmuch as it went on to explain the name Jacob as symbolic of trickery—contrary to correct etymology. And exegetes through the ages have been shaking their heads in disapproval, or taxing their ingenuity for redeeming features. The true explanation, however, lies elsewhere.

The clue is provided again by records about Hurrian society. There, birthright was not necessarily a matter of chronological priority; it could be established by the father's personal decision. Moreover, the most solemn of all testamentary dispositions were those that a man made on his deathbed. And such dispositions were introduced by the formula "I have now grown old."

In the biblical episode, Isaac's impending end is foreshadowed by a comment about his advanced age (vs. 2). The patriarch then transfers to his younger son the rights and privileges of the first-born, which it was within his discretion to do, according to the law of his father's homeland. Tradition took note of the deed, and even preserved the exact introductory formula. But the pertinent social background had become blurred in the meantime; in fact, the practice in question was eventually outlawed altogether (Deut xxi 15 ff.). In the nature of things, another motive was substituted; *J* did not find it adequate, as the tenor of his narrative plainly shows. He could not know that Jacob's preferment did not have to depend on falsehoods. Yet the author's personal feelings on the subject gave him no leave to alter the received data that tradition had shaped and sanctioned long before.

(3) Our third and last case in point revolves about Rachel's surreptitious removal of Laban's house gods (xxxi 19, 30; cf. the fuller COMMENT *ad loc.*). The narrative stems from *E,* who ordinarily takes pains to justify the actions of his principal characters. This time, however, he makes no attempt to account for Rachel's behavior, evidently because he was unable to do so. Innumerable writers since then have tried to find a solution, without coming close to the mark. The correct interpretation calls for detailed knowledge of social conditions in the patriarchal age and center. That information, however, was cut off subsequent to the migration from Mesopotamia; and it was not restored until archaeology had brought to light the necessary evidence from the pertinent sources themselves.

According to Hurrian family law—which played a prominent role in patriarchal society, as we have seen—property passed normally to male descendants. If a daughter, however, was to share in the inheritance for one reason or another, it was customary for the father to hand over his house gods to the woman's husband, as proof that the disposition was legitimate, though exceptional. In this case, Rachel had no illusions about her father's honesty (see xxxi 15 f.). By going off with Laban's images—and thus taking the law, or what she thought to be the law, into her own hands—she evidently hoped to make sure that her husband would not be done out of his rightful dividends from a marriage for which he had labored so long. Tradition remembered the deed, but not its motivation. And the writer could neither ignore tradition nor presume to edit its content.

Taken together, these three old and familiar themes acquire new significance by reason of their special bearing on the subject of biblical origins. Each is an authentic reflection of the complex social conditions to which it alludes. Since the biblical writers had no direct access to the ultimate sources, they must have obtained this material through some such medium as "T." But that intermediary was no longer able to hand over the complete story; the motivation, which could be taken for granted at the outset, had ceased to be self-evident in the course of the intervening centuries. The necessary background has to be retraced to Haran, where the patriarchal clan had lived in intimate symbiosis with Hurrian society. In other words, it was there that "T" itself must have gotten its start. The uniform evidence of the illustrations that have just been given, not to mention others that could have been cited, surely rules out the remotest possibility of coincidence.

One question still remains to be posed, a question that is basic to this entire discussion. Granted that an authentic patriarchal tradition originated in Central Mesopotamia, some time before the middle of the second millennium B.C.—what was it that gave that tradition the ability to remain virtually intact, and the appeal that was to make it canonical in due time? The answer to this question is bound up with the experience itself which gave biblical tradition its original momentum.

GENESIS OF THE BIBLICAL PROCESS

We have seen that various details of the patriarchal story in Genesis are now confirmed and elucidated by outside sources. The data have come from the very area to which the book refers, the portion of Mesopotamia which the patriarchs called their home. Since the background has thus emerged as authentic, one is prompted to ask whether the foreground, too, may not be factual on the whole. And the foreground in this instance is the dramatic content of the story.

At the start of this analysis, it was logical to begin with the biblical data and go on to outside sources. Now conditions are reversed, since the focal event, the migration that set the whole process in motion, originated in Mesopotamia—precisely where both biblical and outside testimony have led us. Accordingly, the patriarchs will now be viewed against the pertinent Mesopotamian setting; the results will then be compared with biblical statements on the subject.

Although there is as yet no firm basis for dating the patriarchal period—which must technically be put down as prehistoric until a direct synchronism with the outside world can be established—conservative estimates would anchor that age in the second quarter of the second millennium B.C. (approximately the eighteenth–sixteenth centuries). In terms of equally conservative Mesopotamian chronology, such a span would take in much of the Old Babylonian Dynasty, from Hammurabi[11] down. Now the reign of Hammurabi dovetails with that of another outstanding monarch, Shamshi-Adad I of Assyria, and it parallels an illustrious stage at Mari. All these phases are richly illuminated by a great variety of sources. For the decades that immediately followed, we now have, among other sources, the new material from the Syrian center of Alalakh. And for the transition from Old to Middle Babylonian times, there is the vivid evidence of the Nuzi records, which were composed by Hurrians who had long been exposed to Babylonian influence; and this source has recently been supplemented by texts from later levels at Alalakh.

Thanks to this manifold and extensive testimony, we now have a balanced picture of Mesopotamian conditions in the first half of the second millennium, not just in Babylonia but also in the peripheral areas to the north and west, where Amorites and Hurrians were entrenched. The over-all yield is that of a cosmopolitan, progressive, and sophisticated civilization: a common heritage of law and government, a legacy stabilized by the use of the same script and language, safeguarded social gains and facilitated international relations. Writing was ubiquitous, not only as the medium of law, administration, and business, but also as a vehicle for literary and scientific endeavors. Aside from jurisprudence, outstanding advances had been achieved in such disciplines as linguistics, mathematics, and the study of history. Architecture and the arts flourished, agriculture and animal husbandry were highly developed, and far-flung commercial enterprises added to the material prosperity. Indeed, on most of these counts, the classical lands of a thousand years later appear as yet primitive by comparison. In short, the Mesopotamia of Hammurabi and his neighbors was the most advanced land in the world—a vigorous force at home and a magnet to other countries near and far.

Yet, if the record in Genesis is to be given credence, it was at

---

[11] The correct transliteration is *Hammurapi;* but the form with *b* has been retained as the more familiar of the two.

that juncture that Abraham turned his back on his homeland and set out for a destination unfamiliar and unsung. What could have prompted him to make such a move? According to Gen xii 1, it was a call from the Deity. To be sure, tradition was bound to look upon the remote past in reverent and idealized retrospect. This is why Abraham emerges as a simple nomad devoted to pastoral ways, although a product of the urban society of Mesopotamia. Yet the same tradition, as we just saw, succeeded in preserving much of the background detail with remarkable accuracy. Moreover, the fact of migration from Mesopotamia is borne out by a mass of circumstantial evidence too vast to itemize here. Since the setting was not invented, and the migration is amply supported, the stated reason for the journey should not be dismissed offhand. And that reason, reduced to basic terms, was a spiritual one.

So far, our inquiry into the remoter reaches of biblical history has not been unduly hazardous. Every so often along the way there have been markers by which we could check our bearings. The common subject matter of the *J* and *E* narratives pointed to an underlying predocumentary stage ("T"). The essential trustworthiness of "T" was vouched for, in turn, by the evidence of cuneiform records. Finally, the starting point of the biblical process—that is, Central Mesopotamia in the age of Hammurabi—was found to be brightly illuminated by various contemporary sources.

Now, however, we can no longer count on such tangible support. The task before us is to re-enact in our minds the experience that impelled Abraham to break with his past and set out on an epic journey, thereby setting in motion a process that was to be sustained throughout the entire course of biblical history. Does such an assignment hold out much hope of worth-while results? There is clearly a limit beyond which circumstantial evidence ceases to afford reasonably safe conduct and lets one proceed only at ever-increasing risk. That limit has now been reached.

Although there is no proof so far of Abraham's historicity, many biblical historians would probably agree that if some such figure had not been recorded by the ancients, it would have to be conjectured by the moderns. But it is one thing to concede Abraham's existence, and quite another thing to attempt to read his mind at a critical juncture in his life. Nevertheless, the effort is worth making, for two reasons: first, because a great deal is at stake, namely, the genesis of the biblical process; and second, because there are still some resources available for checking such an assumption. To be sure, the controls in this case are general rather than specific. Yet the same test must fit so many different conditions that a wrong turn at any one point would show up soon enough. If the hypothesis, however, stands up throughout, if it helps to account for much that would be incomprehensible otherwise, its usefulness, if not its absolute accuracy, will have been validated.

Since the first problem before us is to establish the motive for Abraham's break with his homeland, the clues that we require have to be sought in Mesopotamia. And if the reason for the migration was spiritual, as the Bible asserts, the cause should be traceable to the society that Abraham abandoned. Or to state it differently, we start with the assumption that Abraham found the spiritual solution of Mesopotamia wanting, and that the biblical process began as a protest against that failure.

The vibrant character of Mesopotamian civilization as a whole, and particularly so during the period under discussion, has already been stressed. By the time of Hammurabi, that civilization had established itself as a dynamic force at home and abroad. Nor can there be much doubt that social progress was the overriding factor in that advance. The Mesopotamian concept of the cosmos, which barred autocracy even in heaven, also made for a regime on earth whereby the law was above the ruler and thus stood guard over the rights of the individual. In various ways, this social system was responsible for the country's balanced progress in governmental, intellectual, and scientific matters.[12] And it sustained the historic civilization of Mesopotamia—as opposed to its several prehistoric stages—throughout its long career, from its dawn at the turn of the fourth millennium to the sudden collapse some twenty-five centuries later. The age of Hammurabi was thus approximately the halfway mark along that impressive span. It was also the high-water mark in a cultural sense. Yet Abraham appears to have viewed it as a failure.

To ascribe such disenchantment to the patriarch's West Semitic antecedents would not do justice to known facts. Hammurabi himself was a member of a West Semitic dynasty, although in his case that foreign background was too remote to have made a difference.

[12] E. A. Speiser, "Some Sources of Intellectual and Social Progress in the Ancient Near East," *W. G. Leland Volume*, 1942, pp. 51–62.

But there were other Amorite rulers to the west and north of Babylonia who had not had enough time to become assimilated; yet most of them became ardent converts to the Babylonian way of life. The celebrated Shamshi-Adad I, for example, could be described as Babylon's cultural missionary to Assyria. And correspondence from outlying regions, including the district of Har(r)an itself, and even distant and powerful states like Aleppo, testifies to the eager acceptance by Amorites of the civilization of Southern Mesopotamia. Hence it would scarcely be normal for a native of Mesopotamia, whatever his ethnic origins, to look for greener pastures elsewhere.

Now it is true that Genesis portrays Abraham as a nomad of simple tastes, for whom the refinements of urban life held little charm, unlike his nephew Lot (xiii 12). Would not this attitude be reason enough for pulling up stakes and going off to a land where kindred Amorites still maintained their ancient mode of life? Perhaps so, provided that this particular image of Abraham is in true focus. Actually, however, tradition's views of the distant past became at times oversimplified in nostalgic retrospect. A more realistic picture of the patriarch is reflected in Gen xiv, precisely because that chapter departs sharply from the traditional mold. In that account, Abraham—or rather Abram, as he was then called—appears as a prosperous settler who can mobilize on short notice a sizable troop from among his own retainers and put an invading horde to rout. Clearly, therefore, there must have been more to the patriarch's migration than a vague impulse to revert to the idyllic ways of his distant ancestors. Moreover, the whole tenor of the Abraham story reflects a concern about the future rather than the past. Mesopotamia, it would seem, was not a suitable base for planning ahead.

Yet the inferred shortcomings cannot be laid to prevailing social conditions, as we have seen. The evolving Hebrew society had enough in common, in this respect, with the historic society of Mesopotamia to presuppose not only generic affiliation but also basic accord. In both instances we find the same reverence for law impersonally conceived, and the identical concept of non-autocratic government on earth. Such fundamental agreements would scarcely argue for a rejection of the Mesopotamian social system on the part of the Hebrew patriarchs. But in the ancient world in general, and the Near East in particular, the social aspect of a civilization was intimately related to its religious aspect: the two interlocked. If it was not, then, the social climate that drove Abraham from Mesopotamia, could local religion provide a plausible motive?

The answer may not be far to seek. In Mesopotamia, the very tenets that stimulated the social growth of the country proved to be a source of weakness in its spiritual progress. The terrestrial state was non-autocratic because man took his cue from the gods; and in the celestial state no one god was a law unto himself, not even the head of the pantheon. All major decisions in heaven required approval by the corporate body of the gods. And since nothing was valid for all time, the upshot was chronic indecision in heaven and consequent insecurity on earth. Man's best hope to get a favorable nod from the cosmic powers lay, it was felt, in ritualistic appeasement. And as the ritual machinery grew more and more cumbersome, the spiritual content receded ever farther, until it all but disappeared from the official system. When social gains could no longer balance the spiritual deficit, Mesopotamian civilization as a whole ceased to be self-sustaining.

To be sure, the golden age of Hammurabi, with which the early patriarchal period has to be correlated, was more than a millennium away from the collapse of Assyria and Babylonia; it would not appear to be a ripe time for spiritual forebodings. Nevertheless, there must have been occasional doubts even then about the religious solution which local society had evolved. As a matter of fact, the earliest known composition on the subject of the Suffering Just—or the Job theme—dates from Old Babylonian times. Thus Abraham would not have been alone in his religious questioning. However, if the biblical testimony is anywhere near the mark, he was the first to follow up such thoughts with action.

Since the Mesopotamian system was vulnerable chiefly because of its own type of polytheism, a possible remedy that an inquiring mind might hit upon would lie in monotheism. But to conceive of such an ideal initially, without any known precedent in the experience of mankind, called for greater resources than those of logic alone. It meant a resolute rejection of common and long-cherished beliefs, a determined challenge to the powers that were believed to dominate every aspect of nature, and the substitution of a single supreme being for that hostile coalition. The new belief, in short, would call for unparalleled inspiration and conviction. Without that kind of call, Abraham could not have become the father of the biblical process.

To summarize the reasoning thus far, the genesis of the biblical way is bound up with the beginnings of the monotheistic concept; both converge in the age, and presumably also the person, of Abraham. To this extent, the present reconstruction is in broad accord with the tenor of biblical tradition. Unlike traditional tenets, however, a historical hypothesis cannot be accepted on faith; it must meet the test of independent controls. In the present instance, the controls are implicit in the internal evidence of biblical history as a whole. But before the test is attempted, one important point needs to be clarified in passing.

In adducing monotheism and polytheism as contrasting factors in the story of mankind, the student of history must steer clear of subjective involvement with these theological systems in the abstract. His sole business is to ascertain what the respective concepts contributed pragmatically. The judgment must be based of necessity on what the given system accomplished in the long run. The question of independent validity cannot be at issue in this instance.

The effects of Mesopotamian polytheism on the local civilization have already been outlined. Because the cosmos was viewed as a state in which ultimate authority was vested in the collective assembly of the gods, mortals were, paradoxically enough, both gainers and losers. Human society followed the lead of the gods in adopting an anti-authoritarian form of government. But since heaven itself was subject to instability, mankind too lacked the assurance of absolute and universal principles.

Monotheism, on the other hand, is predicated on the concept of a God who has no rivals, and is therefore omnipotent. As the unchallenged master of all creation, he has an equal interest in all of his creatures. Since every nation has the same claim to his care, each can aspire to just and impartial treatment in conformance with its conduct. The same holds true of individuals. It is thus causality and not caprice that is the norm of the cosmos. Impersonal justice, moreover, is conducive to objective standards of ethics and morality.

The history of the biblical process is ultimately the story of the monotheistic ideal in its gradual evolution. That ideal was first glimpsed and pursued by a single society in resolute opposition to prevailing beliefs. In the course of that quest, certain truths emerged which proved to possess universal validity, hence their progressive recognition and acceptance; hence, too, the abiding appeal of the Bible as the comprehensive record of that quest. The inception of the underlying process becomes thus a matter of unique interest and significance. As has been emphasized repeatedly, all signs so far have pointed to Abraham as the pioneer. To what extent is this borne out by the internal evidence of biblical history?

Once Israel had been established as a political entity, any retracement of its spiritual history was bound to operate in the shadow of the towering figure of Moses. This is in no way surprising. Even in the sharper perspective of today, a perspective made possible by an ever-quickening flow of discovery, Moses stands unchallenged as the founder of the Israelite nation. By the same token, however, Mount Sinai emerges as a vital stage on the road to nationhood, but not as its starting point. The biblical concept of a nation stresses three features above all others: (1) a body of religious beliefs; (2) an integral system of law; and (3) a specific territorial base. It was the heroic achievement of Moses to have rallied an amorphous agglomerate of serfs and nomads and imbued them with a will to independent nationhood. To that end he proclaimed Yahweh as the one and supreme God, put together a legal code, and led his fractious followers to the borders of the Promised Land. Yet the religious content is invariably characterized as ancestral, the faith of the forefathers. The law, it is true, becomes a personal revelation from the Deity, in a manner that is traditional with all ancient legislators; but most of the legal provisions involved have demonstrable pre-Mosaic antecedents and can often be traced back paragraph by paragraph, sometimes even word for word. And the theme of the Promised Land is prominent with all the patriarchs, and central to the mission of Abraham. Thus the earlier traditions themselves ascribe the original program to Abraham and credit Moses primarily with its execution. This may not do full justice to Moses' over-all achievement, the strength and the perseverance and the faith that went into it, and the toll that it took. Nevertheless, the ultimate inspiration derived from an earlier vision, a vision that required a long time to incubate, one that Moses set out to validate in all humility. While it is thus true that Israel as a nation would be inconceivable without Moses, the work of Moses would be equally unthinkable without the prior labors of the patriarchs. The covenant of Mount Sinai is a natural sequel to God's covenant with Abraham. The two together become the twin cornerstones of the spiritual history of Israel, and are honored as such throughout the Bible.

When it comes, therefore, to the genesis of the biblical process, the internal evidence of the Bible itself goes hand in hand with the results of modern biblical study based in large measure on the testimony of outside sources. Both sets of data point to the age of Abraham; each in its own way enhances the probability of Abraham as a historical figure. And if the term probability appears too sanguine in this connection, in view of the tenuous and circumstantial nature of the evidence, it should be remembered that the case for Moses is analogous in kind, though not in degree. Furthermore, the argument for Abraham is not as yet exhausted. A significant final point still remains to be cited.

Biblical history proper, as distinct from primeval history, begins in Genesis with chapter xii. This beginning comes with startling suddenness. The preceding chapter concluded with a notice about Abraham's family which betrays the hand of *J,* followed by a typical statement from *P* about Abraham's stopping in Haran, although he had started out for Canaan. Even *P* fails to tell us that Abraham "walked with God," as had Enoch and Noah, or to suggest any reason for the patriarch's journey And when *J* commences his main narrative, Abraham does not know what his destination is to be. We are told only that he has been called, without prior preparation or warning. The opening words are. "Go forth," thus keynoting the theme of migration from Mesopotamia in quest of spiritual values. There could be no way more apt or direct to signal the commencement of the biblical process.

Nor could there be much preparation or warning in the circumstances. As a drastic departure from existing norms, the concept of monotheism had to break new ground. There had to be a first time, and place, and person or group of persons; hence the abruptness of the account in Gen xii. The time has been circumscribed for us by the background data which the patriarchal narratives incorporate. The place is indicated in three ways; the Mesopotamian source of the material involved; the need for a new and different religious solution, a need that could be discerned in Mesopotamia more clearly than anywhere else, as we have seen; and the manifold ties that link Israel to the homeland of the patriarchs. The human factor cannot be reduced independently to a given individual or group of individuals. But tradition has nominated Abraham specifically, and that choice is not contradicted by modern study. Furthermore, the author of the narrative about Abraham's call did not get his information from a researcher's files. And he could not have obtained it from cuneiform texts since, even if his scholarship matched his literary genius, the documents from the pertinent period had by *J*'s time been covered up for centuries, and were to remain buried for nearly three thousand years more. *J* could have gotten his material only from earlier Israelite traditions, which in turn reached back all the way to patriarchal times. That is why the Genesis narrative about the turning point in Abraham's life, favored as it is by the internal evidence from biblical history and the indirect testimony of extra-biblical sources, deserves more than casual attention.

The end result of that religious experience of faraway and long ago cannot be estimated even at this late date, for the end is not yet in sight. From just such a start a society was fashioned, and its continued quest for universal verities inspired three enduring religions, which profoundly affected all subsequent history. As the record of that progressive quest, the Bible became and has remained a factor in cultural life and an influence in world literature.

But if the full results cannot be calculated, an impression of their magnitude may perhaps be suggested by means of indirect comparison. The question has often been posed whether the course of recent history would have changed much if on August 15, 1769, Letizia Bonaparte had given birth to a girl instead of a boy. The answer is obvious when limited to decades. But would it still be true a hundred years later, or a hundred and fifty? The chances are that it would not, and that the deviation from the original course which the advent of Napoleon brought about would have been righted in due time.

Now let us ask the same kind of question about the biblical process and its presumed originator. The answer can be ventured with much greater confidence because the measuring span is twenty times as long. That distant event altered history irrevocably. In the case of Napoleon, the detour rejoined the main road. But in the case of Abraham, the detour became itself the main road.

INTRODUCTION TO THE BOOK OF GENESIS

NATURE OF THE CONTENTS

In terms of subject matter, the Book of Genesis breaks up into two distinct and unequal parts. The first contains chapters i–xi; it is restricted—if allowances are made for the Table of Nations—to what has come to be known as Primeval History. The second part, chapters xii–l, takes up the Story of the Patriarchs.

The following discussion will include some material that has already been cited, or will come up later in the comments on the pertinent sections. Such data need to be brought together under this heading because of their special relevance to the present context.

(1) Primeval History

The break between Primeval History and the Story of the Patriarchs (Parts I and II in this book) is sharper than is immediately apparent. On the surface, the end of chapter xi appears to lead up to the next chapter. Actually, however, the call that set Abraham's mission on its course, and with it the biblical process as a whole (xii 1 ff.), is received without any prior warning, as was stressed above. Everything that precedes is a broadly conceived preface, a prelude to the particular story with which the rest of the Pentateuch is concerned. The difference is underscored by the scope of the two subdivisions of Genesis. The patriarchal narratives take up four-fifths of the entire book, yet they cover only four generations of a single family. Primeval History, on the other hand, has the whole world as its stage, and its time span reaches back all the way to Creation. In other words, Primeval History seeks to give a universal setting for what is to be the early history of one particular people.

Although the content of the prefatory part is thus in effect pre-historic, it could still have originated with Israelites, or been imported from some outside quarter or quarters. In this instance, it can be established that (1) the material was imported for the most part, and (2) that the ultimate source of the borrowings or adaptations can be traced to a single land. The originating center has left its geographic stamp, so to speak, in some cases, and indirect but just as decisive markers in others.

Let us first list the headings of the thirteen sections into which the first eleven chapters of Genesis have been arranged in this work; the respective documentary sources are given in parentheses: 1. Opening Account of Creation (*P*). 2. The Story of Eden (*J*). 3. The Fall of Man (*J*). 4. Cain and Abel (*J*). 5. The Line of Cain (*J*). 6. The Patriarchs before the Flood (*P*). 7. Prelude to Disaster (*J*). 8. The Flood (*J*, *P*). 9. Blessing and Covenant (*P*). 10. Noah and his Sons (*J*, *P*). 11. The Table of Nations (*P*, *J*). 12. The Tower of Babel (*J*). 13. Genealogies from Shem to Abraham (*P*, *J*).

In Sections 2 (Tigris and Euphrates), 11 (Nimrod's lands and cities), 12 (Babylon), and 13 (Ur, Haran), Mesopotamia is designated explicitly. In Sections 6 (antediluvian lists) and 8 (Flood) there is a demonstrable relationship with abundant cuneiform sources. Section 7 echoes concepts of theogony which are ultimately traceable to Mesopotamia. And the remaining topics likewise fall into line by reason of such marked details as Eden or the Flood. In other words, Primeval History is clearly oriented toward Mesopotamia.

One of the significant aspects of this situation is that *P* incorporated outside material, in so far as Primeval History is concerned, no less than *J*. It should be stressed, moreover, that *P* did not utilize *J*'s material in these particular instances. *P*'s account of Creation is fundamentally different from *J*'s, but it shows a far-reaching correspondence in detail with the Babylonian account of Creation as presented in *Enūma eliš* (see COMMENT on Sec. 1). The same holds true of *P*'s approach to antediluvian generations (cf. COMMENT on Sec. 6). It follows, accordingly, that *P* had independent access to traditions that ultimately originated in Mesopotamia. This has a bearing, in turn, on the essential antiquity of at least some of *P*'s data; and it should warn us against discounting *P* when pre-documentary traditions are considered.

Another aspect of the derivative character of Primeval History also deserves careful attention. Native traditions are homogeneous by definition. The themes they feature are bound to reflect local concepts and beliefs; and the language in which such themes have been transmitted lends itself readily to restatement by the eventual chroniclers. It is different, however, with outside motifs which have been taken over for one reason or another. The background is alien, the subject matter is fixed, and the form and expression are inevitably influenced by the original medium. It should come as no surprise, therefore, that a certain degree of dissonance can be detected when Primeval History is compared with native material in the Bible, as is the case, for example, with the mythological content of Section 7, and such passages as iii 22 ff. and xi 6; or that the story about Eden should contain, aside from the theme itself, such Sumerian loanwords as the term Eden or the word for "flow" ('ēd, see Sec. 2). In such cases, the writer was restricted by his source material in more ways than one. Small wonder, therefore, that various critics have found difficulty in recognizing *J*'s hand in these sections of Genesis. But their consequent recourse to other sources (*E,* and even the more speculative *L* and *S*) has proved to be so much tilting at windmills. It is still unmistakably *J,* but a *J* operating under particularly rigid limitations.

Lastly, the fact that the account of Creation was secondary in much of its detail has an important bearing on the "scientific" aspect of the narrative. It means that the data embody Mesopotamian conclusions on the subject, conclusions that had been reached at a remote age by a society which was a pioneer in the gradual advance of science. In this respect, biblical thought reflected the best that was available in contemporary scientific thinking, yet raised such data to its own theological standards. It is a case of authenticity in the second degree, that is, an authentic reflex of an underlying source. And the basic question about any statement in a given source is not whether that statement is true or false, but what it means (cf. concluding COMMENT on Sec. 1).

How is one to evaluate such manifold dependence of Primeval History on Mesopotamian prototypes? One attempted answer can be found in the tenets of a school that sprang up at the beginning of the century under the aegis of the distinguished German Assyriologist Friedrich Delitzsch. In his lectures under the collective title of "Babel and Bibel," Delitzsch drew sharp attention to the Babylonian ingredient in Genesis, and went on to conclude that the

Bible was therefore guilty of crass plagiarism. Ironically enough, the accuser could not know at the time how much more fuel for his theory subsequent discoveries might seem to provide, but that, paradoxically, the increment would refute the theory itself by placing the whole subject in its true perspective.

The added material has demonstrated, among other things, that the background of the patriarchal narratives in Genesis is indeed authentic, so much so in fact that it could have been obtained only in Mesopotamia itself. Accordingly, the traditions about the patriarchs are right in naming that country as the homeland of Abraham. In that case, however, Abraham and the people he led could hardly have remained untouched by the rich culture of the land from which they migrated. They were bound to be influenced by various local customs and practices, and we know now that such was actually the case. In addition, they must have been familiar with the themes that dominated the literature of Mesopotamia. Nor need all such ties have been severed as a result of Abraham's departure. We are told that Jacob had the opportunity to renew them over a period of twenty years. And similar contacts may have been maintained by later generations. In other words, there is nothing surprising about the fact that early Hebrew literature is replete with Mesopotamian motifs, especially motifs relating to pre-Israelite times. It is only lack of such themes that would be grounds for suspicion.

Delitzsch and his followers failed to take due notice of the fact that the Bible never denied the close ties between the patriarchs and Mesopotamia. And they overlooked the further significant fact that there was a spiritual reason for the parting of the ways. The migration, as we have seen, was in protest against the local religious solution. And reflections of that protest can still be detected throughout the account on Primeval History. *P*'s statement about Creation differs from its Mesopotamian analogue by its overriding concept of an omnipotent Creator. *J*'s version of the Flood receives a moral motivation. Most revealing of all is the same writer's narrative about the Tower of Babel. The scene of the episode is Babylon itself, and some passages in that story read as though the author had had the Babylonian prototype before him. Yet the purpose of the tale is not a direct though unacknowledged transcript, but a stern criticism of the builders' monumental presumption. To reverse a familiar saying, the more things are alike in some ways, the greater the differences between them on other counts.

There is, finally, yet another question about Primeval History that remains to be considered. Why was this sketchy introduction included altogether? The career of a given nation is not traced back automatically to Creation, especially when even that nation's forefathers are presented as relative newcomers on the stage of history. The logical beginning in this instance would seem to be Gen xii, or perhaps a few verses earlier. And in fact, the E source does not reach back beyond Abraham, unless one ascribes this late start to accidents of preservation rather than deliberate design.

The answer to this question may be sought in the fact that neither J nor P was interested in national history as such. Rather, both were concerned with the story of a society and, more particularly, a society as the embodiment of an ideal, that is, a way of life. A history of that kind transcends national boundaries and may conceivably be retraced to the beginnings of the world. Such at least is the manifest intent of P, whose system is designed to close any possible genealogical gaps.

Nevertheless, one should not discount another potential reason for the grand preface. Mesopotamian literature was fond of taking many of its themes all the way back to Creation, sometimes even in matters of no great consequence.[13] Understandably enough, this tendency was especially prominent in historical writings. Thus the standard Sumerian king list starts with the dynasties before the Flood,[14] and proceeds from there to eras with which the compiler was better acquainted. We know that the same approach was followed elsewhere in the Near East.[15] Moreover, P's genealogies before the Flood parallel the antediluvian dynasties of the Sumerians in endowing individuals with enormous life-spans; and the names of some of the biblical patriarchs before the Flood display Akkadian formation (see Sec. 6). It would have been no less natural for J, who frequently incorporated Mesopotamian data in his own contribution to Primeval History, to follow time-honored precedent in prefacing his work with sketches about the early stages of mankind

[13] Even a simple incantation against toothache is honored with such a cosmic introduction; cf. ANET, p. 100.

[14] See Thorkild Jacobsen, The Sumerian King List, 1939.

[15] There is, for example, an Old Hurrian text about world rulers starting with primeval times; cf. J. Friedrich, Kleinasiatische Sprachdenkmäler, 1932, p. 35.

as a whole. If the Mesopotamian models were not the sole reason for such an arrangement, they could well have been a contributing factor.

(2) *The Story of the Patriarchs*

The patriarchal narratives in Genesis comprise three major subdivisions: A. The Story of Abraham (xii 1–xxv 18); B. The Story of Jacob (xxv 19–xxxvii 2a); C. Joseph and His Brothers (xxxvii 2b–l 26). What happened to Isaac? Strange as it may seem, Abraham's son and successor does not appear to have inspired a separate cycle of narratives about himself. The death of Abraham is recorded in xxv 8–10. Verses 12–18 are devoted to Ishmael and his descendants. Verse 19 proceeds immediately to Isaac's descendants, and the birth of Jacob and Esau is recorded in 21ff., thus introducing the story of Jacob. Chapter xxvi, to be sure, gathers a number of scattered notices about Isaac. Yet the very fact that these notices are disconnected and meager demonstrates how inconspicuous was the role that Isaac played in the story of the patriarchs as a whole. It is further evident from chapter xxiv that Isaac could not have been a memorable personality.

The story of Abraham contains a secondary theme in the sporadic references to Lot. A companion of the patriarch ever since the migration from Mesopotamia, Lot eventually parts from his uncle and settles in the Jordan Plain where he becomes an eyewitness to the upheaval that wiped out Sodom and the region about it. The Lot narrative comes to a close with the births of the eponymous ancestors of the Moabites and the Ammonites. A unique section within the cycle of narratives about Abraham is chapter xiv, which stands out from the rest by virtue of its distinctive orientation, and provides a picture of the patriarch as viewed from the outside.

The Jacob story is more diversified in its pattern than that of Abraham. Its protagonist lacks his grandfather's stability, and that lack, which heightens the dramatic impact of the story, is brought out primarily through the medium of the continuous rivalry between Jacob and his twin brother Esau. Jacob's flight to Haran turns into twenty years of penance in Mesopotamia, and terminates in an equally hasty return to Canaan. The long stay in Mesopotamia is portrayed against a background of authenticated local conditions.

Significantly, both *J* and *E* prove to have drawn on original data for their respective accounts of this stage in Jacob's life.

Two episodes are recounted in the latter half of Genesis which are nearly as extraneous to their particular contexts as was Gen xiv in the first half. Unlike Gen xiv, however, the authorship of the accounts in question is not a serious problem; each betrays the hand of *J*. One of these later narratives is chapter xxxiv, which centers about Jacob's daughter Dinah; it goes chronologically with the Jacob cycle, and Jacob himself becomes personally involved. The other narrative is chapter xxxviii, which deals with the incident of Judah and Tamar; it happens to be technically a part of the Joseph story, which is introduced in chapter xxxvii. Nevertheless, it has nothing whatever to do with Joseph, and the Judah whom we meet here cannot be synchronized with the Judah of the Joseph story (see COMMENT on xxxviii). The two accounts will be considered here jointly because of their common deviation from the main cycles into which they have been inserted in the text.

The name Dinah occurs twice outside ch. xxxiv, namely, in xxx 21 and xlvi 15; but those passages are textually suspect; they appear to be afterthoughts, which is another term for glosses. This does not mean, of course, that Dinah had no place in the older traditions; it does suggest, however, that notices about Dinah were not part of the main themes with which biblical historians were concerned. Now the story that Gen xxxiv tells about her relates to a very early stage in Hebrew history, which culminated in a clash between the tribes of Simeon and Levi on the one hand, and the city of Shechem on the other. Whatever the immediate results, the long-term effect was ruinous for the two tribes, inasmuch as Simeon was eventually reduced to an insignificant role, while Levi lost its tribal status altogether. Israel looked back on the incident in stern reproof (cf. xlix 5–7).

Gen xxxviii shows no awareness of Judah's presence in Egypt, while displaying a keen interest in the early history of the tribe of Judah. In common, thus, with xxxiv, the narrative under discussion affords an independent and different insight into early historical conditions. *J* was apparently in no position to ignore either of these side views, although he must have been aware of the resulting discrepancies in chronology as regards Judah. One could only wish that both *J* and *E* had had reason to incorporate other such notices, which no doubt must have been current; we would then have had a broader basis for the reconstruction of a dimly illuminated age. But, as stated above, the biblical narrators were interested primarily in recording a progressive spiritual experience; and one can hardly blame them for their preference.

The Joseph story calls for no special comment at this time. As has just been pointed out, chapter xxxviii, although now placed within the Joseph cycle, is not pertinent to it in content. The same is true of the Testament of Jacob (xlix 1) (see COMMENT on Sec. 61). Another intrusive passage in the Joseph story is the list in xlvi 8–27 (P); cf. COMMENT *ad loc*. The last Hebrew word in the Book of Genesis reads "in Egypt," a fitting, though doubtless unintended, catchword which points to the Book of Exodus.

GENESIS EXEGESIS

Over the many centuries that have elapsed since its definitive compilation, Genesis has proved to be by far the most popular book of the Pentateuch, attracting the greatest amount of attention and giving rise to the largest volume of comment. The variety and universal appeal of its contents and the literary quality of its narratives are one reason for this continuous interest. Another reason, of course, lies in the manifold challenge that Genesis has always presented to philosophers and theologians. As a result, references to Genesis began to appear in the later books of the Bible itself, only to swell into an ever-increasing flow of opinions and studies as time went by. The modern age has provided a new stimulus through the dual medium of biblical criticism and archaeology. By now the total extent of publications on the subject is probably beyond computation. The chances are that a latter-day Ecclesiastes would repeat his predecessor's complaint that "of making many books there is no end," but would apply this saying exclusively to the extant material on Genesis.

The following is a sample listing of works, both ancient and modern, that relate in varying degrees to the interpretation of the Book of Genesis. In many instances, the given entry is but one of a number that would have been included if space permitted. The immense periodical literature had to be ignored altogether. Nor is this the place to take up translations as such; that subject will be dealt with in the next section.

Among the oldest works pertaining to Genesis, or at least inspired by the canonical version, are two components of the Pseudepigrapha, both dating from the second century B.C. They are the *Book of Jubilees*, originally written in Hebrew and purporting to be an elaboration of the biblical book; and *Testaments of the XII Patriarchs*, originally composed in Aramaic. Another Aramaic composition is the so-called *Genesis Apocryphon* (abbr. Gen. Apocr.), one of the recently recovered Dead Sea scrolls (published by N. Avigad and Y. Yadin, 1956). More systematic in method and approach is a work by the Jewish-Hellenistic philosopher Philo of Alexandria, who was born toward the end of the pre-Christian era. In his comprehensive Greek study on the Pentateuch which bore the title "Questions and Solutions," Philo paid a great deal of attention to Genesis, inasmuch as the extant material points to at least six books on this subject alone.

Rabbinic literature is replete with references and allusions to Genesis themes. The haggadic (morally instructive) legends on the subject have been collected in L. Ginzberg's *The Legends of the Jews,* 7 vols., 1913–38. A special midrashic (expository) collection on Genesis is the subject of a large work entitled *Bereshit Rabba* Representative of many early studies by the Church Fathers is the Commentary on Genesis by the great third-century scholar Origen

Jewish scholars of the Middle Ages produced various biblical studies—lexicographical, grammatical, and exegetical. The pioneer in this effort was Sa'adia (882–942), who is still celebrated for his translation of the Pentateuch into Arabic; but he was also the author of an Arabic commentary on Gen i–xxviii 7, which unfortunately is extant only in fragments. We do have, however, the complete Arabic commentary by Sa'adia's Karaite (literalist) opponent 'Ali ben Sulaimān (tenth/eleventh centuries) published by S. Skoss, 1928 Of the numerous mediaeval commentaries in Hebrew, the best known, and still useful in many respects, are those of Rashi (eleventh century) and Abraham Ibn Ezra (twelfth century).

We have to skip the next few stages, with their groping for an objective approach to the Bible and the evolution of critical methods, and turn to recent works. The classic formulation of the documentary hypothesis, embracing the Pentateuch and the Former Prophets, is still J. Wellhausen's *Die Composition des Hexateuchs . .* , 1889 For subsequent statements see D. C. Simpson, *Pentateuchal Criticism*, 1924, and especially M. Noth, *Überlieferungsgeschichte des Pentateuchs,* 2d ed., 1948. Representative of the large number of Introductions to the Old Testament are those by S. R. Driver, 10th ed., 1900, R. H. Pfeiffer, 1941, and J. L. McKenzie, 1956. For a special, and elaborate, application of the documentary method to the first book of the Pentateuch, cf. O. Eissfeldt, *Die Genesis der Genesis*, 1958. The views of Y. Kaufmann, as expressed in his monumental Hebrew study on *The Religion of Israel*, may now be gleaned from the English abridgment by M. Greenberg, 1960.

Of the many distinguished commentaries on Genesis published since the last quarter of the nineteenth century, I can only list those that I had occasion to consult frequently. They include A. Dillmann's *Die Genesis*, 6th ed., 1892, which is notable for its sound philological approach, H. Gunkel's *Genesis*, 1902, marked by the author's keen appreciation of literary quality, and S. R. Driver's (abbr. Dr.) *The Book of Genesis* (12th ed., 1926, repr. 1954). The abiding popularity of this last work is a well-deserved tribute to the author's rare combination of learning, lucidity, and plain common sense. But the book was published originally in 1904, and effective revisions were interrupted by Driver's death in 1914. A convenient digest of the textual apparatus is available in J. Skinner's treatment of Genesis in the *International Critical Commentary*, 1910, 2d ed., 1930. Within the past decade there have appeared, among others, U. Cassuto's *From Adam to Noah* (Gen i–v) and *From Noah to Abraham* (Gen vi–xi), both in Hebrew (1953); R. de Vaux's *La Genèse*, as part of La Sainte Bible (abbr. SB), 1953; and G. von Rad's (abbr. von Rad) *Das erste Buch Mose*, 1952–53; the recently published English translation of this thoughtful study substitutes the RSV version of the Hebrew text.

As examples of sectional commentaries on Genesis, I cite in addition to Cassuto's, above (which was intended to cover the entire book), only K. Budde's *Biblische Urgeschichte* (Gen i–xii 5, 1883) and W. Zimmerli's *Die Urgeschichte: 1. Mose 1–11* (2d ed., 1957). J. H. Kroeze's (Dutch) *Genesis Veertien* ("Genesis XIV"), 1937, may serve as an illustration of still more restricted monographic studies.

When it comes to insight into biblical usage, there is nothing that can match A. B. Ehrlich's (abbr. Ehrl.) *Randglossen zur hebräischen Bibel*, Vol. I, 1908 (for Genesis, pp. 1–256). The text of the Hebrew Bible itself is by no means as firmly established as the commonly applied term "Masoretic" (traditional) would seem to imply. The recorded variants, however, are of minor technical significance.

For all general purposes, R. Kittel's edition of Genesis in the same editor's *Biblia Hebraica*, 3d ed., 1937, is fully adequate.

Finally, Israel, as the nation that produced the Bible, was not an island either in space or in time. Hence there is a virtually inexhaustible commentary on the Bible that can be distilled from the literary remains of Israel's contemporaries. For Genesis, the material is spread over a maze of cuneiform documents, echoed in a scattering of West Semitic inscriptions, and implicit in some of the records from Egypt. The fundamental importance of Assyriological sources has been manifest ever since the publication of G. Smith's *The Chaldean Account of Genesis*, 1880; and it received more recent recognition in A. Heidel's *The Babylonian Genesis*, 1945, 2d ed., 1951, and *The Gilgamesh Epic and Old Testament Parallels*, 1946. The West Semitic inscriptions, in so far as they may bear on Genesis times, have yet to be excerpted in a separate book; on the independent area of Ugaritic studies, cf. M. H. Pope, *El in the Ugaritic Texts*, 1955. For the latest evaluation of the meager Egyptological material we have J. Vergote's (abbr. Vergote) *Joseph en Egypte*, 1959. A collection of outside sources pertaining to the Hebrew Bible as a whole is presented in a large volume on *Ancient Near Eastern Texts Relating to the Old Testament* (abbr. ANET), edited by J. B. Pritchard, 2d ed., 1955. But fresh material keeps on turning up all the time, and much more extensive screening will be required in the future.

ON TRANSLATING GENESIS

The main task of a translator is to keep faith with two different masters, one at the source and the other at the receiving end. The terms and thoughts of the original, the impact of sound and phrase, the nuances of meaning, and the shadings of emphasis should all be transposed from one medium into another without leaving any outward sign of the transfer. It is, of course, an ideal goal, one that can never be attained with complete success. Yet the translator must strive to approximate this ideal. If he is unduly swayed by the original, and substitutes word for word rather than idiom for idiom, he is traducing what he should be translating, to the detriment of both source and target. And if he veers too far in the opposite direction, by favoring the second medium at the expense of the first, the result is a paraphrase. The task is an exacting one even with contemporary or relatively recent sources. With ancient sources, the difficulties are compounded as problems of text, usage, and cultural setting increase progressively with age.

The Old Testament shares many such problems with other literary works of comparable antiquity; but it also presents to the modern translator a number of obstacles that are not found elsewhere. Genesis, for example, is itself a stratified book. It was compiled sometime before the middle of the first millennium B.C., after a long period of growth and composition. But the extant manuscripts of Genesis as a whole are many centuries later, so that much could have happened, and some things are actually known to have occurred, after the definitive compilation. In marked contrast, the stele of Hammurabi is still, except for one excised portion, the monument that the legislator ordered.

Far more problematic than the integrity of the text is the accuracy of the transmitted meaning. On this count, Genesis has been vulnerable to a greater degree than any other book of the Bible, since Genesis reaches back to the patriarchal period and contains a substantial amount of authentic material from that age; hence there was ample opportunity for meanings to be lost or mislaid even before the time of compilation. Moreover, later Hebrew usage is by no means identical with early biblical usage. Yet successive interpreters would tend to make the secondary usage retroactive. And because the Bible had become sacred Scripture, such anachronistic interpretations acquired a normative bearing of their own. Thus in course of time the content of the Bible became enveloped in layer after layer of superimposed interpretation; interpretations bequeathed by scribes and Rabbis, ancient versions, the vocalizers of the standard (Masoretic) text, and—not the least formidable of all—the first standard version in the given Western tongue. Each of these accretions has served as a safeguard in some ways, but as a barrier in others, a barrier to the recovery of the original context. The translator of the Bible has to work his way through these successive incrustations, grateful for what each has safeguarded, but wary of their heterogeneous matter. As one gentle critic put it, with tongue in cheek, translations are so much more enjoyable than originals, because they contain many things that the originals leave out. The translator of the Bible must try to avoid such spurious improvements, new or old.

The starting point, naturally, is the received text. Sooner or later the question is bound to arise whether a given passage has been correctly transmitted. On the whole, the textual condition of Genesis is much better than that of a number of other books of the Old Testament. Nevertheless, Genesis has its complement of textual distortions. Some are manifestly late and easily corrected with the help of parallel passages elsewhere in the Bible, the ancient versions, or a combination of both. Thus the received reading *Dōdānīm* in x 4 can be restored to *Rōdānīm* thanks to I Chron i 7 as well as LXX; the letters *R* and *D* are easily and often confused in the standard Hebrew script. The mangled names in xlvi 21 can be reconstructed with the assistance of Num xxvi 38 f. and I Chron viii 4 f. At times, the solution is more roundabout, but not seriously in doubt; this is true, for example, of Gen x 10 ("all of them" for "Calneh"), or the whole of Gen xlix 26. In other instances, an obvious omission can be safely restored from a primary ancient version, usually LXX; cf. xlvii 5 f.

There remains, however, a handful of passages that are obviously wrong as transmitted, yet cannot be righted by any of the means at our disposal. Invariably, these are instances about which the earliest versions and interpreters were already in doubt; the parade example is the "Shiloh" passage in xlix 10c. In such cases—they are fewer than is generally assumed—I deemed it best to adhere to the text, at least in its consonantal form, while relegating possible remedies to the footnotes. If an emendation is to be accorded preferential status, sound methodology requires that it have the balance of the argument in its favor; in other words, to be adopted, an emendation ought to be immediately appealing (as is true of "Calneh" in x 10). Elsewhere, the text is in a better position than the emender to bear the onus of uncertainty; and indeed, incidental discoveries have more than once vindicated a biblical text and refuted modern critics. In strictly technical studies, obstinate cruxes are often left untranslated.

Before we touch briefly on questions of meaning, a comment should be made about the division of the biblical text into chapters and verses; such breaks often affect the syntax of the given passage one way or another. The Masoretic division into verses was slow to solidify, and was not accomplished until the turn of the ninth century of the present era. The division into chapters is still later and non-Masoretic; it was introduced by Christian scholars in the thirteenth century,[16] that is, almost two millenniums after the Book of Genesis had been compiled. In these circumstances, it is not surprising that the now familiar breakdown into chapters and verses does not always accord with the internal evidence of the content. In Genesis, the first chapter should have continued through ii 4a, ending in the middle of what is now marked as a verse; similarly, the beginning of the Joseph story, which surely ought to have been signalized by a new chapter, is now found inside xxxvii 2. Inappropriate verse breaks are naturally more common; note, for example, i 1–3, vi 1/2, xxiii 5/6, 14/15, 17/18. Sometimes, the wrong break occurs in the middle of a word, an echo of a distant period when punctuation was sporadic or non-existent. An example of such a mishap will be found at the juncture of xlix 20 and 21, where we now have "heel: *From* Asher" instead of "*their* heel: Asher" (the border letter *M,* depending on its position, can yield either "from" or "their"). Fortunately, such misdivided words are rare in the text of the Old Testament as a whole.

To go back to the recovery and transfer of meaning, the modern translator of Genesis—and other books of the Old Testament—has to mediate between two sovereign linguistic entities, each with its distinctive equipment developed over a long period of time. The differences are not only chronological but also structural and cultural. In transposing an ancient source, the ultimate task is to translate not just a text but a civilization. In the present instance, the respective media are early biblical Hebrew and modern English. Frequently, it is not a case of a one-to-one correlation; the desired balance has to be achieved indirectly, whether the point at issue is one of construction, semantic range, or idiomatic expression. It should be useful, therefore, to give a few representative illustrations, as proof that a faithful translation is by no means the same thing as a literal rendering; similar lists could, of course, be adduced for any two unrelated languages. Some of the examples cited below have often been commented on before; others have not received adequate recognition.

(1) *The particle wa.* The most common meaning of this ubiquitous particle is "and." But *wa* (usually reduced to *wᵉ*) may also introduce a subordinate clause ("while," xx 1), and then mark the main clause (xx 2; note also i 3: "God said," or "then God said"). It can also be

---

[16] Cf. Pfeiffer, *Introduction* . . . , pp. 101 ff., 200 f.

adversative ("but, however"), explicative ("namely, that is"), or a connective in a hendiadys (see below). At the beginning of a sentence, and particularly of a paragraph, section, or book, the translational equivalent of *wa* is zero. A good illustration of various uses of *wa* is to be found in i 14b, where the particle occurs four times, but each time with a different force: (a) introductory; (b) connective in hendiadys; (c) explicative; (d) plain connective. The relatively literal Authorized Version (KJ) reads: *"and* let them be for signs *and* for seasons, *and* for days *and* years" (italics added). The present translation offers: "let them mark the fixed times, (namely) the days and the years." Aside from the four "and"s, the literal rendering obscures the underlying meaning of two significant details; see the discussion *ad loc.*

(2) *Differences in semantic capacity.* Terms that correspond at the core may differ widely in their later coverage. Hence a given verb or noun in biblical Hebrew may require various English counterparts and, conversely, more than one Hebrew term may best be rendered by the same English word. The Hebrew stem *'mr* coincides by and large with the English verb "to say." But the Hebrew verb in question carries many other nuances: *to tell, promise, threaten, express fear, reflect* (speak to oneself), and the like. A uniform translation would result not only in monotony but also in under-representation. Much the same applies to Heb. *yd'*, basically "to know," but secondarily also "to recognize, learn, experience." Mechanical transposition has saddled English, as distinct from other Western languages, with the far from self-explanatory euphemism "man knew woman" (cf. iv 1). Similar deficits result from our slavish "to hear, to sin, to remember" for the given Hebrew verbs.

The same holds true of translations of Hebrew nouns. Thus, for example, Heb. *zera'*, primarily "seed," lends itself to several derivative connotations. In xxxviii 8 f. this noun occurs three times with as many distinct and significant shadings. KJ reproduces it each time as "seed." But the context calls for, and usage justifies, *"line—seed—offspring"* respectively.

(3) *Flexible idioms.* The Hebrew phrase which means literally "to find favor/grace in one's eyes" often becomes meaningless in rigid translations. An impression of its wealth of nuances may be gathered from the following: "But Noah *found favor* with Yahweh" (vi 8); "if I may *beg* of you this *favor*" (xviii 3); "in the hope of *gaining* your *favor*" (xxxiii 8); "please, *indulge me*" (xxxiii 15);

"he took a fancy to" (xxxix 4); "we are *thankful* to my lord" (xlvii
25). A similar case in point is "to lift one's head," a phrase that is
used, deliberately and with telling effect, in three widely differing applications within the same narrative (ch. xl): "Pharaoh will *pardon* you" (13); Pharaoh "will *lift off* your *head*" (19); "he
singled out" (20). Another good example of elusive idiomatic usage
is provided by the prepositional phrase *lipnē,* normally "before,"
either in space or in time. But there is a residue of occurrences,
several of them in Genesis, in which "before" makes little if any
sense on closer examination; yet this is the translation that is invariably offered. What meaning could an objective reader wrest from
a phrase (in x 8) like "Nimrod was a mighty hunter *before* Yahweh
(the Lord)"? But when all the pertinent instances are viewed jointly,
a common pattern emerges. The term refers to something that happened with one's approval (cf. our "countenanced by"; the literal
meaning of the Hebrew is "to the face of"), or at one's behest. Thus
x 8b becomes "a mighty hunter *by the will* of Yahweh; xvii 18
yields "Let but Ishmael thrive *if you so will it";* in xxvii 7 we find
"that I may . . . bless you *with* Yahweh's *approval* before I die"
(not *"before* Yahweh *before* I die"); and in xliii 33 we obtain the
meaningful "they took their seats *at his direction"* instead of *"before him"* (which does not suit the context in any case). Many
similar examples of demonstrable idiomatic usage are scattered
throughout Genesis.

(4) *Rare verbal forms.* There are two specialized verbal forms in
biblical Hebrew which the grammars underestimate or ignore altogether. One is exactly like the Hebrew causative (or Hiphil) in
formation, but sharply different in meaning, inasmuch as it is intransitive and does not, therefore, take a direct object; it imparts to
the stem a durative or superlative connotation. Thus the forbidden
tree in Eden was not "to be desired to make one wise" (no object
is expressed in the text), but "attractive as a means to (lasting)
wisdom" (iii 6); in vi 19 we are told that the animals were to be
taken into the ark not "to keep them alive" (again no object is
indicated, hence KJ italicizes the pronoun), but to "stay alive"; in
the sense "to quicken," biblical Hebrew would normally use here the
Piel conjugation. In describing the birth of Benjamin (xxxv 16 f.),
the narrative first tells us that Rachel "had hard labor" (Piel), and
then marks the climax by saying "when her labor was at its
hardest . . ." (Hiphil). The standard translations offer: "and she

had hard labor. And it came to pass when she was in hard labor. . . ." Not only do such renderings ignore the difference in conjugations but they miss the climax as well; and many commentators homogenize the verbs by repointing the second occurrence so as to make it agree with the first, thereby compounding the offense. Another case in point is "you shall excel no more" (xlix 4). This time nobody could make the Hiphil causative; but many conscientious critics would repoint the alleged misfit to yield "you shall not survive"!

The other specialized verbal form is outwardly the so-called Hithpael, except that it is neither passive nor reflexive, as Hithpaels should be. What we have in such cases is an old Semitic form, which is durative or iterative in connotation, and has formally coalesced with the Hithpael. One example of this type is a derivative of the stem for "to go," with the meaning of "walk about" (which is a prolonged or iterative activity): it is used of Enoch (v 22, 24) and Noah (vi 9), both of whom "walked with God"; cf. also xiii 17. Another common example is the stem meaning "to mourn," which is again something that lasts a long time. In xxiv 21 the same formation is used most appropriately to express "(the man) stood gaping (at her)," as opposed to a fleeting glance.

(5) *Differing modes of definition.* Biblical Hebrew and modern English have similar means of reference, but they do not always distribute them in the same way. For instance, Hebrew may use the definite article where English prefers the possessive pronoun: e.g., Heb. *"the* young men": Eng. *"my* men" (xiv 24); Heb. *"the* flock": Eng. *"my* flock" (xxxviii 17); and conversely, Heb. *"my* covenant between me and you": Eng. *"the* covenant between you and me" (xvii 7); similarly, Heb. "the men of *her* place": Eng. "the men of *that* place" (xxxviii 21). Just so, Hebrew will often employ the personal pronoun, where English requires or prefers the personal name (e.g., xxix 14), and vice versa.

(6) *Replies to questions.* Since biblical Hebrew lacks a term for "yes," it indicates an affirmative reply by repeating the question without the interrogative particle. A good example is xxix 6. To Jacob's question "Is he well?" the shepherds' reply is literally "Well" (note that the text does not say "He is well"); to reflect the mood of that occasion, we have to say "He is."

(7) *Inversion.* Both Hebrew and English employ inversion of the normal word order as a method of achieving some significant modifi-

cation of meaning. But since the results are not parallel, it would not do merely to transfer the device automatically; neither can the usage be ignored with impunity. Hence the effect of inversion in Hebrew must often be reflected in English by some indirect means. For instance, xxx 40 is a parade example of separating the sheep from the goats. The goats have just been dealt with in the preceding verse. Accordingly, the sequel must read, "The ewes, *on the other hand, . . .";* the italicized phrase is not in the text in so many words, but its semantic equivalent is plainly indicated just the same.

(8) *Hendiadys.* This is a method whereby two formally co-ordinate terms—verbs, nouns, or adjectives—joined by "and" express a single concept in which one of the components defines the other. The usage was especially common in Greek, hence the term for it ("one by means of two"). Nor is it entirely a stranger to colloquial, if not literary, English. The statement "I am good and mad" would be a solecism on the face of it, since one is not apt to be both kind and angry at one and the same time; what this phrase means is "I am very angry."

The point of this digression is to call attention to the fact that hendiadys was also well known to biblical Hebrew, far more so than is generally recognized. Sometimes, the added nuance is a minor one, so that failure to notice it is not necessarily damaging. In xii 1, for example, we have "Go forth from *your native land,"* not "Get thee out of *thy country, and* from *thy kindred"* (KJ); and the favorite Hebrew expression *ḥesed weʾemet* is not "mercy and truth" (KJ), or "steadfast love and faithfulness" (RSV; cf. xxiv 27 and seq.), but simply "steadfast (*ʾemet*) kindness (*ḥesed*)"; in these compounds, or what amounts to compounds, the order of the constituents is immaterial.

There are times, however, when failure to heed a hendiadys results in an illogical or distorted rendition. In iii 16, Eve is told literally, "I will multiply greatly your pain and your conception" (cf. KJ), with the logical order seemingly reversed. The hendiadys, however, yields "pangs in childbearing" (cf. RSV). In xlv 6 the text appears to say, "there will be neither plowing nor harvest," and is so invariably rendered. Yet no farmer will abstain from plowing because there has been a famine; on the contrary, he will try that much harder. What the hendiadys conveys is "there shall be no yield from tilling."

Many other categories of this kind could be cited. But the foregoing sampling should suffice to warn the reader and vindicate the
translator.

STANDARD VERSIONS

This section, which brings the Introduction to a close, will be
limited to two widely separated sets of Old Testament translations,
namely, ancient versions, and translations into English. In both instances the survey will have to be sketchy and selective.

The old versions to be reviewed are the ones that bear a direct
relationship to the Hebrew text. Secondary translations based on the
Septuagint need not detain us here. But no such survey can ignore
the Samaritan Pentateuch (abbr. Sam.), although strictly speaking
this is not a version but a recension.

The Samaritan Bible does not go beyond the Pentateuch, because
that was the only part of the Old Testament that had been actually
canonized by the time of the Samaritan schism (ca. 400 B.C.). Accordingly, Sam. did not participate in any subsequent Masoretic developments, and thus became a valuable witness of relatively early
textual conditions. There are some six thousand cases throughout
the Pentateuch in which Sam. differs from the received text. In
about one-third of these, Sam. has the support of LXX. This means
that both Sam. and LXX made independent use of common earlier
traditions. Far more significant, however, is the overwhelming agreement with the central Masoretic body of material. While some of the
readings were as yet fluid, by far the bulk of the material had firmed
sufficiently, as early as the year 400, to leave scant room for departures within the evolving branches. This is another way of saying
that the Torah had already become a book sacred to all concerned.

Aside from predictable sectarian interpretations and frequent or-
thographic variants, the residual differences between the Samaritan
and the Masoretic texts of Genesis are relatively few. Sam., in common with the *Book of Jubilees,* assigns shorter life-spans to some of
the patriarchs before the Flood (ch. v); but it increases the distance between the birth of Arpachshad and the birth of Abraham
(ch. xi) from 290 to 940 years. More significant, because of their
antiquity, are Sam.'s readings in certain narrative passages, especially where the Masoretic text is obviously defective. Thus Sam.

supplies (in agreement with LXX and other versions) the missing clause "Let us go outside" in iv 8; in x 4, Sam. reads correctly *Dōdānīm* for *Rōdānīm;* and in xxii 13 it offers "a (literally 'one') ram" for "a ram behind" (reading *'ḥD* for *'ḥR;* the Masoretic text reflects the same mechanical confusion of *D* for *R* as in the previous example). The over-all crop (of which this is but a sampling) may not be large; but the value of the Samaritan recension lies not so much in what it corrects as in what it attests.

Because it bears not only on the text but, more especially, on its meaning, the first extant translation of Genesis is bound to be of exceptional importance. That pioneering role belongs to the oldest Greek version, which is known as the Septuagint (LXX); the Pentateuchal part of it goes back to the third century B.C. The subject as a whole is much too rich and complex to be compressed into a brief outline; for a comprehensive treatment, see H. B. Swete's *An Introduction to the Old Testament in Greek,* 2d ed., 1914. Several aspects of the LXX, however, deserve to be stressed in the present context. For one thing, the translators were Alexandrian Jews who approached their task with reverence and were intent primarily on making biblical tradition accessible to a community that was no longer at home in Hebrew. The principal aim of LXX was thus to conserve, and not to change or correct; hence the results reflect neither independent scholarship nor extensive editorializing, but tradition transposed into another linguistic medium. For another thing, however, all disagreements between LXX and the Masoretic text, in spite of the relative antiquity of the former, are not to be adjudged automatically in favor of the Greek version. Such departures may be due to any of a number of factors. For instance, the Samaritan recension has demonstrated that on various points tradition was as yet fluid; in some cases, the data behind the Masoretic text have proved to be superior to those that LXX utilized, while in other cases the translators were on firmer ground. It is worth noting in this connection that not only the Samaritan text but also material from the Dead Sea caves often supports the Septuagint. And for yet another thing, many of the existing differences from the received text are due to inner-Greek processes; the recovery of the original text of LXX is still far from accomplished. In sum, each given instance must be judged by itself and on its own merits.

The Septuagint version was to be but one of several early Greek translations. At least three others appeared within the space of a

few centuries, namely, the new and mutually contrasted translations by Aquila, Symmachus, and Theodotion. Of these efforts, Aquila's is the most curious and, indirectly, also the most valuable. As a relative of Emperor Hadrian, Aquila knew his Greek very well. But subsequent to his conversion to Judaism, his fidelity to the Hebrew text became extreme, so much so that Aquila came to be known as "a slave to the letter." In the third century, the great Christian scholar Origen arranged all four Greek versions in parallel columns, along with the Hebrew text and its transliteration into Greek script. The entire work, called Hexapla because of its six-column arrangement, was a product of precise scholarship as well as immense industry. Unfortunately, only fragments of the Hexapla have survived.

Jewish translations into Aramaic are extant in several versions. The most extensive of these is Targum Onkelos (TO), which dates from the second century of the present era. Although some sections are paraphrased, and anthropomorphisms are shunned throughout, TO is for the most part a literal rendering of the Hebrew embodying not only long-established rabbinical traditions but also a great deal of valuable philological lore. There are also fragments of other Palestinian recensions in Aramaic (TP), and of an extensive periphrastic rendition erroneously attributed to an otherwise unspecified Jonathan (TJ). A Christian translation into Syriac (a subdivision of Aramaic) bears the name of Peshitta. This version (Syr.) is based in part on the Hebrew text and in part on LXX.

Finally, the standard Latin version or Vulgate (Vulg.) is a tribute to the scholarship and devotion of Jerome (late fourth and early fifth centuries). In his task, Jerome utilized, in varying degrees, the translation of LXX, the so-called Old Latin version which was based on LXX, the Hexapla of Origen, and the underlying Hebrew text in the light of contemporary rabbinical exegesis. The Vulgate is thus a rich mine of information; and it remains the official Bible of the Roman Catholic Church.

Passing now to English versions of the Bible, is it proper to describe more than one such translation as standard? Should not this term be reserved for the Authorized Version of 1611, more commonly known as the King James Bible (KJ)? The question is not entirely academic. It is an inescapable fact, for instance, that all subsequent English translations of the Bible, which go back to the original and not, say, to the Vulgate, are loyal revisions of KJ or re-

spectful dissenters from it—a tribute either way to the pre-eminent position of the Authorized Version. Here, however, the term "standard" is not intended to carry a normative connotation; it is used not comparatively but quantitatively, to designate certain major efforts.

The King James Bible has been described as "the noblest monument of English prose." If one amends this to read "the most influential work in the English language," the statement would be valid beyond the remotest shadow of doubt. The influence of the King James Bible on life and letters in the English-speaking world has been all-pervasive. The reported comment of one late discoverer, "It is such an interesting book: there are so many quotations in it," is an excellent—though no doubt apocryphal—summary of the situation.

But success on such an unprecedented scale can lead to loss of perspective. When one distinguished literary critic recently described KJ as "probably the greatest translation ever made," he was laying claim to broader literary and technical knowledge than any individual could possibly command. KJ is the product of a singularly happy stage in the history of English. It was achieved, moreover, by men who showed great sensitivity in their handling of the original media —Hebrew, Aramaic, and Greek. The translators had the further advantage of invaluable spadework by gifted predecessors, especially the martyred William Tyndale. It was a matchless combination of assets, and the result was a truly inspired version, destined for extraordinary influence and acclaim.

All translations, however, are but arrested pursuits of the given source. In each case the chase halts with the publication of the version. But the target does not remain stationary, unless the subject itself is static so that no further progress is possible. With regard to the Bible, the flow of information has never ceased. The King James Version could not go beyond the knowledge and insights of its own age. Yet we have learned more about a book like Genesis in the subsequent 350 years than had been gleaned in the preceding twenty centuries—more indeed in the last 50 years than in any comparable period since the Pentateuch was canonized. In other words, the gap between KJ and its target has been widening constantly and at a steadily accelerating pace.

Relatively few lay readers of the Bible are able to make a firsthand comparison between their favorite translation and the origi-

nal. With a version that possesses the outstanding appeal of the King James Bible, it is not surprising that many of its users should dismiss the original as an unwelcome intruder. Substantive departures from KJ are apt to be resented as so many wanton desecrations. The fact, say, that "the valley of the shadow of death" is an old distortion of the actual text is immaterial to those who have come to cherish the eerie image; and who wants to give up Joseph's "coat of many colors," even though the chromatic effect is illusory? It is almost as if the Psalmist, or Jacob, should have consulted the translators, instead of the other way about. Nevertheless, beyond the interest in any given Bible translation looms the attraction of the original source. For it was the source that inspired the hundreds of versions, ancient and recent, and enabled each of them to shine with refracted glory—not just the King James Bible, but also Luther's older translation into German (1534), and the many similar achievements in other European countries. The constant striving for improved translations is not motivated by mere pedantry; it is stimulated, in the final analysis, by the hope that each new insight may bring us that much closer to the secret of the Bible's universal and enduring appeal. This alone would be reason enough for the growing number of revisions and new translations, in various languages, with all the toll in energy and treasure that such efforts entail.

Recent increase in these activities in English may be judged from the following partial listing of Old Testament versions. Revisions of the King James Bible include the *English Revised Version* (1885), the *American Revised Version* (1901), the *Holy Scriptures,* issued by the Jewish Publication Society (JPS, 1917), and the *Revised Standard Version* (RSV, 1952). Less hampered by ties to the Authorized Version of 1611 are James Moffatt's *The Old Testament* (1922); *The Old Testament: An American Translation* (AT, 1931); and the revised translation by the Jewish Publication Society, *The Torah,* 1962. The same should be true of the forthcoming Old Testament section of the *New English Bible.* And one should note the Catholic Confraternity Version.

It is no accident that all but one of these versions fall within the present century, and that several are either the product of the past decade or are still in preparation. The stepped-up pace of translational effort is but an index of the swelling flow of discovery. Desire to keep up with changing English usage has been a relatively minor factor. It is not the language of this or that version of the Bible that has needed revising, but the underlying image of the biblical age, as reflected in the text, the grammar, the lexicon, and—above all—in the enormous volume of new material on the ancient Near East as a whole.

The translation which is offered in the present work was handicapped by fewer obstacles than "standard" versions normally face. Concentration on a single book of the Bible automatically limits the range of problems. An individual can venture solutions from which a collective body might be expected to shrink. And the addition of extensive notes and comments affords ample opportunity to justify a seemingly far-fetched rendition.

But no biblical version nowadays can be anything else than stuff for transforming. All that a modern translator can hope for is to have progressed here and there beyond his innumerable predecessors, each of whom has had some share in the search. As long as a single pertinent tablet or ostracon remains underground, or has gone unheeded, there can be no definitive translation of a book of the Bible.

I. PRIMEVAL HISTORY

1. OPENING ACCOUNT OF CREATION
(i 1–ii 4a: *P*)

I ¹ When God set about to create heaven and earth—² the world being then a formless waste, with darkness over the seas and only an awesome wind sweeping over the water—³ God said, "Let there be light." And there was light. ⁴ God was pleased with the light that he saw, and he separated the light from the darkness. ⁵ God called the light Day, and he called the darkness Night. Thus evening came, and morning—first day.

⁶ God said, "Let there be an expanse in the middle of the water to form a division between the waters." ᵃAnd it was so.ᵃ ⁷ God made the expanse, and it divided the water below it from the water above it.ᵇ ⁸ God called the expanse Sky. Thus evening came, and morning—second day.

⁹ God said, "Let the water beneath the sky be gathered into a single area, that the dry land may be visible." And it was so. ¹⁰ God called the dry land Earth, and he called the gathered waters Seas. God was pleased with what he saw, ¹¹ and he said, "Let the earth burst forth with growth: plants that bear seed, andᶜ every kind of fruit tree on earth that bears fruit with its seed in it." And it was so. ¹² The earth produced growth: various kinds of seed-bearing plants, and trees of every kind bearing fruit with seed in it. And God was pleased with what he saw. ¹³ Thus evening came, and morning—third day.

¹⁴ God said, "Let there be lights in the expanse of the sky, to distinguish between day and night; let them mark the fixed

ᵃ⁻ᵃ So LXX; transposed in MT to the end of vs. 7.
ᵇ Heb. "expanse" (twice).
ᶜ So several manuscripts and most ancient versions; omitted in MT.

times, the days and the years, 15 and serve as lights in the expanse of the sky to shine upon the earth. And it was so. 16 God made the great lights, the greater one to dominate the day and the lesser one to dominate the night—and the stars. 17 God set them in the expanse of the sky to shine upon the earth, 18 to dominate the day and the night, and to distinguish between light and darkness. And God was pleased with what he saw. 19 Thus evening came, and morning—fourth day.

20 God said, "Let the waters teem with swarms of living creatures, and let birds fly above the earth across the expanse of the sky." ᵈAnd it was so.ᵈ 21 God created the great sea monsters, every kind of crawling creature with which the waters teem, and all kinds of winged birds. And God was pleased with what he saw. 22 God blessed them, saying, "Be fertile and increase; fill the waters in the seas, and let the birds multiply on earth." 23 Thus evening came, and morning—fifth day.

24 God said, "Let the earth bring forth various kinds of living creatures: cattle, creeping things, and wild animals of every kind." And it was so. 25 God made various kinds of wild animals, cattle of every kind, and all the creeping things of the earth, whatever their kind. And God was pleased with what he saw.

26 Then God said, "Iᵉ will make man in my image, after my likeness; let him subject the fish of the sea and the birds of the sky, the cattle and all the wild [animals],ᶠ and all the creatures that creep on earth."

> 27 And God Created man in his image;
> In the divine image created he him,
> Male and female created he them.

28 God blessed them, saying to them, "Be fertile and increase, fill the earth and subdue it; subject the fishes of the sea, the birds of the sky, and all the living things that move on earth." 29 God further said, "See, I give you every seed-bearing plant on earth and every tree in which is the seed-bearing fruit of the tree;

ᵈ⁻ᵈ Restored from LXX.
ᵉ See NOTE.
ᶠ See NOTE.

30 And to all the animals on land, all the birds of the sky, and all the living creatures that crawl on earth [I give] all the green plants as their food." And it was so. 31 God looked at everything that he had made and found it very pleasing. Thus evening came, and morning—sixth day.

II 1 Now the heaven and the earth were completed, and all their company. 2 On the seventh*g* day God brought to a close the work that he had been doing, and he ceased on the seventh day from all the work that he had undertaken. 3 God blessed the seventh day and declared it holy, for on it he ceased from all the work which he had undertaken.

4 Such is the story of heaven and earth as they were created.

NOTES

i 1. On the introductory phrase see COMMENT.

2. The parenthetic character of this verse is confirmed by the syntax of Heb. A normal consecutive statement would have begun with *watt*e*hī hā'āreṣ*, not *w*e*hā'āreṣ hāy*e*tā*.

a formless waste. The Heb. pair *tōhū wā-bōhū* is an excellent example of hendiadys, that is, two terms connected by "and" and forming a unit in which one member is used to qualify the other; cf., for example, vs. 14, iii 16, xlv 6. Here "unformed-and-void" is used to describe "a formless waste."

an awesome wind. Heb. *ru*a*h* means primarily "wind, breeze," secondarily "breath," and thus ultimately "spirit." But the last connotation is more concrete than abstract; in the present context, moreover, it appears to be out of place—see H. M. Orlinsky, JQR 47 (1957), 174–82. The appended *'*e*lōhīm* can be either possessive ("of/from God"), or adjectival ("divine, supernatural, awesome"; but not simply "mighty"); cf. xxx 8.

sweeping. The same stem is used in Deut xxxii 11 of eagles in relation to their young. The Ugaritic cognate describes a form of motion as opposed to a state of suspension or rest.

4. *was pleased with [what] he saw.* This phrase, which serves as a formal refrain, means literally "saw that it was good," or rather "saw how good it was" (cf. W. F. Albright, *Mélanges Robert*, 1956, pp. 22–26); but Heb. "good" has a broader range than its English equivalent.

5. *came.* Literally "was, came to be"; Heb. repeats the verb with "morning." The evening marks the first half of the full day.

g See NOTE.

first day. In Semitic (notably in Akkadian, cf. Gilg., Tablet XI, lines 215 ff.) the normal ordinal series is *"one,* second, third," etc., not *"first,* second, third," etc.; cf. also ii 11.

6. *expanse.* Traditionally "firmament," one of the Bible's indirect contributions to Western lexicons. It goes back to the Vulg. *firmamentum* "something made solid," which is based in turn on the LXX rendering of Heb. *rāqīaʻ* "beaten out, stamped" (as of metal), suggesting a thin sheet stretched out to form the vault of the sky (cf. Dr.).

And it was so. This clause is correctly reproduced here by LXX but misplaced in Heb. at the end of vs. 7. The present account employs it normally after each of God's statements; cf. vss. 9, 11, 15, 24, 30, and textual note *d–d*.

9. *area.* Literally "place," Heb. cons. *mqwm,* for which LXX reads *mqwh* "gathering," the same as in vs. 10, perhaps rightly (cf. D. N. Freedman, *Zeitschrift für alttestamentliche Wissenschaft* 64 [1953], 190 f.).

14. *let them mark the fixed times.* Heb. literally "let them be for signs and for seasons (and for days and for years)," which has been reproduced mechanically in most translations (most recently RSV). Some of the moderns (e.g., von Rad, SB), realizing that signs do not belong in this list, take the first connective particle as explicative: they shall serve as signs, that is, for seasons, and days, and years; but the sun and the moon cannot be said to determine the seasons proper; moreover, the order would then be unbalanced (one would expect: days, seasons, years). The problem solves itself once we take the first pair as a hendiadys (cf. vs. 2): they shall serve a sign for the fixed time periods, or in other words, they shall mark the fixed times, that is, the days and the years. The use of the particle (Heb. $w^e/\bar{u}$) in each of these functions (hendiadys, explicative, connective) is amply attested elsewhere.

15. *lights.* Heb. $m^{e'}\bar{o}r\bar{o}t$, differentiated from $m^{e'}\bar{o}r\bar{o}t$ in vs. 14, literally "sources of light, luminaries."

20. The creation of the fifth day was deemed to comprise creatures (Heb. *nepeš*) that might appear in swarms (*šereṣ*) in the water, on the ground, or in the air. But their ultimate breeding place was traced to the waters, since land creatures come under the sixth day. The process is described indirectly: let the waters teem with . . . (stem *šrṣ*, with cognate accusative).

21. The same Heb. stem (*rmś*) is used for "crawl" (as in this instance) and "creep" (as in 24 ff.). The underlying sense, however (which is shared by the Akk. cognate *namāšu*), is "to have locomotion"; cf. vs. 28, vii 21, ix 2. And just as Heb. *remeś* is contrasted here with

larger animals in 24 ff., so, too, in Gilg. (Tablet I, column ii, lines
40 ff.) the small creatures of the steppe (Akk. *namaššū*) are juxtaposed
to the larger beasts.

24. Heb. *bᵉhēmā* "cattle" covers here the domestic animals in general,
or animals due to be domesticated.

26. For the singulars "my image, my likeness" Heb. employs here
plural possessives, which most translations reproduce. Yet no other
divine being has been mentioned; and the very next verse uses the singular
throughout; cf. also ii 7. The point at issue, therefore, is one of grammar
alone, without a direct bearing on the meaning. It so happens that the
common Heb. term for "God," namely, Elohim (*'ᵉlōhīm*) is plural in
form and is so construed at times (e.g., xx 13, xxxv 7, etc.). Here God
refers to himself, which may account for the more formal construction
in the plural.

wild [*animals*]. Reading [*ḥyt*] *h'rṣ* as in vs. 25.

28. *move*. Same Heb. verb as for "creep"; see NOTE on vs. 21.

30. [*I give*]. In Heb. the predicate may carry over from 29; but the
translation has to repeat it for clarity.

ii 1. The relatively recent division into chapters, which dates from
medieval times, disturbs in this case the inner unity of the account. In
vs. 4, below, the much older division into verses proves to be equally
misleading.

company. Heb. *ṣābā'* generally stands for "army, host," but this is by
no means the original meaning of the term; the basic sense of the stem
is "to be engaged in group service" (cf. Exod xxxviii 8; I Sam ii 22;
Isa xxix 7, 8). The cognate Akk. noun *ṣābu* denotes not only "soldier,"
but also "member of a work gang, laborer." The Heb. term is collective;
in the present context it designates the total made up of the various
component parts in the planned design of creation; hence array, ranks,
company.

2. Since the task of creation was finished on the sixth day, the text
can hardly go on to say that God concluded it on the seventh day. It
follows therefore that (a) the numeral is an error for "sixth," as assumed
by LXX, Sam., and other ancient versions; (b) the pertinent verb is
to be interpreted as a pluperfect: God had finished on the sixth day and
rested on the seventh; or (c) the verb carries some more particular
shade of meaning. The present translation inclines to the last choice.
Under circumstances that are similar in kind if not in degree, Akk.
employs the verb *šuteṣbû* in the sense of "inspect and approve"; this is
applied to the work of craftsmen (masons in the Code of Hammurabi
233) and even to the birth of Marduk (ANET, p. 62, line 91). In this
account, God inspects the results of each successive act and finds them

pleasing. The end result could well be described as work "brought to a (gratifying) close." A. Heidel, *The Babylonian Genesis,* p. 127, proposes "declared finished," which appears to point in the same direction.

4. *story.* Heb. *tōlᵉdōt,* traditionally "generations" in the etymological sense of "begettings," that is, "genealogy, line" in modern usage (cf. Note on vs. 1); hence the derived meaning "history," or more simply "story," as in the present context.

COMMENT

This opening statement about the creation of the world is assigned by nearly all critics to the P(riestly) source. There is a marked difference between the present section and the accounts that follow, accounts which most scholars regard as typical of the J source. Although the subject matter is roughly parallel in both instances, there is scarcely any similarity in general treatment or specific emphasis. No less noteworthy is the stylistic contrast between the respective sections, which cannot be ignored even in translation, as the subsequent chapters will show. The version before us displays, aside from P's characteristic vocabulary, a style that is impersonal, formulaic, and measured to the point of austerity. What we have here is not primarily a description of events or a reflection of a unique experience. Rather, we are given the barest statement of a sequence of facts resulting from the fiat of the supreme and absolute master of the universe. Yet the account has a grandeur and a dramatic impact all its own.

The stark simplicity of this introductory section is thus by no means a mark of meager writing ability. It is the result of special cultivation, a process in which each detail was refined through endless probing and each word subjected to minutest scrutiny. By the same token, the end product cannot have been the work of an individual, but must be attributed to a school with a continuous tradition behind it. The ultimate objective was to set forth, in a manner that must not presume in any way to edit the achievement of the Creator—by the slightest injection of sentiment or personality—not a theory but a credo, a credo untinged by the least hint of speculation.

In these circumstances, the question that immediately arises— one that is necessarily more acute here than in nearly any other

context—is the basic question that has to be raised about any statement in a given source; and this is not whether the statement is true
or false, but what it means (R. G. Collingwood, *The Idea of History*, 1946, p. 260). In other words, the point here is not whether
this account of creation conforms to the scientific data of today, but
what it meant to, and how it was arrived at by, the writer concerned. It is on this score, among many others, that the results of
recent discovery and research afford us the means for an improved
perspective.

Genesis i–xi in general, and the first section in particular, are a
broad introduction to the history which commences with Abraham.
The practice of tracing history back to antediluvian times is at least
as old as the Sumerian king list (see above, p. LVII). Biblical
tradition had ample reason to be familiar with Mesopotamian cultural norms. Indeed, the Primeval History is largely Mesopotamian
in substance, implicitly for the most part, but also explicitly in such
instances as the Garden of Eden or the Tower of Babel. Thus biblical authors were indebted to Mesopotamian models for these early
chapters not only in matters of arrangement but also in some of the
subject matter.

Is the treatment of creation in Genesis a case of such indebtedness? We have two separate accounts of this theme, the present
section which stems from *P*, and the one following which goes back
to *J*, as was indicated above. Yet neither source could have borrowed directly from the other, since each dwells on different details.
Accordingly, both must derive from a body of antecedent traditions.
It follows that the present version of *P* should have connections with
old Mesopotamian material. This premise is borne out of actual
facts.

Mesopotamia's canonical version of cosmic origins is found in the
so-called Babylonian Creation Epic, or *Enūma eliš* "When on High"
(ANET, pp. 60–72). The numerous points of contact between it
and the opening section of Genesis have long been noted. There is
not only a striking correspondence in various details, but—what is
even more significant—the order of events is the same, which is
enough to preclude any likelihood of coincidence. The relationship
is duly recognized by all informed students, no matter how orthodox
their personal beliefs may be. I cite as an example the tabulation
given by Heidel, *The Babylonian Genesis*, p. 129:

Enūma elish	*Genesis*
Divine spirit and cosmic matter are coexistent and coeternal	Divine spirit creates cosmic matter and exists independently of it
Primeval chaos; Ti'amat enveloped in darkness	The earth a desolate waste, with darkness covering the deep (*těhōm*)
Light emanating from the gods	Light created
The creation of the firmament	The creation of the firmament
The creation of dry land	The creation of dry land
The creation of luminaries	The creation of luminaries
The creation of man	The creation of man
The gods rest and celebrate	God rests and sanctifies the seventh day

Except for incidental differences of opinion in regard to the exact meaning of the first entry in each column (see below, and cf. NOTE on vs. 2), the validity of this listing is not open to question. What, then, are the conclusions that may be drawn from these and other relevant data?

It is clear that the biblical approach to creation as reflected in *P* is closely related to traditional Mesopotamian beliefs. It may be safely posited, moreover, that the Babylonians did not take over these views from the Hebrews, since the cuneiform accounts—among which *Enūma eliš* is but one, and a relatively stereotyped, formulation—antedate in substance the biblical statements on the subject. Nor is there the slightest basis in fact for assuming some unidentified ultimate source from which both the Mesopotamians and the Hebrews could have derived their views about creation. It would thus appear that *P*'s opening account goes back to Babylonian prototypes, and it is immaterial whether the transmission was accomplished directly or through some intermediate channel; in any case, *J* cannot have served as a link in this particular instance.

The date of the take-over cannot be determined within any practical limits. Although much in *P* is demonstrably late, there is also early material in that same source. The Primeval History in particular was bound to make use of old data. At the same time, however, a distinction must be made between basic subject matter and its final form in the collective version. The creation account could have entered the stream of biblical tradition sometime in the latter half of the second millennium, without taking final shape until a number of centuries later. In the present connection, however, the question of date is a relatively minor one. Of far greater importance are (1) the established borrowing of the general version of creation, and (2) the ultimate setting into which biblical tradition incorporated the received account.

Derivation from Mesopotamia in this instance means no more and no less than that on the subject of creation biblical tradition aligned itself with the traditional tenets of Babylonian "science." The reasons should not be far to seek. For one thing, Mesopotamia's achievements in that field were highly advanced, respected, and influential. And for another, the patriarchs constituted a direct link between early Hebrews and Mesopotamia, and the cultural effects of that start persisted long thereafter.

In ancient times, however, science often blended into religion; and the two could not be separated in such issues as cosmogony and the origin of man. To that extent, therefore, "scientific" conclusions were bound to be guided by underlying religious beliefs. And since the religion of the Hebrews diverged sharply from Mesopotamian norms, we should expect a corresponding departure in regard to beliefs about creation. This expectation is fully borne out. While we have before us incontestable similarities in detail, the difference in over-all approach is no less prominent. The Babylonian creation story features a succession of various rival deities. The biblical version, on the other hand, is dominated by the monotheistic concept in the absolute sense of the term. Thus the two are both genetically related and yet poles apart. In common with other portions of the Primeval History, the biblical account of creation displays at one and the same time a recognition of pertinent Babylonian sources as well as a critical position toward them.

Such in brief is the present application of the precept that when faced with a statement in a significant source—and especially a statement about such matters as creation—we ask first what the statement means, before we consider whether it is true or false from the vantage point of another age.

It remains to discuss, in passing, the structure of the introductory verses of this section, since their syntax determines the meaning, and the precise meaning of this passage happens to be of far-reach-

ing significance. The problem could not be fully elucidated in the
NOTES, which is why it is being considered here.

The first word of Genesis, and hence the first word in the Hebrew
Bible as a unit, is vocalized as *bᵉrēʾšīt*. Grammatically, this is evidently
in the construct state, that is, the first of two connected forms which
jointly yield a possessive compound. Thus the sense of this particular
initial term is, or should be, "At the beginning of . . . ," or "When,"
and not "In/At the beginning"; the absolute form with adverbial
connotation would be *bārēʾšīt*. As the text is now vocalized, therefore, the Hebrew Bible starts out with a dependent clause.

The second word in Hebrew, and hence the end-form of the indicated possessive compound, appears as *bārāʾ*, literally "he
created." The normal way of saying "at the beginning of creation
(by God)" would be *bᵉrēšīt bᵉrōʾ* (*ʾelōhīm*), with the infinitive in the
second position; and this is indeed the precise construction (though
not the wording) of the corresponding phrase in ii 4b. Nevertheless,
Hebrew usage permits a finite verb in this position; cf. Hos i 2. It is
worth noting that the majority of medieval Hebrew commentators
and grammarians, not to mention many moderns, could see no
objection to viewing Gen i 1 as a dependent clause.

Nevertheless, vocalization alone should not be the decisive factor
in this instance. For it could be (and has been) argued that the
vocalized text is relatively late and should not therefore be unduly
binding. A more valid argument, however, is furnished by the syntax
of the entire first paragraph. A closer examination reveals that vs. 2
is a parenthetic clause: "the earth being then a formless waste
. . . ," with the main clause coming in vs. 3. The structure of the
whole sentence is thus schematically as follows: "(¹)When . . .
(²)—at which time . . . —(³)then . . ." Significantly enough, the
analogous account (by *J*) in ii 4b–7 shows the identical construction, with vss. 5–6 constituting a circumstantial description. Perhaps more important still, the related, and probably normative, arrangement at the beginning of *Enūma eliš* exhibits exactly the same
kind of structure: dependent temporal clause (lines 1–2); parenthetic clauses (3–8); main clause (9). Thus grammar, context, and
parallels point uniformly in one and the same direction.

There is more to this question, of course, than mere linguistic
niceties. If the first sentence states that "In the beginning God created heaven and earth," what ensued was chaos (vs. 2) which
needed immediate attention. In other words, the Creator would be

charged with an inadequate initial performance, unless one takes the whole of vs. 1 as a general title, contrary to established biblical practice. To be sure, the present interpretation precludes the view that the creation accounts in Genesis say nothing about coexistent matter. The question, however, is not the ultimate truth about cosmogony, but only the exact meaning of the Genesis passages which deal with the subject. On this score, at least, the biblical writers repeat the Babylonian formulation, perhaps without full awareness of the theological and philosophical implications. At all events, the text should be allowed to speak for itself.

2. THE STORY OF EDEN
(ii 4b–24: *J*)

II ⁴ᵇ At the time when God Yahweh made earth and heaven—
⁵ no shrub of the field being yet in the earth and no grains of the
field having sprouted, for God Yahweh had not sent rain upon
the earth and no man was there to till the soil; ⁶ instead, a flow
would well up from the ground and water the whole surface of
the soil—⁷ God Yahweh formed man[a] from clods in the soil[b]
and blew into his nostrils the breath of life. Thus man became a
living being.

⁸ God Yahweh planted a garden in Eden, in the east, and
placed there the man whom he had formed. ⁹ And out of the
ground God Yahweh caused to grow various trees that were a
delight to the eye and good for eating, with the tree of life in
the middle of the garden and the tree of knowledge of good and
bad.

¹⁰ A river rises in Eden to water the garden; outside, it forms
four separate branch streams. ¹¹ The name of the first is Pishon;
it is the one that winds through the whole land of Havilah,
where there is gold. ¹² The gold of that land is choice; there is
bdellium there, and lapis lazuli. ¹³ The name of the second
river is Gihon; it is the one that winds through all the land of
Cush. ¹⁴ The name of the third river is Tigris; it is the one that
flows east of Asshur. The fourth river is the Euphrates.

¹⁵ God Yahweh took the man and settled him in the garden
of Eden, to till and tend it. ¹⁶ And God Yahweh commanded
the man, saying, "You are free to eat of any tree of the garden,

---

[a] MT *'ādām*.
[b] Heb. *'ᵃdāmā*, in assonance with *'ādām*.

17 except only the tree of knowledge of good and bad, of which you are not to eat. For the moment you eat of it, you shall be doomed to death."

18 God Yahweh said, "It is not right that man should be alone. I will make him an aid fit for him." 19 So God Yahweh formed out of the soil various wild beasts and birds of the sky and brought them to the man to see what he called them; whatever the man would call a living creature, that was to be its name. 20 The man gave names to all cattle, all*e* birds of the sky, and all wild beasts; yet none proved to be the aid that would be fit for man.*d*

21 Then God Yahweh cast a deep sleep upon the man and, when he was asleep, he took one of his ribs and closed up the flesh at that spot. 22 And God Yahweh fashioned into a woman the rib that he had removed from the man, and he brought her to the man. 23 Said the man,

This one at last is bone of my bones and flesh of my flesh. She shall be called Woman,*e* for she was taken from Man.*f*

24 Thus it is that man leaves his father and mother and clings to his wife, and they become one flesh.

c So several manuscripts and ancient versions; MT omits.
d MT "Adam."
e Heb. *'iššā.*
f Heb. *īš,* in assonance with *'iššā.*

NOTES

ii 4b. *At the time when.* Literally "on the day when"; Heb. *beyōm,* cognate with Akk. *enūma,* the opening word of the Babylonian Genesis (*Enūma eliš*).

God Yahweh. Although this combination is the rule in ii 4b–iii 24, it is found only once in the rest of the Pentateuch (Exod ix 30). Critical opinion inclines to the assumption that the original version used "Yahweh" throughout, in conformance with *J*'s normal practice, the other component being added later under the influence of the opening account (by *P*). One cannot, however, discount the possibility that these personal name of a deity with a determinative for "god," except that such a qualifier would follow the name in Hebrew rather than precede it.

The personal name itself has come down in the consonantal text (*K^{e}thib*) as YHWH. The vocalized text (*Q^{e}re*) has equipped this form with the vowels *^{e}-ō-ā*, thus calling for the reading *'^{a}dōnāy* "Lord" (the difference between the initial vowels is secondary). The reluctance to pronounce the personal name, which is not yet reflected in the consonantal sources but is already attested in LXX, is directly traceable to the Third Commandment (Exod xx 7; Deut v 11), which says actually, "You shall not swear falsely by the name of Yahweh your God," but has been misinterpreted to mean "You shall not take the name of Yahweh your God in vain." Lev xxiv 16 deals with an entirely different issue (specifically, an insult to Yahweh).

5. In *'ādām* "man" and *'^{a}dāmā* "soil, ground" there is an obvious play on words, a practice which the Bible shares with other ancient literatures. This should not, however, be mistaken for mere punning. Names were regarded not only as labels but also as symbols, magical keys as it were to the nature and essence of the given being or thing (cf. vs. 19). The writer or speaker who resorted to "popular etymologies" was not interested in derivation as such. The closest approach in English to the juxtaposition of the Hebrew nouns before us might be "earthling: earth."

6. *flow.* Heb. *'ēd*, apparently Akk. *edû* (Sum loanword), cf. my note in BASOR 140 (1955), 9 ff.; for a slightly different view see W. F. Albright, JBL 58 (1939), 102 f. The sense would be that of an underground swell, a common motif in Akkadian literary compositions. The only other occurrence of the term, Job xxxvi 27, "mist" or the like, need signify no more than the eventual literary application of this rare word.

7. *clods.* The traditional "dust" is hard to part with, yet it is inappropriate. Heb. *'āpār* stands for "lumps of earth, soil, dirt" as well as the resulting particles of "dust." For the former, cf., for example, xxvi 15; note also vs. 19, where the animals are said to have been formed "out of the soil." On the other hand, "dust" is preferable in iii 19.

8. *Eden.* Heb. *'ēden*, Akk. *edinu*, based on Sum. *eden* "plain, steppe." The term is used here clearly as a geographical designation, which came to be associated, naturally enough, with the homonymous but unrelated Heb. noun for "enjoyment."

in the east. Not "from"; the preposition (Heb. *min*) is not only partitive but also locative.

9. See iii 5.

10–14. On the general question of the Rivers of Eden see COMMENT.

10. *rises in.* Not the traditional "went out of" (wrong tense), nor

even "comes out of, issues from," since the garden itself is in Eden. Hence, too,

outside. Heb. literally "from there," in the sense of "beyond it," for which cf. I Sam x 3. What this means is that, before reaching Eden, the river consists of four separate branches. Accordingly,

branch streams. In Heb. the mouth of the river is called "end" (Josh xv 5, xviii 19); hence the plural of *rō'š* "head" must refer here to the upper course (Ehrl.). This latter usage is well attested for the Akk. cognate *rēšu*.

11. *winds through*. The customary "compasses, encircles" yields a needlessly artificial picture. The pertinent Heb. stem *sbb* means not only "to circle" but also "to pursue a roundabout course, to twist and turn" (cf. II Kings iii 9), and this is surely an apt description of a meandering stream.

Havilah. There was evidently more than one place, as well as tribe, by that name (Dr., pp. 119, 131).

12. *lapis lazuli*. For this tentative identification of Heb. *'eben haššoham*, cf. my discussion "The Rivers of Paradise" in *Festschrift Johannes Friedrich*, 1959, pp. 480 f.

14. *Tigris*. This modern form is based on the Greek approximation to the native name, which appears as *(I)digna* in Sumerian, *Idiqlat* in Akkadian, *Ḥiddeqel* in Hebrew, *Deqlat* in Aramaic, and *Dijlat* in Arabic.

Asshur. Elsewhere in Heb., either the land of Assyria or its eponymous capital. Here evidently the latter; the Tigris flows east of the city of Ashur, but it never constituted the entire eastern border between Assyria and Babylonia (Cush).

16. *you are free to eat*. Or "you may eat freely." Heb. employs here the so-called "infinitive absolute" construction, in which the pertinent Heb. form is preceded by its infinitive. The resulting phrase is a flexible utterance capable of conveying various shades of meaning; cf. next vs.

17. *the moment*. Heb. literally "on the day"; cf. 4b.

you shall be doomed to death. Another infinitive absolute in Hebrew. The phrase need not be translated "you shall surely die," as it invariably is. Death did not result in this instance. The point of the whole narrative is apparently man's ultimate punishment rather than instantaneous death.

18. *an aid fit for him*. The traditional "help meet for him" is adequate, but subject to confusion, as may be seen from our "helpmate," which is based on this very passage. The Heb. complement means literally "alongside him," i.e., "corresponding to him."

19. *a living creature.* In this position this phrase does violence to Heb. syntax, it could well be a later gloss.

20. *proved to be.* Traditionally "was found to be." In this construction, however, the Heb. stem *mṣ'* usually means "to suffice, reach, be adequate" (Ehrl.), as is true also of its cognates in Akkadian and Aramaic.

21. *at that spot.* Heb. literally "underneath it," or "instead of it," with the idiomatic sense of "then and there."

22. *to the man.* In Heb. the defined form *hā'ādām* is "man," the undefined *'ādām*, "Adam," since a personal name cannot take the definite article. With prepositions like *lᵉ-* "to," the article is elided and only the vowel marks the difference between "to Adam" (*lᵉ'ādām*) and "to the man" (*lā'ādām*), so that the consonantal text is bound to be ambiguous (*l'dm* in either case). Since the form without preposition appears invariably as *hā'ādām* in ii–iii (the undefined form occurs first in iv 25), and is not mentioned until the naming of Adam v 2, the vocalized "to Adam" (also vs. 20, iii 17) is an anachronism. In iii, LXX favors "Adam" even in the presence of the consonantal article.

23. The assonance of Heb. *'īš* and *'iššā* has no etymological basis. It is another instance of symbolic play on words, except that the phonetic similarity this time is closer than usual. By an interesting coincidence, Eng. "woman" (derived from "wife of man") would offer a better linguistic foil than the Heb. noun.

COMMENT

The brief Eden interlude (ii 4b–iii 24) has been the subject of an enormous literature so far, with no end in sight. One study alone takes up over 600 pages (cf. the comment by J. L. McKenzie, "The Literary Characteristics of Genesis 2–3," *Theological Studies* 15 [1954], 541–72). Here there is room for only a few paragraphs.

The account before us deals with the origin of life on earth, as contrasted with the preceding statement about the origin of the universe as a whole. The contrast is immediately apparent from the respective initial sentences. The first account starts out with the creation of "heaven and earth" (i 1). The present narrative begins with the making of "earth and heaven" (ii 4b). The difference is by no means accidental. In the other instance the center of the stage was heaven, and man was but an item in a cosmic sequence of majestic acts. Here the earth is paramount and man the center of interest; indeed, an earthy and vividly personal approach is one of the outstanding characteristics of the whole account. This far-reaching divergence in basic philosophy would alone be sufficient to warn the reader that two separate sources appear to be involved, one heaven-centered and the other earth-centered. The dichotomy is further supported by differences in phraseology (e.g., "create" : "make") and in references to the Deity ("God" : "God Yahweh"); and the contrast is sustained in further pertinent passages. In short, there are ample grounds for recognizing the hand of *P* in the preceding statement, as against that of *J* in the present narrative.

Yet despite the difference in approach, emphasis, and hence also in authorship, the fact remains that the subject matter is ultimately the same in both versions. We have seen that the *P* version, for its part, derived much of its detail from Mesopotamian traditions about the beginnings of the world. The account by *J* points in the same direction, as is immediately apparent from the following comparison of opening lines:

"At the time when God Yahweh made earth and heaven—" (ii 4b)

"When God set about to create heaven and earth—" (i 1)

"When on high heaven had not been named,

Firm ground below had not been called by name—" (ANET, pp. 61 f., I, lines 1 f.).

In each case the temporal clause leads up to a parenthetic description, and is then resumed with the proper sequel. Thus, however much *J, P,* and their Mesopotamian sources may differ ultimately from one another, they are also tied to common traditions.

That *J* incorporated Mesopotamian data in his treatment of the origin of man—most of which, incidentally, are missing in *P*—is shown by much more compelling evidence than the mere agreement of initial clauses. To begin with, the narrative before us features two telltale loanwords. One is the word for "flow" (vs. 6), Akk. *edû*, from Sum. *a.dé.a* (see NOTE *ad loc.*). The other is the geographical term "Eden" (cf. NOTE on vs. 8), Akk. *edinu*, Sum. *eden*, which is especially significant in that this word is rare in Akk. but exceedingly common in Sum., thus certifying the ultimate source as very ancient indeed. The traditions involved must go back, therefore, to the oldest cultural stratum of Mesopotamia.

Next comes the evidence from the location of Eden which is furnished by the notices about the rivers of that region. Recent data on the subject demonstrate that the physical background of the tale is authentic (see the writer's "The Rivers of Paradise," *Festschrift Johannes Friedrich,* pp. 473–85). All four streams once converged, or were believed to have done so, near the head of the Persian Gulf, to create a rich garden land to which local religion and literature alike looked back as the land of the blessed. And while the Pishon and the Gihon stand for lesser streams, which have been Hebraized into something like "the Gusher" and "the Bubbler" respectively, the Tigris and the Euphrates leave no doubt in any case as to the assumed locale of the Garden of Eden. The chaotic geography of ancient and modern exponents of this biblical text can be traced largely to two factors. One is the mistaken identification of the land of Cush in vs. 13 (and in x 8) with the homonymous biblical term for Ethiopia, rather than with the country of the Kassites; note the spelling *Kuššū-* in the Nuzi documents, and the classical Gr. form *Kossaios.* The other adverse factor is linked with specialized Heb. usage. In vs. 10 (see NOTES) the term "heads" can have nothing to do with streams into which the river breaks up after it leaves Eden, but designates instead four separate branches which have merged within Eden. There is thus no basis for detouring the Gihon to Ethiopia, not to mention the search for the Pishon in various remote regions of the world.

There is, finally, the motif of the tree of knowledge which likewise betrays certain Mesopotamian links. The discussion, however, may best be combined with the COMMENT on iii 5. For the present, it need only be remarked in passing that the Heb. for "the tree of life in the middle of the garden and the tree of knowledge of good and bad" is extremely awkward syntactically, especially in a writer who is otherwise a matchless stylist. Moreover, vs. 17 has nothing to say about the tree of life, and speaks only of the tree of knowledge. There is thus much in favor of the critical conjecture that the original text had only "and in the midst of the garden the tree of knowledge."

Would so much dependence on Mesopotamian concepts be strange in an author of *J*'s originality and caliber? Not at all. For it should be borne in mind that the Primeval History is but a general preface to a much larger work, a preface about a remote age which comes to life in Mesopotamia and for which that land alone furnishes the necessary historical and cultural records. In these early chapters, *J* reflects, in common with *P,* distant traditions that had gained currency through the ages.

3. THE FALL OF MAN
(ii 25–iii 24: *J*)

II 25 The two of them were naked, the man and his wife, yet they felt no shame.

III 1 Now the serpent was the sliest of all the wild creatures that God Yahweh had made. Said he to the woman, "Even though God told you not to eat of any tree in the garden . . ." 2 The woman interrupted the serpent, "But we may eat of the trees in the garden! 3 It is only about the fruit of the tree in the middle of the garden that God did say, 'Do not eat of it or so much as touch it, lest you die!'" 4 But the serpent said to the woman, "You are not going to die. 5 No, God well knows that the moment you eat of it your eyes will be opened and you will be the same as God in telling good from bad."

6 When the woman saw that the tree was good for eating and a delight to the eye, and that the tree was attractive as a means to wisdom, she took of its fruit and ate; and she gave some to her husband and he ate. 7 Then the eyes of both were opened and they discovered that they were naked; so they sewed fig leaves together and made themselves loincloths.

8 They heard the sound of God Yahweh as he was walking in the garden at the breezy time of day; and the man and his wife hid from God Yahweh among the trees of the garden.

9 God Yahweh called to the man and said to him, "Where are you?" 10 He answered, "I heard the sound of you in the garden; but I was afraid because I was naked, so I hid." 11 He asked, "Who told you that you were naked? Did you, then, taste of the tree from which I had forbidden you to eat?" 12 The man replied, "The woman whom you put by my side—it was she who gave me of that tree, and I ate." 13 God Yahweh said to the

woman, "How could you do such a thing?" The woman replied, "The serpent tricked me, so I ate."

14 God Yahweh said to the serpent:

> "Because you did this,
> Banned shall you be from all cattle
> And all wild creatures!
> On your belly shall you crawl
> And on dirt shall you feed
> All the days of your life.

15 I will plant enmity between you and the woman,
> And between your offspring and hers;
> They shall strike at your head,
> And you shall strike at their heel."

16 To the woman he said:

> "I will make intense
> Your pangs in childbearing.
> In pain shall you bear children;
> Yet your urge shall be for your husband,
> And he shall be your master."

17 To the man[a] he said: "Because you listened to your wife and ate of the tree from which I had forbidden you to eat,

> Condemned be the soil on your account!
> In anguish shall you eat of it
> All the days of your life.
> 18 Thorns and thistles
> Shall it bring forth for you,
> As you feed on the grasses of the field.
> 19 By the sweat of your face
> Shall you earn your bread,
> Until you return to the ground,
> For from it you were taken:
> For dust you are
> And to dust you shall return!"

a MT, LXX "Adam."

20 The man named his wife Eve,^b because she was the mother of all the living.^c 21 And God Yahweh made shirts of skins for the man and his wife, and clothed them.

22 God Yahweh said, "Now that the man has become like one of us in discerning good from bad, what if he should put out his hand and taste also of the tree of life and eat, and live forever!" 23 So God Yahweh banished him from the garden of Eden, to till the soil from which he was taken. 24 Having expelled the man, he stationed east of the garden of Eden the cherubim and the fiery revolving sword, to guard the way to the tree of life.

^b Heb. *ḥawwā.*
^c Heb. *ḥay.*

NOTES

iii 1. *Even though.* The interrogative sense which is generally assumed for Heb. *'ap kī* in this single passage would be without parallel; some critics emend accordingly to *ha'ap kī.* But the corresponding *gam kī* is used for "although," cf. Ps xxiii 4, and the meaning suits the context admirably (Ehrl.). The serpent is not asking a question; he is deliberately distorting a fact.

not to eat. Heb. literally "you shall not eat," since the language has no simple way to express indirect discourse.

2. *interrupted.* Literally "said"; the Heb. stem *'mr* is capable of describing varying types of utterance.

3. *touch it.* In her eagerness to make her point, the woman enlarges on the actual injunction; cf. ii 17.

5. *No.* For this use of *kī* (as opposed to the normal conjunctive force), cf. xxxi 16; Deut xiii 10; Job xxii 2; Ruth i 10 etc.; see KB, p. 431, No. 7.

God. Since Heb. *'elōhīm* is grammatically a plural, and may be used not only for "God," but also for "gods, divine beings," the context is sometimes ambiguous; nor is a modifying plural form, such as the participle "who know" in the present instance, necessarily conclusive. In vs. 22 "one of us" would seem to imply a celestial retinue, but there the speaker is God himself. The serpent might aim at a different effect. In these circumstances no clear-cut decision is possible; "celestials, immortals," or the like would be just as appropriate.

6. *a means to wisdom.* Literally "(to be coveted) in order to become (not 'to make') wise." The so-called causative conjugation of

Heb. is often intransitive (ee JCS 6 [1952], 81 ff.); cf. vi 19 f., xxxv 17, xlix 4.

8. *walking.* A good example of the special durative conjugation in Heb.; cf. vs. 24, v 22, 24, and see JAOS 75 (1955), 117 ff.

at the breezy time of day. The Heb. preposition *l*ᵉ- may be used of time (cf. viii 11), but not temperature; hence the memorable "in the cool of the day" lacks linguistic support. The time involved is toward sundown, when fresh breezes bring welcome relief from the heat.

9. *Where are you?* The question is obviously rhetorical.

11. *then.* Suggested by the inversion in Heb. for added emphasis.

13. *How could you . . . ?* Cf. xii 18.

14. *Banned.* The Heb. stem *'rr* is regularly translated as "to curse," but this sense is seldom appropriate on closer examination. With the preposition *mi(n)*, here and in vs. 17, such a meaning is altogether out of place: "cursed from the ground" (*ibid.*) only serves to misdirect, and "cursed above all cattle and all the beasts of the field" (present instance) would imply that the animal world shared the serpent's guilt. The basic meaning of *'rr* is "to restrain (by magic), bind (by a spell)"; see JAOS 80 (1960), 198 ff. With *mi(n)* the sense is "to hold off, ban" (by similar means). In vs. 17 the required nuance is "condemned."

15. *offspring.* Heb. literally "seed," used normally in the collective sense of progeny. The passage does not justify eschatological connotations. As Dr. put it, "We must not read into the words more than they contain."

16. *pangs in childbearing.* A parade example of hendiadys in Heb. (cf. i 2 and see above, p. LXX). The literal rendering would read "your pangs and your childbearing," but the idiomatic significance is "your pangs that result from your pregnancy."

17. *man.* Cf. NOTE on ii 20.

Condemned. See above, vs. 14.

on your account. LXX translates "as you till it," reflecting *b'bDk*, whereas Heb. reads *R/D;* the two letters are easily confused.

19. *earn your bread.* Literally "eat your bread"; but the effort described is in the producing of grain to be eaten (Ehrl.), not in the eating of it.

22. *Now that.* Heb. *hēn . . . w*ᵉ*'attā* introduce the protasis and the apodosis, so that the two clauses cannot be interpreted as independent.

one of us. A reference to the heavenly company which remains obscure.

24. *cherubim.* Cf. Akk. *kāribu* and *kuribu* which designate figures of minor interceding deities (cf. S. Langdon, *Epic of Creation*, 1923, p. 190, n. 3).

fiery revolving sword. Although the description pertains to an act of

Yahweh, the detail appears to be derived from Mesopotamian traditions. Most of the gods of that land had distinctive weapons of their own, such as the dagger of Ashur or the toothed sword of Shamash. Another illustration may be found in the concluding lines of *Enūma eliš* I (ANET, pp. 63, 160 f.); there the rebel gods are said "to make the fire subside" and "to humble the Power-Weapon." The fire would seem to characterize the weapon, a metaphorical description apparently of the bolt-like or glinting blade. The magic weapon was all that stood between the insurgent gods and their goal.—The Heb. for "revolving" (or "constantly turning") is another instance of the special durative conjugation; cf. NOTE on vs. 8.

COMMENT

Now that the stage has been set, the author can hit his full stride. There is action here and suspense, psychological insight and subtle irony, light and shadow—all achieved in two dozen verses. The characterization is swift and sure, and all the more effective for its indirectness.

Everything is transposed into human terms. The serpent is endowed with man's faculties, and even God is pictured in subjective and anthropomorphic fashion. When Adam has been caught in his transparent attempt at evasion, Yahweh speaks to him as a father would to his child: "Where are you?" In this context, it is the same thing as, "And what have you been up to just now?" This simple phrase—a single word in the original—does the work of volumes. For what *J* has thus evoked is the childhood of mankind itself.

Yet the purpose of the author is much more than just to tell a story. *J* built his work around a central theme, which is the record of a great spiritual experience of a whole nation. But a nation is made up of individuals, who in turn have their ancestors all the way back in time. When such a composite experience is superbly retraced and recorded, the result is also great literature.

Behind the present episode lay many traditions which provided the author with his raw material. In the end product, however, the component parts have been blended beyond much hope of successful recovery. Speculation on the subject has been going on for thousands of years and takes up many tomes. The following comment will confine itself to one or two of the more prominent details.

The focal point of the narrative is the tree of knowledge. It is the tree "in the middle of the garden" (vs. 3), and its fruit imparts to the eater the faculty of "knowing good and bad" (vs. 5; cf. vs. 22). In the last two passages, the objective phrase "knowing/to know good and bad" is faultless in terms of Heb. syntax. But the longer possessive construction "the tree of knowledge of good and bad" (ii 9, 17) is otherwise without analogy in biblical Hebrew and may well be secondary.

More important, however, than those stylistic niceties is the problem of connotation. The Heb. stem yd^c signifies not only "to know," but more expecially "to experience, to come to know" (cf. COMMENT on Sec. 4); in other words, the verb describes both the process and the result. In the present phrase the actual sense is "to distinguish between good and bad"; cf. II Sam xix 36, where "between" is spelled out; see also I Kings iii 9. The traditional "good and evil" would restrict the idiom to moral matters. But while such an emphasis is apparent in I Kings iii 9 and Isa vii 15, 16, and might suit Deut i 39, it would be out of place in II Sam xix 36. In that context, the subject (Barzilai) shows very plainly that he is a keen judge of right and wrong. At the age of eighty, however, his capacity for physical and aesthetic pleasures is no longer what it used to be: he has lost the ability to appreciate "good and bad." The same delicate reference to physical aspects of life is implied in our passage, which leads up to the mystery of sex (cf. Ehrl., and see McKenzie, *Theological Studies* 15 [1954], 562 f.). For so long as the man and his wife abstain from the forbidden fruit, they are not conscious of their nakedness (ii 25); later they cover themselves with leaves (iii 7). The broad sense, then, of the idiom under discussion is to be in full possession of mental and physical powers. And it is this extended range of meaning that the serpent shrewdly brings into play in iii 5.

Such motifs as sexual awareness, wisdom, and nature's paradise are of course familiar from various ancient sources. It is noteworthy, however, that all of them are found jointly in a single passage of the Gilgamesh Epic. There (Tablet I, column iv, lines 16 ff., ANET, p. 75), Enkidu was effectively tempted by the courtesan, only to be repudiated by the world of nature; "but he now had wisdom, broader understanding" (20). Indeed, the temptress goes on to tell him, "You are wise Enkidu, you are like a god" (34); and she marks his new status by improvising some clothing for him (column ii, lines 27 f., ANET, p. 77). It would be rash to dismiss so much detailed correspondence as mere coincidence.

This is not to imply that *J* had direct access to the Gilgamesh Epic, even though *J*'s account of the Flood reflects a still closer tie with the same Akkadian work (Tablet XI, see comment *ad loc.*). Such affinities, however, lend added support to the assumption that in his treatment of Primeval History *J* made use of traditions that had originated in Mesopotamia. Now derivative material of this kind is sometimes taken more literally than the original sources intended it to be; note, for example, the narrative about the Tower of Babel. It is thus conceivable that the poetic "You are wise Enkidu, you are like a god" (see above) might give rise to the belief that in analogous circumstances man could become a threat to the celestials. And if the concept reached ancient Hebrew tradition, in common with patriarchal material, *J* would in such an instance be no more than a dutiful reporter. He could only articulate the transmitted motifs.

The concluding verses of the present section appear to be a case in point. On the evidence of vs. 22, the serpent was right in saying that God meant to withhold from man the benefits of the tree of knowledge (vs. 5); the same purpose is now attributed to Yahweh. Yet all that this need mean is literal application of a motif that Hebrew tradition took over from Mesopotamia centuries earlier. In any event, the specific source and the precise channel of transmission would remain uncertain; nor have we any way of knowing how the author himself interpreted these notions.

We are on slightly firmer ground when it comes to the subject of God's resolve to keep the tree of life out of man's reach. In later narratives, starting with Abraham, the point is never brought up, since man knows by then his place in the scheme of things, and Yahweh's omnipotence precludes any fear of competition from whatever quarter. In other words, here is again a motif from the Primeval Age based on foreign beliefs. And once again, the center of dissemination is Mesopotamia, which provides us this time with at least two suggestive analogues: the tale of Adapa (ANET, pp. 101 ff.) and, once more, the Epic of Gilgamesh with its central emphasis on man's quest for immortality. Inevitably, both attempts end in failure. To be sure, an exception was made in the case of Utnapishtim, the local hero of the Flood, but that special dispensation was not to be repeated: "Now who will call the gods for you to Assembly, / That you may find the life you are seeking?" (Gilg.,

Tablet XI, lines 197 f.). In the end, Gilgamesh is favored with a concession: he is permitted to take back with him a magic plant which offers the sop of rejuvenation (Tablet XI, line 282), if not the boon of immortality. But he is soon to be robbed of it—by a serpent.

As a whole, then, our narrative is synthetic and stratified. Thanks, however, to the genius of the author, it was to become an unforgettable contribution to the literature of the world.

4. CAIN AND ABEL
(iv 1–16: *J*)

IV 1 The man had experience of his wife Eve, and she conceived and bore Cain, as she said, "I have added[a] a life[b] with the help of Yahweh." 2 Next she bore his brother Abel. Abel became a keeper of flocks, and Cain became a tiller of the soil. 3 In the course of time, Cain brought an offering to Yahweh of fruit of the soil. 4 For his part, Abel brought the finest of the firstlings of his flock. Yahweh showed regard for Abel and his offering, 5 but for Cain and his offering he showed no regard. Cain resented this greatly and his countenance fell. 6 Yahweh said to Cain, "Why are you resentful, and why has your countenance fallen? 7 Surely, if you act right, it should mean exaltation. But if you do not, sin is the demon at the door, whose urge is toward you; yet you can be his master."

8 Cain said to his brother Abel, ["Let us go outside."].[c] And when they were outside, Cain set upon his brother Abel and killed him. 9 Then Yahweh asked Cain, "Where is your brother Abel?" He replied, "I don't know. Am I my brother's keeper?" 10 And he said, "What have you done! Listen! Your brother's blood cries out to me from the soil. 11 Hence you are banned from the soil which forced open its mouth to take your brother's blood from your hand. 12 When you till the soil, it shall not again give up its strength to you. A restless wanderer shall you be on earth!"

13 Cain replied to Yahweh, "My punishment is too much to bear. 14 Now that you have banished me this day from the soil,

[a] Heb. *qānītī*, literally "I acquired," in assonance with "Cain."
[b] Literally "man, individual."
[c] So with Sam., LXX, and other ancient versions; MT omits.

and I must hide from your presence and become a restless wanderer on earth, anyone might kill me on sight!" 15 "If soᵈ," Yahweh said to him, "whoever kills Cain shall suffer vengeance sevenfold." And Yahweh put a mark on Cain, lest anyone should kill him on sight.

16 Thereupon Cain left Yahweh's presence and settled in the land of Nod, east of Eden.

ᵈ See COMMENT.

NOTES

iv 1. *had experience of.* See COMMENT.

Cain. If the name is cognate with Ar. *qayin* "metalworker," the indicated derivation would be more in order in vs. 22. But this is plainly yet another case of sound symbolism (cf. ii 5). The assonance in Heb. *qayin* : *qny(ty)* may be reflected in English by "Cain : gain(ed)."

a life. Heb. אׁישׁ stands for "man" in the sense of an individual being, whereas *'ādām* (see ii 5) is undifferentiated and generic. Ordinarily the term is applied to adults. Yet there is no warrant for suspecting the text, as is sometimes done. In the circumstances, Eve is fully justified in hailing the arrival of another human being.

with the help of. Heb. *'et* "with," which has drawn considerable suspicion and speculation. It is worth mentioning, therefore, that Akk. personal names often employ the corresponding element *itti*, e.g., *Itti-Bēl-balāṭu* "With Bel there is life."

2. *Abel.* The Heb. common noun *hebel* means "puff, vanity." If the combination is pertinent, the name may be suggestive of the shepherd's losing struggle against the farmer. But speculations of this sort are often more intriguing than convincing.

4. *the finest.* Heb. has literally "namely ('and'), of their fattest parts," not "and their curds," which the text iself does not preclude. The manifest contrast, however, is between the unstinted offering on the part of Abel and the minimal contribution of Cain.

showed regard for. The Akk. cognate *šeû* signifies "to look closely into."

5. *resented.* Literally "his anger was kindled."

7. See COMMENT.

8. *said.* The original must have contained Cain's statement, but the text was accidentally omitted in MT, owing, no doubt, to the repeated

"outside" (literally "the field"); the ancient versions supply the missing clause.

11. *banned*. See NOTE on iii 14.

12. *strength*. Used poetically for "produce," cf. Job xxxi 39.

restless wanderer. Literally "totterer and wanderer." Another instance of hendiadys (cf. i 2).

13. *punishment*. Literally "iniquity," and its consequences.

14. *Now that*. See iii 22.

on sight. Literally "who reaches, finds me."

15. *If so*. MT *lkn* "therefore," which LXX and most of the other versions understood as *l' kn* "not so," the basis of the above translation.

mark. For various types of protective signs, usually placed on the forehead, cf. Exod xiii 16; Deut vi 8, xi 18; Ezek ix 4, 6 (*taw*); also Exod xxviii 38; cf. JQR 48 (1957), 208 ff.

16. *Nod*. Literally "wandering," a symbolic place name for Cain's retreat, beyond Eden. The retreat of the Mesopotamian Flood hero Utnapishtim is similarly located "faraway, at the mouth of the rivers" (Gilg., Tablet XI, line 196), east of the head of the Persian Gulf.

COMMENT

The story of early man is now carried a step further, embracing the conflict between the pastoral and the agricultural ways of life. The conflict is depicted in terms of the impact on the given individuals. The author's ability to animate a large canvas with a few bold strokes, and his ear for natural dialogue, are again put to highly effective use.

Two problems of a linguistic nature require special discussion. One concerns the translation of a single word, and the other affects the understanding of an entire verse. In both instances the issues exceed the scope of the NOTES.

The reference to connubial relations in vs. 1 is customarily echoed in English by the translation "knew." The rendering is unsatisfactory on several counts. The underlying Heb. stem *yd'* is applied not only to normal marital situations (cf. vss. 17, 25), but also to clandestine conduct (e.g., xxxviii 26, where the traditional "and he knew her again no more" is inept), and even homosexuality (xix 5). It is thus not a matter of delicate usage, as is sometimes alleged. Nor is the usage confined to Hebrew. Akkadian, for example, extends it to dogs.

There has never been any doubt as to the exact meaning of the idiom. Its semantic basis, moreover, is independently attested by the analogous use of the Akk. verb *lamādum* "to learn, experience" (e.g., Code of Hammurabi rev., column ix, lines 69, 75; column x, line 6), which is identical with Heb. *lmd*. It was indicated earlier that Heb. *yd'* itself has a broader range than our verb "to know" and shares with *lmd* the connotation "to experience" (see COMMENT on iii 5). The slavish English reproduction falls thus short of the Hebrew as well. And unlike so many other English terms that are rooted in biblical usage, this one has never become self-sufficient; for when used in the sense here required, "to know" is still felt to be in need of such props as "carnally, in the biblical sense," or the like.

The problem, then, is strictly translational and peculiar by and large to English. German can get by with its *erkannte,* and French with *connut;* but our "knew" corresponds to *wusste* or *savait,* which would be unthinkable in the present instance. The difficulty is aggravated by the need for suitable equivalents for other related Heb. expressions (see vi 4, xix 31, 32). Accordingly, we are restricted to the concepts of experience and intimacy, depending on the particular context; "had experience of" is right semantically, if not stylistically.

A problem of much greater complexity is posed by vs. 7, where the reading and meaning of the original remain very much in doubt. The oldest versions are no less perplexed than the most recent interpreters. The consonantal text had come down apparently in reasonably good shape, since LXX, for one, differs from MT only in regard to a single letter: *lNth* instead of *lPth;* but the Greek reflects wide differences in word division and vocalization. There, the troubling clauses read, "Is it not true that, when you sacrifice correctly but dissect incorrectly, you are a sinner? Subside then." The standard Aram. translation of Onkelos (TO) presupposes the received Masoretic text, but furnishes a paraphrase rather than a translation and is guilty of some violence to the grammar.

In these circumstances, the best procedure is to adhere consistently to the received text before any departures are attempted. Surprisingly enough, this has not been the standard traditional practice. The two adjacent words *ḥṭ't rbṣ* (unvocalized) have generally been taken to mean "sin couches," although the first (vocalized as *ḥaṭṭā't*) is feminine and calls for a corresponding predicate (*rōbeṣet*); assumed dittography (*ḥṭ't [t]rbṣ*) will not solve the difficulty, since in that case the two possessive suffixes in the sequel

should likewise be feminine instead of masculine. The only way that the present reading can be grammatically correct is in a predicative phrase: "sin is a *rbṣ*," with the following possessives referring to *rbṣ*, a masculine form.

Now the stem *rbṣ* in Hebrew signifies "to couch." A pertinent noun is otherwise unattested in this language, but is well known in Akkadian as *rābiṣum*, a term for "demon." These beings were depicted both as benevolent and malevolent, often lurking at the entrance of a building to protect or threaten the occupants. Phonologically, *rābiṣum*, both noun and participle, would be matched in Hebrew by *rōbēṣ*. The adjective is independently attested. The noun is not; it would have to be regarded in the present instance as an early loanword from Akkadian. There can be no inherent objection to such a derivation, especially in the narrative before us, the locale of which is still in the vicinity of Eden, with the principal character settling eventually "east of Eden." It would thus be the *rōbēṣ* whose "urge" is directed toward Cain, but whom Cain could still thwart if he would control his jealous impulses—all expressed with faultless syntax.

Once the basic difficulty has been removed, the rest falls readily into place. The abstract infinitive *śeʾēt*, from the stem *nśʾ* "to lift up," is in purposeful (and long assumed) contrast to the "fallen" countenance in the preceding verse: good conduct should result in exaltation, not dejection! The whole would then be a "wisdom" motif, suitably applied to the case in question. The consonantal text, it is worth repeating, is well attested, in spite of the far-reaching differences in its interpretation. The ultimate culprit was apparently the above *rōbēṣ*, a malevolent demon in more ways than one.

5. THE LINE OF CAIN
(iv 17–26: *J*)

IV   17 Now Cain had experience of his wife, who conceived and bore Enoch. He was the founder of a city, and he named the city after the name of his son Enoch. 18 To Enoch was born Irad, and Irad begot Mehujael; Mehujael*a* begot Methusael, and Methusael begot Lamech. 19 Lamech took two wives; the name of one was Adah, and the name of the other was Zillah. 20 Adah bore Jabal; he was the ancestor of those who keep tents and cattle. 21 His brother's name was Jubal, who was the ancestor of all who handle lyre and pipe. 22 And Zillah, for her part, bore Tubal-cain, who forged various implements of copper and iron; Tubal-cain had a sister Naamah.

23 Lamech said to his wives,

> "Adah and Zillah, hear my voice,
> O wives of Lamech, give ear to my speech:
> I have killed a man for wounding me,
> A boy for injuring me.
> 24 If Cain be avenged sevenfold,
> Then Lamech seventy-sevenfold."

25 As for Adam, he again had experience of his wife, and she bore a son whom she called Seth, meaning, "God has granted*b* me other issue, because Cain killed Abel." 26 To Seth, in turn, a son was born, and he named him Enosh. It was then that the name Yahweh was first invoked.

a MT (cons.) writes this time *Mehijael.*
b Heb. *šāt*, in assonance with *"Seth."*

NOTES

iv 17. *Enoch*. Cf. v 22.

18. *Mehujael*. The two variant spellings of MT reflected some textual uncertainty. The traditional form with *-j-* is misleading. It should be *-y-*, here and in all other instances where the same consonant is involved (cf. "J" for "Yahwist," and in "Jehovah"). But so many old spellings of biblical names have become part of our culture that their modernization at this late date would only result in greater confusion.

Lamech. This form is particularly regrettable in that its *-a-* is "pausal," coming as it does here at the end of the sentence. The normal Heb. form is "Lemech," as in 19, 23 (*bis*).

20. *keep*. Heb. literally "dwell in," the stem being applied to both tents and cattle. The translation attempts a commonly acceptable bridge in English. It is worth noting that the Mesopotamian king lists sometimes interrupt their statistics with similar incidental comment about a given entry; cf. the Khorsabad List (JNES 13 [1954], 210 ff.), which describes the first seventeen rulers as "dwelling in tents," using an analogous participial form (line 10).

22. *implements*. MT vocalizes the form (*ḥrš*) as an agent noun ("craftsman"), evidently through oversight; the mention of iron, moreover, is an anachronism.

23. *speech:* The colon reflects Heb. *kī*, for which cf. vs. 25.

25. The particle *kī* appears here in two of its several distinctive connotations (cf. xxix 32). The first occurrence is explanatory; it explicates the personal name in question, but is not itself part of the gloss; cf., for example, xli 51 f. A similar use is found in vs. 23, above, where *kī* corresponds to our colon; cf. also xxi 30. The other occurrence supplements *taḥat* with which it is co-ordinated to signify an emphatic "because" (Ehrl.; cf. Prov i 29); alternatively, the whole may be rendered, "in place of Abel, since Cain killed him."

COMMENT

This short section poses many problems. It lists the progeny of Cain (17–24) and appends the beginning of the parallel line of Seth. Yet the next section takes up the Sethite genealogy afresh; what is more, it duplicates some of the Cainite names (Enoch, Lamech), and approximates others. Two separate streams of tradition would thus seem to be indicated, both ultimately derived from the same distant source. The departures may be ascribed to a long period of intervening oral transmission. The critics are agreed on the whole that the next chapter has come down through *P* (except vs. 29), whereas the notices before us go back to a parallel work, evidently by *J*. The latter writer, in turn, has telescoped, perhaps unconsciously, the separate lines of Cain and Seth.

At any event, there can be little doubt as to the background of these genealogical data, or the reason for their inclusion. The lists of antediluvian patriarchs, as recorded here and in the following chapter, cannot be divorced from Mesopotamian traditions about the kings who ruled before the Flood (see Jacobsen, *The Sumerian King List*, pp. 70 ff.). The very fact of the compilations, and the sharp diluvian divide, are significant common features. And the name Methusael is transparently Akk., at least in its components and formation; it reflects *mutu-ša-ili*, apparently "Man of God"; comparable Akk. names that are actually attested include *Mutum-ilum, Muti-ilum,* and *Mutum-el* "(My) god is the husband," perhaps echoing an affirmation by the child's mother (see J. J. Stamm, *Die akkadische Namengebung*, 1939, p. 298). Nevertheless, the names found in the respective lists themselves have nothing in common. It would thus appear that before they reached the Hebrews these entries had gone through a secondary center of dissemination, where they were transformed in accordance with local needs and conditions; see the COMMENT on vi 13, and cf. W. F. Albright, JBL 58 (1939), 91 ff.

J and *P,* then, followed both precedent and source material in incorporating antediluvian notices. The purpose of such data was also much the same in all instances. Just as the Sumerian lists sought to bridge the gap between Creation and the Flood, the biblical writers were intent on tracing the generations between Adam and Noah. The appended cultural details were incidental. While the Cainite line is singled out here as the vehicle for mankind's technological progress, it is evident that the account was not conceived as a summary of cultural achievements. It is derivative in every respect, repeating what tradition managed to hand down. And since some of the sources go back to the third millennium B.C., the scientific perspective is often archaic. At other times the results are anachronistic, notably in vs. 22, which records the use of iron. In a long and complex process of transmission a certain amount of dislocation is bound to take place.

The so-called "Song of the Sword" (23 f.) stands out from the rest in form as well as content. It is generally viewed as the cry of a vengeful tribesman who has triumphed over his enemy. In any case, the poem evidently owes its inclusion in the present context to the mention of Cain in the last couplet. If the song is tribal in origin, its ultimate source has to be sought outside historic Mesopotamia, possibly even to the south of Palestine, where Kenite clans are known to have been at home. It should be added, however, that the available evidence is far from conclusive.

An acute problem is posed, lastly, by the laconic notice at the end of the chapter. The clause reads, "It was then that the name Yahweh began to be invoked"; not "the name *of* Yahweh," since the emphasis is precisely on the personal name and not on its eventual substitute "the Lord." But this statement is directly at variance with Exod iii 14 (*E*) and vi 3 (*P*), which indicate that the name Yahweh had not come into use until the time of Moses. Yet *J* employs this very name throughout Genesis; and the present passage ascribes the usage to very ancient practice.

To be sure, some critics would attribute vss. 25–26 to *P*, in view of the fact that vs. 25 speaks of "Adam" (instead of "the man"), as is *P*'s custom (see v 1 ff.), aside from mentioning Elohim; cf. Noth, *Überlieferungsgeschichte* . . . , p. 12, n. 26. In that case, however, the divergence from Exod vi 3 would be that much more perplexing. (There is, of course, nothing new in *J*'s use of Elohim; cf. ix 26 f.) Everywhere else, each documentary source is consistent on this point; it is only their joint testimony that gives rise to difficulties.

A plausible solution may be in sight, nevertheless. Even though *J* traced back the name Yahweh to the dim past, while *E* and *P* attributed the usage to Moses, both views may be justified depending on the point of vantage. The worship of Yahweh was in all likelihood confined at first to a small body of searchers under the aegis of the patriarchs; it was this movement that found a worthy recorder in *J*. When Moses set out to fashion a nation out of an amorphous conglomerate of sundry ethnic and tribal elements, he had to concentrate on three major features of nationhood: a territorial base, a body of laws, and a distinctive religion. The last was normative in more ways than one; it was necessarily the faith of the same forefathers who had already tied it to the Promised Land, with Yahweh as its fountainhead. To that extent, therefore, Yahweh revealed himself to Moses: and it is this personal revelation that both *E* and *P* celebrate. To *J*, however, who chronicled the progress within the inner circle of the patriarchal pioneers, the personal participation of Yahweh had been the dominant fact from the start.

Little can be said in this connection about the etymology of Yahweh. The fact that attempts to solve the problem are still being made all the time is proof that none of the preceding efforts has carried sufficient appeal. All such ventures start out with the Bible's own explication in Exod iii 14. Yet that name gloss should not be adduced as a technical etymology. It is manifestly a case of sound symbolism no less than the instances in Gen ii 23, iv 1, xi 9, and many other passages. On this score, at any rate, the name of Yahweh is constantly taken in vain.

6. THE PATRIARCHS BEFORE THE FLOOD
(v 1–28, 30–32; *P*; 29: /*J*/)

V 1 This is the record of the line of Adam:
—When God created man, he made him in the likeness of God; 2 he created them male and female. And when they were created, he blessed them and named them Man.—

3 Adam was 130 years old when he begot a son in his likeness, after his image, and he named him Seth. 4 After the birth of Seth, Adam lived 800 years and begot sons and daughters. 5 All the days of Adam's life came to 930 years; then he died.

6 Seth was 105 years old when he begot Enosh. 7 After the birth of Enosh, Seth lived 807 years and begot sons and daughters. 8 All the days of Seth came to 912 years; then he died.

9 Enosh was 90 years old when he begot Kenan. 10 After the birth of Kenan, Enosh lived 815 years and begot sons and daughters. 11 All the days of Enosh came to 905 years; then he died.

12 When Kenan was 70 years old he begot Mahalalel. 13 After the birth of Mahalalel, Kenan lived 840 years and begot sons and daughters. 14 All the days of Kenan came to 910 years; then he died.

15 Mahalalel was 65 years old when he begot Jared. 16 After the birth of Jared, Mahalalel lived 830 years and begot sons and daughters. 17 All the days of Mahalalel came to 895 years; then he died.

18 Jared was 162 years old when he begot Enoch. 19 After the birth of Enoch, Jared lived 800 years and begot sons and daughters. 20 All the days of Jared came to 962 years; then he died.

21 Enoch was 65 years old when he begot Methuselah. 22 Enoch walked with God. After the birth of Methuselah,

[Enoch lived]ª 300 years and begot sons and daughters. 23 All the days of Enoch came to 365 years. 24 Enoch walked with God, then was no more, because God took him.

25 Methuselah was 187 years old when he begot Lamech. 26 After the birth of Lamech, Methuselah lived 782 years and begot sons and daughters. 27 All the days of Methuselah came to 969 years; then he died.

28 Lamech was 182 years old when he begot a son. /29 He named him Noah, which is to say, "This one will bring us reliefᵇ from our work and the toil of our hands, out of the very soil which Yahweh had placed under a ban."/ 30 After the birth of Noah, Lamech lived 595 years and begot sons and daughters. 31 All the days of Lamech came to 777 years; then he died.

32 Noah was 500 years old when he begot Shem, Ham, and Japheth.

ª So with LXX and some manuscripts; see COMMENT.
ᵇ In assonance with "Noah."

NOTES

v 1. *line.* Heb. *tōlᵉdōt* means literally "begettings." The traditional "generations" is etymologically correct, but has come to be specialized in an entirely different connotation. In Hebrew the emphasis rests on genealogy, and extends to "story" (ii 4a), and later to history in general. The actual "record" begins with vs. 3.

2. This passage tells at last of the naming of Adam. As a personal name, the noun is common in *P*. For *J*'s usage, see NOTE on ii 20; cf. also the COMMENT on iv 25, where the documentary source is not clear cut.

and named them Man. The author's way of saying, "This is how mankind began."

3 ff. *was . . . years old.* Literally "(had) lived . . . years."

begot a son. Heb. normally uses the verbal form *hōlīd* (the basis of *tōlᵉdōt*) with a direct object, which is the case in vss. 6 ff. Here the usage is absolute, since an immediate object would have been stylistically awkward; the implied object is *yeled* "child," so that "a son" may be supplied in translation without presupposing accidental omission of *bēn*. As for "begot," there is no need for paraphrases in English. The familiar reservation about "all the begats" is aimed not so much at the verb as at the statistics that go with it.

15. *Jared.* This traditional spelling has exactly the same background as "Lamech"; cf. NOTE on iv 18. The correct transliteration is "Yered."

18. *Enoch.* The initial *ḥ* in the Heb. form would seem to preclude any etymological relationship with Sum. Enmeduranna, for which see COMMENT.

22. *walked.* For the durative force of the corresponding Heb. form, cf. JAOS 75 (1955), 117 ff.

Enoch lived. This insert is supported not only by various manuscripts but the formulaic evidence of the chapter as a whole. The omission in MT is an obvious textual oversight.

29. *He named him Noah.* This clause must have been present in *P,* as well as in *J,* to whom the verse is attributed in view of the reference to Yahweh.

will bring us relief. The translation given by LXX may, but need not, reflect Heb. *nwḥ,* rather than *nḥm,* since the context would not differ appreciably. The former stem is, of course, closer to the name "Noah." But biblical etymologies are not guided by linguistic considerations; cf. iv 1.

has placed under a ban. See NOTE on iii 14.

COMMENT

This section is characteristic of *P,* a source which has been silent since ii 4a. The heading "This is the line of X" is *P*'s normal genealogical rubric; see also vi 9, x 1, xi 10, 27, xxv 12, 19, xxxvi 1, 9, xxxvii 2; and Num iii 1. In Gen ii 4a, on the other hand, the same term is employed—by the same source—not in a heading but in a colophon, with the derivative sense of "story, history."

One need not look far for an explanation of this persistent interest in genealogies. To dedicated guardians of cherished traditions, unbroken lineage meant a secure link with the remotest past, and hence also a firm basis from which to face the future. Thus to *P* these were vital statistics in more ways than one.

As was pointed out in the comment on the preceding section, the present Sethite line is related, in some of the names if not in general treatment, to the Cainite line of iv 17–24, which was traced by a different hand. The two lists point back, therefore, to the same ultimate source. The original center of dissemination was manifestly in Mesopotamia. For it is there that we find a firmly embedded tradition about successive antediluvian rulers, a tradition which is attested as early as the end of the third millennium (cf. Jacobsen, *The Sumerian King List*), and as late as the third century B.C. (in the Greek work on Babylonian history by the Babylonian priest Berossus). The number of rulers (including the hero of the Flood) vacillates between nine and ten (sometimes less), and their respective reigns run from 18,600 to nearly 65,000 years. For the same interval, the Cainite list, which gives no ages, records eight patriarchs, and the Sethite genealogy knows of ten. The relatively high figures in *P*'s report turn out to be exceptionally moderate by comparison, since the entire lifetime of even a Methuselah fails to reach a millennium. Of far greater consequence, however, is the fact that the biblical names in either list bear no demonstrable relation to the standard cuneiform series; the difference between patriarchs and kings is likewise worth stressing. It is thus apparent that the underlying tradition had been subjected to considerable modification in some intermediate center.

Where that center may have lain is far from certain. The hints on this point are few and insubstantial. One personage in the very fragmentary Hurrian version of the Flood bears the name *Na-aḥ-ma-su-le-el* (*Keilschrifturkunden aus Boghazköi*, Vol. VIII, No. 61, rev., line 6); it is preceded by the determinative for "god," but this tells us nothing, since the name of Gilgamesh is treated there in the same fashion. Comparison with Noah has been suggested; such a possibility cannot be ruled out, but neither can it be relied upon. It is suggestive, at any rate, that in the biblical account the ark landed on a peak in the Ararat range, whereas the Akkadian version has it grounded on Mount Niṣir, in the vicinity of modern Sulaimaniya. Armenia had various connections with the Hurrians, and the Hurrians had intimate contacts with the Hebrews. On this roundabout reasoning, the Hurrians could have served as intermediaries in the transmission of the antediluvian lists to biblical chroniclers. It may be noted in passing, that the names in question are far from typical in a Hebrew context; cf. the COMMENT on iv 18.

The *P* source, then, did not invent the abnormal life-spans of the Sethite list; if anything, they have been drastically reduced. How such figures were interpreted at the time is something that one may only guess at today. If a specific principle ever underlay these numbers, it is no longer apparent. Moreover, in marked contrast to the names, the numbers were not dependably transmitted or handled, for both the LXX and the Samaritan readings depart from the Hebrew

text, as well as from each other: cf. the convenient tabulation in Dr. Only rarely is there any hint as to how a given figure may have emerged. Thus Enoch's total of years corresponds to the 365 days in the solar year, and is surely related in some way to the notice of his unprecedented treatment by God, with whom Enoch "walked"; hence, too, the prominence of Enoch in apocryphal and apocalyptic writings. Lamech's tally of 777 appears to be linked with the numbers 7 and 77 and his namesake's Song of the Sword (iv 24; cf. also Matt xviii 22). And the number 500 which represents Noah's age at the birth of all three of his sons is plainly a round figure, as is also his age of 600 at the onset of the Flood.

A numerical puzzle of an entirely different sort helps to deepen the already profound mystery of Enoch. As the seventh in the line of antediluvian patriarchs, Enoch parallels the Mesopotamian Enmeduranna, who is the seventh king before the Flood according to the best textual evidence (Jacobsen, op. cit., p. 75). What is more, Enmeduranna's capital city was the ancient center of the sun god of Sippar, which could explain the solar number of 365 that is recorded for Enoch (cf. Dr., pp. 78 f.). Yet the slight similarity in names is apparently coincidental (see NOTE ad loc.).

Finally, prodigious as are the life-spans of the individual patriarchs, they are dovetailed to such an extent that the total elapsed time adds up to no more than 1656 years in the Heb. version. The death of Adam has to be dated to the generation of Noah's father Lamech. In turn, Noah himself would have witnessed the sixtieth birthday of Abraham. All such results have to be evaluated in terms of the limited chronological horizons of the age that produced them.

7. PRELUDE TO DISASTER
(vi 1–4: J)

VI ¹ Now when men began to increase on earth and daughters were born to them, ² the divine beings saw how beautiful were the human daughters and took as their wives any of them they liked. ³ Then Yahweh said, "My spirit shall not shield man forever, since he is but flesh; let the time allowed him be one hundred and twenty years."

⁴ It was then that the Nephilim appeared on earth—as well as later—after the divine beings had united with human daughters to whom they bore children. Those were the heroes of old, men of renown.

NOTES

vi 2. *divine beings*. Literally "sons of God/gods." The term *'elōhīm* is here clearly differentiated from Yahweh (vs. 3). Elsewhere *E* employs the former in the sense of "Fate, Providence," and the like (see NOTE on xx 13). Here, however, the main stress is on "immortals" as opposed to "mortals."

human daughters. Literally "the daughters of man," in balanced contrast to the above.

3. *shield*. The traditional "abide in" is a guess lacking any linguistic support. For this interpretation, based on Akk. *dinānu* "substitute, surrogate," see JBL 75 (1956), 126 ff.

since he is but flesh. This clause stands for Heb. *bešaggam*, which is obscure except for the preposition *be-*. A different analysis of the components yields "by reason of their going astray [he is but flesh]." But the first interpretation is superior, though still highly uncertain.

4. *Nephilim*. Named also as a giant race in Num xiii 33. There, however, the context implies that the people found by the spies were like the very Nephilim of old.

united with. Literally "came to," in the idiomatic sense of "cohabited with." This idiom appears to match the circumlocution used in iv 1.

Actually, however, there is one outstanding difference. Whereas "to have experience of" can be applied to either sex, "to come to" refers in this connection only to the male who visits a woman's quarters; cf. xxx 16, xxxviii 16.

men of renown. Literally "men with a name"; cf. Gilg., Yale Tablet, column v, line 7: "a name that endures will I make for myself."

COMMENT

The undisguised mythology of this isolated fragment makes it not only atypical of the Bible as a whole but also puzzling and controversial in the extreme. Its problems are legion: Is what we have here an excerpt from a fuller account? Why was such a stark piece included altogether? Does its present place in the book imply a specific connection with the Flood? Is the stated period of 120 years meant as a deadline for mankind to mend its ways? On these and many similar points arising from the all too laconic passage before us there have been innumerable conflicting opinions, with few if any concrete gains. Of late, however, thanks mainly to the discovery of pertinent literary links, some of the scattered pieces of the puzzle have begun to fall into place. To be sure, the nature of the fragment is such as to discourage confident interpretation. But a semblance of an intelligible pattern appears to be indicated at long last.

The passage is dated explicitly to the time of the initial appearance of the Nephilim, who are described as "the heroes of old"; the LXX version translates the noun as "giants." Now Greek mythology (Hesiod, Pseudo-Apollodorus) recalls an unsavory stage in the history of the gods, which involves the leading triad of the pantheon: Uranus (Sky) wars against his children, but is defeated and emasculated by his son Cronus, who is vanquished in turn by his own son Zeus. The latter, however, must then do battle with a group of giants known as Titans, and subsequently with a particularly menacing monster named Typhon.

A closely related Phoenician tradition is reported by Philo of Byblos, in the name of a much older author, a certain Sanchunyathon. This relationship is so prominent that ultimate derivation of the Phoenician material from Greek sources has been suggested more than once (cf. E. G. Kraeling, "The Significance and Origin of Gen. 6:1–4," JNES 6 [1947], 193 ff., especially 205). It was further assumed that the biblical account under discussion may allude to a

similar commingling of primeval giants and celestial turpitude. Nevertheless, Sanchunyathon was regarded as an apocryphal figure, while
the other Phoenician and Greek sources were too late to have been
utilized by *J;* and so this hypothesis could not make headway.

The whole perspective, however, has recently changed with the
discovery of Hittite texts containing translations of Hurrian myths.
These myths parallel the Uranid cycle in such striking detail as to
preclude any possibility of coincidence. Here, too, the sky god (Anu)
is fought and emasculated by his son (Kumarbi), who in turn is
vanquished by the storm god (Teshub). But before his victory is
assured, Teshub must face a formidable stone monster (Ullikummi).
The decisive battle takes place near Mount Ḫazzi, the classical
Mount Casius, which is also the scene of Typhon's battle with Zeus
(see H. G. Güterbock, "Oriental Forerunners of Hesiod," AJA 52
[1948], 123 ff.; cf. also JCS 5 [1951], 145). Since the Hurrian
original goes back to the middle of the second millennium B.C., it has
to be the source of the Phoenician and Greek versions as well as of
the Hittite adaptation. (For possible Ugaritic parallels, cf. M. H.
Pope, *El in the Ugaritic Texts,* 1955, pp. 4 f.) The Hurrians, for
their part, are known to have utilized in this group of epics a number
of Mesopotamian elements (e.g., the god Anu). The whole cycle,
then, with all its bloodthirsty detail, was by *J*'s time familiar to much
of the ancient world. It could hardly have been a stranger to *J* or
his own immediate sources.

It is evident, moreover, from the tenor of the Hebrew account
that its author was highly critical of the subject matter. It makes
little difference whether *J* took the contents at face value or, as is
more likely (cf. vs. 5), viewed the whole as the product of man's
morbid imagination. The mere popularity of the story would have
been sufficient to fill him with horror at the depravity that it reflected. A world that could entertain such notions deserved to be
wiped out.

In these circumstances, the present position of the fragment immediately before the account of the Flood can scarcely be independent of that universal catastrophe. The story of the primeval
titans emerges as a moral indictment, and thereby as a compelling
motive for the forthcoming disaster. And the period of 120 years
becomes one of probation, in the face of every sign that the doom
cannot be averted. All of this accords with the separately established
fact that the Flood story in Genesis, unlike its Mesopotamian analogues, was morally motivated.

8. THE FLOOD
(vi 5–viii 22: *J*, /*P*/)

VI 5 When Yahweh saw how great was man's wickedness on earth, and how every scheme that his mind devised was nothing but evil all the time, 6 Yahweh regretted that he had made man on earth, and there was sorrow in his heart. 7 And Yahweh said, "I will blot out from the earth the men that I created, man and beast, the creeping things, and the birds of the sky; for I am sorry that I made them." 8 But Noah found favor with Yahweh.

/9 This is the line of Noah.—Noah was a righteous man; he was without blame in that age; Noah walked with God.— 10 Noah begot three sons: Shem, Ham, and Japheth.

11 The earth was corrupt in the view of God, and it was full of lawlessness. 12 And God saw how corrupt the earth was, for all flesh had corrupted their ways on earth.

13 Then God said to Noah, "I have decided to put an end to all flesh, for the earth is filled with lawlessness because of them. So I am about to destroy both them and the earth. 14 Make yourself an ark of gopher wood; make it an ark with compartments, and cover it inside and out with pitch. 15 This is how you shall build it: the length of the ark shall be three hundred cubits, its width fifty cubits, and its height thirty cubits. 16 Make a sky light for the ark, terminating it within a cubit of the top. Put the entrance in the side of the ark, which is to be made with lower, second, and third decks.

17 For my part, I am about to bring on the Flood—waters upon the earth—to eliminate everywhere all flesh in which there is the breath of life: everything on earth shall perish. 18 But with you I will establish my covenant, and you shall enter the ark— you, your sons, your wife, and your sons' wives. 19 And of all

else that is alive, of all flesh, you shall take two of each into the ark to stay alive with you; they must be male and female. 20 Of the birds of every kind, cattle of every kind, every kind of creeping thing—two of each shall come inside to you to stay alive. 21 For your part, provide yourself with all the food that is to be eaten, and store it away to serve as provisions for you and for them."

22 This Noah did. Just as God commanded him, so he did./

VII 1 Then Yahweh said to Noah, "Go into the ark, you and all your household, for you alone have I found to be truly righteous in this age. 2 Of every clean animal take seven pairs, a male and its mate; and of the animals that are unclean, one pair, a male and its mate; 3 but seven pairs again of the birds of the sky, male and female, to preserve issue throughout the earth. 4 For in seven days' time I will cause it to rain upon the earth for forty days and forty nights; and I will blot out from the surface of the earth all existence that I created."

5 Noah did just as Yahweh commanded him. /6 Noah was in his six hundredth year when the Flood came—waters upon the earth./

7 Then Noah, together with his sons, his wife, and his sons' wives, went inside the ark because of the waters of the Flood. 8 Of the clean animals and the animals that are unclean, the birds of the sky and everything that creeps on earth, 9 [two of each]ᵃ, male and female, came inside the ark to Noah, as God had commanded Noah. 10 As soon as the seven days were over, the waters of the Flood were upon the earth.

/11 In the six hundredth year of Noah's life, in the second month, on the seventeenth day of the month—on that day—

> All the fountains of the great deep burst forth
> And the sluices in the sky broke open./

12 Heavy rain fell upon the earth forty days and forty nights. /13 On the aforesaid day, Noah and his sons, Shem, Ham, and Japheth, Noah's wife, and the three wives of his sons had entered the ark—14 they as well as every kind of beast, every kind

ᵃ Evidently a gloss, see NOTE.

of cattle, every kind of creature that creeps on earth, and every kind of bird, every[b] winged thing. 15 They came inside the ark to Noah, two each of all flesh in which there was the breath of life. 16 Those that entered comprised male and female of all flesh, as God had commanded Noah./ Then Yahweh shut him in.

/17 The Flood came down upon the earth/forty days.[c] As the waters increased, they bore the ark aloft, so that it rose above the earth. /18 The waters swelled and increased greatly upon the earth, and the ark drifted on the surface of the water. 19 The waters continued to swell more and more above the earth, until all the highest mountains everywhere were submerged, 20 the crest reaching fifteen cubits above the submerged mountains. 21 And all flesh that had stirred on earth perished—birds, cattle, beasts, and all the creatures that swarmed on earth—and all mankind./ 22 All in whose nostrils was the faintest breath of life, everything that had been on dry land, died out. 23 All existence on earth was blotted out—man, cattle, creeping things, and birds of the sky; they were blotted out from the earth. Only Noah was left, and those that were with him in the ark.

/24 When the waters over the earth had maintained their crest one hundred and fifty days, **VIII** 1 God remembered Noah and all the beasts and cattle that were with him in the ark, and God caused a wind to sweep across the earth. The waters began to subside. 2 The fountains of the deep and the sluices in the sky were stopped up,/ and the heavy rain from the sky was held back. 3 Little by little the waters receded from the earth. /By the end of one hundred and fifty days the waters had diminished so that 4 in the seventh month, on the seventeenth day of the month, the ark came to rest on the Ararat range. 5 The waters went on diminishing until the tenth month. In the tenth month, on the first day of the month, the peaks of the mountains became visible./

6 At the end of forty days Noah opened the hatch of the ark that he had made, 7 and released a raven; it went back and forth waiting for the water to dry off from the earth. 8 Then he sent out a dove, to see if the waters had dwindled from the ground.

[b] LXX, and others, read "and every winged bird."
[c] See NOTE.

9 But the dove could not find a place for its foot to rest on, and returned to him in the ark, for there was water all over the earth; so putting out his hand, he picked it up, and drew it inside the ark toward him. 10 He waited another seven days and again released the dove from the ark. 11 The dove returned to him toward evening, and there in its bill was a plucked olive leaf! Noah knew then that the waters had dwindled from the ground. 12 He waited yet another seven days and released the dove; it did not return to him again.

13 /In the six hundred and first year [of Noah's life],*d* in the first month, on the first day of the first month, the waters had begun to dry from the earth./ Noah removed the covering of the ark and saw that the surface of the ground was drying. /14 In the second month, on the twenty-seventh day of the month, the earth was dry.

15 Then God spoke to Noah, saying, 16 "Come out of the ark, together with your wife, your sons, and your sons' wives. 17 Bring out with you every living being that is with you—all flesh, be it bird or cattle or any creature that creeps on earth—and let them swarm on earth, and breed and increase on it." 18 So Noah came out, with his sons, his wife, and his sons' wives. 19 And every animal, every creeping thing, and every bird —everything that stirs on earth—left the ark, group by group./

20 Then Noah built an altar to Yahweh and, choosing from every clean animal and every clean bird, offered burnt offerings on the altar. 21 As Yahweh smelled the soothing odor, he said to himself, "Never again will I doom the world because of man, since the devisings of man's heart are evil from the start; neither will I ever again strike down every living being, as I have done.

> 22 So long as the earth endures,
> Seedtime and harvest,
> Cold and heat,
> Summer and winter,
> And day and night
> Shall not cease."

d LXX supplies the required text, cf. vii 11.

NOTES

vi 5. *Yahweh*. A clear sign in this composite account that the passage stems from *J*.

6. *regretted*. The Heb. stem *nḥm* describes a change of mind or heart, either in an intransitive sense (as here and in 7), or transitive "to comfort."

8. *found favor with*. Literally "won favor (not 'grace') in the eyes of," cf. Akk. *īnam maḫārum* "to receive the eye, attract, please." The Heb. idiom is highly flexible and varies in shading from context to context, as will be apparent from later occurrences; cf. pp. LXVII f.

9–12. A long consecutive passage from *P*. The typical introductory *tōleḏōt* refers to Noah's sons (10). The intervening notice is parenthetic.

9. *in that age*. The traditional rendering "in his generations" is mechanical and obviously unsuitable. It has been proposed to emend the texts *bdrTyw* to *bdrKyw* "in his ways," with allusion to such passages as Deut xxxii 4; Ezek xxviii 15; and Ps cxix 1. The change of a single letter would not be major. Nevertheless, the close parallel in vii 1 (*J*) argues in favor of the received text. The difficulty is largely translational. Heb. *dōr*, in common with its Sem. cognates, signifies "duration, age span"; the meaning "generation" (in the current sense) is secondary. And since the possessive pronoun of Hebrew often corresponds to our definite article or demonstrative pronoun (and vice versa), the present form stands for "in his times, in that age."

10. *Japheth*. It may be of interest that the apparently identical Greek name *Iapetos* is borne by one of the Titans in a context that could be indirectly related to that of vi 1–4; see COMMENT *ad loc.*

11. *in the view of*. The Heb. prepositional term *lipnē* means literally "to the face of." Its normal connotation is either spatial ("in front of") or temporal ("before"). There is, however, still another important meaning which the customary translation "before" can only distort. What is involved in such instances is the attitude of the party concerned, in terms of judgment, will, approval, and the like; cf. vii 1, and see also x 9, xvii 18, xxvii 7 (followed by a temporal *lipnē*), xliii 33. Not infrequently, *lipnē Yahweh* is like our *deo volente;* cf., for example, the four co-ordinate instances in Num xxxii 20 ff. In the present passage the indicated meaning is: according to God's (regretful) conclusion; in vii 1, the equally plain sense is: in my approving view; cf. pp. LXVII f.; cf. the Akk. idiom *pānušūma* "if he chooses."

lawlessness. Heb. *ḥāmās* is a technical legal term which should not be automatically reproduced as "violence"; cf. xvi 5.

13. *I have decided.* Literally "it is in front of me."

14. The Babylonian Flood hero Utnapishtim receives his instructions in a dream.

gopher. The timber in question has not been identified.

compartments. Literally "cells." It is sometimes argued that Heb. *qinnīm* should be repointed as *qānīm* to yield "reeds," on the mistaken assumption that "reed hut—wall" in the pertinent Gilg. passage (Tablet XI, lines 21 f.) shows the material that was used in the construction of the ark. The sense of that passage, however, is altogether different. The reed hut is the venerated shrine in which the Flood hero received his instructions from the friendly god Ea.

pitch. The same substance and the cognate term for it are found in the corresponding cuneiform passage.

15. The stated dimensions (approximately $440 \times 73 \times 44$ feet) suggest a vessel of some 43,000 tons; cf. A. Heidel, *The Gilgamesh Epic and Old Testament Parallels*, 1946, p. 236.

16. *terminating.* For similar technical use of the verb, see Deut xxvi 12. The specific detail remains obscure.

17. *everywhere.* Literally "under the sky."

18. *covenant.* A solemn agreement between two parties providing sanctions in the event of non-compliance.

19. *all else that is alive.* The definite article in Heb. (here in *haḥay*) often contrasts the defined thing with the preceding; cf. xiv 16.

two of each. This number is invariable with P. J specifies seven pairs of all animals that are ritually clean (cf. vii 2) and one pair of those that are unclean.

stay alive. Also in vs. 20; not "maintain life." This is another instance of the intransitive Hiphil (cf. iii 6); the causative sense is generally expressed by the Piel (cf. vii 3); cf. p. LXVIII.

21. *food that is to be eaten.* Necessarily, not "food that is eaten, edible," since the inedible kind would not be called food. The Heb. form is capable of either nuance; cf. Lev xi 34.

vii 1. *I found to be truly righteous.* On the force of Heb. *lipnē* cf. NOTE on vi 11.

2–3. Were the aquatic creatures left out because they were immune from the Flood?

6. *in his six hundredth year.* Cf. vs. 11, from the same hand (P). The Heb. construction with *ben-* "son of," i.e., "participant in," can be either cardinal or ordinal.

9. [*two of each*]. If this statement came from J, it would be at variance with J's figures elsewhere in this account; the words are attributed, therefore, to a later redactor who sought to bring the passage into harmony with P. The same would apply to the use of Elohim in this verse rather than Yahweh; but the latter reading is given by Sam., Syr., and Vulg.

(manuscripts). Some of the critics regard all of vss. 8–9 as a later addition.

12. *Heavy rain.* Heb. *gešem,* unlike *māṭār,* signifies abnormal rainfall; cf. also viii 2. The period of forty days is a feature of J.

16. *comprised.* Literally "came as." The final clause is from J (note "Yahweh"); these words may have stood originally after vs. 10.

17. *forty days.* LXX adds "and forty nights"; the whole phrase, however, was probably carried over from vs. 12.

18. *swelled.* Literally "grew mighty/mightier"; a slightly different nuance ("the crest reaching") is found in vs. 20.

21. *that had stirred.* Here the Heb. verb refers to all life in general, and not merely reptiles; see NOTE on i 28, and cf. viii 17.

22. *the faintest breath of life.* Literally "the breath of the spirit of life."

23. *was blotted out.* The traditional vocalization takes the verb as active. Taken literally, "he blotted out" would leave the pronoun without antecedent. The passive form, however, would be made up of exactly the same consonants (*wymḥ*). Moreover, Hebrew often employs actives in an impersonal sense (cf. ix 6). Either way, therefore, the translation here given may be safely adopted.

viii 1. *subside.* The pertinent Heb. verb is isolated in this account and rare elsewhere.

4. *the Ararat range.* The terminology ("mountains of Ararat") alludes clearly to range as opposed to a particular peak. For the significance of this location see the COMMENT on Sec. 6.

6. *forty days.* In the original narrative by J this was the full length of the Flood; cf. vii 4. In the present sequence, however, the text appears to refer to an interval following the specific date just given in vs. 5 (P).

9. *its foot.* Literally "flat part, sole of its foot."

13. The Heb. stem for "to be dry" (*ḥrb*) denotes "to be or to become free of moisture"; complete dryness is signified by *ybš* (14).

17. *on it.* MT repeats "on the earth."

19. LXX has here the preferable reading: "All the beasts, all the cattle, all the birds, and all the creeping things on earth" (cf. vii 21).

21. *doom.* Heb. uses the Piel form of the stem *qll,* which denotes not so much "to curse" as "to belittle, slight, mistreat," and the like.

from the start. Literally "from his (i.e., man's) childhood/youth." This is ambiguous because we are not told whether what is involved is the early age of mankind as a whole, or that of each individual. In xlvi 34 the same term is applied by Jacob's sons both to themselves and to their ancestors, which can best be reflected in English by "from the beginning." The same kind of neutral phraseology commends itself in this instance.

COMMENT

The received biblical account of the Flood is beyond reasonable doubt a composite narrative, reflecting more than one separate source. One of the sources goes back to *P,* and is easy enough to identify except for a clause or two. But the identity of the narrator or narrators other than *P* has caused considerable trouble and debate. Nevertheless, if one is prepared to overlook a few highly technical details—as one must in a comprehensive study—it should not be too hazardous to accept *J* as the only other author involved.

More serious for our immediate purposes is the fact that the respective versions of *P* and *J* have not been handed down in connected form, as was the case, for example, with Sec. 1 (*P*) and Sec. 2 (*J*). Here the two strands have become intertwined, the end result being a skillful and intricate patchwork. Nevertheless—and this is indicative of the great reverence with which the components were handled—the underlying versions, though cut up and rearranged, were not altered in themselves. The upshot is that we are now faced not only with certain duplications (e.g., vi 13–22 : vii 1–5), but also with obvious internal contradictions, particularly in regard to the numbers of the various animals taken into the ark (vi 19–20, vii 14–15 : vii 2–3), and the timetable of the Flood (viii 3–5, 13–14 : vii 4, 10, 12, 17, viii 6, 10, 12).

To show the diverging accounts at a glance is not a simple task. A number of modern treatments resort to the expedient of reshuffling the text, but this does violence, in turn, to a tradition that antedates the LXX translation of twenty-two centuries ago. The arrangement followed here reproduces the exact order of the received ("Masoretic") text. At the same time, however, everything that can be traced to *P* has been placed between diagonals. This way the two components can be distinguished at a glance, or they may be followed consecutively if one wishes to do so. No attempt, however, has been made to mark in *J* the possible ministrations of *R*(edactor), in the few instances where such "joins" appear to be indicated; minimal remarks on this subject have been included in the NOTES.

That the biblical account as a whole goes back ultimately to Mesopotamian sources is a fact that is freely acknowledged by most modern scholars; see the detailed discussion in Heidel's *Gilgamesh*

Epic . . . , pp. 224–89. But the actual ties are more complex than is generally assumed.

The primeval Flood is echoed in a variety of cuneiform sources; cf. S. N. Kramer, *From the Tablets of Sumer,* 1956, pp. 176 ff. The most extensive prototype, and the best known by far, is found in Tablet XI of the Gilgamesh Epic. It is with this celebrated narrative that the biblical account has most in common.

In both instances there is a Flood hero who has been singled out for deliverance from the impending universal catastrophe. Each is told to construct an ark according to detailed specifications. There follow related descriptions of the elemental cataclysm, the annihilation of all life outside the ark, and the eventual grounding of the strange vessel on top of a tall mountain. Both Noah and Utnapishtim, his Babylonian counterpart, release a series of birds at appropriate intervals to test the subsidence of the waters; each account mentions a dove and a raven. Lastly, when dry land has reappeared in the now desolate world, each principal gives expression to his boundless relief through a sacrifice of humble thanksgiving.

So much correspondence in over-all content is inescapable proof of basic interrelationship. There are, however, also significant differences in detail. The biblical Flood, as was noted earlier (see COMMENT on Sec. 7) is given strong moral motivation, whereas the cuneiform version—at least the one that is incorporated in the Gilgamesh Epic—fails to suggest a plausible cause; one might ascribe the awesome interlude to mere whims of heaven. There are, furthermore, dissimilarities with respect to the occupants of the two arks (the Mesopotamian personnel includes "all the craftsmen") and the order of the test flights (raven–swallow–dove in Gilg.). Above all, there is the immediately apparent difference in names: Noah as against Utnapishtim; the mountains of Ararat as opposed to Mount Niṣir. It is thus clear that Hebrew tradition must have received its material from some intermediate, and evidently northwesterly, source, and that it proceeded to adjust the data to its own needs and concepts.

The ultimate inspiration for the Mesopotamian cycle of Flood narratives can only be a matter of guesswork at this time. Perhaps the best chance of a likely solution lies in the recent disclosures concerning the geological background of Lower Mesopotamia (cf. J. M. Lees and N. L. Falcon, "The Geological History of the Mesopotamian Plains," *Geographical Journal* 118 [1952], 24–39). It now appears that not very long ago, as geological ages are reckoned, waters from the Persian Gulf submerged a large coastland area, owing probably to a sudden rise in the sea level. If that rise was precipitated by extraordinary undersea eruptions, the same phenomenon could also have brought on extremely heavy rains, the whole leaving an indelible impression on the survivors. All this, however, must remain in the realm of speculation.

9. BLESSING AND COVENANT
(ix 1–17: *P*)

IX ¹ God blessed Noah and his sons, and said to them, "Be fertile and increase and fill the earth. ² Dread fear of you shall possess all the animals of the earth and all the birds of the sky— everything with which the ground is astir—and all the fishes of the sea: they are placed in your hand. ³ Every creature that is alive shall be yours to eat; I give them all to you as I did with the grasses of the field. ⁴ Only flesh with its lifeblood still in it shall you not eat. ⁵ So, too, will I require an accounting for your own lifeblood: I will ask it of every beast; and of man in regard to his fellow man will I ask an accounting for human life.

> ⁶ He who sheds the blood of man,
> By man shall his blood be shed;
> For in the image of God
> Was man created.
> ⁷ Be fertile, then, and increase,
> Abound on earth and subdue*ᵃ* it."

⁸ God said to Noah, and to his sons also: ⁹ "Furthermore,*ᵇ* I now establish my covenant with you and with your offspring to come, ¹⁰ and with every living being that was with you: birds, cattle, every wild animal that was with you, all that came out of the ark—*ᶜ*every living thing on earth.*ᶜ* ¹¹ And I will maintain my covenant with you, that never again shall all flesh be cut off by the waters of a Flood; neither shall there be another Flood to devastate the earth.

ᵃ So LXX (manuscripts), reading *ureᵈū,* cf. i 28; Heb. *urᵉbū* (dittography).
ᵇ Literally "And I" (emphatic).
ᶜ⁻ᶜ LXX omits.

12 "And this," God said, "is the sign of the covenant that I institute between me, and you and every living being along with you, for all ages to come: 13 I have placed my bow in the clouds, and it shall be the sign of the covenant between me and the earth. 14 When I bring clouds over the earth, and the bow appears in the clouds, 15 I will recall the covenant which is in force between me, and you and all living beings comprising all flesh, so that waters shall not again become a Flood to destroy all flesh. 16 As the bow appears in the clouds, I will see it and remember the eternal covenant between me[d] and every living being, comprising all flesh that is on earth. 17 That," God told Noah, "shall be the sign of the covenant which I have established between me and all flesh that is on earth."

[d] So LXX; MT has "God."

Notes

ix 1. The statement begins with one of *P*'s favorite phrases; cf. i 28.

2. *Dread fear*. Literally "the fear and the dread," another example of hendiadys.

is astir. The verbs *rmś* (cf. i 21) is used here in its broader sense of "to move, have motion." In the next verse, the corresponding noun *remeś* is employed for animal life in general, as a new source of food for man who will now be carnivorous. The Akk. cognate stem *namāšu* shares the same range of meaning.

4. *flesh*. *P*'s term for "mortals."

with its lifeblood. Literally "whose blood is in the/its being."

5. *in regard to his fellow man*. Literally "from the hand of man his brother," i.e., one another. Significantly, the principle that animals are held accountable for homicide is found also in the Covenant Code, Exod xxi 28.

7. *Abound*. The normal sense of Heb. *śrṣ* is "to swarm, teem with."

subdue. Heb. repeats "increase" from the first half of the verse.

9. *covenant*. On the institution in general see G. E. Mendenhall, BA 17 (1954), 50–76; for the Heb. term see Note on xv 18.

10. The absence of the concluding phrase in LXX may imply a marginal gloss in MT. Yet such a recapitulation is entirely in order and should not be automatically ruled out.

11. *maintain*. Heb. uses here the same stem as in vss. 9 and 17, where the translation employs "to establish." The original carries both

meanings; the translation, however, has to distinguish between the initial act and the subsequent renewals.

15. *the covenant which is in force.* Literally "my covenant which is."

comprising. Literally "in," i.e., entering into the totality of mortal life on earth.

COMMENT

The Flood's aftermath in this biblical episode is much the same as in the cuneiform sources. The survivors are treated with solicitude and favored with divine blessing (cf. Gilg., Tablet XI, lines 192 ff.). There are also differences, to be sure, but these are in keeping with the ways and beliefs of the societies involved. Utnapishtim is granted immortality and settles in the region of Dilmun— or approximately the same general locality that the Bible describes as "east of Eden" (iv 16). Noah, on the other hand, must remain mortal. The sanctity of all future life is given forceful emphasis, but it is terrestrial and limited. Man's food supply, however, may now be supplemented from the animal kingdom. Finally, the rainbow is introduced as a bright and comforting reminder that the race shall endure, however transient the individual.

10. NOAH AND HIS SONS
(ix 18–27: *J*; 28–29: /P/)

IX 18 The sons of Noah who came out of the ark were Shem, Ham, and Japheth—Ham being the father of Canaan. 19 These three were the sons of Noah, and from them the whole world branched out.

20 Noah, a man of the soil, was the first to plant a vineyard. 21 He drank of the wine, became drunk, and lay uncovered inside the tent. 22 Ham, the father of Canaan, saw his father naked,ᵃ and he told it to his brothers outside. 23 Then Shem and Japheth took a cloth, held it against both their backs and, walking backward, covered their father's nakedness; their faces were turned the other way, so that they did not see their father naked.

24 When Noah woke up from his wine and learned what his youngest son had done, 25 he said,

> "A curse on Canaan!
> The lowest of slaves
> Shall he be to his brothers."

26 He went on,

> "Blessed be Yahweh,
> The God of Shem.
> Let Canaan be slave to the others.
> 27 May God make roomᵇ for Japheth,
> That he dwell among the tents of Shem.
> And let Canaan be their slave."

/28 Noah lived 350 years after the Flood. 29 All the days of Noah came to 950 years; then he died./

ᵃ LXX adds "he came out."
ᵇ Heb. *yapt*, a play on the name *Yepet* "Japheth."

NOTES

ix 18. *Ham being the father of Canaan.* The apparent purpose of this remark is to relate Ham to the subsequent curse against Canaan.

20. *was the first to plant a vineyard.* If MT intended to say "Noah was the first man of the soil" (as it is generally taken to mean), we should expect *hēḥēl lihyōt*, exactly as in x 8. Moreover, Cain had been introduced as the first farmer (iv 2). Thus both text and context require the translation here offered, which is entirely consistent with Heb. idiomatic usage. The present notice harks back to v 29, with its reference to the fruits of the soil.

22. *saw his father naked.* Literally "saw his father's nakedness." The specific reference is to the *pudenda;* see the various injunctions in Lev xviii 6 ff. The term itself relates to exposure (cf. xlii 9, 12) and does not necessarily imply sexual offenses; cf. ii 25 and Exod xx 26.

25. *The lowest of slaves.* Literally "slave of slaves," one of the Heb. ways to express the superlative. The phrase points evidently to the inferior social and political status of Canaanites. Was this an accomplished fact at the time of composition, or is the allusion no more than a wishful projection into the future, as the context would seem to suggest?

26. One expects this blessing to be aimed at Shem rather than Yahweh; hence various changes in the pointing have been proposed. Nevertheless, the ancient versions support the received text, which does not lack champions among modern critics (cf. von Rad, p. 114).

28–29. This postscript from the hand of *P* supplements the list in ch. v, if it does not indeed belong there directly after v 32.

COMMENT

This short piece constitutes a link between *J*'s account of the Flood and the same author's version of the Table of Nations in ch. x. It may even go back all the way to v 29, where the name Noah was explained as that of the patriarch who was destined to wrest comfort out of the very soil which Yahweh had placed under a ban. The Flood story would then stand out all the more as an awesome and elemental break in the gradual progress of mankind.

Connecting passages can be puzzling precisely because they are meant to bridge gaps, and they are usually laconic. We have had one such example in iv 17–24. In the present instance the question arises whether what we have before us is merely a splinter from a more substantial narrative. A fuller account, for example, would not have been likely to telescope Ham and Canaan, as is now the case. For if it was Ham who was guilty of such disrespect toward his incapacitated and exposed father, why is Noah's curse directed at Canaan (25)? And why is Ham spoken of as the youngest son in vs. 24, whereas vs. 18 lists him as the second of three? Have two divergent traditions been fused, or was Canaan the original offender? At all events, the moral of the story is actually aimed at Canaan and, by extension, at the Canaanites. And the burden of it is not so much to justify an accomplished political fact, as it is to stigmatize distasteful practices on the part of the older inhabitants of the land.

The passage thus supplies more questions than answers. One point, however, is abundantly clear: the background is distinctly local, in marked contrast with the bulk of Primeval History, for which the ultimate inspiration came from Mesopotamia.

To come back briefly to the villain of this tale, the explicit order of the sons of Noah, which indicates age, is invariably Shem–Ham–Japheth; see v 32, vi 10, vii 13, ix 18, x 1. Accordingly, one is not prepared for the notation in 24 that Ham was the youngest. At most, he should have been called "the younger," but Hebrew cannot be forced to yield this meaning. Two possible explanations suggest themselves: (1) the passage before us derives from a different tradition, one in which either Ham or Canaan was cited as the third son of Noah; this is the view of most modern critics. (2) The statement refers not to Noah's youngest son, but Ham's; and on the evidence of x 6, that individual was Canaan. This view is expressed already in the commentary of Ibn Ezra (twelfth century) *ad loc.* Ham himself, then, would be the offended party, and his son Canaan the perpetrator of some base deed, the details of which were either accidentally lost or deliberately suppressed. The omission led in turn to the disturbed text that is now before us. It can be seen that both views leave much to be desired. The problem remains unresolved.

No less perplexing in its own way is the statement that Japheth shall dwell in the tents of Shem (27). This must allude to some form of co-operation between the two groups, with Canaan condemned to enslavement by both. What, then, is the historical background of the verse in question? The most likely period that would seem to fit the conditions here reflected is the turn of the twelfth century B.C., when the Israelites were struggling against the entrenched Canaanites at the same time that the recently arrived Philistines were trying to consolidate their hold on the coastal strip. By the end of the eleventh century, the Canaanites were no longer a major political factor in Palestine, and the advantageous coalition of Philistines and Israelites gave way to bitter conflict between the two successors. If these deductions are correct (cf. also A. Van Selms, OTS 12 [1958], 187), we would have here a criterion for dating the verses with reasonable accuracy. By the same token, however, the Japhethites of the present account would differ considerably from their namesakes in the Table of Nations (x 2–5: P). For by then, the Philistines too had ceased to be a politically significant group; and they had been settled long enough to be classed with the Hamites (x 14).

11. THE TABLES OF NATIONS
(x 1–32: /P/, J)

X /¹ These are the lines of Noah's sons, Shem, Ham, and Japheth, to whom sons were born after the Flood.

² Descendants of Japheth: Gomer, Magog, Madai, Javan, Tubal, Meshech, and Tiras. ³ Descendants of Gomer: Ashkenaz, Riphath, and Togarmah. ⁴ Descendants of Javan: Elishah, Tarshish, the Kittim, and the Rodanim.ᵃ ⁵ [These are the descendants of Japheth],ᵇ and from them branched out the maritime nations, in their respective lands—each with its own tongue—by their clans within the nations.

⁶ Descendants of Ham: Cush, Mizraim, Put, and Canaan. ⁷ Descendants of Cush: Seba, Havilah, Sabtah, Raamah, and Sabteca. Descendants of Raamah: Sheba and Dedan./

⁸ Now Cush begot Nimrod, who was the first potentate on earth. ⁹ He was a mighty hunter by the will of Yahweh, hence the saying, "Like Nimrod, a mighty hunter by the will of Yahweh." ¹⁰ The mainstays of his kingdom were Babylon, Erech, and Accad, ᶜall of themᶜ in the land of Shinar; ¹¹ from that land came Asshur. And he built Nineveh, Rehoboth-ir, Calah, ¹² and Resen, between Nineveh and Calah, the latter being the main city.

¹³ Mizraim begot the Ludim, the Anamim, the Lehabim, the Naphtuhim, ¹⁴ the Pathrusim, the Casluhim, and the Caphtorim,ᵈ from whom the Philistines descended.

¹⁵ Canaan begot Sidon, his first-born, and Heth; ¹⁶ also the Jebusites, the Amorites, the Girgashites, ¹⁷ the Hivites, the

ᵃ So with LXX and I Chron i 7; Heb. Dodanim.
ᵇ Accidental omission in MT; cf. vss. 20 and 31.
ᶜ⁻ᶜ MT cons. *wklnh;* see NOTE.
ᵈ See NOTE.

Arkites, the Sinites, 18 the Arvadites, the Zemarites, and the Hamathites. Later on, the clans of the Canaanites spread out, 19 until the Canaanite borders extended from Sidon all the way to Gerar, near Gaza, and to Sodom, Gomorrah, Admah, and Zeboyim, near Lasha. /20 These are the descendants of Ham, according to their clans and tongues, by their lands and nations./

21 To Shem for his part—ancestor of all the children of Eber and Japheth's older brother—sons were born. /22 Descendants of Shem: Elam, Asshur, Arpachshad, Lud, and Aram. 23 Descendants of Aram: Uz, Hul, Gether, and Mash./

24 Arpachshad begot Shelah, and Shelah begot Eber. 25 Two sons were born to Eber: the name of the first was Peleg, because it was at that time that the world was dispersed*; his brother's name was Joktan. 26 Joktan begot Almodad, Sheleph, Hazarmaveth, Jerah, 27 Hadoram, Uzal, Diklah, 28 Obal, Abimael, Sheba, 29 Ophir, Havilah, and Jabab; all these were descendants of Joktan. 30 Their settlements extended from Meshah all the way to Sephar, the hill country to the east. /31 These are the descendants of Shem, according to their clans, tongues, and lands, by their nations.

32 Such are the groupings of Noah's descendants, according to their origins, by their lands. And from these branched out other nations of the world after the Flood./

*See NOTE.

NOTES

x 1. For the ethnic list as a whole cf. my discussion in *The Interpreter's Dictionary of the Bible*, III, 1962, pp. 235 ff.

2. *Descendants.* Literally "sons," but the list includes not only obvious eponyms but also outright ethnic names (Kittīm, Rōdānīm), which are plurals.

Japheth. The same name is apparently reflected in *Iapetos* (cf. COMMENT on Sec. 7), who was one of the Titans. It is significant, therefore, that the descendants of Japheth include the Ionians (Javan, i.e., *Yāwān*). In general, the Japhethite line may be said to comprise various ethnic groups that were settled at the time in Anatolia, the Aegean region, and beyond. The principal criterion was geographic. But it so happened that most of the groups involved were of Indo-European stock, so that the list becomes ethnogeographic and ethnolinguistic in effect, as is actually indicated in vs. 5.

Gomer. See also Ezek xxxviii 6. These are the *Gimirray* of the Assyrians, the Cimmerians of classical sources, a name still in use apparently for the Welsh (*Cymry*).

Magog. This is the land of Gog (Ezek xxxviii 2), who has been compared with Gyges of Lydia, the ruler whose reign coincided with the period of Assyrian campaigns against the Cimmerians.

Tubal, Meshech. Both are familiar from Ezekiel (xxvii 13, xxxii 26, xxxviii 2, xxxix 1) and were located in eastern Anatolia.

Tiras. Probably to be compared with Eg. *Tur(u)sha* and Gr. *Tyrsenoi,* perhaps the Aegean counterpart of the Etruscans.

3. *Ashkenaz.* Also Jer li 27. The name is evidently connected with cun. *Ashguza* "Scythians."

Togarmah. Cf. Ezek xxvii 14, xxxviii 6; cun. *Tegarama,* near Carchemish (see A. Goetze, *Kizzuwatna,* 1940, pp. 19 f.).

4. *Elishah.* Corresponds to cun. *Alashiya* "Cyprus."

Rodanim. Inhabitants of the island of Rhodes. The miswritten "Dodanim" of MT (see textual note *a*) is readily explained by the graphic similarity of "D" and "R" in the "square" Heb. script.

Of the two remaining names in this verse,

Kittim is the *Kition* of the Greeks, which is modern Larnaka, in Cyprus. In that case,

Tarshish, might be sought, analogously, on the island of Rhodes, or perhaps in western Anatolia. Yet the usual practice is to adduce Gr. *Tartessos,* in Spain (for other occurrences see Ezek xxvii 12; Isa lxvi 19; Ps lxxii 10; Jon i 3); cf. W. F. Albright, BASOR 83 (1941), 21 f., for a namesake in Sardinia. The biblical name may well refer to more than one place.

5. *maritime nations.* Literally "the isles (or 'coastlands') of the nations."

6. *Cush.* This geographic term is used in the Bible for two widely separated lands whose names happen to be similar by coincidence: (1) Ethiopia, as here. (2) Cossaea, the country of the Kassites, as in vs. 8, below, and ii 13; see COMMENT on Sec. 2). The present combination of Ethiopia, Egypt (Mizraim), and

Put, which is either Punt, or Libya (JNES 2 [1943], 309), corresponds thus to ethnolinguistic facts.

Canaan. In a strictly linguistic sense, the term designates a people who spoke a language that was closely related to Heb., or some specifically the Phoenicians. And indeed, vs. 15 (*J*) lists Sidon as the first-born son of Canaan. Moreover, Isa xix 18 calls Hebrew (but on other ground) "the tongue of Canaan." For the earliest uses and background of this term attention may be called to my paper in *Language* 12 (1936), 121–26; the cun. occurrences have recently been increased by instances from Alalakh. In these circumstances, the subsuming of Canaan under Hamites appears at first to be strange. The solution is to be sought apparently in geographic and political connection rather than in ethnolinguistic relations.

7. The list proceeds now from the African to the Asiatic side of the Red Sea; on Dedan see especially W. F. Albright, *Festschrift Albrecht Alt,* 1953, pp. 1–12. The combination of Cush and Havilah is known also from ii 11, 13, in the context of the rivers of Eden. There, however, the locale is the head of the Persian Gulf, and the Cush in question is heterogeneous.

8–12. These five verses constitute a fragment from, or a summary of, an account dealing with the exploits of Nimrod. The immediate source is readily identified as *J;* note the repeated mention of Yahweh in 9. The piece owes its position to the occurrence of the other Cush in vss. 6–7, and the same circumstance has contributed to the confusion that has long centered about the figure of Nimrod.

8. *potentate.* Literally "mighty man, hero." The allusion, however, is political, as can be seen from 10–12; the effect is that of "mighty conqueror."

9. *by the will of Yahweh.* See NOTE on vi 11.

10. *mainstays.* Heb. $r\bar{e}'\check{s}\hat{\imath}t$, which has been translated regularly as "beginning," or the like. Yet three ancient and authentic capitals cannot all have been the beginning of a famous ruler's career. One need not look farther than Jer xlix 35 to find the same noun in the sense of "mainstay (of their might)"—and so actually rendered in modern translations.

all of them. The cons. text is pointed $w^e kaln\bar{e}h$ "and Calneh," but no such south Babylonian city, let alone capital, is attested in cun. records; it should be noted that the mention of Accad points up the soundness of the source, since that city, while most important at one time, had lost is preeminence as far back as the end of the third millennium. Accordingly, the repointing of Heb. to $kull\bar{a}n\bar{a}(h)$, which is known independently from xlii 36, has everything in its favor (cf. W. F. Albright, JNES 3 [1944], 254 f.).

Shinar. The biblical counterpart of cun. *Šumer(u)* "Sumer"; see xi 2, xiv 1.

11. *from that land came Asshur.* The transition would be smoother if the clause read "from that land he went forth to Ashur"; but this would make for awkward syntax. At any rate, it was obviously Nimrod and not some ruler by the name of Ashur who went on to found the Assyrian

centers that are here listed. The debt of Assyria to Sumer is, of course, an established cultural fact.

Rehoboth-ir. In all likelihood, this is not a city name but a phrase which describes Nineveh as a city of broad streets; the Gilgamesh Epic speaks analogously, and repeatedly, of *Uruk-rēbītu* "Uruk of the spacious markets," the Akk. epithet being actually a cognate of Heb. *rᵉḥōb* (singular). The prepositional *wᵉʾet* could just as readily express "namely" as a serial accusative.

12. *Resen.* No such place of suitable prominence has as yet been identified in that particular region. This entry, too, may have served originally as a parenthetic description rather than an additional place name. Some impressive engineering or military construction, perhaps some kind of water works (**rēš ēni*, which would become *rēsēn* in Heb.) might have inspired such a comment. The next-named place actually lay at the confluence of the Tigris and the Upper Zab.

Calah. There is no question about the importance or impressive appearance of this place, Akk. *Kalḫu.* The city was built, interestingly enough (cf. COMMENT), by Shalmaneser I, father of Tukulti-Ninurta I. It was a major center in the days of Tiglath-pileser I (at the end of the twelfth century), and Ashurnasirpal II (884–859 B.C.) made it the capital of Assyria. Its palaces and temples have yielded enormous treasure to several generations of excavators. It is suggestive, moreover, in the present context that the modern name of the site is *Nimrud.*

the latter being the main city. When this was committed to writing (by J. hence not later than the tenth century), Calah certainly outranked Nineveh in political importance. The final clause, therefore, should apply to Calah, as the word order of MT demands, and not to Nineveh, as is commonly assumed.

13–14. All the names in these two verses have the plural form in *-īm*, thereby emphasizing the ethnic character of the entries.

13. *the Ludim.* Although mentioned elsewhere (Isa lxvi 19; Jer xlvi 9; Ezek xxvii 10, xxx 5), they are yet to be identified. Described sometimes as mercenaries, the Ludim could have been recruited from distant parts; cf. "Lud" in vs. 22. Similar uncertainty characterizes some of the other listings in this portion of the Table.

14. *the Pathrusim.* Based on Eg. "the people of the south land," i.e., Upper Egypt; see Isa xi 11; Jer xliv 1, 15; Ezek xxix 14, xxx 14.

the Caphtorim. Since Caphtor, evidently "Crete," is recorded as the home or staging center of the Philistines (Deut ii 23; Amos ix 7; Jer xlvii 4), the clause "from whom the Philistines issued/descended" cannot be applied to the preceding Casluhim, as the word order of MT indicates, and should be transposed to the end of the verse.

the Philistines. If origin had been the criterion (see above), this people should have been listed among the "maritime nations" descended from Japheth (vs. 5). But that part of the record stems from *P*, whereas the present notice derives from *J*. Since the historic Philistines were settled along the coastal approaches to Egypt, the classification here given is evidently geographic. It is worthy of special mention that the Philistines are never mentioned with the stereotyped groups of pre-Israelite nations (e.g., xv 19 f.). This reflects sound chronology inasmuch as the Philistine invasion occurred in the twelfth century, by which time the Israelites had already been settled in the land.

15. *Heth.* The indicated family relationship between "Hittites" and Phoenicians (Sidon) would be cause for surprise only if the Table of Nations, or its *J* section in any case, set out to offer ethnolinguistic data. What the present passage is saying depends, of course, on the meaning of the term Heth: does this name describe the pre-Indo-European Hattians, the "Hittites" of ca. 1450–1200 B.C., or the Hurrians? In favor of the last-named connection is the fact that by the middle of the second millennium the population of Syria and north-central Palestine was largely a mixture of Semitic and Hurrian elements. The present notice might well reflect just such a condition. It may be noted in passing that LXX and MT between them confuse Hurrians, Hittites, and Hivites more than once. Cf. also Ezekiel's reference to Jerusalem, "Your father was an Amorite and your mother a Hittite" (Ezek xvi 3); see further the COMMENT on xxiii.

16–18. These verses can be distinguished at a glance from the rest of the Table inasmuch as all the names which they list are formal ethnica (with the adjectival suffix *-î*). On this and other counts the passage is considered to be a later addition, perhaps by *R*(edactor). Some of the names remain obscure and are passed over without comment.

16. *the Jebusites.* The ruling Hurrian element in Jerusalem during the Amarna age (ca. 1400 B.C.).

the Amorites. Cun. *Amurrû,* a West Semitic group related to, but not identical with, the Canaanites. In the Bible, these two designations vary considerably depending on the documentary source.

17. *the Hivites.* See above, under *Heth.*

18. *the Arvadites.* So named after a town built on an island off the northern coast of Phoenicia; it is familiar also from Assyrian historical records.

19. *all the way.* Literally "as you come," in an impersonal sense.

21–31. The line of Shem, as recorded by both *J* and *P*. *P* continues his list in xi 18–27.

21. *the children of Eber.* They are singled out for special attention

and cited in more detail in 24–30. Eber is the eponymous ancestor of the Hebrews. On the complex question of possible connection between Hebrews and the extra-biblical Ḫapiru or Ḫabiru, see J. Bottéro (ed.), *Le problème des Ḫabiru*, 1954, and M. Greenberg, The *Ḫab/piru*, 1955.

22. *Elam*. Eastern neighbor and traditional rival of Mesopotamian states since the dawn of history. The name reflects the native term *Ḫaltam(tu)*; see A. Poebel, AJSL 48 (1931), 20 ff. The Elamite language is not related to Semitic, Sumerian, Hurrian, or Indo-European. The present grouping under Shem is due to political and geographic considerations.

Arpachshad. This name (also in xi 10 ff.) continues to defy linguistic analysis. As the father of Eber, Arpachshad should be transparently Semitic, yet such is certainly not the case. The name has often been compared with cun. *Arrapḫa* (modern Kirkuk); but the cons. transliterated as *ch* (spirantized *k*) does not correspond to *ḫ;* and the last two letters would remain unaccounted for. To be sure, the first part of the name could reflect Hurrian *Arip-*, which is a common element in personal names; but the rest would not be a demonstrably Hurrian component. The best that one can say today is that Arpachshad, if correctly transmitted, has to be regarded as non-Semitic. This would fit well enough with what we know today about the composite ethnic background of the Hebrews; but could the ancient source be credited with such knowledge? For the present, at any rate, the problem appears to be insoluble.

Lud. See vs. 13. Here the name seems to point to the Lydians of Anatolia. If it was homogeneous with *Ludim*, the duplication might be due to the circumstance that the earlier passage goes back to *J*, whereas this one stems from *P*.

Aram. Eponymous ancestor of the Aramaeans, the most widespread of all the Semitic groups. Speakers of Aramaic (or Syriac) dialects are still to be found in Syria, the region of Mosul, and in the mountains of Kurdistan.

25. Nothing is said here about the descendants of Peleg because his genealogy, starting with Arpachshad, is taken up in detail later on (by *P*, xi). There can be little doubt that *J*, too, had something to say about it at this point, but his data were later omitted in view of the detailed statement by *P* (who ignores Joktan altogether).

was dispersed. Heb. *niplᵉgā*, literally "divided, broke up," wordplay on Peleg; for the meaning cf. ix 19.

26–30. *J*'s list of Joktan's descendants, consisting of various Arabian tribes. Hazarmaveth is modern *Ḥaḍramaut*, in southern Arabia. Sheba (which duplicates *P*'s entry in vs. 7) is located in the Yemen, and Ophir points to the east coast of Arabia. Finally, Havilah (29) is the same place as the one in xxv 18, and perhaps in vs. 7, above. But the entry in ii 11 is manifestly a different locality, associated with the Kassite homophone of Cush, whereas the present passage and more particularly vs. 7 are linked with the South Arabian and Ethiopian Cushites.

COMMENT

The Table of Nations, as we now have it, is devoted specifically to matters of ethnographic import. The various groups may be traced to individuals in certain instances, yet their collective character is plainly indicated by the frequent plural forms (4, 13 f.), and still more so by gentilic adjectives (16–18). The Table incorporates material from both *J* and *P;* the sections attributed to *P* have been set off by means of diagonals. *P*'s list, in particular, was conceived as a catalogue of states, as opposed to tribal units. Hence the summaries stress the term *gōy* "nation" (5, 20, 31, 32), whereas *'am* does not occur at all; on the far-reaching difference between the two, see JBL 79 (1960), 157–63. Subsidiary criteria of classification include country, language, and ethnic affinities (cf. the verses just cited). The whole is thus noteworthy for its wide scope and analytical approach. As such, the Table stands out as a pioneering effort among the ethnographic attempts of the ancient world.

The fact, however, that the Table shows a keen awareness of the need for method does not guarantee correct results in the light of modern findings. Although modern scholarship continues to operate with the traditional terms "Semitic" and "Hamitic," the current groupings depart considerably from those that are given in the Table. This is largely because the modern principle of classification is strictly linguistic, whereas the Bible employs several criteria concurrently, which cannot lead to uniform results. Thus, for example, the Canaanites and the "Hittites" are listed with Hamites on grounds that are partly political and partly geographic; yet all three are linguistically distinctive.

Another source of confusion is bound up with the composite character of the Table. The Japhethite group as recorded by *P* is not later than the seventh century B.C., since it was known to Jeremiah and Ezekiel, directly or indirectly. Yet much of the same information is too late for *J*'s times. Small wonder, therefore, that *J* appears to identify Japheth with the Philistines (see COMMENT on Sec. 10), whom *P* does not even mention. The Philistines, in turn, are relatives of the Egyptians (13–14), according to *J;* in *P,* however, Egypt is grouped with Canaan (6) under Ham, and hence is kept apart from Japheth.

The omission of Peleg's descendants from the Table may appear surprising at first glance, inasmuch as Peleg was the direct ancestor not only of the Israelites, but also of the Ammonites, Moabites, and Edomites. Verse 25 (*J*), where this elder son of Eber is cited, breaks off abruptly, and what follows is a detailed list of the descendants of Joktan, who was Peleg's younger brother. In all likelihood, however, the *J* document had originally dealt with Peleg at greater length, but the details were later left out in favor of *P*'s parallel genealogy in xi 18–27. Another noteworthy omission is that of the Babylonians. The chances are that such an entry was once included under the Mesopotamian Cush (8 ff.), the eponym of the Kassites who were long-time masters of Babylonia. If this is true, the verses in question would have to be dated not later (in terms of source material) than the end of the Kassite period (end of twelfth century). For a fuller discussion of these and related problems cf. the writer's study on "Ethnic Divisions of Man" in *The Interpreter's Dictionary of the Bible,* III, 1962.

On the subject of Nimrod (8–12), I had occasion to write more fully in a paper entitled "In Search of Nimrod," *Eretz-Israel* V (Mazar Volume, 1958), 32*–36*. Various details have already been taken up in the NOTES *ad loc.* Here it will suffice to comment only on the historical model behind the legend. For all his prodigious deeds, Nimrod is depicted in our passage as a recognizably mortal ruler. Hence various attempts to trace the name back to the Mesopotamian god Ninurta must be ruled out. The appended detail, moreover, is obviously authentic. The mention of such celebrated southern capitals as Babylon, Uruk, and Accad, in the land of Shinar (Sumer and Babylonia), and of such northern capitals as Calah and Nineveh, in the land of Ashur, is clear proof of a sound historical background. The biblical Nimrod is said to have combined effective authority over both Babylonia and Assyria. The first Mesopotamian ruler to do so on a solid basis was Tukulti-Ninurta I (thirteenth century B.C.); he was certainly the first Assyrian conqueror of Babylonia. Aside from his conquests, this king was celebrated also for his building activities, and an epic extolling his exploits is one of the literary legacies of Assyria.

Compound Akk. names were often reduced in speech to one of their components. Indeed, classical sources appear to commemorate Tukulti-Ninurta I under the legendary figure of Ninus. Post-biblical sources for their part independently link Nimrod with Ninus, and the same identification is quoted in the name of the late Babylonian historian Berossus. The chain of evidence would thus seem to be complete.

12. THE TOWER OF BABEL
(xi 1–9: *J*)

XI [1] The whole world had the same language and the same words. [2] As men migrated from the east, they came upon a valley in the land of Shinar and settled there. [3] They said to one another, "Come, let us mold bricks and burn them hard." Brick served them for stone, and bitumen for mortar. [4] Then they said, "Come, let us build ourselves a city, and a tower with its top in the sky, to make a name for ourselves; else we shall be scattered all over the world."

[5] Yahweh came down to look at the city and the tower that the earthlings had built. [6] And Yahweh said, "If this is how they have started to act, while they are one people with a single language for all, then nothing that they may presume to do will be out of their reach. [7] Let me, then, go down and confound their speech there, so that they shall not understand one another's talk." [8] Yahweh dispersed them from there over the whole earth, and they stopped building the city. [9] That is why it was named Babel, since Yahweh confounded[a] the speech of the whole world, as he[b] dispersed them from there over the whole world.

[a] Heb. *bālal* "mixed, confused," a wordplay on *Babel* "Babylon."
[b] Heb. *Yahweh.*

NOTES

xi 1. *the same.* Heb. uses the adjectival "one" in the plural.
2. *Shinar.* Cf. x 10.
4. *to make a name for ourselves.* Cf. NOTE on vi 4.
5. *the earthlings.* Literally "sons of man," as opposed to "man" used

collectively. This lends emphasis to the terrestrial status of man, and his presumptuous ways.

6. For the protasis with *hēn* and the apodosis with *we'attā* cf. iv 14.

presume. The Heb. stem *zmm* denotes "to scheme," and the like.

7. *me.* Heb. employs the plural pronoun, apparently because the subject is understood to be analogous to "God," which is grammatically plural; or this may be a plural of majesty. If it were not for the singular in vs. 5, the present instance could also be interpreted as an allusion to Yahweh's celestial staff; see NOTE on i 26.

talk. Same Heb. noun as "speech ('lip')" in the first clause.

COMMENT

This is an exceptionally significant narrative on two separate counts. For one thing, the episode points more concretely to Babylonia than does any other portion of Primeval History, and the background that is here sketched proves to be authentic beyond all expectations. Yet, for another thing, the author's handling of his material is not only independent but critical.

Scholars have been inclined, understandably enough, to trace the original inspiration of this narrative to one of the celebrated temple towers of Mesopotamia, preferably Entemenanki, the ziggurat of Babylon itself. Such an interpretation, however, is ruled out by chronology. For the towering structure that the Greeks saw and described was the final achievement of Nabopolassar and Nebuchadnezzar, in the seventh/sixth centuries B.C. It could not have been known in that very form to *J,* whose work dates to the tenth century, let alone to *J's* sources which have to be older still.

What inspired the present biblical theme in the first instance was not monumental architecture but literary tradition (see the writer's statement in *Orientalia* 25 [1956], 317–23). We need look no farther than the account of the building of Babylon and its temple that is given in *Enūma eliš* VI, lines 60–62 (ANET, p. 69). In describing the construction of Esagila, as the sacred precinct was called, the Akk. text says: "The first year they molded its bricks (*libittašu iltabnū*). And when the second year arrived / They raised the head of Esagila toward Apsû." Apsû is, among other things, a poetic term for the boundless expanse of the sky conceived as one of the cosmic sources of sweet water. It so happens, moreover, that the Sumerian name Esagila means literally "the structure with upraised head." The Akk. for "they raised its (Esagila's) head" (*ullū rēšišu*) is merely a play on Esagila. It is to this particular phrase in a well-known canonical composition, transmitted either directly or indirectly, that the biblical phrase "with its top (literally 'head') in the sky" obviously harks back. The connection is confirmed by the preceding clause (vs. 3) "let us build bricks." In a normal Heb. context such a reference would be out of place and confusing; it thus called for an explanatory reference about the building customs of the Babylonians. As a rendition, however, of an Akk. original, the remark is self-explanatory. For the ceremonial and year-long preparation of the sacral bricks and the solemn laying of the first brick were standard practices bound up with the religious architecture of Mesopotamia.

Our narrator, however, was concerned with more than learned quotations from traditional Mesopotamian sources. He employed these data solely as a basis for his criticism of man's folly and presumption, by giving the original statement a strictly literal interpretation. At the same time, the author finds in his quotation a means for explaining the multiplicity of languages throughout the world. To that end he makes good use of the flexible and ever popular tool of sound symbolism or word play (cf. NOTE on ii 5). It is immaterial whether this particular juxtaposition of similar, yet unrelated, words was first introduced by some Mesopotamian rival of Babylon, or whether it originated on Palestinian soil. Of far greater consequence are the positive results: first, that the biblical story about the Tower of Babel had a demonstrable source in cuneiform literature; and second, that the narrator utilized this source to answer a perplexing question and point a significant moral. The episode has thus a twofold bearing on the nature of the comprehensive work in which it came to be incorporated.

13. GENEALOGIES FROM SHEM TO ABRAHAM
(xi 10–27, 31–32: *P;* 28–30: /*J*/)

XI 10 This is the line of Shem:

Shem was 100 years old when he begot Arpachshad, two years after the Flood. 11 After the birth of Arpachshad, Shem lived 500 years and begot sons and daughters.

12 At 35 years of age, Arpachshad begot Shelah. 13 After the birth of Shelah, Arpachshad lived 403 years and begot sons and daughters.

14 At 30 years of age, Shelah begot Eber. 15 After the birth of Eber, Shelah lived 403 years and begot sons and daughters.

16 At 34 years of age, Eber begot Peleg. 17 After the birth of Peleg, Eber lived 430 years and begot sons and daughters.

18 At 30 years of age, Peleg begot Reu. 19 After the birth of Reu, Peleg lived 209 years and begot sons and daughters.

20 At 32 years of age, Reu begot Serug. 21 After the birth of Serug, Reu lived 207 years and begot sons and daughters.

22 At 30 years of age, Serug begot Nahor. 23 After the birth of Nahor, Serug lived 200 years and begot sons and daughters.

24 At 29 years of age, Nahor begot Terah. 25 After the birth of Terah, Nahor lived 119 years and begot sons and daughters.

26 And when Terah reached the age of 70, he had begotten Abram, Nahor, and Haran.

27 This is the line of Terah: Terah begot Abram, Nahor, and Haran. And Haran begot Lot.

/28 Haran died in the lifetime of his father Terah, in his native land, in Ur*a* of the Chaldeans. 29 Abram and Nahor took wives; the name of Abram's wife was Sarai, and that of Nahor's

---

a LXX "the land."

wife was Milcah daughter of Haran, the father of Milcah and Iscah. 30 Sarai was barren; she had no child./

31 Terah took his son Abram, his grandson Lot son of Haran, and his daughter-in-law Sarai the wife of his son Abram, and *they all left* Ur of the Chaldeans to move to the land of Canaan; but when they reached Haran, they settled there. 32 The days of Terah came to 205 years; Terah died in Haran.

b-b See NOTE.

NOTES

xi 10. According to x 22, Arpachshad was the third of Shem's five sons. His own branch is now singled out as the line to which Abraham belonged.

12–17. The corresponding notices from *J* are found in x 24–25.

20. *Serug.* For the pertinent Mesopotamian city and district of *Sarug-* (in the region of Harran) cf. Dr., p. 139.

22. *Nahor.* For the city of *Nahur* in the Mari documents, see ARM XV, p. 130.

26. Cf. v 32. [The two sentences are identical in structure, listing the patriarch and the age at which he had three sons, who are named, i.e., Noah at 500 and his three sons; Terah at 70 and his three sons. NF]

28. *in the lifetime of.* Literally "upon the face/in the presence of," cf. also Num iii 4.

Ur of the Chaldeans. The rendering "land" (for "Ur") in LXX suggests Heb. *'rṣ* instead of *'(w)r*. But this variant could have been influenced by the mention of "land" in the phrase immediately preceding. As the present passage indicates, the place name is given by *J*, as well as *P* (31), so that the problem involved antedates LXX by many centuries.

29. Nahor marries the daughter of his deceased brother Haran. Juridically, cases of this kind involve adoption (here of an orphaned niece) followed by marriage. The pertinent document in Nuzi would be called *ṭuppi mārtūti u kallatūti* "document of daughter- and daughter-in-law-ship," since the husband was also the adoptive father and thereby father-in-law. Interestingly enough, nothing is said here about the parentage of Sarah; cf. the discussion of the wife-sister problem in Secs. 15 and 25. These laconic notices by *J* presuppose a very ancient tradition precisely because they seem to be pointless in the present context. To be sure, it has been argued that the background of Nahor's wife was significant on account of Nahor's son Lot. But what reason could there

be for the inclusion of Iscah, other than the fact that such a tradition had been handed down to *J*, who had no choice but to record it?

31. *Lot son of Haran.* This is not an appositional construction in Heb. (Lot, the son of Haran) but a serial name (Lot-*ben*-Haran, Lot-son-of-Haran, or Lot "Haranson." Similarly, Milcah-*bat*-Haran (30), and so *passim.*

they all left. MT literally "and they left with them," which is obviously in error; either "he brought them out" (with Sam., LXX, Old Latin, Vulg.), or "he went with them" (with Syr.) which is idiomatically the same as "he took them." All these readings are merely a matter of vocalization, the original consonantal text (which did not express the final -*ū*) remaining unaffected.

Haran. Name of an old and prominent city in Central Mesopotamia, situated on the left bank of the Balikh, a tributary of the Euphrates; cun. *Ḫarrānu(m)*, with double -*rr*- which is still reflected in LXX. The Heb. form *Ḫārān*, follows the rules of Hebrew phonology. The traditional transliteration of the place name is not to be confused with the personal name Haran, Heb. *Hārān* (where the initial consonant is a different phoneme).

32. The Sam. version gives Terah a total of only 145 years (cf. Acts vii 4). On this reckoning, the year of Terah's death would be the same as that of Abraham's departure from Haran (cf. Gen xii 4).

COMMENT

This section resumes the genealogical record that was interrupted at the end of ch. v. It is again the work of *P*, except for a brief but important insert from *J* (28–30). In the meantime, we have had other passages from *P*, notably a distinctive account of the Flood and a portion of the Table of Nations—passages that are now interposed between segments of the genealogy. It is thus likely that the genealogical record (or "The *Tōleḏōt*") was once a separate and continuous work which was broken up in course of time and fitted into a larger whole.

There can be little doubt today that the material before us is based in large part on very old traditions, some of which may date to the period of Abraham himself. This is evident especially from the name Nahor (attributed to the grandfather and to a brother of Abraham). As we know now from the Mari records, there was in the patriarchal age a city by the same name (cun. *Naḫur*) lo-

cated in the region of Haran (see NOTE on 22). Significantly
enough, the population cf Naḫur in Mari times included demonstrably West Semitic elements. Another place name in the same
general area was *Sarug-*. manifestly analogous with the patriarch
(vs. 20; see NOTE) who was the father of Nahor the older. Such
borrowings from names of places are, of course. a well-known and
universal practice.

On the other hand, the statistics cited by *P* do not commend themselves as the product of a dependable tradition. On this point, MT,
Sam., and LXX have each their own detailed answers. One can
see at a glance that MT is transparently schematic. Thus Shem was
exactly 100 years old at the birth of Arpachshad, and he went on
living precisely 500 years In turn, both Arpachshad and Shelah survived the births of their respective oldest sons by identical spans of
just 403 years. And Shelah, Peleg, and Serug were each an even
30 when their first sons were born. All of this indicates a certain
amount of leveling in so far as numbers were involved. If any
particular system of computation was employed in arriving at these
figures, its nature is no longer apparent.

The mention of Ur of the Chaldeans brings up a problem of a
different kind. The ancient and renowned city of Ur is never ascribed
expressly, in the many thousands of cuneiform records from that site,
to the Chaldean branch of the Aramaean group. The Chaldeans,
moreover, are late arrivals in Mesopotamia, and could not possibly
be dated before the end of the second millennium. Nor could the
Aramaeans be placed automatically in the patriarchal period. Yet
the pertinent tradition was apparently known not only to *P* (31)
but also to *J* (28). And even if one were to follow LXX in reading
"land" for "Ur," the anachronism of the Chaldeans would remain
unsolved.

The one fact beyond serious dispute is that the home of the
patriarchs was in the district of Haran, and not at Ur. According
to xii 1 and 5, Haran was Abraham's birthplace. The toponymic
models for the names of Abraham's close relatives have been found
in Central Mesopotamia (see above). And the cultural background
of many of the later patriarchal narratives is intimately tied up with
the Hurrians of Haran and the regions nearby rather than with the
Sumerians and Babylonians in the south. Thus Ur proves to be intrusive in this context, however old that intrusion may have been.

How then did such an anachronism originate? Any explanation is bound to be tenuous and purely conjectural. With these reservations, the following possibility may be hazarded. Both Ur and Haran were centers of moon worship, unrivaled in this respect by any other Mesopotamian city. It is remotely possible, therefore, that this religious distinction, which was peculiar to Ur and Haran, caused the two cities to be bracketed together, and then to be telescoped in later versions, at a time when the Chaldeans had already gained prominence. At all events, the correction required affects only incidental passages that are no more than marginal footnotes to the history of the patriarchs. That history starts at Haran (xii 5), as is evident from its very first episode.

II. THE STORY OF THE PATRIARCHS

A. The Story of Abraham

14. ABRAHAM'S CALL AND MIGRATION
(xii 1–4a, 6–9: *J*; 4b–5: /*P*/)

XII 1 Yahweh said to Abram,

"Go forth from your native land
And from your father's home
To a land that I will show you.
2 I will make of you a great nation,
Bless you, and make great your name,
That ᵃit may beᵃ a blessing.
3 I will bless those who bless you,
And curse thoseᵇ who curseᵇ you;
And through you shall bless themselves
All the communities on earth."

4 Abram went as Yahweh told him, and Lot went with him.
/Abram was 75 years old when he left Haran. 5 Abram took
his wife Sarai, his brother's son Lot, all the possessions that
they had acquired, and all the persons they had obtained in
Haran. They set out for the land of Canaan and arrived in the
land of Canaan./ 6 Abram traveled in the land as far as the
siteᶜ at Shechem, by the terebinth of Moreh. The Canaanites
were then in the land.

7 Yahweh appeared to Abram and said, "I will give this land
to your offspring." He built there an altar to Yahweh who had
appeared to him. 8 From there he moved on to the hill country
east of Bethel, where he pitched his tent, with Bethel to the

ᵃ⁻ᵃ Reading wᵉhāyā; Heb. wehyḗ (second person).
ᵇ Singular in MT, but plural in some manuscripts and various ancient versions.
ᶜ Literally "place."

west and Ai to the east. And he built there an altar to Yahweh and invoked Yahweh by name. 9 Then Abram journeyed by stages to the Negeb.

NOTES

xii 1. *from your native land.* Literally "from your land and your birthplace," a clear case of hendiadys (cf. i 2).

2. *nation.* The term is significantly *gōy*, not *'am* "people." For the important distinction between the two, see JBL 79 (1960), 157 ff. Unlike *'am*, *gōy* requires a territorial base, since the concept is a political one (cf. COMMENT on Sec. 11); note also xvii 20, xviii 18, xxi 13, 18, xlvi 3; Exod xxxii 10; Num xiv 12; Deut xxvi 5.

that it may be. MT is pointed to yield "and you shall be," and the ancient versions concur. Nevertheless, the second person is syntactically unacceptable; it would have to read **wᵉhāyītā* (Ehrl.). The consonantal text remains the same either way.

3. *shall bless themselves.* The Heb. form is often translated "shall be blessed," inasmuch as it is Niphal, which is generally, though not always, passive. There are, however, parallel passages with the Hithpael (see xxii 18, xxvi 4), a form that can be reflexive or reciprocal, but not passive. What the clause means, therefore, is that the nations of the world will point to Abraham as their ideal, either in blessing themselves (Dr.), or one another (Ehrl.). The passive, on the other hand, would imply that the privileges to be enjoyed by Abraham and his descendants shall be extended to other nations. The distinction may be slight on the surface, yet it is of great consequence theologically. Nor may one disregard the evidence from linguistic usage.

communities. Heb. *mišpāḥā* is generally translated as "family." Its basic meaning, however, is demonstrably "category, class, subdivision." The accent here is on political communities; "families" would be expressed by *'ammē-;* cf. xxviii 3.

4b–5. A brief insert that is typical of *P* in emphasis and phraseology.

6. *the site at Shechem.* Not the city as such but a venerated spot within it or nearby, which owed its local prominence to a certain tree (see below). The ancient city by that name, modern Tell Balāṭah, gave way to Flavia Neapolis, modern Nāblūs.

terebinth. LXX, followed by various later translators, renders "oak," here and elsewhere; but the best technical evidence favors "terebinth"; see *Encyclopaedia Biblica* (Heb.) I, 294 f. It is worth noting that TO renders "plain," evidently to avoid the pagan implications of a sacred tree.

Moreh. Tradition regards this as a personal name. The original meaning, however, was probably "guiding, oracular"; LXX renders "lofty"; similarly Vulg. Note the pertinent "Soothsayers' terebinth" in Judg ix 37.

The Canaanites were then in the land. This brief sentence played a large part in the early history of biblical criticism. The famous medieval Jewish commentator Abraham Ibn Ezra states guardedly that this statement could not have been written by Moses, since it implies that the situation had changed in the meantime; it can hardly mean that the Canaanites were already in the land at that time (cf. his comment on Deut i 5). Ibn Ezra concludes by remarking, "there is a mystery here, but the wise had best keep silent." See I. Husik, JAOS 55 (1935), Suppl., 31 ff.

8. *Bethel.* Modern Beitin, 10 miles north of Jerusalem, with *Ai,* modern et-Tell, close by. For the archaeological problem of these two sites, and the possible interchange of their names at certain times, see G. E. Wright, *Biblical Archaeology,* 1959, pp. 31 f.

invoked Yahweh by name. Cf. iv 26 and COMMENT *ad loc.*

9. *the Negeb.* Literally "dry land," a geographic term for the southern part of Palestine.

COMMENT

The fundamental significance of this brief passage was stressed in the Introduction. The first three verses signal the beginning of the integral history of a particular group as opposed to background episodes in the prehistory of the race as a whole. The story commences with one individual, and extends gradually to his family, then to a people, and later still to a nation. Yet it is not to be the tale of individuals or a family or a people as such. Rather, it is to be the story of a society in quest of an ideal. Abraham's call, in short, marks the very beginning of the biblical process.

There was nothing in the preceding accounts to prepare us for Abraham's mission. *P* had done no more than trace the Pelegite genealogy down to Abraham, whom he left in Haran. *J* had noted a few meager details about Abraham's immediate family. Now, however, with startling suddenness, a call comes to Abraham, bidding him to pull up stakes and leave for a destination as yet undisclosed. The mandate means a complete break with Abraham's immediate environment. The spiritual objective of the journey is implicit at the outset; it is to be confirmed time and again in the narratives that follow. Nor were later generations in doubt on this point. The cause is summed up succinctly in Josh xxiv 2: "They had served other gods."

Abraham's journey to the Promised Land was thus no routine expedition of several hundred miles. Instead, it was the start of an epic voyage in search of spiritual truths, a quest that was to constitute the central theme of all biblical history. The all-important commencement is recorded by *J*, who introduces it fittingly with the imperative "Go forth." A brief insert by *P* (4b–5) shows that this source, too, was aware of the epochal bearing of the event, but could add nothing of moment to *J*'s account.

15. ABRAHAM AND SARAH IN EGYPT
(xii 10–20: J)

XII 10 There was a famine in the land; so Abram went down to Egypt to sojourn there, for the famine in the land was severe. 11 As he was about to enter Egypt, he said to his wife Sarai, "Look, I know what a beautiful woman you are. 12 When the Egyptians see you, they will say, 'She is his wife!' And they will kill me, but let you live. 13 Please, say therefore that you are my sister, so that it may go well with me on account of you and that I may retain my life thanks to you."

14 When Abram entered Egypt, the Egyptians saw how very beautiful the woman was. 15 And when Pharaoh's courtiers saw her, they praised her to Pharaoh, and the woman was taken into Pharaoh's household. 16 And on account of her it went very well with Abram, and he came to own sheep and cattle and he-asses, male and female slaves, she-asses and camels.

17 But Yahweh afflicted Pharaoh and his household with extraordinary plagues, because of Abram's wife Sarai. 18 Then Pharaoh summoned Abram and said, "See what you have done to me! Why did you not tell me that she was your wife? 19 Why did you say, 'She is my sister,' so that I took her for my wife? Now, here is your wife. Take her and be gone!"

20 Then Pharaoh put men in charge of him, and they sent him on his way, with his wife and all his possessions.

NOTES

xii 10. *went down*. Heb. regularly describes travel from Palestine to Egypt as "going down," and the reverse trip as "going up," because of the respective elevations of the two countries.

Egypt. With the mention of this land so soon after its parting glance at Mesopotamia, the very first chapter on patriarchal history has something to say about the two great centers that were always to loom large in biblical thought.

to sojourn. Heb. *gūr* describes residence that is limited in duration, privileges, or both; cf. xix 9.

11. *I know*. MT (consonants) *yd'ty*, normally first person perfect. It is worth noting, however, that Sam. has *'ty* for the customary *'t* "thou (feminine)" at the end of the verse. It is thus possible that the verb before us was similarly written as an archaic second person with final *-y*, as is actually the case in Judg v 7. If so, the sense would be "you are well aware that you are beautiful," which would suit the context admirably.

beautiful. Here "comely of appearance," as compared with the simple adjective in vs. 14. The companion phrase is "comely of figure," e.g., xxix 17. Apocryphal literature had much to say about Sarah's exceptional beauty; cf. especially Gen. Apocr., column xx.

12. *let . . . live*. Piel, or factitive, form in Heb. The Hiphil of this verb is often intransitive, cf. vi 19 f. "to stay alive."

15. *courtiers*. Not necessarily "princes," as Heb. *śar(īm)* is usually translated, but dignitaries, high officers of the crown.

household. Heb. *bayit*, normally "house," but often also home, palace, family, and the like.

16. *it went very well*. Here Heb. employs the intransitive Hiphil (cf. NOTE on vs. 12) with emphatic connotation; in vs. 13 the verb appears in its simple stem.

The list of Abraham's acquisitions appears to have been subjected to some reshuffling in the course of transmission, as is indicated by the separation of he-asses and she-asses. The mention of camels, moreover, although by no means isolated in the patriarchal narratives (see xxiv 10), is chronologically suspect, since camels did not become an economic factor until the end of the second millennium. The author may thus be guilty of an anachronism. Alternatively, the camel may have come into limited use at an earlier time (as did also the horse), but required centuries before it ceased to be a luxury.

17. *extraordinary.* Literally "great"; but when the adjective describes unusual phenomena, it has the sense of "strange, wondrous, awesome."

18. Heb. *mah-zōt* is not "what is this?" but merely the interrogative indefinite reinforced by a determinative pronoun emphatically applied. For the unaugmented form with the same verb see iv 10.

20. It is characteristic of this author that he does not indulge in justification or face-saving; contrast xx 11 ff. (*E*). Abraham does not open his mouth in self-defense. For all that *J* knew, Abraham had no defense. His silence is a most effective dramatic touch, given the facts that the author had. That he did not have all the facts is another matter altogether; see COMMENT.

COMMENT

The present account is one of three closely related narratives, the other two being xx 1–18 (*E*) and xxvi 6–11 (*J*). The three together have an important bearing on the documentary hypothesis, as was pointed out in the Introduction; see also COMMENT on Sec. 25. Of much broader significance, however, is the joint evidence of these narratives in regard to patriarchal traditions in general. I have presented the material in due technical detail in a paper entitled "The Wife-Sister Motif in the Patriarchal Narratives"; cf. p. XL, fn. 10. The matter was also broached in the Introduction, although in a different context. The following is a summary of the salient points.

All three passages give essentially the same story: a patriarch visits a foreign land in the company of his wife. Fearing that the woman's beauty might become a source of danger to himself as the husband, the man resorts to the subterfuge of passing himself off as the woman's brother.

This recurrent wife-sister theme in Genesis has been the subject of innumerable comments and speculations. Interpreters through the ages have found the material both puzzling and disturbing. This is not surprising in the light of the data that are now available. For it can be shown on internal grounds that the narrators themselves were no longer aware of the full import of their subject matter. The pertinent customs were peculiar to Hurrian society and practiced in such centers as Har(r)an, where Western Semites, from whom the patriarchs branched out, lived in closest cultural symbiosis with Hurrians. On Palestinian soil, however, these exotic customs gradually lost their original meaning. Tradition retained the details but not their import. Small wonder that they came to be reinterpreted in the light of local circumstances and practices.

In Hurrian society the bonds of marriage were strongest and most solemn when the wife had simultaneously the juridical status of a sister, regardless of actual blood ties. This is why a man would sometimes marry a girl and adopt her at the same time as his sister, in two separate steps recorded in independent legal documents. Violations of such sistership arrangements were punished more severely than breaches of marriage contracts. The practice was apparently a reflection of the underlying fratriarchal system, and it gave the adoptive brother greater authority than was granted the husband. By the same token, the adopted sister enjoyed correspondingly greater protection and higher social status. Indeed, the wife-sister relationship is attested primarily among the upper strata of Hurrian society. It goes without saying that a blood brother had automatically the same kind of authority over his sister when the father died; cf. xxiv 55 ff. And when a brother, whether natural or adoptive, gave his sister in marriage, the law regarded the woman as a wife-sister in such cases as well.

It is worth stressing that these particular wife-sister customs were peculiar to the Hurrians—and hence also to groups that took over Hurrian practices. There is not a trace of such usage among the Akkadians, and it was expressly stigmatized by the Hittites, who otherwise had so much culturally in common with the Hurrians. The institution of the levirate affords no parallel whatsoever, since it is solely concerned with maintaining the line of a deceased brother. Nor can that institution be compared with the brother-sister marriages of the ruling houses of Egypt, and later those of Persia and certain Hellenistic states, for the Hurrian practice extended also to women who were sisters by law but not by blood.

To return to our three narratives, the wife-sister theme is confined here to two successive generations, those of Abraham and Isaac. In the case of Abraham, we find a few laconic notices about his family in xi 27–30. His brother Nahor married Milcah, who was the daughter of a younger brother named Haran. Under the law of such Hurrian centers as Ḥarran and Naḫur, a marriage of this type would carry with it the wife-sister provisions. We have fewer details in regard to Sarah, except that xx 12 (E) describes her indirectly as the daughter of Terah, but not by Abraham's own mother.

This alone would make Sarah eligible for "sistership" status under the law of the land from which Abraham had set out on his journey to Canaan, with all the attendant safeguards and privileges which that law afforded.

In Isaac's case, the situation is appreciably clearer. Not only was Rebekah a native of Hurrian-dominated Har(r)an, but she was actually given as wife to Isaac, through an intermediary, by her brother Laban. As a matter of fact, the details as recorded in xxiv 53–61 are remarkably like a transcript of a Hurrian "sistership" document (see COMMENT *ad loc.*). There are thus sufficient grounds for placing the two marriages, those of Abraham and Sarah and of Isaac and Rebekah, in the wife-sister category.

The problem of the biblical accounts under discussion narrows down, therefore, to the question of how this material was understood by the narrators. Tradition had apparently set much store by these incidents, but the key to them had been lost somewhere in the intervening distances of time and space. In such circumstances, an interpretation was bound to be improvised, one that would be in keeping with more familiar conditions and with common human inclinations. It is not surprising, therefore, that the indicated recourse to half-truth, if not outright deception, was just so much anachronism.

We have, of course, no way of telling what really happened on those visits to Egypt and Gerar, assuming that they did take place. A plausible guess, however, may not be amiss. Both Abraham and Isaac were married to women who enjoyed a privileged status by the standards of their own society. It was the kind of distinction that may well have been worthy of emphasis in the presence of their royal hosts, since it enhanced the credentials of the visitors. Status has always played a role in international relations, as far back as available records can take us. But popular lore has seldom been internationally oriented.

Lastly, why was tradition so interested in the matter, enough so to dwell on it repeatedly? We know now that the wife-sister position was a mark of cherished social standing. This kind of background would be an implicit guarantee of the purity of the wife's descendants. The ultimate purpose of biblical genealogies was to establish the superior strain of the line through which the biblical way of life was transmitted from generation to generation. In other words, the integrity of the mission was to be safeguarded in transmission, the purity of the content protected by the quality of the container. This is why the antecedents of the wife—the mother of the next generation—in the formative early stages were of particular significance. Hence, too, all such notices would be obligatory entries in the pertinent records.

16. LOT'S SEPARATION FROM ABRAHAM
(xiii 1–18: *J,* /*P*/)

XIII ¹From Egypt Abram went up to the Negeb, with his wife, all his possessions, and Lot. ²Now Abram was very rich in livestock, silver, and gold. ³From the Negeb he went by stages toward Bethel, to the place between Bethel and Ai where his tent had stood formerly— ⁴the site of the altar that he had built there the first time; and there he invoked Yahweh by name.

⁵Lot, who accompanied Abram, also had flocks and herds and tents. /⁶The land could not support them if they remained together, for their wealth was abundant, so that they could not stay together./ ⁷There were disputes between the herdsmen of Abram's stock and those of Lot's stock. The country was occupied at the time by Canaanites and Perizzites.

⁸So Abram said to Lot, "Let there be no strife between you and me, and between your herdsmen and mine, for we are kinsmen. ⁹Is not all the land open to you? Then separate from me: if it is to the left, I will go to the right; and if it is to the right, then I will go to the left." ¹⁰Lot looked about and saw how thoroughly watered was the whole Jordan Plain, all the way to Zoar—this was before Yahweh had destroyed Sodom and Gomorrah—like Yahweh's own garden, or like the land of Egypt. ¹¹So Lot chose for himself the whole Jordan Plain, and set out eastward. /Thus they separated from each other: ¹²Abram remained in the land of Canaan, and Lot settled amidst the cities of the Plain,/ pitching his tents near Sodom. ¹³Now the inhabitants of Sodom were very wicked sinners against Yahweh.

¹⁴After Lot had parted, Yahweh said to Abram, "Glance

about you and from where you are look to the north and south,
to the east and west; 15 for all the land that you can see I give
to you and to your offspring forever. 16 I will make your offspring
like the dust of the earth, so that if one could count the dust
of the earth, then your offspring too might be counted. 17 Up,
walk in the land, through its length and breadth, for I give it to
you."

18 Abram then moved his tent and proceeded to settle near
the terebinths*a* of Mamre, which are at Hebron. There he
built an altar to Yahweh.

a Singular in LXX and Syr.; so too in xiv 13, xviii 1.

NOTES

xiii 2. *rich in*. Literally "weighty with."

livestock. Literally "acquisitions," specialized to denote domestic animals. The passage describes the patriarchs as pastoral folk, in full agreement with xlvi 32, 34, xlvii 3; see NOTE on xxxiv 10.

6. An insert from *P,* in common with 11b–12a.

7. *Canaanites and Perizzites*. One of the shorter descriptions of the
pre-Israelite nations of Palestine; see also xxxiv 30; Judg i 4 f. The
shortest cites the Canaanites alone (xii 6); the longest gives ten names
(xv 19 f.). In the present combination, the Perizzites comprise all the
groups that are not subsumed under the Canaanites. The specific connotation and derivation of the term remain obscure. The clause as a
whole appears to point up the dangers of dissension among Abraham's
followers at a time when the land was ruled by others.

8. *between you and me*. So in conformance with English usage; the
order in MT is reversed.

9. *open to you*. Literally "before you," i.e., at your disposal, for
you to choose from.

left . . . right. Also "north . . . south." But the more specific direc-
tional names are cited in vs. 14, so that their equivalents have here been
given their primary meanings. The first alternatives are construed adverbially, and are governed by "separate"; the others are expressed by
cognate verbs.

10. *Plain*. Not "Circle," as the Heb. is often translated, since "the
Circle of the Jordan" would be difficult to justify topographically. The
Heb. noun *kikkār* is used for the typical flap of bread, as well as the

weight known as "talent." Both objects are round as well as flat. Here, however, it was evidently the latter feature that influenced the geographic application.

all the way to Zoar. MT has this phrase at the end of the verse, which may imply a marginal gloss or a measure of stylistic flexibility.

12. *near.* Necessarily not "as far"; for this force of the Heb. particle see H. L. Ginsberg, BASOR 122 (1951), 12 ff.; cf. x 19.

13. *wicked sinners.* Literally "wicked and sinful" (hendiadys).

14. From the heights of Bethel large stretches of Palestine are open to view; cf. F. M. Abel, *Géographie de la Palestine,* I, 1933, p. 372, and Gen. Apocr., column xxviii.

17. *walk.* On the Heb. form see NOTE on v 22. A close Akk. parallel, both in form and content, is found in Gilg., Tablet XI, line 303. In both instances, a tour of inspection is involved.

18. *the terebinths of Mamre.* Probably not to be compared with "the terebinth of Moreh," xii 6, even though LXX and Syr. give the singular here and also in xiv 13 and xviii 1. Since Mamre reappears as a personal name in xiv 13, the phrase could mean here something like "the terebinth grove of Mamre."

COMMENT

The best of the biblical narrators, whether they deal with the prehistory of a people or the history of a state, have the knack of depicting broad events in terms of their impact on the leading actors. *J* is an unsurpassed master of this art, and the present episode is a case in point.

The slow process of striking root in the Promised Land had begun. The recent immigrants from Mesopotamia have prospered greatly, thanks to their expanding pastoral economy. Their very success, however, entails problems and dangers. There are frictions within the group, which must be resolved before the dominant Canaanite population is aroused to action.

So much for the background, with its social and political features. In addition, the reader is being prepared for the presence in Transjordan of two close relatives of Israel, viz., the Moabites and the Ammonites, both of whom will be traced back to Lot in due time. Nor is the ultimate spiritual objective ignored; for the view from Bethel takes in much of the land in which the future of Israel is destined to unfold.

But history, as our author views it, is expressed in the last analysis through individuals; hence it is essentially personal history—vivid, concrete, and direct. In the present instance attention centers on the relations between Abraham and Lot. Having been orphaned early in his life (xi 28), Lot was brought up at first by his grandfather Terah (xi 31). The task was then taken over by Abraham (xii 5), who went on to treat his nephew with unfailing solicitude and tenderness. Now the two must part, since each requires a large grazing and watering radius for his flocks and herds. Although the choice of territory rests with the older man, Abraham generously cedes this right to his ward. Nor does Lot fail to take advantage of this unforeseen opportunity. He picks the greener and richer portion. How was he to know what fate lay in store for Sodom and Gomorrah, or how glorious was to be the future of the rugged hill country to the west? The narrative ends thus on a note of gentle irony, the ever-present irony of history.

17. INVASION FROM THE EAST. ABRAHAM AND MELCHIZEDEK
(xiv 1–24: X)

XIV ¹ When*a* Amraphel king of Shinar, Arioch king of Ellasar, Chedorlaomer king of Elam, and Tidal king of Goiim ² made war on Bera king of Sodom, Birsha king of Gomorrah, Shinab king of Admah, Shemeber king of Zeboiim, and the king of Bela—that is, Zoar— ³ all the latter joined forces in the Valley of Siddim—now the Dead Sea.*b* ⁴ For twelve years they had served Chedorlaomer, but in the thirteenth year they rebelled. ⁵ In the fourteenth year, Chedorlaomer and the kings allied with him came and defeated the Rephaim in Ashteroth-karnaim, the Zuzim in Ham, the Emim in Shaveh-kiriathaim, ⁶ and the Horites in the*c* hill country of Seir, near El-paran, which is on the edge of the wilderness. ⁷ They then swung back to En-mishpat—now Kadesh—and subdued all the territory of the Amalekites, and also the Amorites who dwelt in Hazazon-tamar. ⁸ Thereupon the king of Sodom, the king of Gomorrah, the king of Admah, the king of Zeboiim, and the king of Bela— or Zoar—marched forth and engaged them in battle in the Valley of Siddim: ⁹ Chedorlaomer king of Elam, Tidal king of Goiim, Amraphel king of Shinar, and Arioch king of Ellasar— four kings against five.

¹⁰ Now the Valley of Siddim was one bitumen pit after another. The kings of Sodom and Gomorrah flung themselves into these in their flight; the others escaped into the hills. ¹¹ [The invaders]*d* seized all the possessions of Sodom and

a See NOTE.
b Literally "Salt Sea."
c So most versions; MT "their."
d Literally "They."

Gomorrah and all their food, and departed, 12 taking with them
Lot, the son of Abram's brother, together with his possessions;
he had been living in Sodom.

13 A fugitive brought the news to Abram the Hebrew, who
was camping at the terebinths of Mamre the Amorite, kinsman
of Eshkol and Aner, these being confederates of Abram.
14 When Abram learned that his kinsman Lot had been captured, he called up his retainers, born into his household, in the
number of 318, and gave chase as far as Dan. 15 He and his servants deployed against the others at night, defeated them and
pursued them as far as Hobah, which lies north of Damascus.
16 He recovered all the possessions, and he also brought back his
kinsman Lot and his possessions, along with the women and
other personnel.

17 When he returned from his victory over Chedorlaomer and
the kings who were allied with him, the king of Sodom came
out to the Valley of Shaveh—that is, the King's Valley—to
greet him. 18 And Melchizedek king of Salem brought out
bread and wine; he was priest of El-Elyōn. 19 He blessed him,
saying,

> "Blessed be Abram by El-Elyōn,
>   Creator of heaven and earth.
> 20 And praised be El-Elyōn,
>   Who has delivered your foes to you."

And [Abram]ᵉ gave him a tenth of everything.

21 Then the king of Sodom said to Abram, "Give me the persons, and you may keep the property." 22 But Abram replied to
the king of Sodom, "I have sworn to Yahweh, God Most High,ᶠ
Creator of Heaven and earth, 23 that not so much as a thread or
a sandal strap would I take of anything that belongs to you, lest
you say, 'I made Abram rich.' 24 Nothing for me, save what my
men used up; but as for the men who joined me—Aner, Eshkol,
and Mamre—let them take their share."

ᵉ MT "he."
ᶠ See NOTE on *Yahweh* re *'l 'lywn*.

NOTES

xiv 1. *When*. The first clause is unacceptable by normal Heb. standards. It appears to date the proceedings to four named foreign kings who then go on to make war against five local rulers. In that case, however, the sequel would lack a subject; the same form cannot be construed as both possessive and subject at one and the same time. We should expect, following the initial narrative *wayhī* (cf. Judg i 1; Esther i 1), "In the days of . . . , [these/the above] made war on. . . ." But Heb. lacks the resumptive pronoun [*hēm*], unlike the alleged parallel in Esther i 1; and a dangling predicate would have been supplied with [*wa-*] in any case. The omission is hard to gloss over even in translation; Vulg. resumes with "in those days," and most moderns smuggle in "these/these kings," or the like.

But even if the syntax were faultless, the context would still be unmanageable. Date formulas specify one particular person or event, not four kings of as many separate countries. Theoretically, of course, the first of the four names could have marked the date, and the other three the invaders. But the context, not to mention the syntax, will not permit such a solution, since the narrative speaks repeatedly of four invaders by name and number.

All the difficulties, however, vanish once it is assumed that Heb. *bym*(*y*) stood here not for the construct form "in the day(s) of," but as a rendition of the cognate Akk. conjunction *e/inūma/i* "when," originally "in the day, at the time"; the final *-y* would not have appeared in early consonantal writing in any event. This could not have happened most readily in a translation from an Akk. account; for an initial *inūma* in a historical document from Syria, see D. J. Wiseman, *The Alalakh Tablets*, 1953, No. 1.1. The traditional *bīmē* would be a natural attempt to adjust the Akkadianism to Heb. usage. Nor would this be an isolated borrowing in this unique document; see COMMENT.

On the various names in this verse, see COMMENT.

2. All but the last of the local cities are found in x 19 and Deut xxix 22; cf. Hos xi 8 where only Admah and Zeboiim are mentioned. The names of the first two kings are evidently pejorative: Bera is based on *ra'* "evil," and Birsha on *reša'* "injustice," in symbolic censure of Sodom and Gomorrah. The significance of Shinab and Shemeber, whether original or secondary, is no longer apparent; for the latter, Sam. and Gen. Apocr. give *-d* as final consonant. The place name Bela is otherwise unknown; the name of its king is lacking.

3. *Valley of Siddim*. Apparently the authentic name of the area at the southern end of the Dead Sea, which was later submerged.

4. Here and in the next verse Chedorlaomer emerges as the head of the foreign coalition; note especially vs. 17.

5. The Gen. Apocr. (column xxi, line 28) puts the starting point of the invasion somewhere on the Euphrates.

the Rephaim. A prehistoric race of giant stature. It is worth noting that elsewhere (see especially xv 20; Deut ii 11, iii 11) this element is identified as pre-Israelite, which accords well with the indicated early date of the present account.

the Zuzim. Evidently the same as the Zamzummim of Deut ii 20 f., the name of a giant pre-Ammonite people. The Gen. Apocr. (column xxi, line 29) actually speaks of "the Zamzummim of Ammon" in the present context.

the Emim. Giant forerunners of the Moabites according to Deut ii 10 f.

6. *the Horites.* In the OT, the name of two unrelated elements: (1) the non-Semitic Hurrians (LXX in xxxiv 2; Josh ix 7); and the Semitic predecessors of Seir/Edom (xxxvi 20, Deut ii 12, 22, and present passage); cf. *The Interpreter's Dictionary of the Bible, sub voce.*

El-paran. The first element in this place name is not to be confused with the divine appellative El; the cons. text is *'yl*, a variant form of the Heb. word for "terebinth," and was so translated by LXX.

7. *swung back.* Literally "returned." Assyrian rulers often use the phrase "on my return" to introduce additional victories.

En-mishpat. Literally "Spring of Decision," another name for Kadesh, equated with modern 'Ayn Qadeis, some fifty miles south of Beer-sheba. The invaders appear to have made a wide turn to the right before starting on their way home.

territory. Normally, "field, open country."

the Amalekites. Traditional enemies of Israel; cf. Exod xvii 8–16; I Sam xv, xxx.

the Amorites. See x 16.

Hazazon-tamar. Equated in II Chron xx 2 with En-gedi, on the west shore of the Dead Sea.

10. *flung themselves.* Literally "fell"; but the Heb. stem (*npl*) often carries a reflexive connotation, notably in the phrase "to fall on one's neck" (xxxiii 4, xlv 14, xlvi 29), which describes a voluntary act; see also xvii 3.

11. The bracketed words do not imply an omission in MT. They are required in English for clarity, whereas Heb. is more liberal with its pronominal references.

13. *the Hebrew.* LXX translates this occurrence alone as "the one from across," in what is apparently an attempt to give an etymological rendering based on the Heb. verb *'br* "to pass, cross"; elsewhere, the gentilic

"Hebrew" is regularly employed. The special bearing of this one passage is thus clearly recognized by the Greek translation.

The question of possible connection between Heb. *'ibrî* "Hebrew" and cun. *Ḫab/piru* and its cognates or counterparts has been fully discussed in two recent monographs, one by Bottéro, ed., *Le problème des Ḫabiru*, and the other by Greenberg, *The Ḫab/piru*. The evidence remains ambiguous; and within the Bible itself, the matter is complicated by the legal phrase "Hebrew slave" (Exod xxi 2; cf. Deut xv 12). At any rate, the present instance accords more closely than any other with cun. data on the Western Ḫabiru; note especially the date formula in *Alalakh Tablets* 58 (eighteenth/seventeenth centuries), 28 ff., which mentions a treaty with Ḫabiru warriors; and the *Statue of Idrimi* (fifteenth century Alalakh), line 27, which tells how the royal fugitive found asylum among Ḫabiru warriors.

Of more immediate significance, however, is the fact that the designation "Hebrew" is not applied elsewhere in the Bible to Israelites, except by outsiders (e.g., xxxix 14), or for self-identification to foreigners (xl 15; Jon i 9). Hence the fac that the author himself refers here to Abraham as a Hebrew is strong presumptive evidence that the document did not originate with Israelites. This deduction receives independent support from various other details in the chapter before us, and it opens up in turn unexpected vistas which bear on the historicity of Abraham; see COMMENT.

camping. The Heb. stem *škn* is applied primarily to dwelling in tents, cf. xvi 12; hence the derived noun *miškān* "tabernacle."

kinsman. Literally "brother." But the same term is used in the next verse with Lot, who was Abraham's nephew. There is no way to determine Mamre's exact relationship to the other two men.

Aner. Cons. Heb. *'nr*; Gen. Apocr. gives *'rnm*, which recalls Sam.'s *'nrm*.

confederates. Heb. "members of/in a covenant." Since a covenant involved obligations under solemn oath (cf. the analogous Akk. *bēl adē u māmīt* "participant in a compact under solemn oath" and note Heb. *'ālōt habbᵉrīt* "curses/sanctions of the covenant," Deut xxix 20), "confederates" comes closer to the required meaning than "allies."

14. *he called up.* Heb. gives the cons. *wyrq*, pointed to yield literally "emptied"; but the pertinent form is used elsewhere of drawing or unsheathing a sword, which is not the same as mobilizing warriors. LXX has "mustered," not necessarily because it read *wypqd*, but more likely because it so interpreted the traditional text. Sam. offers *wydq*, which could be a case of the frequent confusion of the letters *R* and *D*, though Sam. employs a different script. There is, however, another possibility, though admittedly a remote one. If Sam.'s reading is correct, it could be

an Akkadianism (for etymological *wydk*), Akk. *dekû* being the normal verb for "mobilize, call up." But whatever the background, the above translation cannot be far off the mark.

retainers. Cf. T. O. Lambdin, JAOS 73 (1953), 160.

born into his household. As opposed to slaves obtained through purchase, this class ranked close enough to members of the family to be entrusted with tasks of considerable importance and responsibility; cf. xxiv 23. The number involved is not too small for a surprise attack; by the same token, it enhances the authenticity of the narrative. But it is a large body of picked servants for the patriarch as he is described in the remaining narratives. In the present instance, Abraham appears as a powerful sheikh, which could be the aspect that was best known to his contemporaries. Elsewhere we see him in idealized retrospect. Once again, therefore, the account before us proves to be unique.

16. *other personnel.* For the differentiating force of the article in Heb., cf. vi 19 and Ehrl. at iii 2; note further "other flesh," Lev vii 19, and "the rest of the blood," Lev viii 24. For the use of *'am* for military personnel, with the emphasis on the individual rather than the group (the latter is *ṣābā'*), cf. especially I Sam xiii 5; II Chron xii 3.

18. *Melchizedek.* The Canaanite counterpart of Akk. *Šarru(m)kên* "Sargon," literally "the king is just, legitimate"; cf. Ps cx 4.

Salem. Identified with Jerusalem in Ps lxxvi 3; also the Targumim and Gen. Apocr.

El-Elyōn. Both elements (*'el* and *'elyōn*) occur as names of specific deities, the first in Ugaritic (Pope, *El in the Ugaritic Texts*) and the second in Phoenician; the Aram. inscription from Sujin combines the two into a compound (*ibid.,* 54 ff.). Though appellatives at first ("god" and "supreme" respectively), both are thus attested also as personal names of deities. Elsewhere in the OT, *'el* is used as a literary or poetic synonym for Elohim; and *'elyōn* occurs either separately (Isa xiv 14; Ps ix 3), or as a divine epithet (Pss vii 18, xlvii 3, lvii 3, lxxviii 56). But these are relatively late passages which conceivably could hark back to the instances before us. The question, then, is how to interpret the latter.

Now that this chapter is amply attested as a source unto itself, it is not only unnecessary but fallacious to harmonize its contents with other portions of the OT. As a Canaanite priest, Melchizedek would invoke his deity or deities by name; and this is what the above translation has sought to reproduce. Abraham, on the other hand, would just as naturally turn to Yahweh, especially in an oath (vs. 22; see below).

19. *Creator.* For *qn 'rṣ* in Phoenician, see Pope, *op. cit.* pp. 51 f.; the verb occurs in the same sense in Ugaritic (*ibid.*).

22. *I have sworn.* Literally "I raised up my hand," followed (in 23) by

the negative oath formula: "if I take" – "I will not take," i.e., may so-and-so happen to me if I do.

Yahweh. LXX, followed by Syr., omits, which does not automatically presuppose a superior text, and thereby a late insert of the divine name; see NOTE on 18. Nor would the use of "Yahweh" prove *J*'s authorship at this point, in a document concerning which there are still so many question marks. In any case, no conclusions should be based on this particular occurrence. The accompanying *'l 'lywn,* on the other hand, is textually impeccable. But as used by Abraham, the phrase appears to be descriptive, especially in apposition to "Creator of Heaven and earth," whereas a Canaanite priest would be expected to employ the same words in the personal sense in which they are independently attested.

23. *so much as.* Literally "from – to, whether – or," here to convey the idea of "no matter how trifling." The corresponding idiom in Akk. is *ḫāmu u ḫuṣābu u mimma* "a stalk of straw, or a twig, or whatever" (cf. CAD, Vol. 6, p. 259), and the Aram. analogue is *mn ḥm w'd ḥwṭ* (see the comprehensive discussion JAOS 54 [1934], 200 ff.). It is noteworthy that both Akkadian and Aramaic make good use of alliteration (cf. our "bag and baggage," and German Mann und Maus). Heb. is thus a paraphrase, evidently because Sem. *ḫām* was not current in Heb. This again argues for outside influence.

24. *my men.* Literally "the boys."
used up. Heb. "ate"; for a similar connotation cf. xxxi 15.

COMMENT

Genesis xiv stands alone among all the accounts in the Penta-teuch, if not indeed in the Bible as a whole. The setting is international, the approach impersonal, and the narration notable for its unusual style and vocabulary. There is still much about this chapter that is open to wide differences of opinion. On one point, however, the critics are virtually unanimous: the familiar touches of the established sources of Genesis are absent in this instance. For all these reasons the chapter has to be ascribed to an isolated source, here marked *X.*

Since Genesis xiv constitutes an intrusive section within the patriarchal framework, and since it contains, moreover, an assortment of extraneous data, the chapter has long enjoyed more than its proportionate share of scholarly attention. A comprehensive treatment of the various problems at issue was offered long ago by W. F. Albright in his paper on "The Historical Background of Genesis XIV" (*Journal of the Society of Oriental Research* [1926], 231–69); see also BASOR 88 (1942), 33 ff. There is also a separate monograph on the subject by Kroeze (in Dutch), entitled *Genesis Veertien* ("Genesis XIV"), 1937. Only the briefest outline and comment can be attempted in the next few paragraphs.

The chapter consists in effect of two loosely connected parts: (1) the attack by four foreign kings against five local rulers; and (2) the Melchizedek episode. The link is provided by Abraham's= Abram's intervention. The patriarch's success is hailed not only by the king of Sodom, leader of the local coalition, but also by Melchizedek of Salem, a place not otherwise involved in the hostilities. It is this exploit by Abraham, in the otherwise unfamiliar role of a warrior, that evidently led to the inclusion of the chapter with the regular patriarchal material in Genesis.

The date of the narrative has been variously estimated. A ranking documentary critic is inclined to dismiss the story as a late scholastic reconstruction (Noth, *Überlieferungsgeschichte* . . . , p. 170). Others would regard it as the product of living tradition. A fresh re-examination of all the available scraps of evidence, both internal and external, favors an early date, scarcely later in fact than the middle of the second millennium. For one thing, the account is admittedly not the work of *J,* or *E,* let alone *P.* Who, then, could have had an interest in learned speculations of this sort? For another thing, Sodom, Gomorrah, and three neighboring towns are still very much in the picture; except for the apparently tendentious distortion of the names of two of their rulers (vs. 2), these are not places doomed as yet to disaster. Most important of all, the names of the foreign invaders and their respective countries are not made up. They have an authentic ring, in spite of all the hazards of transliteration and transmission; one of them at least (Arioch) takes us back to the Old Babylonian age, with which the period of Abraham has to be synchronized. These onomastic data call for a brief review.

(1) *Amraphel king of Shinar.* For Shinar (Heb. *Shin'ār,* Akk. *Šumeru,* perhaps Sum. *Kiengi(r)*), see x 10, xi 2. Both TO and Gen. Apocr. render, appropriately enough, "Babylon." The linguistic associations of Amraphel are obscure. The once popular identification of this king with the celebrated Hammurabi of Babylon is most precarious and probably untenable: for the final *-l*

would have to be an error for -y, and the initial 'aleph a mistake for 'ayin, which is scarcely credible. The Heb. form, however, accords well with several possible Amurrite (Amorite) or even Akkadian combinations; in that case, the bearer could well have been some minor prince from Lower Mesopotamia.

(2) *Arioch king of Ellasar.* The name of the land can only be guessed at at this time; Gen. Apocr. (column xxi, line 23) identifies it with *Kptwk,* evidently "Cappadocia." But the ruler's name is transparently clear: it is linguistically the same as *Arriwuk,* the name of a vassal of Zimri-lim of Mari (a contemporary of Hammurabi), and perhaps also Nuzi *Ariukki.* The linguistic background is Hurrian. The form is comparatively rare, and not attested after the middle of the second millennium. Its appearance in the present context thus presupposes an ancient and authentic tradition. No late Hebrew writer would be likely to invent such a name and to assign it correctly to a neighbor of Babylonia.

(3) *Chedorlaomer king of Elam.* For the country, see NOTE on x 22. The ruler's name contains tangible Elamite components, but no such historical figure has as yet been found in the documents; see BASOR 88 (1942), 33 ff. It is interesting to note, and perhaps significant, that our text makes Chedorlaomer, and not Amraphel, the leader of the invaders (vss. 4, 5, 9, 17), which further weakens the proposed identification of the latter with Hammurabi.

(4) *Tidal king of Goiim.* Scholars are agreed that Tidal (cons. *td'l*) represents cun. *Tudḫaliya.* There were, however, no fewer than five Hittite rulers by that name; the only one who would fit the chronological requirements is Tudḫaliya I, but we know next to nothing about him. The name itself goes back to pre-Hittite Anatolia. Once again, this is not the kind of name that could be improvised by a late Hebrew writer. The political term Goiim (Heb. *gōyīm*) is the same as the Hebrew word for "nations." A possible link between the two is provided by cun. *Ummān-Manda* ("Manda-people(s)" in Akkadian), a name used since Old Babylonian times, if not earlier, to describe the spearhead of a barbarian irruption that destroyed the empire of Akkad. From that time on, the Ummān-Manda were virtually synonymous with a divine scourge aimed at Mesopotamia. Occasionally they are associated with the Elamites, which could be pertinent to the present passage. Their background, however, points to Anatolia (cf. JAOS 72 [1952], 100 ff.), and the Hittite Code cites them by name. Thus the combination of Tidal

and Goiim has more than one fact in its favor. But if Goiim reflects Akk. *Ummān-*, the Heb. name is actually a translation, which in turn has a bearing on the possible source of Gen xiv.

There are other plausible indications of Akkadian influence. The first sentence is syntactically hopeless without the aid of a cognate Akk. conjunction (see NOTE on vs. 1). Other such possibilities have been noted in vss. 7, 14, and 23. None of these would carry enough persuasion by itself; but taken together, they cannot be dismissed offhand. There are also additional details which point independently to extraneous influences. The narrative is unique in its international orientation. Abraham is glimpsed incidentally, through the eyes of outsiders, and he is depicted as a resolute and powerful chieftain rather than as an unworldly patriarch. What is more, he is identified as "Abram the Hebrew," which an Israelite source would not do in such circumstances (see NOTE on 13). All of this adds up to an impressive cumulative argument in favor of a foreign source for this chapter, from which the present narrative was either excerpted or adapted. A good analogue would be the so-called Spartoli Tablets in Akkadian, which have been often adduced in this connection, notably by Albright. Equally pertinent is the cun. cycle of historical legends about Naram-Sin, famous ruler of the Dynasty of Akkad. These compositions were popular in such distant lands as Anatolia, no less than in Mesopotamia proper. They tell, moreover, of rival coalitions of various rulers (just as the present narrative does), with good historical support; cf. H. G. Güterbock, ZA 42 (1934), 78 ff., and my comments in JAOS 72 (1952), 97 ff.

All this imposes one conclusion above all others which can be of outstanding importance for the study of biblical origins. If Abraham was cited in a historical or quasi-historical narrative that was written not by Israelites but by outsiders, it necessarily follows that Abraham was not a nebulous literary figure but a real person who was attested in contemporary sources. Short of a non-Israelite text mentioning an Abram son of Terah, or an Isaac son of Abram, this is as close as we can as yet come to a direct epigraphic witness of the patriarch.

The geographic detail that marks the route of the invaders, and the casual listing of the Cities of the Plain, lend further support to the essential credibility of the narrative. Who the foreign invaders were remains uncertain. It is highly improbable, however, that they were major political figures. The mere fact that Abraham could rout them with no more than 318 warriors at his disposal (the force is just small enough to be realistic) would seem to suggest that the outlanders were foreign adventurers bent on controlling the copper mines south of the Dead Sea (cf. Wright, *Biblical Archaeology,* pp. 50 f.). The most likely date for such an expedition would be approximately the eighteenth century B.C.

Finally, the notice about Melchizedek merits a measure of confidence in its own right. He invokes an authentic Canaanite deity (see NOTE) as a good Canaanite priest would be expected to do. Abraham, on the other hand, refers to Yahweh, using the Canaanite name or names in suitable apposition, which is no less appropriate in his particular case. That later religious Hebrew literature should have identified El-Elyōn with Yahweh, quite probably on the basis of this passage, is readily understandable. But this appears to be the only late reflex of Gen xiv. The narrative itself has all the ingredients of historicity.

18. PROMISE AND COVENANT
(xv 1–21: *J*, /*E*?/)

XV ¹ Some time afterward, this word of Yahweh came to Abram, in a vision:

> "Fear not, Abram!
> I am your shield;
> Your reward shall be very great."

² But Abram answered, "O Lord Yahweh,ᵃ to what purpose are your gifts, when I continue childless, /and the successor to my house is Dammesekᵇ Eliezer? ³ Since you have granted me no offspring," Abram continued,/ a member of my household will become my heir." ⁴ Then Yahweh's word came back to him in reply, "That one shall not be your heir; none but your own issue shall be your heir." /⁵ He took him outside and said, "Look up at the sky and count the stars if you can. Just so," he added, "shall be your offspring."/ ⁶ He put his trust in Yahweh, who accounted it to his merit.

⁷ He then said to him, "I am Yahweh who brought you out from Urᶜ of the Chaldeans to give you this land as a possession." ⁸ He replied, "O Lord Yahweh,ᵃ how shall I know that I am to possess it?" ⁹ He answered, "Bring me a three-year-old heifer, a three-year-old she-goat, a three-year-old ram, a turtledove, and a young pigeon." ¹⁰ He got them all and slit them through the middle, placing each half opposite the other; but he did not cut the birds. ¹¹ When birds of prey swooped down upon the carcasses, Abram drove them off. ¹² As the sun was

ᵃ Vocalized in MT to read (Qrē) Elohim.
ᵇ See COMMENT.
ᶜ LXX "land"; cf. xi 28.

about to set, a trance fell upon Abram, and a deep dark dread descended upon him.

/ 13 He said to Abram, "You should know that your offspring shall be strangers in a land not theirs, to be enslaved and oppressed for four hundred years. 14 But I will bring judgment on the nation they must serve, and in the end they shall leave with great wealth. 15 As for you, you shall join your forefathers in peace; you shall be buried at a happy old age. 16 And the others shall return here in the fourth time span, for the iniquity of the Amorites will not have run its course until then." /

17 When the sun had gone down and it was very dark, there appeared a smoking fire pot and a flaming torch which passed between those pieces. 18 That day Yahweh concluded a covenant with Abram, saying, "To your offspring I give this land, from the river of Egypt to the great river, the river Euphrates: 19 the Kenites, the Kenizzites, the Kadmonim, 20 the Hittites, the Perizzites, the Rephaim, 21 the Amorites, the Canaanites, the Girgashites, and the Jebusites."

NOTES

xv 2. *Lord Yahweh.* The consonants YHWH are vocalized this time (and in vs. 8) to be read "God" instead of the customary "the Lord," because the latter word is already present.

to what purpose are your gifts. Literally "what will/can you give me?" But this question refers to the promise of rewards in the preceding verse, and the Heb. verb *ntn* often signifies "to present," as is plain from the derived noun *mattānā* "gift."

successor. The term *ben-mešeq* does not occur elsewhere in the Bible, and the clause as a whole is generally regarded as hopeless. Nevertheless, its approximate sense can be gathered from two separate sets of circumstances. (1) The present clause, which may stem from E (see COMMENT) is duplicated by 3b (J), where the meaning is not in doubt: since Abraham has no descendants, his estate will pass to a member of his household. (2) The clause itself contains, in all probability, an internal gloss, with deliberate wordplay on *bn mšq : dmśq*. The old place name *Dimašgi* "Damascus" (non-Semitic) was etymologized in Aramaic as *di mašqyā* "having water resources," to judge from the Assyrian paraphrase of the name (cf. JAOS 71 [1951], 259 f.).

On this basis, Heb. *ben mešeq* (one of *mešeq*) would be an analogue of the Aramaic phrase. In like fashion, the two were further juxtaposed to signify hereditary succession: a servant by the name of Eliezer, apparently a Damascene by birth, was the only prospective heir to Abraham's estate. A semblance of linguistic support for such a connotation may be found in the term *mi-mšaq-* (Zeph ii 9) "province, sphere of X."

This linguistic interpretation is by no means definitive. There can be little doubt, however, about the legal aspect of the passage. We know now that in Hurrian family law, which was also normative for the patriarchs (see COMMENT on Secs. 15, 19, 35, 42), two types of heir were sharply distinguished. One was the *aplu* or direct heir; and the other was the *ewuru* or indirect heir, whom the law recognized when normal inheritors were lacking. Such an *ewuru* could be a member of a collateral line, and at times even an outsider, depending on the circumstances. Consequently, our Dammesek Eliezer—whoever he may have been and whatever the first word might mean—was juridically in the position of an *ewuru*. Here, then, is another instance of Hurrian customs which the patriarchs followed, but which tradition and its later expounders were bound to find perplexing.

4. *your own issue.* Literally "what comes from your body."

6. *put his trust.* The invariable translation of Heb. *he'emīn* as "believed" does not always do justice to the original. The basic sense of the form is "to affirm, recognize as valid." In other words, the result is not so much a matter of objective faith as of absolute fact. Our "Amen" derives from the same Heb. root.

7. For the problems posed by the mention of Ur in MT, see COMMENT on Sec. 13.

9. The ritual details that accompany the conclusion of a covenant are ultimately derived from sympathetic magic. The contracting parties—so at least in an agreement between equals; otherwise perhaps only the weaker of the two—passed between the sections of the dismembered animals (cf. Jer xxxiv 19 ff.) and thus left themselves open, by extension, to the fate of the sacrificed victims in the event of future violation. The specified age of the animals was a matter of ritual maturity; cf. I Sam i 24 (where MT misreads "three bulls" for "a three-year-old bull"), and the discussion in BASOR 72 (1938), 15 ff. The choice of the animals used for the purpose was governed by ritual custom and economic conditions. The Amorites of the Mari documents used asses, with the result that in their terminology "to slay an ass" was idiomatic for "to enter into a compact"; cf. G. E. Mendenhall, BASOR 133 (1954), 26 ff., and M. Noth, *Gesammelte Studien*, 1957, pp. 142 ff. It is this prominence of the ass in pagan cults that caused the Israelites to proscribe the custom in their own

ritual practices (cf. Exod xiii 13, xxxiv 20). The Hurrians of Nuzi resorted on solemn occasions to a fixed combination of "one bull, one ass, and ten sheep": see the writer's analysis in *Orientalia* 25 (1955), 9 ff. Lastly, turtledoves and pigeons are cited repeatedly among the ritual provisions of Leviticus; see especially xiv 22; hence the above "young pigeons" to render a Heb. noun that normally means "young bird(s)."

13–16. The documentary source of this passage is still unclear. There can be no doubt, however, about the significance of the contents in Israelite historical thought. The covenant between God and Israel was the charter on which Israel's national position was founded.

15. *in peace.* But Heb. *šālōm* seldom means "peace" in the usual sense of the term; the emphasis is rather on security, satisfaction, or fulfillment; in other words, here "in peace of mind, untroubled." This special nuance is underscored in the next clause.

a happy old age. The opposite connotation is unambiguously conveyed by the phrase "to send one's old age (literally 'white hair/head') down to Sheol in grief," cf. xlii 38, xliv 29, 31. Accordingly, the present expression is qualitative rather than quantitative.

16. *time span.* See NOTE on vi 9. Heb. *dōr* signifies "duration, age, time span," and only secondarily "generation" in the current sense of the term. The context does not show specifically how the author used the term in this instance; it could have been any of several round numbers of years. No conclusions can therefore be drawn from this passage in regard to the date of the Exodus.

Amorites. Normally the name of a specific people (cf. x 16, and NOTE), but sometimes also the collective term for the pre-Israelite population of Canaan (*E*). For the same comprehensive use of the term "Canaanites," cf. xii 6 (*J*).

17. The smoking fire pot (literally "oven") and flaming torch (to keep the fire going in the brazier) were not just fanciful inventions by the author or his immediate source. Both these details are recorded in Akk. texts pertaining to magic. They are listed together in an incantation against witches: "I sent out against you repeatedly a 'going' (i.e., lighted) oven (*āliku tinūru*), a fire that has caught"; cf. *Maqlû* II lines 190 f. and W. von Soden, *Orientalia* 26 (1957), lines 127 f. The combination is almost exactly the same as in the present instance. It was evidently believed to be highly efficacious, which may explain the archaic use of "oven" in the sense of "brazier," since no detail of an occult practice, or of the wording that goes with it, must be disturbed; actual ovens would not have the required mobility. Very likely, therefore, Heb. *tannūr* in this particular context was due to similar considerations, if not directly to the use of *tinūru* in Akkadian. And a

combination that worked so well against witches would be no less impressive as an ominous feature in a covenant.

18. *concluded a covenant.* The Heb. verb in question (*krt*) means "to cut." The noun, Heb. *bᵉrīt*, lacks an established etymology. M. Noth has suggested recently (*Gesammelte Studien,* pp. 146 ff.) that this term may go back to Akk. *bīrīt* "between," which appears in the Mari description of a covenant as "the slaying of an ass between X and Y." Thus an Akk. preposition descriptive of the mutual character of the agreement would have become in Heb. a technical term for the compact itself, the "co-" in "covenant," so to speak. For partial confirmation we need look no farther than vs. 10, which employs different words to describe the process, but they mean much the same thing, namely, "he slit/cut (them) in the middle." And alongside Mari "to kill an ass," Heb. "to cut between" would not seem too far-fetched as a technical term for so significant and serious an institution.

the river of Egypt. Normally, this phrase designates the Nile. The border of Egypt is elsewhere (e.g., Num xxxiv 5; Josh xv 4, 47) demarcated by a wadi or brook (Heb. *naḥal*), modern Wādi el-'Arīsh. There is reason to assume, therefore, that an original cons. *nḥl* was misread in this instance as *nhr* "river."

19. The Kenites and the Kenizzites were tribal groups in the Negeb, eventually absorbed by Judah.

the Kadmonim. Literally "Easterners," cf. xxix 1.

20. *the Hittites.* Cf. x 15, xxiii 3, xxxvi 2.

the Perizzites. See NOTE on xiii 7.

the Rephaim. Cf. xiv 5.

21. *the Jebusites.* See x 16.

COMMENT

While this chapter shows no trace of the *P* source, it exhibits nevertheless, for the first time in Genesis, other marked departures from the usual manner of *J.* Vss. 2–3 combine two separate forms of the same statement. It is nighttime in vs. 5 but still daylight in 12. Vs. 16 employs "Amorites" as the comprehensive term for the pre-Israelite population of Canaan, whereas *J* is known to speak of Canaanites in such cases (cf. xii 6). Repeated occurrences of the name Yahweh (1, 6, 7, 8, 18) permit us to attribute certain portions to *J* with relative confidence. The evidence concerning the rest is mainly circumstantial, since the term Elohim is absent throughout. But the whole is clearly not of a piece, though now intricately blended; cf. Noth, *Überlieferungsgeschichte* . . . , p. 29, n. 85, and L. A. Snijders, "Genesis XV The Covenant with Abram," OTS 12 (1958), 261 ff.

In its present fused form, the chapter consists of two interrelated parts. The first (1–6) takes up the increasingly urgent matter of Abraham's succession. The patriarch's original call (xii 1 ff.) implied that the mandate was to be taken over by Abraham's descendants. Thus far, however, Abraham has remained childless. The ultimate success of his mission was therefore in danger. Moreover, he had cause for personal anxiety, for in ancient Near Eastern societies it was left to a son to ensure a restful afterlife for his father through proper interment and rites ("he shall lament him and bury him" say the Nuzi texts). God's reaffirmed promise of a son now sets Abraham's mind at rest on both counts.

The remainder of the chapter (7–21) places the preceding incident in a broader perspective. Above and beyond personal considerations, the birth of an heir to Abraham is essential to God's scheme of things. It involves a nation to be, and its establishment in the Promised Land. That land shall extend from Egypt to Mesopotamia (18). The emphasis shifts thus to world history, and the importance of the episode is underscored by the conclusion of a covenant. In secular practice, this is normally a binding compact between states. This time, however, we are witnessing a covenant between the Creator of the universe and the ancestor of a nation ordained in advance to be a tool for shaping the history of the world. Small wonder, therefore, that the description touches on magic (cf. NOTE on 17) and carries with it a feeling of awe and mystery which, thanks to the genius of the narrator, can still grip the reader after all the intervening centuries.

19. THE BIRTH OF ISHMAEL
(xvi 1–16: *J*, /*P*/)

XVI 1/Abram's wife Sarai had borne him no children./ Now she had an Egyptian maidservant whose name was Hagar. 2 So Sarai said to Abram, "Look, Yahweh has restrained me from bearing. Cohabit then with my maid. Maybe I shall reproduce[a] through her." And Abram heeded Sarai's plea. /3 Thus, after Abram had lived ten years in the land of Canaan, his wife Sarai took her maid, Hagar the Egyptian, and gave her to her husband Abram as concubine./ 4 He cohabited with her, and she conceived. And when she saw that she was pregnant, she looked upon her mistress with contempt. 5 So Sarai told Abram, "This outrage against me is your fault! I myself put my maid in your lap. But from the moment she found that she had conceived, she has been looking at me with contempt. Yahweh decide between you and me!" 6 Abram answered Sarai, "Your maid is in your hands. Do to her as you like." Sarai then abused her so much that she ran away from her.

7 Yahweh's angel found her by a desert spring, the spring on the road to Shur, and he asked, "Hagar maid of Sarai, from where have you come and where are you going?" 8 She replied, "I am fleeing from my mistress Sarai." 9 But Yahweh's angel said to her, "You must go back to your mistress and submit to abuse at her hand. 10 For," Yahweh's angel told her, "I will make your offspring so numerous that they shall be too many to count." 11 And Yahweh's angel further said to her,

> "You are now with child and shall bear a son;
> You shall name him Ishmael,[b]

---

[a] See NOTE.
[b] Literally "God heard."

For Yahweh has paid heed to your woes.
12 He shall be a wild colt of a man,
His hand against everyone,
And everyone's hand against him;
And in the face of all his kin he shall camp."

13 And Yahweh who had spoken to her she called by the name "You are El-ro'i,"* by which she meant, "Did I not go on seeing here after he had seen me?"* 14 That is why the well is called Beer-lahai-roi,* it is between Kadesh and Bered.

╱ 15 Hagar bore Abram a son, and Abram gave the son whom Hagar bore him the name Ishmael. 16 Abram was 86 years old when Hagar bore him Ishmael. ╱

c Or "God of seeing" (cons.).
d So MT literally; see NOTE.
e Literally "Well of the Living One who sees me"; see NOTE.

NOTES

xvi 2. *Cohabit.* See NOTE at vi 4.
I shall reproduce. The verb as it stands (Heb. *'ibbānê*) can only mean "I shall be built up" (see especially xxx 3); and the usage is confirmed by Deut xxv 9. At the same time, however, it is an obvious word play on *bēn* "son," alluding to "I shall have a son," although this would not be grammatically correct. The above translation seeks to convey some of the same double meaning. For the legal background see COMMENT.
3. A typical insert from *P.*
concubine. Like its Akk. cognate *aššatum*, Heb. *'iššā* may signify either "wife" or "concubine." For the principal wife, however, in non-legal contexts Akkadian uses the term *ḫīrtum* "chosen woman."
4b. The literal meaning of the clause is "her mistress was lessened in her eyes," i.e., she lost caste in her estimation.
5. *This outrage.* Literally "my injustice" in objective construction: the injustice done to me; the possessive is adequately reflected by "this," as happens so often in interchanging possessive and defined forms, cf. "the boys" : "my men," xiv 24. For Heb. *ḥāmās* "lawlessness, injustice," cf. vi 11; it is a strictly legal term, which trad. "violence" fails to show adequately. The same force is reflected in the Akk. verb *ḫabālum* "to deprive someone of his legal rights," adjective *ḫablum* "wronged." The Code of Hammurabi states explicitly that a slave girl who was elevated to the status of concubine must not claim equality with her mistress

(par. 146). Sarah is thus invoking her legal rights, and she holds her husband responsible (literally "it is against you") for the offense.

I myself put my maid in your lap. This is not just a fanciful expression, but recognized legal phraseology. For the identical usage, cf. the old Sum.-Akk. dictionary of legal expressions known as *ana ittišu* (B. Landsberger, MSL I, 1937): "he placed his daughter in [the other's] lap," Tablet 3, column iv, line 34.

6. *abused her.* Literally, applied force to her, treated her with violence.

7. *Yahweh's angel.* The Heb. noun meant originally "messenger," exactly as its Gr. equivalent *'angelos.* In association with a divine term, the noun refers to a manifestation of the Deity, but not necessarily a separate being. In the present chapter, for instance, the angel is later identified with Yahweh himself (vs. 13). For one reason or another, an angel is interposed, in human form as a rule, to avoid direct contact between Yahweh and mortals. The concept was obviously familiar to *J* (cf. xix 13); the corresponding manifestation in *E* is "angel of God" (cf. xxi 17, xxxi 11). The use of the term to describe a distinct class of supernatural beings is of later date.

Shur. A locality near the Egyptian border; cf. xx 1, xxv 18.

12. *a wild colt of a man.* The qualifying Heb. noun *pere'* could stand either for wild ass or wild horse; cf. also Job xi 12 and, in variant form, Gen xlix 22. The phrase recalls Akk. *lullū-awēlu,* approximately "savage of a man," which the Akkadians used to describe both Enkidu and the first primitive man created by the gods.

in the face of. One of the idiomatic uses of Heb. *'al p^{e}nē* (literally "upon/against the face of") is "to the face" (cf. Job i 11, vi 28, xxi 31), and more particularly "in defiance/disregard of," as proved by Deut xxi 16: "he shall not be able to give the birthright to the (younger) son of the loved wife, in disregard of (*'al p^{e}nē*) the (older) son of the unloved wife." For the present occurrence, cf. the parallel reference to Ishmaelites in xxv 18: "they shall make raids against (*'al p^{e}nē*) all their kinsmen"; what is thus described is a typically Bedouin mode of life which the preceding clauses sum up so vividly. Such customary translations as "in the presence of," or "to the east of" ignore both idiom and context.

13. *El-ro'i.* MT is pointed defectively (*'El-r^o'ī*), perhaps on purpose, to leave the reader a choice between this, i.e., "God of seeing," one whom it is permitted to see, and the *rō'ī* of the last clause, "one who sees me." The explanatory gloss that follows is hopeless as it now stands. Its original form, however, can be inferred from the next verse, which starts out with "That is why." On the use of *kī* in this verse, cf. iv 25.

14. *Beer-lahai-ro'i.* The meaning is relatively clear, and it may thus

furnish the key to the interpretation of the enigmatic last clause of 13, which reads unvocalized *hgm hlm r'yty 'hry r'y*. As J. Wellhausen realized nearly a century ago, some part of this sequence should anticipate "the Living One," Heb. cons. *lhy*, in the commemorative name of the well. The only suitable spot for it is the received *'hry*, which Wellhausen emended accordingly to *w'hy* "yet I lived." The logical next step was to change the unmanageable *hlm* "here" to *'lhm* "God," and to assume that the concluding *r'y* was copied from the place name after *w'hy* had been corrupted to *'hry*. The gloss would thus have read originally *hgm 'lhm r'yty w'hy* "Did I really see God, yet remained alive?" an excellent paraphrase of the name of a well that could be translated to mean "Well of the living sight." At all events, the disfigurement of the text is old enough to be witnessed in LXX. It is not surprising in aetiological explanations of very ancient names. The well itself is independently attested in xxiv 62.

15–16. These concluding verses bear the unmistakable stamp of *P*. Vital statistics are always important to that source; cf. v, xi 10–26.

COMMENT

Except for marginal notices by *P*, the narrative goes back to *J*, as is immediately apparent from the repeated use of the name Yahweh (5, 7, 9, 10, 11, 13). Moreover, the author is here at the peak of his art.

The twin themes that *J* follows throughout his work—the societal and the personal—are again intertwined, each tied up in its own way with the matter of Abraham's successor. But whereas the broader aspect was featured in the previous episode, the writer now restores the balance, as it were, by permitting the individuals to move to the fore. In so doing, he utilizes his material to create an interlude of acute suspense: Abraham is indeed to have an heir; not by Sarah, however, but by her slave girl Hagar. Is this not contrary to earlier hints and expectations, a disappointing anticlimax? The reader can only wait and see.

At the personal level, from which the author starts out, the basic conflict is between certain specific legal rights and natural human feelings. We know now the pertinent legal measures as illustrated by the Laws of Hammurabi and the Nuzi documents. The juridical background of the issue before us is as complex as it is authentic, a circumstance that makes the unfolding drama at once more poignant and intelligible. All three principals in the case have some things in their favor and other things against them. Sarah is thus not altogether out of order when she bitterly complains to Abraham that her rights have not been honored (5). Beyond all the legal niceties, however, are the tangled emotions of the characters in the drama: Sarah, frustrated and enraged; Hagar, spirited but tactless; and Abraham, who must know that, whatever his personal sentiments, he may not dissuade Sarah from following the letter of the law.

For the legal background in the case, we. were limited until recently to the provisions of par. 146 of the Code of Hammurabi, which are pertinent only in part: A priestess of the *naditum* rank, who was free to marry but not to bear children, gives her husband a slave girl in order to provide him with a son. If the concubine then tries to arrogate to herself a position of equality with her mistress, the wife shall demote her to her former status of slave; but she may not sell her to others.

This law is applicable to the case before us in that (a) the childless wife must herself provide a concubine; (b) the successful substitute must not forget her place. But these provisions are restricted to certain priestesses for whom motherhood was ruled out. No such limitations applied to Sarah. Her case, however, is covered in full by the family law of another society; one document in particular combines all the requisite details save only for the inescapable difference in names. It is a text from Nuzi, which was published in HSS V (1929) as No. 67, and which I presented in transliteration and translation in AASOR 10 (1930), 31 ff. Because this text is of outstanding significance for our present purposes, and because its original treatment needs to be brought up to date, it will not be amiss to take up the relevant portions afresh, but necessarily in all brevity.

The document as a whole records the adoption of a certain Shennima and his concurrent marriage to Gilimninu. It is the marriage alone that we are concerned with here. These are the stated provisions (lines 17 ff.): "If Gilimninu bears children, Shennima shall not take another wife. But if Gilimninu fails to bear children, Gilimninu shall get for Shennima a woman from the Lullu country (i.e., a slave girl) as concubine. In that case, Gilimninu herself shall have authority over the offspring (*u šerri Gilimninu-ma uwār*)." In other words, in this socially prominent lay family, the husband may not marry again if his wife has children. But if the union proves to be childless, the wife is required to provide a concubine, but would then have all the legal rights to the offspring. This must be the exact bearing of the term *'ibbānê* ("I shall reproduce/be built up") in vs. 2 above. The other provisions of the Nuzi case are likewise paralleled in our narrative: Sarah is childless, and it is she herself who has pressed a concubine on Abraham (vs. 5). What Sarah did, then, was not so much in obedience to an impulse as in conformance with the family law of the Hurrians, a society whose customs the patriarchs knew intimately and followed often.

The extra-biblical material gives new meaning also to the next phase in the story as described in vs. 6. Although Abraham told Sarah to do to Hagar as she pleased, Sarah stops short of expelling her slave. Hammurabi Law 146 would forbid it in these circumstances, and Deut xxi 14 also imposes certain restraints upon the owner. But there is nothing in either source (the meaning of the key verb in Deut is "to pledge for debts," not "to treat brutally") to discourage intolerable abuse, which eventually drove Hagar to flight.

But our author must not dwell too long on personalities. Presently he shifts to a different plane and larger issues. It is time to account for the place of the Ishmaelites in the scheme of things, the role of the Bedouin who are always in evidence on the border between the desert and the sown, a group as defiant and uncontrollable as the young woman from whom the narrative derives them. *J* handles both episodes, with all their wealth of facts and overtones, in a bare dozen verses.

20. COVENANT AND CIRCUMCISION
(xvii 1–27: *P*)

XVII 1 When Abram was 99 years old, Yahweh*a* appeared to Abram and said to him, "I am El Shaddai. Follow my ways and be blameless. 2 I will grant a covenant between myself and you, and will make you exceedingly numerous."

3 Abram threw himself on his face, as God continued speaking to him, 4 "And this is my covenant with you: You are to be the father of a host of nations. 5 Nor shall you be called Abram any longer: your name shall be Abraham, meaning that 'I make you the father of a host of nations.'*b* 6 I will cause you to be exceedingly fertile, and make nations of you; and kings shall stem from you. 7 And I will maintain the covenant between myself and you, and your offspring to follow, through the ages, as an everlasting pact to be God to you and to your offspring to follow. 8 And I will give to you, and to your offspring to follow, the land in which you are now sojourning—the whole land of Canaan—as an everlasting possession. And I will be their God."

9 God further said to Abraham, "For your part, you must keep my covenant, you and your offspring to follow, through the ages. 10 And this shall be the covenant between myself and you, and your offspring to follow, which you must keep: every male among you shall be circumcised. 11 You shall circumcise the flesh of your foreskin, and that shall be the mark of the covenant between me and you. 12 At the age of eight days, every male among you, through the ages, shall be circumcised, even houseborn slaves as well as those whom you have acquired for money from any outsider who is not of your blood*c*— 13 yes, houseborn slaves and those that you purchase must be circum-

a See NOTE.
b Wordplay on "Abraham"; see NOTE.
c Literally "seed."

cised.—Thus shall my covenant be marked on your flesh as an everlasting pact. 14 An uncircumcised male, one who has not been circumcised in the flesh of his foreskin—such a person shall be cut off from his kin: he has broken my covenant!"

15 God also said to Abraham, "As for your wife Sarai, do not call her Sarai, for her name shall be Sarah.*d* 16 I will bless her; moreover, I will give you a son by her, *e*whom I will bless also.*e* And she shall give rise to nations; rulers of peoples shall issue from her.*f* 17 Abraham threw himself on his face, and he smiled*g* as he said to himself, "Can a child be born to one who is 100 years old, and could Sarah give birth at 90? 18 Then Abraham said to God, "Let but Ishmael thrive if you so will it." 19 But God replied, "Still, your wife Sarah is to bear you a son, and you shall name him Isaac; and I will sustain my covenant with him, and*h* with his offspring to follow, as an everlasting pact. 20 Furthermore, I will heed*i* you as regards Ishmael: I hereby bless him. I will make him fertile and exceedingly numerous; he shall bring twelve chieftains into being, and I will make of him a great nation. 21 But my covenant I will maintain with Isaac, whom Sarah shall bear you by this time next year." 22 And as soon as he finished speaking with him, God was gone from Abraham.

23 Then Abraham took his son Ishmael and all his slaves, whether houseborn or acquired—every male in Abraham's household—and he circumcised the flesh of their foreskins on that same day, as God had told him. 24 Abraham was 99 years old when he was circumcised in the flesh of his foreskin, 25 and his son Ishmael was 13 years old when he was circumcised in the flesh of his foreskin. 26 Thus Abraham, together with his son Ishmael, was circumcised on that very day; 27 and all his retainers, his houseborn slaves as well as those that had been acquired for money from outsiders, were circumcised with him.

d Heb. for "princess"; cf. NOTE.
e–e MT "and I will bless her"; see NOTE.
f Some versions read "him"; see NOTE.
g Heb. yiṣḥaq, play on "Isaac."
h So with many manuscripts, Sam., and LXX.
i MT šāma'tî, wordplay on "Ishmael."

NOTES

xvii 1. *Yahweh.* Since the rest of the chapter has Elohim consistently, this single exception appears to be a slip under the influence of the preceding narrative. For an analogous carry-over in an introductory verse, cf. xxi 1.

El Shaddai. According to the present author, this was the only divine appellation known to the patriarchs prior to the time of Moses (Exod vi 3); see COMMENT on iv 26. The traditional translation of Shaddai as "Almighty" goes back to an early rabbinic etymology ("Self-sufficient"). Modern scholarship leans toward Albright's derivation from Akk. *šadū* "mountain" employed as a divine epithet (JBL 54 [1935], 180 ff.). But the comparison runs into phonologic difficulties (the same stem has an initial *š* in Heb.); and in Akkadian itself, the epithet was but one of hundreds like it. Thus a satisfactory explanation of this term (significantly enough, Exod vi 3, does not call it a name) is yet to be proposed, just as is that of *Yahweh.*

Follow my ways. In the light of vi 11 and x 9, *lᵉpānāy* has here a concessive connotation: conduct yourself in a way I approve: see especially vs. 18.

2. *I will grant a covenant.* The verb in Heb. is literally "give, set." A lasting covenant must be established or concluded before it can be maintained. An initial step was recorded in xv 18, but by a different source (*J*). This is the first such reference to Abraham in *P* (on the covenant with Noah, cf. ix 9 ff.); for the follow-up *P* uses here *hēqīm* "to maintain" (7,21).

3. *threw himself.* Cf. NOTE on xiv 10.

4. *host.* Or "multitude," Heb. *hᵃmōn* (construct state), the initial *h* explicating symbolically the added *-ha-* in *"Abraham"* (5).

5. *Abraham.* Linguistically, the medial *-ha-* is a secondary extension in a manner common in Aramaic. The underlying form *Abram* and its doublet *Abiram* are best explained as "the (not 'my') father is exalted"; the supposed Akk. cognate *Abam-rāmā* is not to be adduced, since it is unrelated and means "love the father."

For the premise that a change in name signifies a change in status, see COMMENT.

7. *your offspring to follow.* Literally "your seed after you"; a favorite phrase in *P.*

ages. Trad. "generations," cf. vi 9 and NOTE; the possessive pronoun in Hebrew has here, as elsewhere, the force of our definite article.

pact. Same Heb. noun as "covenant"; but some such variation is desirable in English.

8. *in which you are now sojourning.* Heb. "of your sojournings," where the plural stands for a collective abstract. On the meaning of the stem *gūr,* see xii 10, xix 9.

12. *houseborn slaves.* Cf. xiv 14.

13. *shall . . . be marked.* Literally "shall be."

15. *Sarah.* Linguistically, *śārā* embodies the common feminine ending (Sem. **-at*). whereas *śāray* preserves an old and specialized feminine form.

16. *whom I will bless also.* So with LXX, Syr., Vulg., reading the pronominal suffix as masculine and applying it to Isaac. The last clause, however, need not be shifted, with the same ancient versions, from Sarah to Isaac. This would involve not merely a repointing but an emended cons. text (*whyh* for *whyth*); moreover, the passage is concerned with Sarah, whereas her son is as yet incidental. Indeed, if it were not for redundancy in the Heb. verse as it stands (the repetition of "I will bless her"), no reference to the blessing of Isaac would have been suspected at this point. There is also the inherent possibility that the second instance is to be construed as part of a subordinate clause: "And when I have blessed her, she shall give rise to nations."

17. *he smiled.* Heb. *way-yiṣḥaq* anticipates, of course, the personal name Isaac (*Yiṣḥaq*). P does this here, J offers a variant explanation in xviii 12, and E still another in xxi 6. Each allusion operates with the verb *ṣḥq,* which covers a wide range of meanings, including "to play, be amused," and notably also "to rejoice over, smile on (a newborn child)." A Hurro-Hittite tale describes the father (Appu) as placing his newborn son on his knees and rejoicing over him (ZA 49 [1956], 220, line 5). Such acts were often the basis for naming the child accordingly. The shortened form Isaac (with the subject left out) undoubtedly reflects some such symbolic gesture: (X) rejoiced over, smiled on (the child).

To judge from the three separate explanations in our documentary sources, this last application was no longer familiar at the time of the writing, even as far back as the time of J. Tradition was thus reduced to speculations based on the later connotations of the verb. The meaning chosen varied with the source and the context. In the earthy treatment by J, an incredulous Sarah could well be shown as laughing bitterly to herself (xviii 12). But the concept of Abraham in a derisive attitude toward God would be decidedly out of keeping with P's character. The above translation, therefore, should come close to the spirit of the received text, though not the original use of the pertinent verb.

18. *thrive.* Literally "live," with the force of "stay well, prosper."

if you so will it. Cf. "follow my ways," vs. 1, NOTE.

20. *chieftains*. Literally "elevated (in the assembly)," cf. Num i 16; see the full discussion in CBQ 25 (1963), 111–17.

22. *was gone from*. Literally "rose from upon," with a suggestion of suddenness, which "departed" would not convey.

COMMENT

The entire chapter is from the hand of *P*. As a unit of considerable length, and richer in content than the genealogical lists, this section affords a better picture of *P*'s scope and approach. At the same time, the contrast with other sources stands out all the more sharply in view of *J*'s parallel treatment of the covenant theme in xv.

P's concern about chronological detail is reaffirmed at the outset (vs. 1); and it is worth stressing that all other statistics about Abraham or Sarah stem from the same source (xvi 3, 16, xxi 5, xxi 4f., xxiii 1, xxv 7, 17; cf. von Rad). The over-all chronological scheme remains obscure. It is apparent, however, that the round figure of 100 played a part in this tradition. This is obviously the reason for stressing that Abraham was exactly 99 years old at the start of this episode, for that would make him 100 at the time of Isaac's birth. Analogously, Shem was an even 100 when Arpachshad was born (xi 10). If *J* was familiar with these computations, he did not consider them germane to his story.

The most striking difference, however, between *P* and *J* lies, here and elsewhere, in their contrasting treatments of the same event and their dissimilar approach to the individual. Both here and in xv the central theme is the covenant. *J* saw the covenant as a future factor in world history. It was set against a fearsome background which helped to bring out the numinous character of Yahweh's partnership with Abraham. Yet for all his bewilderment, Abraham was presented as a sensitive participant in an intensely dramatic process. Just as in the Eden account, *J*'s handling of the episode was earth-centered. In the present account by *P,* on the other hand, the overriding feature of the covenant is circumcision. And much of the chapter is devoted to a formal pronouncement by God. *P*'s approach, in short, is ritualistic and impersonal.

Circumcision is an old and widely diffused practice, generally linked with puberty and premarital rites. In the ancient Near East it was observed by many of Israel's neighbors, among them the Egyptians, the Edomites, the Ammonites, the Moabites, and certain other nomadic elements (cf. Jer ix 25). But the Philistines did not follow it (cf. II Sam i 20), and neither did the "Hivites" (i.e., Horites) of Central Palestine (xxxiv 15). Nor was the custom in vogue in Mesopotamia. Thus the patriarchs would not have been likely to adopt circumcision prior to their arrival in Canaan, which is just what the present account says in another way. The terse passage in Exod iv 24–26 suggests a primitive religious connection. Eventually, the rite became a distinctive group characteristic, and hence also a cultural and spiritual symbol. To P, however, it was essential proof of adherence to the covenant. (For a comprehensive recent summary, see R. de Vaux, *Les Institutions de l'Ancien Testament* I, 1958, pp. 78 ff.)

Another feature of the present chapter is the formal change of the names Abram and Sarai to Abraham and Sarah respectively. But this motif is not peculiar to P. It is found also in other sources, for instance, xxxii 29 (*J*). Such a change is viewed as the external sign of an important turn in the life or function of the bearer. A similar milestone is signaled by the recorded transition from El Shaddai to Yahweh (Exod vi 3: P). The underlying concept was probably much the same as in a king's assumption of a special throne name. The event marked a new era. Such notices are not to be confused with frequent wordplays on original names; for P's own paranomasia on "Isaac," see Note on vs. 17.

21. ABRAHAM AND HIS MYSTERIOUS VISITORS
(xviii 1–15: *J*)

XVIII ¹ Yahweh appeared to him by the terebinths[a] of Mamre; he was sitting at the entrance of his tent as the day was growing hot. ² Looking up, he saw three men standing beside him. When he saw them, he rushed from the entrance of the tent to greet them and, bowing to the ground, ³ he said, "My lord,[b] if I may beg of you this favor, please do not go on past your servant. ⁴ Let a little water be brought, then bathe your feet and rest yourselves under the tree. ⁵ And I will fetch a morsel of bread, that you may refresh yourselves before you go on—now that you have come right by your servant." They answered, "Very well, do as you have said."

⁶ Abraham hastened into the tent and called to Sarah, "Quick, three seahs of the best flour! Knead and make rolls! ⁷ With that, Abraham ran to the herd, picked out a tender and choice calf, and gave it to a boy, who lost no time in preparing it. ⁸ Then he got some curds and milk, and the calf that had been prepared, and set these before them; and he stood by under the tree while they ate.

⁹ "Where is your wife Sarah?" they asked him. "In there, in the tent," he replied. ¹⁰ Then one said, "When I come back to you when life would be due, your wife Sarah shall have a son!" Sarah had been listening at the tent entrance, [c]which was just behind him.[c] ¹¹ Now Abraham and Sarah were old, advanced in years; Sarah had stopped having a woman's periods. ¹² So Sarah laughed to herself, saying, "Withered as I am, am I still to know

---

[a] LXX, Syr. "oak" (singular); cf. xiii 18.
[b] See NOTE.
[c–c] Cf. NOTE.

enjoyment—and my husband so old!" 13 Yahweh said to Abraham, "Why did Sarah laugh, saying, 'Shall I really give birth, old as I am?' 14 Is anything too much for Yahweh? I will be back with you when life is due, and Sarah shall have had a son!" 15 Sarah dissembled, saying, "I didn't laugh," for she was afraid. But he answered, "Yes, you did."

NOTES

xviii 1. *as the day was growing hot.* With this short comment (only two words in Hebrew) the author evokes a complete picture. The old patriarch is resting in front of his tent on a typically hot day, when the landscape turns hazy and one's vision is blurred.

2. *he rushed.* No exertion, even in behalf of total strangers, is too much were hospitality is concerned.

3. Cons. Heb. *'dny* can represent *'ᵃdōnī* "my lord" (singular), *'ᵃdōnay* "my lords" (ordinary plural), or *'ᵃdōnāy*, the special form with long third vowel, which is reserved for the Deity, i.e., "my/the Lord," the pointing that is applied to YHWH in the received text. The versions support traditional Hebrew. Nevertheless, at this stage Abraham is as yet unaware of the true identity of his visitors, so that he would not address any of them as God; and he cannot mean all three, because the rest of the verse contains three unambiguous singulars. What the text indicates, therefore, is that Abraham has turned to one of the strangers whom he somehow recognized as the leader. In vss. 4–5 he includes the other two as a matter of courtesy. His spontaneous hospitality to seemingly ordinary human beings is thus all the more impressive. Later on, in vss. 27, 32–33, the divine appellation is in order, because by then it is clear that Abraham's guests are out of the ordinary. The present pointing was probably influenced by the explicit mention of Yahweh in vs. 1. But this is the author's aside to the reader who is thus prepared at the outset for the surprise that is in store for Abraham.

if I may beg of you this favor. See NOTE on vi 8.

4. *a little water.* Like the "morsel of bread" in the next verse, an attempt by the host to minimize his own efforts.

5. *before you go on.* Literally "(and) you shall continue later"; the initial *wᵉ-* is missing in MT but supplied by some manuscripts and reflected in the versions.

now that. Heb. *kī 'al kēn,* for which see Ehrl.

6–8. The actual performance is in sharp contrast with the deprecating references in 4–5.

6. *three seahs.* A seah was a third of an ephah, or approximately thirteen liters.

the best flour. Heb. *solet,* a kind of semolina.

7. *With that.* Heb. is inverted for special emphasis.

curds. Actually a type of yoghurt, Ar. *leben.*

8. *that had been prepared.* Heb. uses here the active verb with impersonal force.

10. *one said.* One of the visitors now acts as spokesman, and his statement is the first direct intimation that the visitors might not be what they seemed at first.

when life would be due. Heb. literally "at about a life's interval," i.e., at the end of the period of pregnancy; cf. Ehrl.

which was just behind him. MT "he/it was behind him/it," which is far from clear. Sam. and LXX read the first pronoun as feminine; this would mean that Sarah was not far from the speaker; in Heb., however, the pronominal suffix at the end is more likely to refer either to the tent or the entrance, so that the received version is to be preferred.

11. *a woman's.* Plural in MT.

13. *Yahweh.* This time the speaker is plainly identified. Sarah's reference to her husband's age is not repeated; either the speaker or the author has chosen to disregard it.

14. *too much for.* The Heb. stem *pl'* refers to things that are unusual, often beyond human capabilities.

15. *dissembled.* The stem *kḥš* denotes subservience (cf. Deut xxxiii 29, Niphal) or deceit (Piel).

Yes, you did. In Heb. a reply often repeats the wording of the pertinent question or statement (cf. xxix 6); here literally ". . . you did laugh." The verbal form is preceded by *lō' kī.* The particle *kī* is, among many other things, an adversative. When it follows a positive or rhetorical statement, its sense is often "No," cf., for example, xxxvii 35, Deut xiii 10, Job xxii 2, and see KB, p. 431, No. 7; in conjunction with the negation *lō',* it conveys the opposite meaning, hence here "Yes," cf. xlii 12.

COMMENT

Chapters xviii–xix present a continuous and closely integrated narrative which, with the sole exception of xix 29, is the work of J throughout. The author not only maintains the high quality of the earlier sections, but introduces, in his account of Abraham's intercession for Sodom, a new moral and philosophical dimension.

The present section begins with the appearance of three strangers who materialize in front of Abraham's tent as if from nowhere. The heat of the Palestinian summer lends a dreamlike touch to the scene. Abraham is startled, but recovers quickly, and the generosity of his welcome is enhanced by his attempt to disparage his efforts. He knows as yet neither the identity of the strangers nor the nature of their errand.

One of the visitors appears to be the leader, and it is through him that Abraham extends his invitation to all three (see vs. 3, NOTE). Gradually, however, it dawns on the host (vs. 10) that the *'ᵃdōni* (approximately "sir," cf. NOTE on 3) to whom he had been speaking is no mere mortal; and vs. 14 shows him to be Yahweh himself, so that Abraham can now address him deferentially as *'ᵃdōnāy* "the Lord." The reader, on the other hand, is made aware from the start that Yahweh is present, but not how to distinguish him from the other two. To that extent, therefore, we are made to share Abraham's uncertainty and thus re-enact the patriarch's experience. It is not until xix 1 that the narrative speaks of angels as such. By then, however, the grim nature of the errand is all too evident.

There is nothing equivocal, on the other hand, where Sarah is concerned. She is depicted as down-to-earth to a fault, with her curiosity, her impulsiveness, and her feeble attempt at deception. It must not be forgotten, however, that this vivid sketch has been colored, at least in part, by the supposed origin of the name Isaac. On this point, *J*'s interpretation is entirely different from *P*'s (xvii 17). For all that Sarah knew, the promise of a child was a gesture made by meddlesome travelers; her impetuous reaction was one of derision. This is what *J*'s play on the verb *ṣḥq* plainly implies. The traditional connection with "laugh" is therefore closer in this instance than it was on the previous occasion. That neither *J*'s etymology nor *P*'s happens to be right is beside the point, since the underlying cultural context had been lost in the meantime.

22. ABRAHAM INTERCEDES FOR SODOM
(xviii 16–33: *J*)

XVIII 16 The men set out from there and faced toward Sodom, Abraham walking with them to see them off. 17 And Yahweh reflected, "Shall I conceal from Abraham what I am about to do, 18 now that Abraham is due to become a great and populous nation, and all the nations of the world are to bless themselves through him? 19 For I have singled him out in order that he may instruct his sons and his future family to keep the way of Yahweh by doing what is just and right, so that Yahweh may achieve for Abraham the promises he made about him." 20 Then Yahweh said, "The outrage of Sodom and Gomorrah is so great, and their sin so very grave, 21 that I must go down and see whether their actions are at all like the*a* outcry that has reached me, *b*or not. Then I will know."*b*

22 The men left from there for Sodom, *c*but Yahweh paused in front of Abraham.*c* 23 Abraham came forward and said, "Will you stamp out the innocent along with the guilty? 24 Suppose there are in the city fifty who are innocent; would you still level the place, rather than spare it for the sake of the fifty innocents inside it? 25 Far be it from you to do such a thing, to make the innocent perish with the guilty, so that innocent and guilty fare alike. Far be it from you! Shall he who is Judge of all the world not act with justice?" 26 Yahweh replied, "If I find in the city of Sodom fifty who are innocent, I will spare the whole place on their account." 27 Abraham spoke up again, "Here I am presuming to speak to the Lord, I who am but dust and

a MT "her."
b–b For an alternative word division see NOTE below.
c–c See NOTE.

ashes: 28 What if the fifty innocent should lack five? Would
you destroy the whole city because of those five?" "I will not
destroy it," he replied, "if I find there forty-five." 29 But he
persisted, and said, "What if only forty are found there?" He
answered, "I will not do it, for the sake of the forty." 30 Said he,
"Let not the Lord be impatient if I go on: What if only thirty
are found there?" He answered, "I will not do it if I find there
but thirty." 31 But he persisted, "Again I presume to address the
Lord: What if there are only twenty?" "I will not cause destruction," came the reply, "for the sake of the twenty." 32 Still
he went on, "Please, let not the Lord be angry if I speak this
last time: What if there are no more than ten?" He answered,
"I will not bring destruction, for the sake of those ten."

33 As soon as Yahweh finished speaking with Abraham, he
departed. And Abraham went back home.

Notes

xviii 16. *faced toward.* Literally "looked down upon the face of."
After "Sodom" LXX adds "and Gomorrah." But in this narrative,
Sodom is used for the whole area, except in vs. 20.

17. *reflected.* Literally "said." The verb *'mr,* however, covers a wide
range of meaning. The translation (cf. "persisted, replied," and the
like in subsequent passages) has to be guided by the context.

18. *populous.* Heb. *'āṣūm* stresses numbers rather than strength.

For the last clause, cf. xii 3, NOTE.

19. *I have singled him out.* Another aspect of the flexible stem *yd';*
cf. COMMENT on iv 1. Here the stress is on "to acknowledge." The
verse as a whole gives an excellent summary of the way of life ("way of
Yahweh") that is expected of Abraham and his descendants.

future family. Literally "his house after him"; cf. P's "your seed after
you," xvii 7 and *passim.*

20. *outrage.* The noun *ze'āqā* is subtly distinguished from its doublet
ṣe'āqā (21), which is construed objectively to yield "the outcry against
one."

21. *I must go down and see.* For the phrase cf. xi 5.

at all. Heb. *kālā.* The same form occurs also in the sense of "destruction" (e.g., Jer iv 27, v 10), which TO applies here as well, perhaps

rightly. Some moderns would emend cons. *klh* to *klm* "all of them": "are all of them guilty?"

like the outcry. The Heb. noun (cf. NOTE on 20) is vocalized to read "her outcry" (the feminine possessive pronoun *-tah*, with the *-h* sounded). But the pronoun has no antecedent. The same final letters could stand for an archaic feminine suffix without possessive. LXX and TO read the last letter as *-m* and render "their outcry," i.e., the indictment against them.

or not. Then I will know. Alternatively, "And if not, I will find out." For a similar use of the verb, cf. Exod ii 25.

22. *the men.* This time, the two companions of Yahweh.

left from there. Literally "turned . . . and went." In this combination, the first verb describes not so much a turn as a specific direction.

Yahweh paused in front of Abraham. So the original text. But the passage is listed among the rare instances of Masoretic interference known as *Tiqqūnē sōfᵉrīm* "scribal corrections," whereby the text was changed to "Abraham paused before Yahweh," for deferential reasons. The change is already witnessed in LXX.

23–32. In this dialogue several of the recurrent phrases have been varied in translation on stylistic grounds.

24. *innocent . . . guilty.* Not "righteous . . . wicked"; for the legal emphasis, cf. Exod xxii 8.

25. *Judge . . . act with justice.* Heb. uses the form *šōpēṭ* and the derived noun *mišpāṭ*. The basic sense of the stem *špṭ* is "to exercise authority" in various matters, hence "govern, decide," and the like; and the noun signifies norm, standard, manner. The legal connotations are at best incidental. The title *šōpēṭ*, as used in the Book of "Judges," has nothing to do with the judiciary. In the highly significant Foundation Inscription of Yaḫdun-lim of Mari (slightly earlier than Hammurabi) the cognate term *šāpiṭum* is distinct from *dayānum* "judge" (*Syria*, 1955, p. 4, lines 4, 9). In the present instance, however, "Judge" and "justice" can be employed in a non-technical sense; cf. also xix 9.

27. *I presume.* Also in 31. The basic sense of Heb. is "to undertake" (Deut i 5), hence also to venture, presume.

the Lord. Here, and in vss. 32–33, cons. *'dny* refers to Yahweh, although Abraham knows by now who his visitors are. The author remains consistent throughout this narrative. When he speaks for himself, he refers to God as Yahweh; but when Abraham is the speaker, the appellation is "the Lord."

33. *home.* Literally "his place," that is Mamre, cf. vs. 1.

COMMENT

The rebuke to Sarah, as the author records it (vs. 14), was enough to reveal to Abraham the true character of his guests, but not the nature of the mission which his hospitality had delayed for the time being. He now escorts the travelers to a spot outside Mamre, where the Hebron hills overlook the Dead Sea and the bordering district to the south. While his companions take the road to Sodom, Yahweh pauses to talk to Abraham. There can no longer be any doubt as to the visitors' objective. The ensuing dialogue takes place in the gathering dusk (cf. xix 1), within sight of Sodom, still lush and thriving, yet doomed to be reduced before sunrise to a smoldering ruin.

In Yahweh's soliloquy (vss. 17–19), and the colloquy with Abraham that follows, *J* appears in a new role. What the author sets down is not so much received tradition as personal contemplation. The result is a philosophical aside, in which both Yahweh and the patriarch approach the issues of the moment as problems in an enduring scheme of things. Specifically, the theme is the relation between the individual and society. For Yahweh, the individual who matters is Abraham. Having chosen Abraham as the means for implementing his will, and as the spearhead in the quest for a worthy way of life ("the way of Yahweh," vs. 19), should he not now take Abraham into his full confidence? The patriarch, on the other hand, in his resolute and insistent appeal on behalf of Sodom, seeks to establish for the meritorious individual the privilege of saving an otherwise worthless community.

The correlation between merit and fate is not a question which *J* is the first to broach. The basic issue is only one aspect of the theme of the Suffering Just, which Mesopotamian literature wrestled with as early as the Old Babylonian age (cf. AOS 38 [1955], 68 ff.); the OT has treated it most eloquently in the Book of Job. *J*'s own answer is an emphatic affirmation of the saving grace of the just. And even though the deserving minority proves to be in this instance too small to affect the fate of the sinful majority, the innocent—here Lot and his daughters—are ultimately spared.

23. DESTRUCTION OF SODOM. LOT'S ESCAPE
(xix 1–28: *J*; 29: /*P*/)

XIX 1 The two angels arrived in Sodom in the evening, as Lot was sitting in the gate of Sodom. When Lot saw them, he rose to greet them and, bowing low with his face to the ground, 2 he said, "Please, my lords, turn aside to your servant's house for the night, and bathe your feet; you can then start early on your way." They said, "No, we will rest in the square." 3 But he urged them so much that they turned toward his place and entered his house. He prepared for them a repast, and baked flat cakes, and they dined.

4 Before they could lie down, the townspeople, the men of Sodom, young and old—all the people to the last man—closed in on the house. 5 They called out to Lot and said to him, "Where are the men who came to you tonight? Bring them out to us that we may get familiar with them." 6 Lot met them outside at the entrance, having shut the door behind him. 7 He said, "I beg you, my friends, don't be wicked. 8 Look, I have two daughters who never consorted with a man. Let me bring them out to you, and you may do to them as you please. But don't do anything to these men, inasmuch as they have come under the shelter of my roof." 9 They answered, "Stand back! The fellow," they said, "came here on sufferance, and now he would act the master! Now we'll be meaner to you than to them!" With that, they pressed hard against the person of Lot and moved forward to break down the door. 10 But the men put out their hands and pulled Lot inside, shutting the door. 11 And the people who were at the entrance of the house, one and all, they struck with blinding light, so that they were unable to reach the entrance.

12 Then the men asked Lot, "Who else belongs to you here? Sons,ᵃ daughters, anybody you have in the city—get them out of the place! 13 For we are about to destroy this place; the outcry to Yahweh against those in it has been such that he has sent us to destroy it." 14 So Lot went out and spoke to his sons-in-law, who had married his daughters, and urged them, "Up, leave this place, for Yahweh is about to destroy the city." But his sons-in-law looked at him as if he were joking.

15 As dawn broke, the angels urged Lot on, saying, "Hurry, remove your wife and the two daughters who are here, or you shall be swept away in the punishment of the city. 16 Still he hesitated. So the men seized his hand, and the hands of his wife and his two daughters—Yahweh being merciful to him—and led them to safety outside the city. 17 When they had brought them outside, he was told, "Flee for your life! Do not look behind you or stop anywhere in the Plain. Flee to the hills, or you will be swept away." 18 But Lot replied,ᵇ "Oh no, my lord!ᶜ 19 If you would but indulge your servant, having shown so much kindness in what you did for me by saving my life—I cannot flee to the hills, or disaster will overtake me and I shall die. 20 This town ahead is near enough to escape to, and it is scarcely anything! Let me flee there—it is a mere nothing—that my life may be saved." 21 He answered, "I will bear with you in this matter also, by not overthrowing the town you speak of. 22 Hurry, flee there, for I can do nothing until you arrive there." This is how the town came to be called Zoar.ᵈ

23 The sun rose upon the earth just as Lot entered Zoar. 24 Then Yahweh rained down upon Sodom and Gomorrah sulphurous fire from Yahweh in heaven. 25 He overthrew those cities and the whole Plain, with all the inhabitants of the cities and the vegetation on the ground. 26 As Lot's wife glanced back,ᵉ she turned into a pillar of salt.

ᵃ MT adds "son-in-law"; see NOTE below.
ᵇ MT adds "to them."
ᶜ MT "Lord"; see NOTE.
ᵈ Interpreted as "Little (town)," and connected with the repeated *miṣ'ār* of vs. 20, literally "little thing."
ᵉ MT "behind him"; see NOTE.

27 Next morning, Abraham hurried back to the spot where he had stood before Yahweh. 28 As he looked down toward Sodom and Gomorrah and the whole area of the Plain, he could see only smoke over the land rising like the fumes from a kiln. /29 And so it was that, when God destroyed the cities of the Plain and overthrew the cities amidst which Lot had lived, God was mindful of Abraham by removing Lot from the midst of the upheaval./

NOTES

xix 1. *The two angels.* This identification is meant for the reader, who knows that Yahweh stayed behind with Abraham (xviii 22) in order to tell him of the melancholy mission. The author was equally direct in introducing the other visit (xviii 1). But Lot must discover the truth for himself, as Abraham did earlier. It is only in the light of the *sanwērīm* (11), that the "men" (5, 8, 10) are revealed as angels (15). By thus viewing the action through the eyes of the actors, the spectator also is caught up in the unfolding drama, in spite of his advance knowledge.

in the evening. The southern tip of the Dead Sea is approximately forty miles from Hebron. The angels left after their sumptuous meal, hence in late afternoon at the earliest. Normal traveling time for that distance would be about two days.

in the gate. The focal point of all communal activities in an urban center like Sodom.

with his face to the ground. This is how courtiers and clients address their superiors in the Amarna Letters. In the corresponding case of Abraham (xviii 2), the term for "face" (*'appayim*) is significantly missing.

2. *house.* In contrast to Abraham's tent; cf. xviii 1, 6, 9, 10.

early. The Heb. verbal form *hiškīm* is used adverbially when coordinated with another verb, as it is here. In conjunction with *babboqer* (27), it is not of itself "to rise early in the morning," since a second verb is implied there; cf. xx 8, xxi 14, etc. Moreover, as an adverbial complement, *hiškīm* signifies not only "early," but also "persistently, diligently," or the like (e.g., Jer vii 13, 25, xxv 3, 4; Zeph iii 7, etc.). The independent finite usage is rare; cf. 27, where the sense is "he proceeded promptly" (with the preposition *'el* "to").

No. The reply is abrupt. The angels' grim errand leaves no room for the usual amenities.

3. *urged.* Heb. *pṣr* describes various types of pressure; in vs. 9 the verb is rendered "pressed hard." For our "urged . . . on" in vs. 15, Heb. uses a different stem.

they turned toward his place. Literally "they turned aside to him," with the nuance of "chez lui"; cf. "turn aside" in vs. 2.

repast. Heb. *mištê,* also "feast, banquet" (cf. xxi 8); but here the reception is far from elaborate.

flat cakes. Heb. *maṣṣōt* "unleavened bread." The description is meant to contrast with the semolina biscuits of xviii 6; hurriedly baked flat flaps of bread are the daily fare of the region. "Unleavened" now tends to emphasize ritual rather than expediency.

4. *to the last man.* Heb. *miqqāṣê* "(even) from the fringe(s)," i.e., everybody.

closed in on. Literally "placed themselves around." The Heb. Niphal used with the preposition '*al* "upon, against" can describe hostile moves; cf. "to gather, combine against" (verb *qhl*), Exod xxxii 1; Num xvi 3, xvii 7, xx 2, and "to bear down on" (verb *kbd*); Exod xiv 4; Lev x 3 (not "to be glorified"); see Ehrl., Vol. I, p. 316.

5. *get familiar with.* The same circumlocution for sexual relations as in iv 1, but used under different circumstances.

6. *met them outside at the entrance.* Literally "went out to them to the entrance." The entrance is the doorway, which in well-appointed houses was protected by solid and costly doors; cf. 9.

7. *be wicked.* The Hiphil form without object is generally intransitive; cf. NOTE on iii 6, vi 19; see also vs. 9.

8. *consorted with.* Same Heb. idiom as in vs. 5.

9. *on sufferance.* Heb. *lāgūr* "to sojourn," cf. NOTE on xii 10. The sojourner lacked the privileges and protection enjoyed by citizens.

act the master. Heb. stem *špṭ;* see xviii 25, NOTE.

the person of Lot. Literally "the man Lot." The same idiom is used also in the sense of "X as a person, individual," e.g., Num xii 3.

11. *one and all.* Literally "whether little or big"; cf. "young and old," vs. 4.

blinding light. Heb. *sanwērīm* is a loanword based on Akk. *šunwurum,* an adjectival form with superlative or "elative" force: "having extraordinary brightness" (cf. my discussion in JCS 6 [1952], 81 ff., esp. p. 89, n. 52). For ordinary blindness Heb. employs native terms (stem '*wr*), cf. Lev xxii 22; Deut xxviii 28; Zech xii 4. But these would not be suitable in the present instance, since what is involved is not the common affliction, not just "total blindness," as the word before us is generally rendered, but a sudden stroke. And that is just what the term suggests: a blinding flash emanating from angels—who thereby abandon their human disguise—which would induce immediate, if temporary,

loss of sight, much like desert or snow blindness; the same is true of
II Kings vi 18, the only other passage where this noun is used (Elisha
and the Aramaeans). Thus the very word evokes a numinous image. It
is a matter of magic as opposed to myopia.

they were unable. Heb. *wyl'w,* which is not "they wearied themselves."
In Exod vii 18 the Niphal form describes a condition of helplessness, as
is proved by the parallel "they could not" later on (vs. 24). In all
probability, the present occurrence should also be pointed as Niphal:
*wayyillā'ū.

12. *the men.* Sam. reads "the angels," which is now appropriate; Heb.
does the same in vs. 15.

Before "Sons, daughters . . ." the text has "son-in-law," which is
immediately suspect: the singular is inconsistent with what follows
(LXX has plural), the pronominal suffix is lacking (restored in Syr.,
TJ), and above all, a son-in-law would not be mentioned before direct
descendants. The word in question is obviously intrusive, evidently from
vs. 14.

13. *the outcry . . . against those in it.* MT literally "the outcry against
them," the pronoun referring not to "the place," which is the actual antecedent, but—by extension—to the inhabitants; for the noun, cf. xviii 20.
The original is self-explanatory, but in translation a concession has to be
made to clarity.

14. *who had married.* Heb. employs the agent form "takers of," which
could refer to the past (as interpreted by LXX), or (with Vulg.) the future, i.e., those who were due to marry the two girls. The ambiguity
would disappear if we knew the technical meaning of *hannimṣā'ōt* in the
next verse: literally "within reach, present, at hand," which could mean
either pledged but still at home, or unattached altogether. The traditional
translation that has here been followed presupposes that two older daughters had to be left behind with their husbands, who had every legal right,
however, to oppose their departure. But the alternative interpretation is
by no means improbable.

15. *in the punishment.* Or "because of the iniquity"; on Heb. *'āwōn* see
iv 13.

16. *he hesitated.* The text has a pause sign after the verb. Lot is thus
pictured as hesitant to abandon his possessions.

led them to safety. Literally "brought them out and deposited them"
(hendiadys).

17. *Flee.* The Heb. stem *(n)mlṭ* is used five times in this short passage
(17–22), evidently because of its assonance with the name Lot (*lwṭ*).

he was told. Literally "he (the speaker) said"; cf. xviii 10, as contrasted with the preceding verse. The subject in such situations is often

left ambiguous in Heb. The same is true of vs. 21, below, but there Lot had already addressed one of the two angels; see below.

18. *But Lot replied.* The text reads "said to them," which cannot be right, since immediately afterward Lot is addressing himself to a single companion. The error is probably traceable to the ambiguous '*dny,* which must have been read as plural; cf. NOTE on xviii 3. The context, however, favors '*ᵃdōnī.*

19. *If you would but indulge your servant.* Another nuance of the flexible "to find favor in the eyes of . . ."; see vi 8, NOTE.

20. *town.* Heb. '*īr* ranges all the way from "city" to "depository" (cf. I Kings ix 19). The present occurrence describes a small settlement.

ahead. Literally "that, yonder."

to escape to. For once Heb. departs from *nmlṭ* and substitutes *lānūs.*

scarcely anything . . . a mere nothing. Heb. *miṣ'ār* (both times), a skillful wordplay on the place name Zoar (*ṣ'r*). Aetiological explanations were always popular, but seldom as plausible as this one is, at least on the surface.

24. *sulphurous fire.* While sentiment favors the traditional "brimstone and fire," the context points plainly to hendiadys.

25. The repeated use of the verb "to overthrow" may well hark back to an earthquake; cf. Dr. On the problem of location see Wright (*Biblical Archaeology,* p. 50), who assumes, with Albright, that the destroyed cities were buried beneath the shallow waters of the southern tip of the Dead Sea. This view has been questioned by E. G. Kraeling, *Bible Atlas,* 1956, p. 71; see also J. P. Harland, BA 5 (1942), 41 ff.

26. *glanced back.* MT has "(Lot's wife,) behind him, looked." The verb itself does not indicate direction. Unless, therefore, something like "(who followed) behind him" is intended, the pronominal suffix was originally feminine; cf. also vs. 17. The present translation leaves the matter open.

27. *hurried back.* Not "rose early (in the morning)," which cannot be construed with "*to* the place," in any case; some such verb as "and went/hastened" is implied, cf. NOTE on vs. 2.

28. *smoke . . . fumes.* Heb. does not employ here its regular term for smoke, but uses instead, both times, a noun cognate with the term for "incense." The emphasis is thus on dense vapors, such as might be caused by the firing of lime or the burning of fat or incense.

COMMENT

The focus of attention now shifts from Abraham to Lot, whose part in the impending drama was foreshadowed in chapter xiii and gained substance in xviii. By taking advantage of his uncle's kindness and staking out the Plain for himself (xiii 10 f.), Lot became an unwitting accessory to Sodom's guilt. The story of Lot, which is a subplot in the history of Abraham, is now coming to a close. *J* never loses sight of the fact that history, in the last analysis, is made by individuals. But the individual, in turn, mirrors larger issues and events.

At the present juncture, the author is leading up to the origins of Moab and Ammon, two of Israel's close kin. And since these were Transjordanian groups, *J* combines a popular tradition about them with a geographic upheaval south of the Dead Sea. His approach is normative, and the judgment is apparently calculated to point up by indirection the sterner moral values of Israel as compared with those of its neighbors. National history as a vehicle for a way of life remains *J*'s central objective; and that history is at this point personified by Abraham and Lot.

To judge from xiii 10 and vs. 29 here, a major natural catastrophe must have destroyed the settlements at the southern tip of the Dead Sea some time after the patriarchal period had commenced. This could well have been an earthquake, accompanied perhaps by an eruption of petroleum gases underground. The event could not but be ascribed to the delinquency of the local population. But there was no uniform tradition as regards the nature of the offense. Isaiah stresses lack of justice (i 10, iii 9), Jeremiah cites moral and ethical laxity (xxiii 14), and Ezekiel speaks of Sodom's disregard of the needy (xvi 49). To *J*, however, it was the city's sexual depravity, the manifest "sodomy" of its inhabitants, that provided the sole and self-evident reason for its frightful fate.

The action is swift and grim, inevitable yet suspenseful. Nor is it surprising, given the author's insight and skill, that in the personal equation between Abraham and Lot the latter should emerge a poor second. Having met the strangers before, the reader will not need to ask how they could cover the distance between Hebron and Sodom, normally a two-day journey, in the brief interval between midafternoon and sundown. Lot is dutiful in his hospitality. His manner with the visitors, however, appears servile ("with his face to the ground," vs. 1), as contrasted with the simple dignity of Abraham (xviii 2), and both his invitation and subsequent preparations lack his uncle's spontaneity. But true to the unwritten code, Lot will stop at nothing in his effort to protect his guests. Presently, the identity of the visitors is revealed in a flash of supernatural light (vs. 11). The angels' intercession serves to bring out the latent weaknesses in Lot's character. He is undecided, flustered, ineffectual. His own sons-in-law refuse to take him seriously (14). He hesitates to turn his back on his possessions, and has to be led to safety by the hand (16), like a child—an ironic sidelight on a man who a moment earlier tried to protect his celestial guests (von Rad). Lot's irresoluteness makes him incoherent (20). Small wonder that his deliverance is finally achieved without a moment to spare. Had the sun risen an instant sooner, Lot might have shared the fate of his wife; for God's mysterious workings must not be looked at by man.

As Abraham peered anxiously at the scene of the disaster, from the distant heights of Hebron, he had his answer to the question he had posed the night before. A pall of dense vapors was all that could be seen. All life was extinguished. The author is much too fine an artist to spell out the viewer's thoughts, and the close of the narrative is all the more eloquent for this omission.

P's one-sentence summary of the episode (29)—unmistakable in its wording, style, and approach—is an example of scholastic succinctness at its best.

24. LOT'S DAUGHTERS
(xix 30–38: *J*)

XIX 30 Lot went up from Zoar with his two daughters, and settled in the hill country; he was afraid to stay in Zoar. And he lived with his two daughters in a cave. 31 The older one said to the younger, "Our father is growing old, and there is not a man on earth to unite with us as was the custom throughout the world. 32 Come, let us ply our father with wine, then lie with him, in order that we may preserve life through our father."

33 That night, after they had plied their father with wine, the older one went in and lay with her father; he was not conscious of her lying down or her getting up. 34 Next morning the older said to the younger, "Look, last night it was I who lay with father. Tonight let us again ply him with wine, and you go in and lie with him, so that we may preserve life through our father." 35 So after they had plied their father with wine that night also, the younger went in and lay with him; nor was he conscious of her lying down or her getting up.

36 Thus both Lot's daughters came to be with child by their father. 37 The older bore a son, whom she named Moab[a]; he is the father of the Moabites of today. 38 And the younger also bore a son, whom she named Ben-Ammi[b]; he is the father of the Ammonites of today.

[a] Heb. *mō'āb,* equated with *mē'āb* "from father."
[b] "Son of my kin," equated with "children of Ammon."

NOTES

xix 30. *cave*. Vocalized with definite article to signify "a certain cave."

31. *growing old*. The inchoative aspect is necessary in order to point up the urgency of the situation.

unite with. Cf. NOTE on vi 4.

32. *ply . . . with wine*. The primary meaning of the Heb. verb is "to irrigate the ground" (ii 10), then to furnish drink to animals (xxiv 14, xxix 7) or humans (e.g., xxiv 18 f.). Here the object of the scheme is not just to make Lot drink but to get him drunk.

preserve life. Literally "keep seed alive."

34. *with father*. Heb. literally "my father," but the possessive in this case is more stylistic than proprietary. LXX has "our father," without necessarily implying a variant reading.

COMMENT

Popular tales about neighboring peoples are encountered the world over. The product of traditional rivalries, local pride, and raw folk humor, they often tend to place the neighbor's character and origin in an uncomplimentary, if amusing, light. Was the narrative before us inspired by similar considerations? What little evidence there is would seem to contradict such an assumption.

As they are here portrayed, Lot and his two daughters had every reason to believe that they were the last people on earth. From the recesses of their cave somewhere up the side of a canyon formed by the earth's deepest rift, they could see no proof to the contrary. The young women were concerned with the future of the race, and they were resolute enough to adopt the only desperate measure that appeared to be available. The father, moreover, was not a conscious party to the scheme. All of this adds up to praise rather than blame.

The account itself, of course, was colored to a substantial degree by the popular etymology of the ethnic terms for the Moabites and Ammonites. Did the derivations here recorded originate with Israelites, or with the natives themselves whose dialects differed very little from Hebrew? Such points could be argued either way, and with equally inconclusive results. More practical is the question as to why

J incorporated such a tale about outsiders in a story of his own people's past. The likeliest answer would seem to be that these neighbors were too important to be ignored. Yet there is little evidence of such prominence in extant historical records, certainly not in records that *J* could have known. *J* might have been familiar with the substance of I Sam xi, and quite probably with the background of Judg iii 12 ff. and xi 4 ff. But the folk tale before us presupposes a longer period of incubation. It may go back to the thirteenth century, when both Transjordan and Palestine were being settled by related tribes, at which time their relative strengths appear to have been more on a par than was later the case; cf. Deut ii 9, 19. *J*'s parallel treatment of the histories of Abraham and Lot is added proof that interrelationship was particularly intimate and important in early times.

In short, the anonymous Dead Sea cave with which this tale is concerned entails its own full complement of intriguing issues.

25. ABRAHAM AND SARAH AT GERAR
(xx 1–18: *E*)

XX 1 Abraham journeyed on to the region of the Negeb and settled between Kadesh and Shur. While he was sojourning in Gerar, 2 Abraham said of his wife Sarah, "She is my sister." So Abimelech king of Gerar had Sarah brought to him. 3 But God came to Abimelech in a dream one night and said to him, "You are due to die because of the woman you have taken, for she is a married woman." 4 Abimelech, who had not come near her, asked, "O Lord, would you slay one*a* even though he be innocent? 5 The fact is that he told me, 'She is my sister'; and she herself stated, 'He is my brother.' I did it in good faith and with clean hands!" 6 God answered him in a dream, "Yes, I know that you did this in good faith; I myself kept you from sinning against me, which is why I would not let you touch her. 7 But you must now return the man's wife—since he is one who speaks up, he will intercede for you—to save your life. If you do not restore her, know that this means death for you and all yours."

8 Early next morning, Abimelech called all his attendants and told them everything that had happened; and the people were deeply shocked. 9 Then Abimelech summoned Abraham and said to him, "See what you have done to us! Wherein did I fail you that you should have brought such great guilt upon me and my kingdom? You have behaved toward me in an unforgivable manner. 10 What then," Abimelech demanded of Abraham, "was your purpose in doing such a thing?"

11 "I thought," Abraham replied, "there is surely no fear of God in this place, and they will kill me because of my wife. 12 Besides, she is in truth my sister—my father's daughter though

not my mother's—who became my wife. [13] So when Heaven[b] caused me to wander far from my father's home, I said to her, 'I want you to do me this kindness: whatever place we come to, say there of me, He is my brother.'"

[14] Abimelech got sheep and oxen, and male and female slaves, and gave them to Abraham; and he restored his wife Sarah to him. [15] Said Abimelech, "Here, my land is open to you: settle wherever you please." [16] And to Sarah he said, "I have given your brother a thousandworth of silver. Let that serve you as a blind[c] to everybody who is with you; you have been publicly vindicated."[d]

[17] Abraham then interceded with God, and God restored full health to Abimelech, namely, his wife and his maidservants, so that they could bear again. [18] For God[e] had closed fast every womb in the household of Abimelech on account of Sarah, wife of Abraham.

[b] Literally "God"; cf. NOTE.
[c] Literally "covering for the eyes."
[d] See NOTE.
[e] So Sam., LXX manuscripts; MT "Yahweh."

NOTES

xx 1. (*journeyed*) *on*. The text has "from there," which in the present context could only refer to Lot's cave. In the original context of *E*, the nearest antecedent would be xv 5, assuming that nothing from that source is missing at this juncture. The translation seeks to reflect some of the Heb. without making it meaningless.

While he was sojourning. The received verse division causes trouble, at least on the surface. It suggests that to be settled between Kadesh and Shur was the same thing as sojourning in Gerar. By taking 1c as a temporal protasis to vs. 2, we obtain a statement that is immediately clear: in the Negeb, Abraham ranged with his herds from Kadesh to Shur; in the course of that stay, he paid a visit to Gerar. This natural interpretation has the added advantage of automatically clearing up a geographic problem, since Gerar (near Gaza) does not fit readily "between Kadesh and Shur."

3. *a dream*. In *E*, the normal means of communication between God and man; cf. vs. 6 and xxxi 10.

one night. Definite article in Heb. with the force of our "a certain
. . ."; cf. xix 30, NOTE.

You are due to die. In the original, the periphrastic construction with
*hinn*ᵉ*kā.*

4. *one.* The text for the interrogative clause gives the consonants
hgwy gm ṣdyq thrg. Here (*h*)*gwy* presents an old crux, as old as the
ancient versions, which attest the reading but cannot solve it. The noun
stands for "nation" (cf. xii 2, NOTE) as a collective, political, and
territorial concept. No such meaning can be forced into the present
context; and "people" is ruled out by the fact that even for a group of
individuals the required Heb. term would be *'am,* which is sharply
demarcated from *gōy* (cf. JBL 79 [1960], 157 ff.). The respective
usages are established by some 2350 occurrences in the OT. Not one
of them favors "person" or "persons" for *gōy;* the connotation "other-
national, gentile" is post-biblical and predicated on the fact that Israel
was no longer a nation.

The combined evidence thus points overwhelmingly to an old textual
corruption. The original must have read either *hgm,* which came to be
expanded to *hgyhgm* through dittography (the *-w-,* as vowel letter, would
not be used in very old texts), or *h. .gm,* wherein the lacuna was first
taken up by some reinforcing particle, but later displaced by dittography.
The first of these alternatives seems preferable and is reflected in the
translation; for an analogous case of haplography involving *gōy,* see xxi
13.

5. *The fact is.* Translating the rhetorical *h*ᵃ*lō'* "is it not?"

6. *in good faith.* Literally "in the integrity of my heart."

7. *one who speaks up.* Heb. *nābī',* normally "prophet," in the sense
of one who speaks (stem *nb'*) on behalf of another, specifically God;
note especially Deut xviii 18; but the *nābī'* can also represent, be spokesman for, a mortal, cf. Exod vii 1. Here the allusion is apparently to the
latter function.

9. For the first clause, cf. xii 18.

fail. The primary meaning of *ḥṭ'* is "to be deficient," hence ultimately,
but in a restricted sense, "to sin."

unforgivable. Literally "not to be done," cf. xxxiv 7.

10. *What . . . was your purpose.* Literally "What . . . did you (fore)-
see?"

11. *fear of God.* In general, respect for moral and social obligations.

my father's daughter though not my mother's. It is noteworthy that
a Hittite treaty which concerns itself with a similar case of wife-sister,
uses virtually the same terminology (uterine sister : sister "germane"; cf.
P. Koschaker, ZA 41 [1933], 10 ff.). According to xi 29 (*J*), Abraham's
brother Nahor married his niece, whom he had evidently adopted. The

same verse tells of Abraham's marriage to Sarah without, however, indicating her family background, conceivably because she was already a member of Terah's family; cf. NOTE *ad loc.*

13. *Heaven.* Literally "God." The accompanying verb is in the plural, which is grammatically permissible, but not customary with *Elohim* "God"; cf. xxxv 7; II Sam vii 23. Here the construction may hint independently at a related but broader connotation, something like our Heaven, Fate, Providence.

15. *settle.* As opposed to "sojourn," vs. 1.

16. *a thousandworth of silver.* Heb. literally "a thousand of/in silver"; but the figure is obviously a round number, and what Abraham actually received (vs. 14) was not in currency.

a blind. Literally "a covering for the eyes," which appears to describe a method for diverting or forestalling suspicion. Whether the phrase carries special overtones cannot, of course, be determined.

publicly. This represents the vocalized text, literally "before all." But neither the pointing nor the cons. text inspires confidence.

you have been . . . vindicated. The causative stem of the indicated root *ykh* means "to decree" (xxiv 14, 44), "to set right, give judgment" (xxxi 42); and other passages carry a similar legal or disciplinary connotation (e.g., xxi 25). The Niphal (passive or reflexive) is rare, but not unrelated in meaning (Isa i 18; Job xxiii 7). The present occurrence, if correctly recorded, points in the same direction.

17. *restored full health.* Not "healed," as traditionally rendered, but "cured," or the like.

namely. Explicative use of Heb. *we-;* cf. i 14, NOTE; as the following verse demonstrates, only the women were involved.

18. *God.* So correctly in Sam., LXX manuscripts. The "Yahweh" of MT must be a copyist's error influenced by YHWH in the next line (xxi 1).

COMMENT

This is the first connected narrative from the hand of *E* (for probable earlier fragments cf. xv), and it has most of the characteristics which go with that source: Elohim instead of Yahweh; dreams as a medium of communication; a marked tendency to explain and justify. The contrast with *J* is particularly sharp in this instance because the account before us parallels *J*'s narrative in xii 10–20. The external differences stand out, therefore, that much more clearly. What is more, even without the discrepancies in vocabulary, style, and treatment, internal evidence from content would still show independently that the two accounts could not have been written by the same author. The present section thus adds up to a strong argument in favor of a distinct narrative source that is not to be confused with *J;* cf. pp. xxxi ff.

Actually, the episode before us is paralleled not once but twice. The first incident, (a), xii 10–20, involved the encounter of Abraham and Sarah with the ruler of Egypt; the writing was seen to bear all the earmarks of *J.* The other parallel, (c), xxvi 6–11, echoes an identical experience by Isaac and Rebekah with Abimelech of Gerar; it too can be traced to *J.* There is, however, complete separation of cast, locale, and generations: Abraham-Sarah-Pharaoh-Egypt as against Isaac-Rebekah-Abimelech-Gerar. The two narratives are thus entirely appropriate in a work by an individual author.

The present account, (b), on the other hand, juxtaposes Abraham and Sarah with Abimelech of Gerar; it crosses the visitors of (a) with the host and locale of (c). Moreover, if all three reports stemmed from the same source, it would follow (1) that Abraham learned nothing from his experience in Egypt, and (2) that Abimelech was in no way sobered by his all but fatal involvement with Sarah, an affair in which he went to such lengths to protest his innocence. Furthermore, Abimelech would have had to be either a fool or a knave to accept Isaac's subsequent pretense at face value; yet this passage depicts him as both wise and sincere. Lastly, our king of Gerar would be much too old as a candidate for Rebekah's attentions. In short, the three episodes viewed together cannot be homogeneous. As soon, however, as they are traced back to two separate sources, all the contradictions and inconsistencies are resolved automatically.

J knew of two occasions (a, c) when a patriarch thought it necessary to introduce his wife as a sister; there is in them no duplication of principals, locale, or generations. In *E,* however, the two episodes became telescoped, with the result that Abraham and Sarah were shifted from Egypt to Gerar, while Isaac and Rebekah did not participate at all. Thus each source remains entirely consistent within itself; between the two, however, two original incidents branched out into three. Fluctuations in underlying oral tradition would readily account for the eventual confusion.

Where the evidence from content agrees so completely with independently established criteria of terminology and general approach, the combined results may be accepted without serious misgivings. The narrative before us becomes thus a parade example of *E*'s work. It is immediately apparent that this writer, too, has outstanding gifts as a storyteller. He also had access to, and respect for, authentic detail. But *E* cannot match *J*'s economy of speech, and he lacks *J*'s ability to let actions speak for themselves. Whereas Abraham makes no reply to Pharaoh's stinging indictment (see NOTE on xii 20), he has here a great deal to say to Abimelech in self-defense (vss. 11–13, above).

On the significance of the theme which constitutes the subject matter of all three narratives under discussion, see COMMENT on Sec. 15 and, for the whole, cf. pp. xxxi ff.

26. BIRTH OF ISAAC AND EXPULSION OF HAGAR
(xxi 1–2a: /J/; 2b–5: |P|; 6–21: E)

XXI /¹ Yahweh now took note of Sarah as he had said, and he*a* did for Sarah what he had promised. ² Sarah conceived and bore Abraham a son in his old age,/ |at the set time that God had stated. ³ Abraham gave his newborn son that Sarah had borne him the name Isaac. ⁴ And Abraham circumcised his son Isaac at the age of eight days, as God had commanded him. ⁵ Now Abraham was 100 years old when his son Isaac was born to him./

⁶ And Sarah said,

> "God has brought me laughter*b*;
> All who hear of it will rejoice*c* with me."

⁷ And she added,

> "Who would have said to Abraham
> That Sarah might nurse children!
> Yet I have borne a son in his old age."

⁸ The child grew and was weaned. On the day that Isaac was weaned, Abraham held a great feast. ⁹ When Sarah noticed that the son whom Hagar the Egyptian had borne to Abraham was playing *d*with her son Isaac,*d* ¹⁰ she turned on Abraham, "Cast out that slave with her son! No son of that slave is going to share inheritance with my son Isaac! ¹¹ The matter distressed Abraham very much, for the son was his too. ¹² But God said to Abraham, "Do not be distressed about the boy, or about

a Heb. "Yahweh"; see NOTE.
b Play on the name "Isaac."
c Or "rejoicing."
d–d So with LXX, Vulg. (manuscripts); omitted in MT.

your slave woman. Do whatever Sarah tells you, for it is through
Isaac that your line shall be continued. 13 And as for the maid's
son, I will make of him also a great* nation, for he too is your
offspring.

14 Early next morning Abraham got some bread and a skin of
water *to give to Hagar. He placed them on her back and sent
her away with the child*. She wandered aimlessly in the wilderness of Beer-sheba. 15 When the water in the skin was used up,
she left the child under one of the shrubs, 16 and went and sat
down at a distance, about a bowshot away; for she said to herself, "Let me not look on as the child dies." And as she sat thus
at a distance, she broke into sobs.

17 God heard the boy's cry, and an angel of God called to
Hagar from heaven, "What troubles you, Hagar? Fear not, for
God has heard the cry of the boy *in his present plight*.
18 Come, pick up the boy and comfort him; for I will make of
him a great nation." 19 Then God opened her eyes and she be-
held a well of water. She went and filled the skin with water,
and let the boy drink.

20 God was with the boy as he grew up. He lived in the desert
and became a skilled bowman. 21 His home was in the wilderness of Paran. And his mother got a wife for him from the land
of Egypt.

e So with most versions, cf. vs. 18; omitted in MT.
f–f Text obscure; see NOTE.
g–g See NOTE.

NOTES

xxi 1. The second half of the verse duplicates the first. It appears to
stem from *P*, with a secondary change of Elohim to Yahweh, induced
by the preceding clause. It did not, however, seem practical to reflect
such a possibility in the translation.

now. Some such nuance is demanded by the inverted syntax of Heb.

took note. The primary sense of the common and richly shaded stem
pqd; trad. "visited" is suitable at best in punitive contexts alone.

2b. Elohim is the normal designation of the Deity not only in *E* (vss.
6 ff.) but also in *P* (along with El Shaddai).

5. *100 years old.* Cf. COMMENT on xvii.

6. *laughter . . . rejoice.* A double allusion by E to the name Isaac; see NOTE on xvii 17. The derisive "laugh at" is ruled out by the tenor of vs. 7; note also the unique construction of the verb *ṣḥq* with *ħ*.

7. *said.* The stem *mll* is limited in the OT to poetry.

8. *was weaned.* To this day, weaning may take place in the Near East as late as at three years or more; it is often followed by a celebration.

9. *was playing.* Piel form of the verb *ṣḥq*, in further wordplay on the name Isaac. Traditional "mocking" would require the preposition *b-* to designate the object. To judge, however, from some of the ancient versions, the original text appears to have included "with her son Isaac," which is lacking in MT, perhaps through haplography. According to xvi 16 combined with vs. 5 above (both from P, however), Ishmael would now be at least fifteen years old. But his "playing" with Isaac need mean no more than that the older boy was trying to amuse his little brother. There is nothing in the text to suggest that he was abusing him, a motive deduced by many troubled readers in their effort to account for Sarah's anger.

12. *your line shall be continued.* Literally "your seed shall be called, identified": the important branch of your family will descend through Isaac rather than Ishmael; for an analogous employment of "seed," cf. xvii 12.

14. *on her back.* Heb. literally "on her shoulder," but the term covers also the upper part of the back in general. The middle of the sentence is now distorted. The translation of LXX and Syr., "and he placed the child on her shoulder," would yield an acceptable word order for Heb., yet would not automatically guarantee its authenticity. The real problem is Ishmael's age at the time. If the boy was about fifteen years old (see above, NOTE on 9), his mother would not have carried him on her back. Obviously, the present narrative depicts Ishmael as younger (cf. 15 ff.), but still old enough to play the big brother to a weaned Isaac (8 f.). The various emendations that have been proposed merely substitute one set of problems for another. An acceptable solution has yet to be discovered.

15. *left.* Not necessarily "cast away"; cf. Ehrl.

16. *bowshot.* Heb. *mṭḥwy* is quite probably dual, so that "two bowshots" may be a better translation.

she broke into sobs. LXX, followed by most moderns, substitutes the masculine pronoun, thus making Ishmael the subject, evidently because of vs. 17. There, however, the noun "sound, voice" is not expressly connected with weeping; moreover, the text employs the unambiguous feminine prefix twice, the Heb. idiom in this instance being made up of two verbs ("she lifted up her voice and she wept"), which would mean a double emendation. As for the idiom itself, the tendency to interpret it in the sense of "she wept aloud" is not in accord with good Heb. usage. Elsewhere, the verb *nś'* is used with bodily organs (eyes, *passim;* feet, xxix 1; hands, Hab iii 10) not with the sense of "to lift," to signify degree or volume, but with the shading of "to pick up," to focus attention on the activity involved (cf. Ehrl. at xiii 10); Hagar's weeping was audible but not necessarily loud; the above translation reflects, furthermore, the "ingressive" force of the phrase; cf. xxix 1.

17. *heard.* Another explanation of the name Ishmael; cf. xvi 11.

in his present plight. Literally "where he is"; but the phrase would hardly be much to the point as a topographical reference (Ehrl.), for it is not a question of where the boy is but how he is.

18. *and comfort him.* Literally "make your hand firm upon him," which is idiomatic for lending support and encouragement; the traditional "seize him by his hand," or the like, would require "get hold of his hand" in Heb., for which cf. xix 16 (three times).

20. *a skilled bowman.* Heb. *rōbê qaššāt,* a combination of two agent nouns, hence a bowman (*qaššāt*) who does something, not a person who uses the bow. Moreover, no such meaning as "to shoot" can be established for the first element, which might be connected at best with Heb. for "great," or Aram. for "youth," not without some difficulties in either case. The general type of compound, however, recalls in its construction "a wild colt of a man" (xvi 12), or Akk. "hunter-man," which is familiar from the Gilgamesh Epic. The present translation is conjectural.

21. *got a wife for him.* In ancient Near Eastern society the father had to obtain a wife for his son and assume the costs involved; here it is Hagar who has to take over the responsibility.

COMMENT

Except for the first five verses, the narrative is the work of *E.* The proof goes deeper than the external evidence from the consistent use of Elohim (6, 12, 17, 19, 20). The present account duplicates ch. xvi. More significant, however, is the fact that the reason for Hagar's departure is not at all the same as in the earlier story by *J,* nor does the personality of Hagar as here depicted bear any resemblance to that of her namesake in the other story. So complete a dichotomy would be inconceivable in the work of the same author, or in a fixed written tradition.

According to xvi 5, Sarah's hatred of Hagar stemmed from the concubine's tactless behavior toward her childless mistress; and Abraham was either unable or unwilling to intervene in the bitter rivalry between two headstrong women. Here it is Ishmael who becomes the unwitting cause of Sarah's fury; and Abraham makes an effort to remonstrate with Sarah, while Hagar is the downtrodden slave throughout. Once again, E seeks to explain people and their actions, but he does so with the aid of words rather than deeds. If E's characters do more reasoning than J's, they are also less natural and impulsive.

These differences in depth are independently reflected in the innocuous medium of sound symbolism. All three sources are interested in the aetiology of the name Isaac. P ascribed it to Abraham's surprise at God's announcement that Sarah would bear a son (xvii 17). J traced the name back to Sarah's incredulity (xviii 10–14). E, however, postpones his derivation until after the child has been born, and he bases it on the mother's delight with the event. Nor do J and E agree on the precise reasons behind Ishmael's name. In the former account, Yahweh "heeds" the mother's misery; in the latter, Elohim "hears" the cry of the abandoned child. There is thus much that is the same in the theme as a whole, but also a vast difference in detail and treatment. Both sources drew manifestly on the same underlying tradition. By the time of the writing, however, the material had come to be transmitted through more than one channel, and the individual writers contributed indirectly to the widening gap.

27. ABRAHAM AND ABIMELECH AT BEER-SHEBA
(xxi 22–32, 34: *E*; 33: /*J*/)

XXI 22 At about that time Abimelech, accompanied by Phicol chief of his troops,[a] said to Abraham, "God is with you in everything you undertake. 23 Therefore, swear to me by God here and now that you will not deal falsely with me, or with my kith and kin, but will act as kindly toward me and the land in which you are residing as I have acted toward you." 24 And Abraham replied, "I swear it."

25 Abraham then reproached Abimelech about the well of water that Abimelech's servants had seized. 26 Abimelech answered, "I have no idea who did that thing. You never told me, nor have I heard of it until this moment."

27 Then Abraham took sheep and oxen and gave them to Abimelech, and the two of them concluded a pact. 28 Abraham also set apart seven ewe-lambs of the flock, 29 whereupon Abimelech asked Abraham, "What is the meaning of these seven ewe-lambs that you have set apart?" 30 He answered, "It is this: you will accept the seven ewe-lambs from me as my proof that this well was dug by me." 31 This is why that place was called Beer-sheba,[b] meaning that the two of them swore an oath there. 32 Upon the conclusion of the pact at Beer-sheba, Abimelech and Phicol, chief of his troops, left and returned to Philistine country.

/33 As for Abraham,[c] he planted a tamarisk at Beer-sheba, and there he invoked the name of Yahweh, the Eternal God./ 34 And Abraham resided in Philistine country many years.

[a] LXX, Old Latin add "and Ahuzzath his councilor"; cf. xxvi 26 (*J*).
[b] Literally "Well of Seven," or "Well of the Oath."
[c] Sam., LXX, Syr., Vulg.; MT omits.

NOTES

xxi 22. *Phicol.* See also vs. 32. The same military man is mentioned in xxvi 26 (*J*), together with an adviser whom two ancient versions (LXX and Old Latin) cite in this context as well.

23. *here.* The site of future Beer-sheba, in assonance with *h-šbʿ-h* "swear."

kith and kin. To reflect the alliteration in the Heb. pair *nīnī* : *nekdī*, both nouns referring to progeny.

you are residing. Stem *g-r* in Heb. probably a deliberate reference to inferior political status as an argument for the desired treaty; cf. xix 9. In vs. 34 the same argument would not apply any longer. But that passage is not believed to be original with *E;* see below.

27. *pact.* Same Heb. noun as is used for "covenant," cf. xv 9, NOTE; the latter translation, however, may best be reserved for treaties in which God is one of the parties.

28, 29. *apart.* Literally "by themselves," a pointed allusion to the special purpose which the seven ewe-lambs are to serve.

30. *It is this.* Heb. *kī* is used here to introduce a gloss; cf. NOTE on iv 25.

32, 34. *Philistine country.* An anachronism, cf. COMMENT on ix 27 (*J*); this is one of the reasons why these verses are usually attributed to *J*, or to a *R*(edactor) familiar with *J*.

33. *the Eternal God.* Heb. *ʾēl ʿōlām,* for which cf. Pope, *El in the Ugaritic Texts,* pp. 14 f. This need not, however, refer to the local deity of Beer-sheba, but may be a logical epithet of a deity called upon to support a formal treaty that is expected to be valid for all time.

COMMENT

Except for vs. 33, and possibly also 32 and 34, the narrative stems from *E,* hence the use of Elohim in 22f. The subject matter is the aetiology of the important desert center of Beer-sheba, or rather two distinct aetiologies based on common uses of the element *-šebaʿ.* The first part of the compound means "well"; but the second part could be either "seven" or "oath." Hence an original and entirely appropriate "Well of Seven," i.e., Seven-Wells, lent itself to elaboration as "Well of the Oath," which popular etymology would be loath to ignore. As a matter of fact, all three connotations—well, seven, and oath—figure in the present episode through the medium of popular interpretation: a dispute over a well is resolved by a treaty that is solemnized by seven ewe-lambs, which in turn symbolize a mutual oath.

Many moderns would regard the narrative proper (22–31) as composite and in disorder. Consequently, they would place vs. 27 right after 25, arguing that Abraham used sheep and oxen in one oath, but seven ewe-lambs in another oath—or in another version—all this as a result of disputes over a well. Aside from such drastic manipulation of the text, the hypothesis has to assume two E-like sources. Yet no such measures would seem to be at all necessary. The narrative can be logically interpreted as it stands.

Following his encounter with Abimelech (xx, E), Abraham found a promising base of operations in the oasis of Beer-sheba, a number of miles inland from Gerar. Evidently, the ruler of Gerar sought to extend his jurisdiction to the district of Beer-sheba, but could not back his claim with an adequate show of force. When a dispute over water rights at Beer-sheba threatened to get out of hand, Abimelech deemed it wisest to conclude a treaty with the local settlers, which would assure him a certain degree of authority. It is such a mutual non-aggression pact that the story before us commemorates. Abimelech brings with him his army chieftain, and perhaps also his political councilor (cf. NOTE on vs. 22), to strengthen his position as the stronger party, a claim which Abraham, as a newcomer, does not appear to dispute.

What follows is a description of the ceremonies. The first group of animals symbolizes the basic pact (cf. xv 9 f.). The second group, on the other hand, which consists of seven ewe-lambs, is clearly labeled as a gift, the acceptance of which by Abimelech is to constitute validation (*'ēdā*) of Abraham's claim to the well. In other words, there is only one formal occasion with two parts to it, instead of two separate pacts—or two different sources. That the proceedings are linked to the dual aetiology of the name—seven and oath—is a characteristic of the times, and certainly not inconsistent with the character of the E document.

A new note is added in vs. 33, which ties the worship of Yahweh to the symbolism of a sacred tree. One can only guess at the reason why such a brief excerpt from J was inserted at this particular point. For the epithet *'ēl 'ōlām*, see NOTE *ad loc*.

28. THE ORDEAL OF ISAAC
(xxii 1–19: *E*/*J*[a])

XXII [1] Some time afterwards, God put Abraham to the test. He said to him, "Abraham!"[b] "Ready," he answered. [2] And he said, "Take your son, your beloved one, Isaac whom you hold so dear, and go to the land of Moriah,[c] where you shall offer him up as a burnt offering on one of the heights that I will point out to you."

[3] Early next morning, Abraham saddled his ass, took two of his servant boys along with his son Isaac, having first split some wood for the burnt offering, and started out for the place that God had indicated to him. [4] On the third day Abraham sighted the place from afar. [5] Then Abraham said to his servants, "You stay here with the ass while the boy and I go on yonder; we will worship and then come back to you."

[6] Abraham then took the wood for the burnt offering and put it on Isaac his son; the firestone and the cleaver he carried in his own hand. And the two walked off together. [7] Isaac broke the silence and said to his father Abraham, "Father!" "Yes, my son," he answered. "There is the firestone," he said, "and the wood, but where is the sheep for the burnt offering?" [8] Abraham replied, "God will see to the sheep for his burnt offering, my son." And the two of them walked on together.

[9] They came to the place that God had spoken of to him. Abraham built an altar there. He laid out the wood. He tied up his son Isaac. He laid him on the altar on top of the wood. [10] He put out his hand and picked up the cleaver to slay his son. [11] But an angel of Yahweh called to him from heaven, "Abra-

[a] Cf. 14–16, and see COMMENT.
[b] LXX, Vulg. repeat.
[c] See NOTE.

ham! Abraham!" "Here I am," he answered. 12 And he said,
"Lay not your hand upon the boy, nor do the least thing to him!
Now I know how dedicated you are to God, since you did not
withhold from me your own beloved son." 13 As Abraham
looked up, his eye fell upon a*d* ram snagged in the thicket by its
horns. Abraham went and took the ram and offered it up as a
burnt offering in place of his son. 14 And Abraham named that
site Yahweh-yireh,*e* hence the present saying, "On Yahweh's
mountain there is vision."*f*

15 Yahweh's angel called to Abraham a second time from
heaven, 16 and said, " 'I swear by myself,' declared Yahweh,
'that because you have acted thus, and did not withhold your
beloved son *g*from me*g*, 17 I will therefore bestow my blessing
upon you and make your offspring as numerous as the stars in
heaven and the sands on the seashore; and your descendants
shall take over the gates of their enemies. 18 All the nations of
the earth shall bless themselves by your descendants—all because
you obeyed my command.' "

19 Abraham then returned to his servants, and they left together for Beer-sheba. And Abraham stayed in Beer-sheba.

d MT "behind"; see NOTE.
e "Yahweh sees/finds"; cf. vs. 8.
f Last two words *yhwh yr'h* in Heb. text; see NOTE.
g–g Not here in MT.

NOTES

xxii 1. *God put Abraham to the test.* Heb. is inverted for emphasis, and
the effect is heightened by the definite article with Elohim. The idea is
thus conveyed that this was no ordinary procedure, but that God had a
particularly important objective in mind. But the precise shading is
difficult to determine. It might be that God chose to do so, or that it was
an exceptional test.

Ready. Literally "here I am," a courteous response to a call, which
should not be stereotyped in translation. Here the effect is that of our
"Sir?" or "At your service, at once," much the same as the actual
"Ready" of Arabic; cf. especially xxvii 1. In vs. 7 we obviously need
something like "Yes?" (cf. also xxvii 18). In vs. 11, on the other hand,
"Here I am" is not out of place.

2. *beloved.* Heb. uses a term that is not the regular adjective for "one," but a noun meaning "the unique one, one and only." Isaac, of course, was not an only son (xxi 11). The correct rendering is already found in LXX, and the meaning is reinforced in Heb. by the phrase that immediately follows.

land of Moriah. LXX gives "lofty," the same translation as for Moreh in xii 6; Syr. "of the Amorites"; other versions operate with *mr'h* "sight, vision"; elsewhere only in II Chron iii 1, referring to Temple Hill, cf. vs. 14 below.

3. *started out for.* Literally "rose and went to"; when so construed with another verb, Heb. presents a hendiadys in which *q-m* indicates the start or speed of action; cf. xxxi 21.

4. *sighted.* Literally "lifted up his eyes and saw"; for this function of the verb *nś'*, cf. NOTE on xxi 16.

5. *worship.* Literally "bow low."

6. *firestone.* Heb. "fire," but the flame would scarcely have been kept going throughout the long journey. What is evidently meant here is equipment for producing fire, other than the wood itself, which is separately specified: Akk. uses analogously *(aban) išāti* "fire (stone)."

cleaver. The pertinent Heb. noun (see also Judg xix 29 and Prov xxx 14) is used expressly for butcher knives.

together. Same Heb. term as in vs. 8, with singular possessive suffix in adverbial use. Here the point is that Abraham and Isaac left the servants behind; there the picture is that of two persons walking together in oppressive silence.

7. *broke the silence and said.* Literally "said . . . and said."

8. *will see to.* Literally "will see for himself," in anticipation of the place name *Yahweh-yireh* "Yahweh will see," vs. 14.

my son. Also in vs. 7, both times as a mark of great tenderness.

9–10. For the somnambulistic effect of these successive steps described in staccato sentences, see the sensitive comment by von Rad.

12. *how dedicated you are to God.* Literally "that you fear God, that you are a God-fearing man." But the manifest stress is not so much on fear, or even awe, as on absolute dedication.

13. *his eye fell upon a ram.* Text literally "he saw, and behold, a ram after," which is syntactically no better in Heb. than in word-for-word translation; nor would the ungrammatical "behind him/after" suit the context. Not only the ancient versions but many Heb. manuscripts read *'ḥd* for *'ḥr* (for the common misreading of Heb. letters *R/D,* cf. x 4), which makes immediate sense.

14. This parenthetical notice embodies two separate allusions. One, *Yahweh yir'ê,* points back to *Elohim yir'ê* in vs. 8; the other is connected with Temple Hill in Jerusalem. As now vocalized, the verb in the

descriptive clause is pointed as a passive, i.e., *yērā'ê* "(Yahweh) is seen, appears," which accords with Mount Moriah, but obscures the allusion to vs. 8. If we repoint the verb to *yir'ê*, the balance will shift the other way. The translation given above is intentionally neutral.

17. The phrase "shall take over [or 'possess'] the gates of their enemies" (see also xxiv 60) refers to capture of the opponent's administrative and military centers. Analogously, in Akkadian omen literature, favorable signs promise the conquest of enemy territory, while unfavorable signs indicate surrender to the enemy.

18. *all because.* Literally "on the heels, in consequence of."

COMMENT

The episode before us embodies what is perhaps the profoundest personal experience in all the recorded history of the patriarchs; and the telling of it soars to comparable literary heights. The very essence of the biblical process itself is laid bare here through the medium of a fearful test which Abraham had to face and surmount.

Isaac was to Abraham more than a child of his old age, so fervently hoped for yet so long denied. Isaac was also, and more particularly, the only link with the far-off goal to which Abraham's life was dedicated (see xxi 12). To sacrifice Isaac, as God demanded, was to forego at the same time the long-range objective itself. The nightmare physical trial entrains thus a boundless spiritual ordeal.

The reader's anxiety, to be sure, is allayed at the very outset by the underscored notice (see NOTE on vs. 1) that this is to be only a test, however heroic the scale and the stakes. The suspense is thus shifted from viewers to actors, yet the transfer does little to relieve the tension. There is no way of assuring the father that he need have no fear about the final result; one can only suffer with him in helpless silence.

Each successive moment in that seemingly interminable interval of time is charged with drama that is all the more intense for not being spelled out: the saddling of the pack animal; the unarticulated orders to the servants; the splitting of the wood for the sacrificial fire; the long, wordless trip to the spot from which the chosen site can first be seen; the forced matter-of-factness of Abraham's parting instructions to the attendants. As father and son go off by themselves on the last stage of that melancholy pilgrimage—the boy burdened with the wood for his own sacrificial pyre, and the father fidgeting with the flint and the cleaver—the unwary victim asks but a single question. The father's answer is tender but evasive, and the boy must by now have sensed the truth. The short and simple sentence, "And the two of them walked on together" (8), covers what is perhaps the most poignant and eloquent silence in all literature.

At the appointed site, Abraham goes about his task with abnormal attention to each detail (von Rad), with the speechless concentration of a sleepwalker, as if thus to hold off by every possible means the fate that he has no hope of averting. He constructs the offering stand, arranges the wood, straps the boy, lays him on the altar on top of the wood. The blade is in midair when his hand is stayed by a voice from heaven. A scapegoat is providentially at hand. The harrowing test is over.

What is the meaning of this shattering ordeal? In this infinitely sensitive account the author has left so much unsaid that there is now the danger of one's reading into it too much—or too little. Certainly, the object of the story had to be something other than a protest against human sacrifice in general, or child sacrifice in particular—an explanation that is often advanced. To be sure, the practice is traced to Israel's neighbors (II Kings iii 27, xvii 31), and even to Judah (II Kings xvi 3, xxi 6, xxiii 10; cf. Jer vii 31, xix 5; Isa lvii 5; Ezek xvi 20 f., xxiii 37). It was not unknown in Mesopotamia, as is apparent from the so-called Royal Tombs at Ur, and attested by the murder of substitute kings (H. Frankfort, *Kingship and the Gods,* 1948, p. 264). Yet here the subject comes up indirectly, as something not normally expected, and all the more terrifying because demanded by God himself. More important, the sacrifice is characterized at the outset as unreal, a gruesome mandate to be canceled at the proper time. If the author had intended to expose a barbaric custom, he would surely have gone about it in a different way.

Was it, then, the aim of the story to extol obedience to God as a general principle? Abraham had already proved himself on that count by heeding the call to leave Mesopotamia and make a fresh start in an unknown land (xii 1 ff.). The meaning of the present narrative, therefore, would have to be something more specific. And we can hardly go too far afield if we seek the significance of Abraham's supreme trial in the very quest on which he was embarked. The involvement of Isaac tends to bear this out, since the sole heir to the spiritual heritage concerned cannot but focus attention on the future. The process that Abraham set in motion was not to be accomplished in a single generation. It sprang from a vision that would have to be tested and validated over an incalculable span of time, a vision that could be pursued only with singlemindedness of purpose and absolute faith—an ideal that could not be perpetuated unless one was ready to die for it, or had the strength to see it snuffed out. The object of the ordeal, then, was to discover how firm was the patriarch's faith in the ultimate divine purpose. It was one thing to start out resolutely for the Promised Land, but it was a very different thing to maintain confidence in the promise when all appeared lost. The fact is that short of such unswerving faith, the biblical process could not have survived the many trials that lay ahead.

It is ironic that the writer who distilled this unique affirmation in so unforgettable a manner should himself be more difficult to ascertain than virtually all critics have assumed. The narrative is attributed to *E* with scarcely a dissenting voice, and with only a few minor reservations. Nor can the consensus be held at fault, in view of the repeated mention of Elohim (1, 3, 8, 9, 12) and the seemingly theological tenor of the narrative. Yet Yahweh is also mentioned further down, vss. 11, 15, 16; and if the last two occurrences are credited to *R*(edactor), the same is not the case with the two aetiological references to Yahweh in vs. 14. Furthermore, the style of the narrative is far more appropriate to *J* than to *E,* and the ability to paint a vivid scene in depth, without spelling things out for the reader, is elsewhere typical of *J.* What this amounts to, therefore, is that, on external grounds, *J* was either appended to *E,* or *E* was superimposed upon *J.* There was admittedly some fusion in any case (cf. the perplexed comment by Noth, *Überlieferungsgeschichte* . . . , 38, n. 132). On internal evidence, however, based on style and content, the personality behind the story should be *J*'s. Since the crystallized version was such as to be cited and copied more often than most accounts, it is possible that a hand which had nothing to do with *E* (conceivably even from the *P* school) miswrote Elohim for Yahweh in the few instances involved, sometime in the long course of written transmission. The issue is thus not a closed one by any means. But no such documentary perplexities can disturb the total impact of this unique narrative.

29. THE LINE OF NAHOR
(xxii 20–24: *J*)

XXII ²⁰ Some time later, word reached Abraham, as follows, "Milcah too has borne children—to your brother Nahor: ²¹ Uz his first-born, his brother Buz, and Kemuel (the father of Aram); ²² also Chesed, Hazo, Pildash, Jidlaph, and Bethuel"— ²³ Bethuel being the father of Rebekah. These eight Milcah bore to Nahor, Abraham's brother. ²⁴ And his concubine, whose name was Reumah, also bore children: Tebah, Gaham, Tahash, and Maacah.

NOTES

xxii 20–24. The list contains names of Aramaean tribes traced to Nahor. The total number is twelve, precisely as with Ishmael (xxv 13 ff.) and Jacob. There are obvious parenthetic notices in 21 f., dealing with the next generation.

20. *Milcah too.* Referring apparently to xxi 2 f., where the birth of Isaac was recorded.

21 f. Uz, Buz, and Hazo are attested in later books as settled to the north of Edom. According to x 22 (*P*), Aram was a son of Shem. In view, however, of the wide diffusion of Aramaean elements, such divergencies in the extant traditions are readily understandable. Chesed is probably the eponymous ancestor of the Chaldeans (Heb. *Kaśdīm*), who eventually settled in southern Babylonia.

23. *Bethuel.* A shadowy figure (see NOTES on xxiv 50, xxix 5), but of interest to genealogists as the father of Rebekah.

24. *concubine.* Heb. *pillegeš*. A non-Semitic term, though found in other Semitic languages as well as in Greek and Latin. It was introduced into Heb. evidently in order to relieve the ambiguous *'iššā*, for which see xvi 3, NOTE.

Maacah. The only one of the collateral tribes—descended from a concubine—that can be geographically fixed, namely, to the south of Mount Hermon; cf. Deut iii 14; Josh xiii 11, 13.

30. THE MACHPELAH PURCHASE
(xxiii 1–20: *P/J*)

XXIII ¹ The span^a of Sarah's life came to 127 years. ² Sarah died in Kiriath-arba—now Hebron—in the land of Canaan; and Abraham proceeded to mourn for Sarah and to bewail her.

³ Then Abraham rose from beside his dead and addressed the children of Heth: "⁴ Although I am a resident alien among you, sell me a burial site from your holdings so that I may remove my dead for burial." ⁵ The children of Heth replied to Abraham: "Pray,^b ⁶ hear us, my lord! You are the elect of God amidst us. Bury your dead in the choicest of our burial sites. None of us will deny you a burial ground to bury your dead." ⁷ Thereupon^c Abraham bowed low to the natives, the children of Heth, ⁸ and pleaded with them, saying, "If you really wish to me to remove my dead for burial, you must agree to intercede for me with Ephron son of Zohar, ⁹ that he sell me the cave of Machpelah which he owns, and which is on the edge of his land. Let him sell it to me in your presence, at the full price, for a burial site."

¹⁰ Ephron was on hand with the children of Heth. So Ephron the Hittite replied to Abraham in the hearing of the children of Heth—^dall who sat on the council of that town^d: ¹¹ "But no, my lord, hear me out! I give you that land and the cave that is in it. I make this gift in the presence of my kinsmen. Bury your dead!" ¹² Abraham made a bow before the natives, ¹³ as he addressed Ephron in the hearing of the local people: "If you will please agree with me, I will pay the price of the land. Accept it from me, that I may bury my dead there." ¹⁴ And

---

^a See NOTE below.
^b Reading *lū* for *lō* of MT; see NOTE.
^c Literally "He rose and."
^{d–d} Literally "all who came in at the gate of his city"; see NOTE.

Ephron replied to Abraham, saying "Pray,ᵇ ¹⁵ hear me, my lord!
The land will be four hundred shekels of silver—what is that between you and me? Then you can bury your dead." ¹⁶ Abraham
complied with Ephron's request, and so Abraham weighed out
to Ephron the silver that he spoke of in the hearing of the children of Heth—four hundred shekels of silver at the current merchants' rate.

¹⁷ Thus Ephron's land in Machpelah, facing on Mamre—the
field with its cave and all trees anywhere within the limits of
that field—was made over ¹⁸ to Abraham as his property, in the
presence of the children of Heth—all who sat on the council of
that town. ¹⁹ Abraham then buried his wife Sarah in the cave of
the field of Machpelah, facing on Mamre—now Hebron—in the
land of Canaan. ²⁰ And so the field with its cave passed from
the children of Heth to Abraham, as a burial site.

Notes

xxiii 1. *The span.* Literally "years," for which cf. xlvii 28; omitted in
MT at this point, but included in the phrase "the years of Sarah's life" at
the end of the verse. The latter clause is missing in LXX and Vulg.; it
was evidently dislocated in the received text from the beginning of the
verse.

2. *Kiriath-arba.* Literally "City of Four" (*"the* four" in xxxv 27;
Neh xi 25), remembered as the older name for Hebron (cf. Josh xiv
15; Judg i 10, and COMMENT on vs. 19, below). Some passages (Josh
xv 13, xxi 11) take the second element as a personal name, i.e., Arba,
father of the giants. Not improbably, "four" was merely a popular
adaptation of another name, perhaps non-Semitic, which is exactly
what happened with the celebrated Mesopotamian city of Arbilum
(older Urbilum), incorrectly etymologized as "four gods." In other
words, the possibility of non-Semitic origin of the name cannot be discounted, and this could have some connection with the tradition about
the "children of Heth."

mourn . . . bewail. A reference to formal rites, which has no bearing,
one way or another, on the survivor's personal feelings; just so, a Nuzi
adoption document (JEN, No. 59, lines 19–23) provides that "when A
dies, B shall weep for him and bury him."

3. *children of Heth.* The Heb. compound has been reproduced literally

in this chapter so as not to imply identification with the historical Hittites of the north; here the terminology would seem to come closer to the usage of x 15. Verse 10, however, employs the gentilic form which had to be translated accordingly.

4. *resident alien.* In Heb. a hendiadys construction, literally "sojourner and settler," i.e., a settled sojourner, long-term resident, but one lacking the normal privileges of a citizen (cf. xii 10, xix 9), notably, the right to own land. The concession that Abraham seeks, following the death of Sarah, is to acquire enough land for a burial site.

sell. One of the meanings of the verb *ntn,* basically "to give"; see especially vss. 9, 11.

from your holdings. Literally "with you," but the preposition *'im* has here the technical sense of "under one's authority," for which cf. xxxi 38, Lev xxv 35 ff.

5. *Pray.* Here and in vs. 14 the text (cons. *lw*) is pointed as *lō* "to him," and construed with the preceding "saying/as follows"; but such a construction would be unidiomatic; the only partial analogue is found in Lev xi 1, as against hundreds of instances without a pronoun. The letters stand, no doubt, for the precative particle *lū* "would that," for which cf. xvii 18, xxx 34; here a mark of exaggerated politeness, approximately "but please!" Misinterpretation of the text led to wrong verse division both here and in 14.

6. *elect of God.* Generally translated "prince of God," or "mighty prince." The term *nāśī'* (cf. xvii 20, NOTE) designates an official who has been "elevated" in or by the assembly, hence "elected" (see CBQ 25 [1963], 111–17); here an honorific epithet.

7. *Thereupon.* Literally "he arose," with auxiliary use of the verb "to rise"; cf. xxii 3. It is unlikely that the clause describes rising and bowing at the same time, especially since the petitioner was evidently standing all the time.

8. *you must agree.* One of the common uses of the verb *šm'* "to hear"; cf. vs. 16 ("complied with . . . request").

intercede . . . with. With the nuance of "put pressure on, use influence with."

9. *Machpelah.* Not just the name of the cave, but of the district; cf. vss. 17, 19.

in your presence. So rather than "in your midst, territory," in view of the word order in Heb.

10. *on hand.* Not "sitting, seated," but "present," a common secondary meaning of the verb (*yšb*); cf. especially Deut vi 7; this usage is particularly prominent in Akkadian.

who sat on the council of that town (also vs. 18). Literally "who came in at the gate of his city"; for the analogous idiom with "went out," cf.

xxxiv 24, (*bis*). See the full discussion in BASOR 144 (1956), 20 ff., and for a dissenting view note BASOR 150 (1958), 28 ff.

12. *the natives*. Also vs. 7, and vs. 13, in the latter instance translated "the local people" for stylistic reasons. Literally "the people of the land," here juxtaposed to the resident alien.

14. Sales of whole villages are attested for the patriarchal age in northern Syria; cf. Wiseman, *The Alalakh Tablets*, Nos. 52 ff. Prices ranged from 100 shekels to upward of 1000 shekels, depending on the size of the territory and the services and income involved; the weight of the shekel varied, of course, from one center to another, even during the same period. Nevertheless, 400 shekels for a piece of land containing a cave would seem to be excessive in any circumstances. Omri paid 6000 shekels for the entire site of Samaria (I Kings xvi 24; see von Rad); and Jeremiah gave only 17 shekels for land that was probably no less spacious than the field of Machpelah (Jer xxxii 9). At any rate, the sum here exacted appears to have been abnormally high, yet Abraham was in no position to demur.

15. *Then you can bury your dead*. Note that the word order of Heb. differs significantly from that of vs. 11, although the same words are employed.

16. *at the current merchants' rate*. Literally "that passes to the merchant." That this is an old technical phrase is proved by the parallel Akk. *maḫīrat illaku* "the rate that is current," which is common in Old Babylonian and is used officially as early as the Eshnunna Laws (par. 41; cf. A. Goetze, AASOR 31 [1936], 111 f.). This means that the goods which were offered in payment were computed in terms of silver at the fixed rate that was current at the time. The parallel just cited, together with the idiom discussed in the Note on vs. 10, points up the antiquity of the background of the account before us. The circumstance is suggestive, though not decisive.

17–18. The specifications read as though they followed closely the language of sale transactions. Moreover, the deal was duly witnessed by all the representative members of the community. In short, no effort was spared to make the sale strictly legal and incontestable.

COMMENT

The subject matter of this chapter came to be viewed in retrospect as a very significant milestone in Israel's remote past. The Promised Land was a spiritual grant from God. But the best practical safeguard in terms that everybody could recognize and accept was a clear legal title to the land. The living could get by as sojourners;

but the dead required a permanent resting ground. The Founding Fathers, at least, must not be buried on alien soil. The spot had to be theirs beyond any possibility of dispute.

Abraham's wife was the first member of the patriarch's immediate family to be laid to rest; hence the extraordinary emphasis on the Machpelah purchase with all its legal minutiae. Later on, Sarah was to be joined by Abraham himself (xxv 9), Isaac (xxxv 29), Rebekah and Leah (xlix 31), and lastly by Jacob (l 13). Small wonder, therefore, that tradition had to insist on a title which no law-abiding society would dare to contest and upset.

The first thing was to find a landowner who could be induced to sell to a stranger. There is more to the contrast between "resident alien" (4) and "natives" (7, 12) or "the local people" (13) than appears on the surface. The former evidently lacked the citizen's right to acquire holdings in a routine business transaction. Such a deal required approval by the community council (10), which in turn had to use its influence (*pg'*) with the owner of the property in question. Abraham's bereavement, and the high regard in which he was held by the local population (6), predisposed the citizenry in his favor, but the individual owner was yet to be won over. Ephron knew the score all too well. He felt safe in his pretense that he preferred to present the land to Abraham as a gift. But a gift was the last thing that would answer Abraham's need. He insisted on a formal sale, to which Ephron eventually agreed— at an exorbitant price. Abraham promptly paid the sum as demanded "in the hearing of the children of Heth," at the full exchange rate (of goods for silver), and so the property was officially transferred (*wayyāqom:* 17) to Abraham, at long last, "in the presence of the children of Heth" (18).

In these exceptional circumstances, there is the inherent possibility that "the children of Heth" became a party to the transaction by design rather than by coincidence. For reasons of both history and geography, it is most unlikely that this group name has any direct connection either with the Hattians of Anatolia or with their "Hittite" successors. Much more plausible is some kind of association with the eponymous Heth of x 15. In that case, the people in question belonged to the non-Semitic strain of pre-Israelite Palestine. The assumption gains a measure of support from the pertinent place name Kiriath-arba (which may be non-Semitic; cf. NOTE on vs. 2), later changed to Hebron. The change of names would thus have coincided with a change in ethnic composition. Furthermore, according to Ezek xvi 3, 45, the ethnic background of not too distant Jerusalem was part Amorite and part "Hittite," the Hittites in that reference being the same as Jebusites. On this compound evidence, the present "children of Heth" should also be Jebusites or an element closely related to them: not only non-Canaanite but non-Semitic as well. Would this circumstance help explain the success of Abraham's effort to acquire a parcel of land? In other words, would non-Semitic elements in the settled population of the country be more readily disposed to sell land to outsiders than was the case with Canaanites (cf. also xxxiv)? The fact is that the narrative lays constant stress on the term "children of Heth" (3, 5, 7, 10, 18, 19). It is a working hypothesis, of course; but it appears to work, as far as it goes.

The subject matter of this narrative was bound to loom large in the national tradition of Israel. But when was the account composed, and by whom? What we have before us is certainly not homogeneous. The introductory notice about Sarah's life-span is unmistakably from P. As a whole, however, the story betrays a different hand. With a few deft strokes, the author makes us aware not only of the solemnity of the occasion and the high stakes involved, but also of the humorous aspects of the situation. All of this points strongly to J, and this circumstantial identification is strengthened by a significant idiomatic detail. The technical phrase those "who came in at the gate of his city" (10, 18) has its analogue in the idiom "all who went out of the gate of his city," which is used twice in xxxiv 24 to describe the fighting men of the community; and that narrative is commonly attributed to J, with no sign, moreover, of any interference from P. By the same token of authentic technical usage, however, both passages—this one and the account in xxxiv—prove to go back in substance to earlier traditions. The antiquity, or at least the technical accuracy, of the present account is vouched for independently by the reference to "the current merchants' rate" (16), which can be traced to Old Babylonian legal documents and the Eshnunna Laws (see Note *ad loc.*). What the author did, then, was not to make up a story but retell it in his own inimitable way.

31. ISAAC AND REBEKAH
(xxiv 1–67: *J*)

XXIV 1 Abraham was now old, advanced in years; and Yahweh had blessed Abraham in everything.

2 Abraham said to the senior servant of his household, who had charge of all his possessions, "Place your hand under my thigh, 3 and I will make you swear by Yahweh, God of heaven and God of the earth, that you will not obtain a wife for my son from the daughters of the Canaanites among whom I dwell, 4 but will go to the land of my birth to get a wife for my son Isaac." 5 The servant said to him, "What if the woman refuses to follow me to this land? Should I then take your son back to the land from which you came?" 6 But Abraham told him, "On no account are you to take my son back there! 7 Yahweh God of heaven,*a* who took me from the home of my father and the land of my birth, and who solemnly*b* promised me, saying, 'I will give this land to your offspring'—he will send his angel before you that you may bring my son a wife from there. 8 Should the woman still refuse to follow you, you shall then be absolved of this oath to me; but you must not take my son back there!" 9 So the servant placed his hand under the thigh of his master Abraham and swore to him concerning this matter.

10 The servant took ten of his master's camels and, armed with all kinds of gifts from his master, made his way to the city of Nahor in Aram-naharaim. 11 He made the camels kneel by a well outside the city, it being close to evening, the time when the women come out to draw water. 12 And he said, "O Yah-

---

a LXX adds "and the God of the earth"; see vs. 3.
b Literally "swore to me."

weh, God of my master Abraham, grant me a propitious sign
this day and deal thus graciously with my master Abraham! 13 As
I stand by the spring while the daughters of the townsmen come
out to draw water, 14 let the girl to whom I say, 'Please lower
your jug that I may drink,' and who answers, 'Drink, and I will
also give water to your camels!'—let her be the one you have
decreed for your servant Isaac, and by her shall I know that you
have dealt graciously with my master."

15 He had scarcely finished speaking when Rebekah, who was
born to Bethuel son of Milcah, the wife of Abraham's brother
Nahor, came out, a jug on her shoulder. 16 Now the girl was very
beautiful, a virgin untouched by man. She went down to the
spring, filled her jug, and returned. 17 The servant ran toward
her and said, "Please let me have a little sip of water from your
jug." 18 "Drink, sir," she replied and, quickly lowering the jug
onto her hand, let him drink. 19 When she had let him drink his
fill, she said, "I will draw for your camels, too, until they have
drunk their fill." 20 With that, she quickly emptied her jug into
the trough, and ran back to the well to draw anew, until she
had drawn for all the camels. 21 All the while the man stood
gaping at her, not daring to speak until he learned whether Yahweh had made his errand successful or not.

22 When the camels had finished drinking, the man took out
a gold ring weighing half a shekel, ᶜwhich he put on her nose,ᶜ
and two gold bands weighing ten shekels, for her arms. 23 "Tell
me, please," he asked, "whose daughter are you? And is there
room in your father's house for us to spend the night?" 24 She
answered, "I am the daughter of Bethuel son of Milcah, whom
she bore to Nahor. 25 And there is," she went on, "plenty of
straw and feed in our house, and also lodging for the night."
26 Thereupon the man bowed in homage to Yahweh. 27 Said he,
"Praised be Yahweh, the God of my master Abraham, who has
never withheld his steadfast kindness from my master. Yahweh
has led me straight to the house of my master's brotherᵈ!"

28 The girl went at a run to spread the news in her mother's

ᶜ⁻ᶜ So with Sam. and vs. 47; omitted in MT.
ᵈ So with most ancient versions; plural in MT.

house. 29 Now Rebekah had a brother whose name was Laban. Laban rushed outside to the man at the spring. 30 Having noticed the nose-ring, and the bands on his sister's arms, and having heard his sister say, "Thus and so did the man speak to me," Laban went to the man, who was still standing beside the camels at the spring. 31 Said he, "Come, O blessed of Yahweh! Why do you remain outside, when I have readied the house and a place for the camels?" 32 So the man went inside. The camels were unloaded; straw and fodder were given to the camels. Then water was brought to bathe his feet and the feet of the men who were with him. 33 But when food was set before him, he said, "I will not eat until I have told my tale." "Do so," they told him.

34 "I am Abraham's servant," he began. 35 "Yahweh has richly blessed my master, who has prospered: he has given him sheep and cattle, male and female slaves, camels and asses. 36 My master's wife Sarah bore my master a son after reaching old age; and he has given him everything he owns. 37 Then my master put me under oath, as follows: 'You shall not obtain a wife for my son from among the daughters of the Canaanites in whose land I dwell; 38 instead, you shall go to my father's family, to my own kindred, to get a wife for my son.' 39 I said to my master, 'What if the woman refuses to follow me?' 40 He replied to me, 'Yahweh, in whose ways I have walked, will send his angel with you and make your errand successful, that you may get for my son a wife from my own kindred, my father's family. 41 Thus only shall you be released from my ban: if you come to my kindred, and they refuse—only then shall you be released from my ban.'

42 "When I came today to the spring, I said, 'O Yahweh, God of my master Abraham, if you would really lend success to the errand on which I am engaged! 43 As I stand here by this spring, let the young woman who comes out to draw water, to whom I say, "Please give me a little water from your jug," 44 and who answers, "Not only may you drink, but I will also water your camels"—let that one be the woman whom Yahweh has decreed for my master's son.'

45 "I had scarcely finished saying this in my mind, when out came Rebekah, a jug on her shoulder. When she had been down to the spring to draw, I said to her, 'Please let me have a drink!' 46 She quickly lowered the jug she was carrying, and said, 'Drink, and I will also water your camels.' I drank, and she watered the camels also. 47 I inquired of her, 'Whose daughter are you?' She answered, 'The daughter of Bethuel son of Nahor, whom Milcah bore to him.' I then put the ring on her nose and the bands on her arms. 48 And I bowed in homage to Yahweh, and praised Yahweh, the God of my master Abraham, who had led me by the direct path to obtain the daughter of my master's kinsman for his son. 49 Now then, if you mean to treat my master with true loyalty, tell me; and if not, tell me, that I may *proceed this way or that."*

50 Laban ʹand Bethuelʹ spoke up in reply, "This matter stems from Yahweh: we can neither disapprove nor approve. 51 Rebekah is at your call; take her with you, and let her be a wife to your master's son, as Yahweh has spoken."

52 When Abraham's servant heard their decision, he bowed to the ground before Yahweh. 53 Then the servant brought out objects of silver and gold, and articles of clothing, and presented them to Rebekah; and he gave presents to her brother and her mother. 54 Then he and the men who were with him ate and drank, and they passed the night.

As soon as they were up next morning, he said, "Give me leave to return to my master." 55 Her brother and her mother answered, "Let the girl remain with us ten days or so; then you may leave." 56 But he said to them, "Do not detain me, now that Yahweh has lent success to my errand. Give me leave to return to my master." 57 They replied, "Let us call the girl and ask her own mind." 58 So they called Rebekah and said to her, "Will you go with this man?" She replied, "I will." 59 So they said good-by to their sister Rebekah and her nurse, along with Abraham's servant and his men. 60 And they blessed Rebekah and said to her,

e–e Literally "turn right or left."
f–f Probably intrusive.

"Our sister, may you grow
Into thousands of myriads!
And may your offspring take over
The gates of their enemies."

61 Thereupon⁹ Rebekah and her maids mounted the camels and followed the man. Thus the slave got Rebekah and departed.

62 Isaac, meanwhile, had come back from the vicinityʰ of Beer-lahai-roi, having settled in the region of the Negeb. 63 While Isaac was out walkingⁱ in the fields toward evening, he saw there camels approaching. 64 When Rebekah noticed Isaac, she alighted from her camel 65 and asked the servant, "Who is that man out there in the field walking toward us?" "That is my master," replied the servant. So she took her veil and covered herself.

66 The servant recounted to Isaac all the things he had done. 67 Then Isaac took her into his tent.ʲ He married Rebekah and she became his wife. And in his love for her, Isaac found solace after the death of his mother.

⁹ See xxiii 7, NOTE.
ʰ See NOTE.
ⁱ MT obscure.
ʲ Text adds "his mother Sarah"; see NOTE.

NOTES

xxiv 1. *the senior servant of his household.* Cf. xv 2 for reference to a trusted retainer. But the name Eliezer is never used in the present narrative; nor is it certain that the same domestic was involved both times.

2. *Place your hand under my thigh.* The symbolism of this act is not clear. At any rate, the pledge thus elicited was evidently a most solemn one, for it carried with it a curse or ban (Heb. *'ālā*) in the event of non-compliance. Since sons are said to issue from their father's thigh (xlvi 26; Exod i 5), an oath that involved touching this vital part might entail the threat of sterility for the offender or the extinction of his offspring. The only other instance of the same usage in the Bible, xlvii 29, is linked, like the present, to a man's last request—always a solemn occasion; cf. JBL 74 (1955), 252 ff.

3. *I will make you swear.* This is later summarized as an "oath to me" (vs. 8). In the servant's retelling, however, it becomes "my ban," i.e., a curse (41). In other words, it was more than just a solemn assurance, which is the sense in which the same stem is used in vs. 7. Rather, it was a formal adjuration which carried sanctions against the delinquent party. Abraham chooses the term tactfully; the servant rephrases it realistically; and the author subtly varies the emphasis.

obtain a wife. Not simply "take," but acquire. The father or his representative (in Ishmael's case, the mother, cf. xxi 21) had to pay the bride price, whether the amount was specified or not; see also xxix 20, 27.

6. *On no account.* Literally "beware lest."

7. *home of my father.* Heb. *bẹ̄t 'āb*, which may here be translated literally. Elsewhere, however, (notably so in 38, 40) the phrase often describes a consanguineous unit which may vary in size from immediate family to large tribes (cf., for example, Num vii 2).

10. *ten . . . camels.* The figure may be a round one, in the sense of our "a number," cf. vs. 55, and xxxi 7, 41. Similarly "five" may stand for "several," cf. xliii 34. As regards camels, cf. NOTE on xii 16. In the present narrative, however, these animals are mentioned exclusively; cf. also 61. The writer could, of course, be guilty of an anachronism, or he may have chosen the camel as a symbol of Abraham's great wealth—if widespread use of these animals was still some centuries away. Note, however, the occurrence in an Old Babylonian text from Alalakh, in Wiseman, *The Alalakh Tablets*, plate 32, line 62, and cf. A. Goetze, JCS 13 (1959), 37.

armed with . . . gifts. Literally "with . . . gifts in his hand," a circumstantial clause. The term translated "gifts" means literally "goods, wealth, luxuries," or the like.

made his way. Literally "rose and went," but the latter verb can be terminative, which it obviously is in this instance.

city of Nahor. Is it the place in which Nahor had lived, or the place name Nahor in the district of Haran? For the city *Naḫur,* see xi 22, NOTE.

Aram-naharaim. Central Mesopotamia, originally the area within the great bend of the Euphrates; see J. J. Finkelstein, "Mesopotamia," JNES 21 (1962), 73 ff.

12. *grant me a propitious sign.* That is, bring about an omen/occurrence (cf. Num xxiii 15) in my favor (see xvii 18); for the whole phrase, cf. xxvii 20.

deal thus graciously. For Heb. *ḥesed* see below, vs. 27.

16. *untouched by man.* Heb. "no man had known her," same idiom as at iv 1.

17. *sip.* A different stem from "to drink," and "to water" which are regularly used elsewhere in this narrative; the variation is highly effective.

18. *sir.* Same term as "my lord" in xviii (cf. NOTE on vs. 3); the present context calls for something not quite so formal.

19. *let him drink his fill.* Literally "finished letting him drink"; cf. also xix 32, NOTE.

21. For the initial phrase ("stood gaping") Heb. uses a special stem which describes something continuous or repeated (hence "all the while"); see v 22, NOTE.

not daring to speak. In Heb., the participle of the verbal form meaning "to be stark still" (see JCS 6 [1952], 81 ff.). This can be construed with the preceding (stood gazing in silence), as is generally done. Yet the syntax of Heb. points to what follows, and this is also favored by the context: he waited with bated breath.

made his errand successful. Literally "caused his way/mission to prosper." See also vss. 40, 42, 56.

22. After "took out a gold (nose-) ring," MT must have had originally "and put it on her nose," the same verb also governing the sequel, literally "the two bands on her hands/arms." The additional clause is found in Sam., and MT gives it in the parallel passage, vs. 47; here it must have dropped out accidentally.

25. *in our house.* Literally "with us."

27. *steadfast kindness.* In this frequently used hendiadys, the first noun, *ḥesed* (cf. vs. 12), stands for "kindness, grace, loyalty," and the other noun (*'emet*) is "firmness, permanence, truth." The combined phrase describes thus true or steadfast kindness, grace, loyalty. The traditional "steadfast grace and truth" would thus be redundant as a translation of the Heb. aside from ignoring the idiomatic construction.

Yahweh has led me straight. Literally "As for me, Yahweh has led me on the road (to)"; cf. the parallel "by the direct path" (i.e., "firm, true"; see preceding NOTE) in vs. 48.

brother. The text is vocalized as plural, against the singular in most of the versions. In the parallel passage, vs. 48, Heb. gives the singular, "my master's kinsman" in that instance being Bethuel, that is "a close kin," rather than brother in the literal sense. Here, however, the text speaks of the "house," that is, the family (see "home," vs. 7), which might apply to Nahor. In any case, the pointing of the MT is erroneous, and probably intended to make sure that Laban would not be mistaken for Abraham's brother.

28. *the news.* Literally "all such things."

in her mother's house. This phrase can only mean that Bethuel was no longer alive; hence the immediate reference to Rebekah's brother

(29), whose authority in such circumstances would be an overriding factor in any Hurrian or Hurrianized society; note the order "her brother and her mother" in 53, 55, and even "Laban and Bethuel" in 50, where the second personal name is certainly intrusive for that very reason.

29. Many moderns would move the second part of the verse to vs. 30, after "the man." But the transposition is not supported by the versions and is by no means self-evident from the context, once it is realized that all of vs. 30 is the author's own aside about Laban's character.

32. *So the man went inside.* Vulg. construes Heb. *wyb'* as a causative (which requires no more than changing the final vowel); this would make Laban the subject ("he brought the man inside") throughout the verse. The received text, however, is preferable, with the remaining verbs construed impersonally, as is often the case in Heb. when the verb is used without an explicit subject. Note that at the beginning of vs. 33, while the Kethib has an active form of the verb, the Qere reads the passive.

33. *they told him.* Impersonal, or "[Laban] told him."

34–38. Here the servant restates everything that has happened, repeating much of the preceding narrative, often word for word. Such "epic particularity" is a common practice in ancient literary compositions. It is found, for instance, in *Enūma-eliš,* in successive descriptions of Tiamat's conduct; and it is used similarly in the Gilgamesh Epic, at various stages of the hero's journey to Utnapishtim. Our author, however, employs the device constructively, by introducing a few minor changes which add, nevertheless, very notably to the characterization and general content. Thus in vs. 41, the servant speaks of Abraham's ban or curse, whereas Abraham himself referred only to an oath (8). Similarly, when the speaker addresses Rebekah's family, he alludes to Rebekah as *'almā* "young woman" (43); but in his own mind he used the less distinctive term *na'ªrā* "girl" (14). Nor does the servant mention Abraham's categorical injunction not to take Isaac to Mesopotamia under any circumstances (8), since that would not have been a tactful thing to tell his hosts.

37. *put me under oath.* Not "made me swear," for the words that follow relate to Abraham and not his servant.

49. *true loyalty.* The same Heb. phrase was rendered as "steadfast kindness" in vs. 27; here, however, it is applied to men and not Yahweh.

that I may proceed this way or that. Heb. "to turn to the right or the left" is obviously an idiom for "to know where one stands."

50. *and Bethuel.* As was pointed out in the NOTE on vs. 28, this cannot be original. The consonants *wbtw'l* could represent an earlier *bn btw'l* "son of Bethuel," less probably *wbytw* "and his family." Better still, we may have here a marginal gloss on the part of some ancient

scribe who did not realize that the father had no place in this narrative.

53. *presents*. Although the same term is used elsewhere (Ezra i 6; II Chron xxi 3, xxxii 23) for "valuable gifts," it should have here the technical sense of *mohar* "bride price."

55 *ten days or so*. Literally "days or ten." If correctly transmitted, this is the kind of idiom that makes no sense whatever when it is slavishly reproduced. For the number, see NOTE on vs. 10.

57. *her own mind*. Literally "her mouth," i.e., let us ask her in person.

58. *I will*. Literally "I will go." On the form of reply in Heb., cf. xviii 15, NOTE.

62. *the vicinity of*. MT cons. *mb'*, for which Sam. and LXX read *bmdbr*, as though Isaac had come "into the desert" of Beer-lahai-roi. In this context (*b' mb' b'r*), the middle word is most likely a dittographic corruption for original *mb'r* (Isaac had arrived from B.). But any such assumption is just as conjectural as the above translation.

63. *walking*. For the obscure *lśwḥ* of MT see COMMENT.

67. *into his tent*. MT gives literally "into the tent, his mother Sarah," which is grammatically unmanageable. The words "his mother Sarah" probably stood originally at the end of the verse and were moved up from there through an old scribal error.

after the death of his mother. Heb. literally "after his mother," with the preposition employed in this technical sense in complete agreement with Akk. *arki*, which is both "after," and "after the death of."

COMMENT

The present narrative provides a restful interlude between the story of Abraham's life, which is just coming to a close, and the history of Jacob that will soon unfold. Isaac, who can scarcely be described as a memorable personality in his own right, is important chiefly as a link in the patriarchal chain. Continuity is essential, but the vitality of the line will now depend on the woman who is to become Jacob's mother. While history would thus seem to be marking time, the narrator, who is *J* throughout this long chapter, uses the lull as a welcome occasion to relate in unhurried detail how Rebekah was found and won.

Against an idyllic background, the story is told in a series of delicately balanced scenes. As is typical of *J*, the principal characters—in this instance the servant, Rebekah, and Laban—are shown in action rather than through description. And while certain particulars are restated in the epic manner (vss. 34–48), the repetition is never mechanical, but subtly varied (see NOTE *ad loc.*). The chapter as a whole, the longest in the book by far, is a self-contained unit and an unsurpassed literary masterpiece of its kind.

Abraham has sensed that his end is near. This is apparent from the symbolism of the oath—the hand is placed between the adjurer's thighs; this gesture is duplicated only in xlvii 29, where the text says explicitly "the time approached for Israel to die." And indeed, Abraham is no longer alive when the servant comes back with Rebekah and refers to Isaac as his master (65); cf. COMMENT on Sec. 32. The statement about Abraham's death in xxv 8 is manifestly from another source (*P*). What Abraham does, therefore, at the beginning of this episode has all the impact and solemnity of a deathbed disposition (cf. xxvii).

Abraham's request contains two main points: (1) Isaac must not take a wife from among the Canaanites, for that would affect the purity of the line through which God's covenant is to be implemented; and (2) he is not to be repatriated to Mesopotamia, for the covenant is bound up with the Promised Land. It is worth stressing that the role which is assigned here to Isaac is strictly a passive one.

The man to whom the patriarch delegates such a serious mission is never identified by name in the present account. In xv 2, where we seem to have a reference to the same person, the name is Eliezer; but that text is not free from doubt. Here the emissary is spoken of either as "the servant" or as "the man." The Heb. term *'ebed* "servant" may designate anybody from a common slave to the king's subject or the servant of Yahweh. Juridically, too, the noun covers considerable variations in status. Its Akk. counterpart *wardum*, primarily "slave," could analogously designate persons who had land holdings of their own and owned slaves in turn. A Nuzi document tells of one such "slave" who makes an "old-age" declaration whereby he appoints five men as executors of his estate (HSS IX [1932], No. 37). It is not surprising, therefore, that Abraham should entrust Isaac's future to such a dependent.

The long trip to the city of Nahor—probably from Hebron—which must have taken at least a month, is not permitted to slow down the pace of the narrative; one instant the caravan is loaded, and the next instant it is at its destination (10). The discriminating reader may be relied upon to fill in such details for himself. Nor is it necessary to explain to him why the messenger, as soon as he is within sight of the place, resorts to an omen for a prognosis of his mission's success; everybody would be expected to understand these things. What the servant is saying in so many words (vs. 12) is, Please Yahweh, grant me a "phenomenon" and make it favorable for the sake of my master Abraham. The actual suspense lies in the gradual unfolding of the complex test.

The personalities of Rebekah and her brother are established with a few deft strokes; the servant himself gains in stature with each phase of the story. The girl is friendly, helpful, generous, eager to share her excitement with members of her household; Laban, on the other hand, is greedy and insincere, the sort of person that the reader will find it easy to resent later on. Rebekah's father Bethuel, however, presents some difficulties in the present context. The genealogical references to him (vss. 15, 24; also xxii 22, 23, and xxv 20—the last one from P) are no problem. In vs. 50, however, the text states that "Laban and Bethuel spoke up in reply." The listing of the father after the son is irregular enough; what is worse, no gifts for the father are mentioned in vs. 53, although the recipients include Rebekah's "brother and mother" as well as the young woman herself; similarly, in vs. 55 it is once again "her brother and her mother" who ask that Rebekah postpone her journey, while nothing is said about the father. Hence there can be little doubt that Bethuel was no longer alive at the time, which is why Laban was free to exercise his prerogatives as brother (cf. COMMENT on Sec. 15). The inclusion of Bethuel in vs. 50 is due either to a marginal gloss inspired by the genealogical references, or to some textual misadventure.

The relative freedom, however, which the author could enjoy in this narrative in drawing on his great literary gifts, does not mean that the detail was invented by and large. If there was ever much doubt on this point, it should be dispelled by what we now know of the Hurrian marriage practices—which were normative in the Haran region—when the brother acted in place of the father. The pertinent marriage contract would them come under the heading of *ţuppi ahātūti* or "sistership document." A composite agreement of this kind would embody the following specifications: (a) The principals in the case. (b) Nature of the transaction. (c) Details of payments. (d) The girl's declaration of concurrence. (e) Penalty clause. A close study of vss. 50 ff. should show that what we have there is virtually a restatement, in suitable literary form, of such a "sistership document." For principals we have this time, on the one hand, Abraham's servant as the spokesman for the father of the groom and, on the other hand, Laban as the responsible representative of the prospective bride. The transaction is thus necessarily of the "sistership" type, since it is the girl's brother who acts on the request. The emissary gives presents to the girl, but does not neglect the "gifts" for her brother and mother, which must cover the customary bride payment. Most significant of all, in view of the detailed evidence from Nuzi, is the statement that Rebekah herself should be consulted (57); her reply is in the affirmative: 'ēlēk "I will go" (58). The Nuzi texts says in similar cases ramāniya u aḫūya "myself and my brother (agree to this marriage)" (HSS V [1929], No. 25, lines 14 f.), or irramāniya "(I do this) of my own free will" (JEN, No. 78, lines 23 f.). The only thing, then, that is missing is the penalty clause, which would surely be out of place in a literary transcript.

The final scene of the narrative (62–67) is obscured by textual and linguistic uncertainties. Abraham had presumably died in the course of the intervening months, and the servant could have heard the news as he was approaching home. If we knew the meaning of the key verb in vs. 63 (Heb. lā-śūᵃḥ), we might have a further clue to Isaac's personality; but the guesses of the ancient versions (to chat, pray, meditate, take a walk) leave too wide a choice, to say nothing of the possibility that none may have hit the mark; and neither usage nor etymology is of much help in this instance. It is clear only that Sarah's death had affected her son deeply (67). Rebekah's arrival soon proved to be a source of solace and support.

32. THE SONS OF KETURAH. DEATH OF ABRAHAM. THE LINE OF ISHMAEL
(xxv 1–6, 11b, 18: *J*ᵃ; 7–11a, 12–17: /P/)

XXV 1 Abraham took another wife, whose name was Keturah, 2 and she bore him Zimran, Jokshan, Medan, Midian, Ishbak, and Shuah. 3 Jokshan begot Shebaᵇ and Dedan. The descendants of Dedan were the Asshurim, the Letushim, and the Leummim. 4 The sons of Midian were Ephah, Epher, Hanoch, Abida, and Eldaah; all these were descendants of Keturah.

5 Abraham deeded to Isaac everything he owned. 6 But to his sons by concubinage he made grants while he was still living, as he sent them eastward, away from his son Isaac, to the country of the East.

/7 This was the total span of Abraham's life: 175 years. 8 When Abraham had breathed his last, dying at a happy ripe age, old and fullᶜ of years, he was gathered to his kin. 9 His sons Isaac and Ishmael buried him in the cave of Machpelah, in the field of Ephron son of Zohar the Hittite, which faces on Mamre, 10 the field which Abraham had bought from the children of Heth. There Abraham was buried along with his wife Sarah. 11 After Abraham's death, God blessed his son Isaac./ Isaac settled near Beer-lahai-roi.

/12 This is the line of Ishmael son of Abraham, whom Hagar the Egyptian, Sarah's slave, bore to Abraham. 13 These are the names of each of Ishmael's sons, in the order of their births: Nebaioth, Ishmael's first-born, Kedar, Adbeel, Mibsam, 14 Mishma, Dumah, Massa, 15 Hadad,ᵈ Teman, Jetur, Naphish,

---

ᵃ See COMMENT.
ᵇ LXX adds "and Teiman."
ᶜ Text "full" alone; "(of) days" in manuscripts, Sam., LXX, Syr.
ᵈ Text doubtful.

and Kedmah. 16 These are the sons of Ishmael, and these are their names by their dwelling places and encampments: twelve chieftains of as many tribal groups. 17 And this was the span of Ishmael's life: 137 years. When he had breathed his last and died, he was gathered to his kin./ 18 They ranged from Havilah-by-Shur, which is close to Egypt, all the way to Asshur; and each made forays against his various kinsmen.

NOTES

xxv 2 ff. On the Arabian elements in general, see J. A. Montgomery, *Arabia and the Bible*, 1934.

2. *Midian*. The best-known name in the list. The Midianites ranged from the head of the Gulf of Aqaba to Moab and even Gilead (cf. Judg vi ff.).

Shuah. Cf. the gentilic "Shuhite," Job ii 11.

3. The second clause, which gives the descendants of Dedan, is omitted in the parallel passage in I Chron i 32. The translation "descendants" instead of "sons" is necessitated here by the plural form of the names. On Dedan see Albright, *Festschrift Albrecht Alt*, pp. 1–12.

4. *Ephah*. Cf. Isa lx 6, and for the verse as a whole, Montgomery, *op. cit.* p. 43.

Hanoch. Same name as that of the patriarch Enoch (iv 17, v 18 ff.).

5. *deeded*. Literally "gave"; but the Heb. verb has various other meanings (cf. NOTE on xxiii 4); the explicit "while he was still living" (for which cf. *ina bulṭišu* "in his lifetime," Code of Hammurabi 170.43, 171.61) in the next verse implies that the "gift" in the present instance was a testamentary grant.

6. *his sons by concubinage*. Literally "the sons that Abraham had by concubines"; but the plural is either a grammatical pleonasm, or an abstract, since only one concubine is mentioned in this context, unless Hagar is included. The above translation (cf. Ehrl.) should suit either interpretation.

away from his son Isaac. Literally "from upon . . . Isaac," i.e., to free Isaac from them.

the country of the East. Apparently used here as a vague geographical concept for "desert lands."

8. *kin*. Same Heb. term as the plural for "people," used in its primary connotation of close relative; in this particular idiom the noun may alternate with "fathers," cf. xv 15.

13. *the names of each.* Literally "the names . . . by their names."

Nebaioth. Cf. xxviii 9, xxxvi 3; Isa lx 7; not to be confused with the Nabataeans, see Montgomery, *op. cit.*, pp. 31, 54.

Kedar. Often mentioned in later times as a prominent tribe; cf. Isa xxi 16 f., xlii 11; Jer ii 10, xlix 28; Ps cxx 5.

14. *Dumah.* Connected with the oasis Dumat al-Ghandal in the Syrian desert.

15. *Teman.* Cf. the celebrated oasis of Teima in northwest Arabia. The name is found in an inscription of Tiglath-pileser III, in association with cun. equivalents of Sheba, Ephah, Adbeel, and possibly also Massa and M/Bedan; see Montgomery, *op. cit.*, pp. 58 f. Nabonidus, the last native king (555–39 B.C.) of Babylonia, used Teima as his residence for a number of years.

Jetur. The same as the later Ituraeans (Dr.).

16. *chieftains.* Cf. xvii 20 and xxiii 6.

18. *Havilah-by-Shur.* Since the name Havilah was shared by several localities (cf. ii 11), further identification was necessary at times to avoid confusion.

Asshur. Hardly "Assyria"; perhaps connected with the tribal name Asshurim in vs. 3.

each made forays against his various kinsmen. This clause has to be interpreted in conjunction with the virtually identical passage in xvi 12: "And in the face of all his kinsmen he shall camp." Here the sentence starts with "They ranged/camped," the same verb as in xvi 12, but this time in the plural, referring to various Bedouin tribes; in the clause before us the verb in *npl*, in the singular, evidently distributive, hence the rendering "each." The primary meaning of the stem is "to fall"; but, all other things being equal, "camp" (dwell in tents) and "fall" cannot be very far apart in their present applications. The clue has to be sought in the recurrent preposition *'al pᵉnē*, in its adversative sense of "in disregard, to the detriment of"; cf. NOTE on xvi 12. For the technical sense of *npl*, cf. also Judg vii 12, where the verb is used absolutely, just as here, in the sense of "to be deployed, arrayed," and applied—significantly enough—to Midianites and Amalekites.

COMMENT

The section is made up of fragments, some of which are typical of *P*, while others are excerpts from narrative sources. The only passage that may be safely attributed to *J* is 11b, in view of Beer-lahairoi, for which see xvi 13 f. and xxiv 62. The list in 2–4 may, however, be compared with the *J* portions in x, and vs. 18, as pointed out in the Note *ad loc.,* links up with xvi 12. Nevertheless, in summary notices of this sort, the documentary analysis is more uncertain than elsewhere, and must so be labeled in the present instance.

In any event, the passage as a whole cannot have been intended as a chronological sequel to xxiv. According to xxv 20 (*P*), Isaac was 40 years old when he married Rebekah, at which time the Abraham of the previous chapter (*J*) was scarcely apt to remarry and have more children. But even according to *P*'s own calculations, the data before us cannot be in chronological sequence. If Isaac was 60 at the birth of Jacob and Esau (vs. 26), and Abraham was then 100 years older (xxi 5), the grandfather still had 15 years of life ahead of him (xxv 7) when the twins were born. Consequently, the notice of Abraham's death should have come not at the beginning but at the end of this chapter. It is thus evident that the various details of this chapter have been grouped in such a manner as to interfere as little as possible with the progress of the narrative. All of which lends independent support to the assumption that, according to *J*'s timetable, the death of Abraham occurred prior to Rebekah's arrival.

The descendants of both Keturah and Ishmael represent sundry elements from the northern peripheries as well as the interior of the Arabian peninsula. Some (Sheba and Dedan) were cited in the Table of Nations (x 7); others are listed here for the first time. The line of Ishmael comprises yet another group of twelve tribes, alongside the Nahorites (xxii 20–24) and Israel; cf. M. Noth, *Geschichte Israels,* 1950, pp. 74 ff.

II. THE STORY OF THE PATRIARCHS

B. The Story of Jacob

33. ESAU AND JACOB: THEIR BIRTH AND YOUTH
(xxv 19–20, 26b: /P/; 21–26a, 27–34: J)

XXV /[19] This is the story of Isaac son of Abraham: Abraham begot Isaac. [20] Isaac was 40 years old when he married Rebekah, daughter of Bethuel the Aramaean of Paddan-aram, sister of Laban the Aramaean./

[21] Isaac pleaded with Yahweh on behalf of his wife, since she was barren. Yahweh responded to his plea, and his wife Rebekah conceived. [22] But the children clashed inside her so much that she exclaimed, "If this is how it is to be, why do I go on living?" Finally,[a] she inquired of Yahweh. [23] And Yahweh answered her,

"Two nations are in your womb,
Two peoples at odds while still in your bosom.
But one people shall surpass the other,
And the older shall serve the younger."

[24] When it was time for her to be delivered, there were twins in her womb! [25] The first one emerged reddish,[b] like a hairy[c] mantle all over; so they named him Esau.[d] [26] Next came out his brother, his hand holding on to Esau's heel[e]; so they named him Jacob. /Isaac was 60 years old when they were born./

[27] As the boys grew up, Esau became a skilled hunter, a man of the outdoors; whereas Jacob was a retiring man who kept

[a] Literally "she went (and)."
[b] Heb. *'admōnī*, play on "Edom."
[c] Heb. *śēʿār*, play on "Seir," synonym of Edom.
[d] Eponym of Edom; cf. NOTE.
[e] Heb. *ʿqb*, play on *y-ʿqb* "Jacob."

to his tents. 28 Isaac favored Esau, because he had a taste for game; but Rebekah was fonder of Jacob.

29 Once, when Jacob was cooking a stew, Esau came in from the country, famished. 30 Said Esau to Jacob, "Give me a swallow of that ʲred stuffʲ, for I am famished"—which is why they named him Edom. 31 Jacob answered, "First give me your birthright in exchange." 32 Esau replied, "Here I am at the point of death, so what good is birthright to me!" 33 But Jacob said, "You must swear to me first." So he swore to him, giving up his birthright to Jacob. 34 Jacob then gave Esau some bread and lentil stew. He ate, drank, got up, and went away. Thus did Esau misprize his birthright.

ʲ⁻ʲ Heb. *hā-'ādōm*, repeated, another play on "Edom."

NOTES

xxv 21. *she was barren.* This condition persisted, according to *P*, for twenty years, cf. vss. 20 and 26.

responded to his plea. Niphal of the form for "pleaded," above; for a parallel development, cf. Akk. *šālu* "to ask," reciprocal stem "to respond."

22. The exact meaning of Rebekah's exclamation is difficult to ascertain. Most moderns translate "why do I live?" following Syr., and more particularly with an eye on xxvii 46. But the two passages are by no means analogous; a closer parallel is found in vs. 32, below "what good is . . . !" Rebekah proceeds to consult Yahweh through an oracle (Heb. *drš*), which shows that, though desperate, she was not as yet resigned to her fate.

23. *peoples.* Heb. *lᵉ'ōm*, a poetic synonym for "nation," used here in preference to *'am*, which is not only "people" but more specifically "kin," and would hence be redundant if applied to twins.

at odds while still in your bosom. More specifically, who have been drawing apart ever since (*min*) they were implanted in your womb.

the older shall serve the younger. The normal sense of Heb. *rab* is "numerous, plentiful," rather than "great"; actually, the two adjectives are etymologically distinct. In the latter connotation, *rab* is a cognate of Akk. *rabū*. And it is worthy of special notice that the present pair *rab* : *ṣā'īr* has its exact counterpart, both in etymology and usage, in the Akk. pair *rabū* : *ṣeḫru*, which has a precise function in family law.

The *māru rabū* "elder son" was entitled to an inheritance share which was double that of the *māru ṣeḫru*. However—and this is particularly true of Hurrian law, and hence a likely source of patriarchal customs— the *māru rabū* could be designated as such by the testator contrary to the actual order of birth. In the present instance, we have not only an echo of Akk. linguistic usage but also a significant survival of Mesopotamian legal practice, one which Israel had to outlaw later on; cf. Deut xxi 16. The tradition behind this narrative, as well as behind ch. xxvii, employs thus an authentic and ancient motif in focusing on the joint prehistory of Israel and Edom.

25. *they named him Esau.* This is an indirect word play. To make the aetiology explicit, the text should have said "they named him Seir," since only this synonym for Edom, and not the eponym Esau, is at all evoked by *śē'ār* "hair." The more familiar Esau may have been substituted mechanically; or else, the author left it to the reader to complete the identification.

26. *Jacob.* See COMMENT.

27. The description of the two boys is clearly antithetical. The last parts of the comparison are self-evident: Esau is a man of the outdoors (field, steppe), whereas Jacob prefers the quieter life indoors (literally in the "tents," the plural being used in the abstract; "in the house" would be too urban for the purpose); note the semantically identical Akk. phrase *ašibūti/u kultarī* "dwellers in tents," which in Assyrian king lists (JNES 13 [1954], 210 f., lines 8 f.) summarizes the background of the first seventeen rulers; it was no longer primitive, like Enkidu's (see COMMENT), yet not urban, but pastoral-rural. The first parts of the comparison, however, are less transparent. Esau is given to hunting (literally "experienced in, privy to," cf. Isa liii 3 "familiar with illness"), as opposed to Jacob who is ('*īš*) *tām*, something like "of simple tastes, quiet, retiring." The over-all contrast, then, is between the aggressive hunter and the reflective semi-nomad.

28. *for he had a taste for game.* The exact force of the phrase is not entirely clear; cf. perhaps Job xx 12.

30. Esau is depicted as an uncouth glutton; he speaks of "swallowing, gulping down," instead of eating, or the like.

31. *first.* Heb. *kayyōm* "as of now," also in vs. 33; see Ehrl.

give me . . . in exchange. Traditionally "sell me" does not bring out the fact that the birthright was to be bartered (the basic meaning of Hebrew) for food; in vs. 33, however, "sold" may be retained.

34. The second half of the verse presents a staccato succession of five verbal forms, which is evidently calculated to point up Esau's lack of manners and judgment. But this is merely literary license. In xxxiii 1–17 we get an altogether different picture of Jacob's older brother.

COMMENT

The section starts out with a brief notice by *P*. The initial phrase, traditional "these are the generations of Isaac," leads one to expect a genealogical list, but none is forthcoming. The only birth recorded is that of Isaac himself, so that *tōlᵉdōt*, if applied here in its usual technical sense, should actually have referred to Abraham as begetter, and not to Isaac. Something is obviously out of line here. The term may have been used this time in its broader sense of "story" (cf. ii 4a, from the same source), which the above translation has adopted for the sake of expediency. Or the passage may have been construed originally much like vi 9–10, i.e., with heading, parenthetic clause (19–20), and some such notice as [Isaac begot Esau and Jacob]; but the latter lost out to the narrative by *J* (21 ff.) in the final compilation. One could go on with other conjectures; a convincing conclusion has yet to be found.

The rest of the section is manifestly from *J* (see 21, 23). The author was limited to some extent by the various aetiologies which had to be worked into the account. Three of these involve Esau: "hair" as a roundabout reference to Seir (25); its "reddish" color as an allusion to Edom (25); and the "red stuff" in the bowl as another such allusion (30); the fourth pertains to Jacob, and features *'qb* "heel" as symbolic of *y-'qb* (26), for which see below. Yet *J* is still able to depict Esau as a sort of Enkidu figure: the child emerges "like a hairy mantle all over," which is almost the same as "shaggy with hair was his whole body," applied to Enkidu in Gilg., Tablet I, column ii, line 36 (where the phrase *šuʾur šārta* is cognate with Heb. *ṣēʿār*); and Esau, like Enkidu, is a man of the open spaces. The rest of the narrative sustains the image of uncouthness, which is heightened by the drumbeat effect of five successive verbal forms in vs. 34.

In seeking to assess the meaning of this section, we should bear in mind the following points: (1) Business transactions in the Near East, while always subject to strict legal norms, have also been looked upon to some extent as a game, one in which the contestants match wits with one another (xxiii). Popular lore takes delight in such "gamesmanship," much as official law stresses the ethical and moral side in such dealings (cf. for example, Exod xxii

20 ff.). Abstract judgments could thus be easily misapplied. (2) Tradition, which guided the writers, was influenced in turn by aetiological uses of words and sounds; in this instance, the name Jacob had a ready surface explanation. (3) As was true, however, in so many other cases, the popular explanation is not necessarily, or even usually, the correct one. The original meaning of the name Jacob, shortened from *Y'qb-'l* "may God protect," or the like, was forgotten once the pertinent verb had gone out of general use; all that remained was its apparent connection with "heel," which symbolists could not be expected to leave alone. (4) Above all, the main motif with which tradition had to deal in the case of Isaac's sons was the transfer of birthright from the older to the younger. That this was more than casual word play is evident from the very different and obviously serious background of the narrative in xxvii. Yet the social setting of that transfer was no longer self-evident at the time of the writing, which permitted popular etymology to impose its own interpretation. For a discussion of the underlying social factor, which is the heart of the matter, see COMMENT on Sec. 35 (ch. xxvii).

34. VARIOUS NOTICES ABOUT ISAAC
(xxvi 1–33: *J*; 34–35: /*P*/)

XXVI 1 There was a famine in the land—aside from the previous famine that had occurred in the days of Abraham—and so Isaac journeyed to Abimelech, king of the Philistines in Gerar. 2 Yahweh had appeared to him and said, "Do not go down to Egypt; stay in the land that I will point out to you. 3 You shall sojourn in that land, but I will be with you and bless you; for I will give all these lands to you and to your offspring, in fulfillment of the oath that I swore to your father Abraham. 4 And I will make your descendants as numerous as the stars in the sky, and give all these lands to your offspring, so that all the nations of the earth shall bless themselves by your offspring— 5 all because Abraham heeded my call and kept my mandate: my commandments, my laws, and my teachings."

6 While Isaac stayed thus in Gerar, 7 the men of the place asked questions about his wife. He answered, "She is my sister"; for he was afraid to say, "My wife," thinking, "The men of this place might kill me on account of Rebekah, since she is so beautiful." 8 After he had been there a long time, Abimelech, king of the Philistines, happened to look out of the window, and saw Isaac fondling his wife Rebekah. 9 Abimelech sent for Isaac and said, "Then she is your wife! How could you have said, She is my sister?" Isaac said to him, "Because I thought that I might lose my life on account of her." 10 But Abimelech replied, "Think of what you could have done to us! One of the men might have lain with your wife; you would thus have brought guilt upon us!" 11 Then Abimelech issued orders to all

nally the same sequence as in 15, but one of the nouns dropped out accidentally.

25. *started digging*. See NOTE on 18. The success of the attempt is not reported until 32.

26. *councilor*. An extension of the noun $r\bar{e}^{a'}$ "friend, companion," which has a similar technical connotation in II Sam xv 37, xvi 16, and especially I Kings iv 5. Analogously, Akk. *mūdū* "familiar, expert" becomes a councilor of the crown in the court of Ugarit; cf. JAOS 75 (1955), 163. The parallel account in xxi 22 does not mention this official in the MT version, but he is included in LXX and Old Latin.

28. *a sworn treaty*. Heb. *'ālā* "adjuration, curse" (cf. xxiv 41), but also, by extension, a treaty with sanctions, note especially Deut xxix 20.

between our two sides. Heb. *bēnōt-*, not the preposition "between" but a secondary noun "between two parties," or the like; cf. xlii 23.

29. *Yahweh's blessing upon you!* Not an invocation but a form of welcome (Ehrl.) which cancels the expulsion decree of vs. 16. With the treaty concluded, Isaac is assured of a friendly reception throughout Abimelech's territory.

31. *bade them good-by*. Literally "blessed," but often used in greeting or parting, since pertinent formulas would normally include an appeal for the good will of the deity; cf. xlvii 7, 10.

33. *Shibah*. The cons. text of MT can yield: (a) *šib'ā* "seven" (traditional); (b) *śib'ā* "satedness, plenty" (Syr., Vulg., Aquila, Symmachus); (c) *šᵉbū'ā* "oath" (cf. LXX). Of these choices, (a) does not fit the context at all, since nothing has been said here about the number seven; (b) has a possible indirect connection, inasmuch as the discovery of a new well has a bearing on future crops; the most pertinent of the extant interpretations, however, is (c), since the narrative features a political treaty solemnized by an oath (vss. 28, 31). The pointing of MT was influenced obviously by direct association with the name Beer-sheba, as recalled from the other narrative. The facts before us, however, favor the third interpretation, especially since the parallel account in xxi 27 ff. also lists the oath as one of the reasons for the name of the city.

34–35. This excerpt from P has no connection with the preceding episodes. As now placed, it may be viewed as a later and separate motivation (disappointment with Esau's Canaanite wives) for the narrative in xxvii. One of the two gentilics in vs. 34 is almost certainly an error for "Hivite" or "Horite"; cf. textual note *ʰ*.

his people, saying, "Anyone who touches this man or his wife shall be put to death!"

12 Isaac sowed in that region, and reaped a hundredfold[a] the same year, for Yahweh had blessed him. 13 The man grew richer all the time, until he was very wealthy. 14 He acquired flocks and herds, and a large retinue; and the Philistines were envious of him. 15 So the Philistines stopped up all the wells that his father's servants had dug—back in the days of his father Abraham —and filled them up with earth.

16 Then Abimelech said to Isaac, "You must go away from us, for you have become too big for us by far." 17 So Isaac departed from there and encamped in the wadi[b] of Gerar, where he remained. 18 Isaac next reopened the wells which [c]had been dug in the days of[c] his father Abraham, but were later stopped up by the Philistines after Abraham's death; and he gave them the same names that his father had given them. 19 But when Isaac's servants, digging in the wadi, found there a well with spring water, 20 the herdsmen of Gerar contended with the herdsmen of Isaac, saying, "This water is ours!" So they named that well Esek,[d] because they had bickered with him. 21 Then they dug another well, and there was contention over that one also; so he called it Sitnah.[e] 22 Moving on from there, he dug still another well; and there was no contention over it. So he called it Rehoboth, which is to say, "This time Yahweh [f]has granted us room[f] to increase in the land."

23 From there he went up to Beer-sheba. 24 The same night Yahweh appeared to him, and said,

"I am the God of your father Abraham.
Fear not for I am with you.
I will bless you and increase your offspring,
For my servant Abraham's sake."

[a] See NOTE.
[b] Not "valley," see NOTE.
[c–c] Versions differ, see NOTE.
[d] Literally "challenge," an allusion to "contended."
[e] "Opposition."
[f–f] Heb. hi-rḥīb, play on "Rehoboth."

COMMENT

The section groups together several episodes in the life of Isaac, a further unifying factor being the presence of Abimelech of Gerar. Except for the last two verses (34–35, for which see NOTE), the whole is essentially the work of *J*. This is attested directly by the use of the name Yahweh (2, 12, 22, 25, 29); and indirectly, by the anachronism of the Philistines (cf. NOTE on vs. 1) and, more particularly, by divergencies from duplicate accounts which can be attributed to *E* on internal grounds.

The recurring themes fall into two classes: (1) a wife-sister episode at Gerar (vss. 6–11 : xx 1–18); and (2) the Treaty of Beer-sheba (vss. 15–33 : xxi 22–32), with pertinent aetiologies. On the former, see the detailed COMMENT on Sec. 25. In *J*'s version, this is the only episode to involve Abimelech with a patriarchal couple; nor do Abraham and Sarah repeat the naïve deception which they attempted with Pharaoh (Sec. 15). Abimelech is thus absolved of any charge of insincerity, or short memory; nor is the author guilty of inconsistencies in characterization. By the same token, *E*'s account in xx is likewise self-consistent.

The same basic factor of two distinct sources accounts also for the problems raised by the respective versions of the Treaty of Beer-sheba. The facts are similar in substance but different in some of the details (cf. COMMENT on Sec. 27), notably as regards the aetiology of that place name. Evidently, tradition had preserved an old report of a treaty between one of the patriarchs and a local ruler of Gerar. In the version utilized by *E*, the patriarch in question was Abraham, whereas the material handed down to *J* placed Isaac in that position. It may be regarded as certain that no two such events actually did take place. For even if one were to grant that a pact entered into by Abraham was subsequently renewed by Isaac, it is improbable in the extreme that the same Abimelech participated in both agreements; and since Phicol is the Gerar troop chieftain in both instances, one can hardly posit two rulers who happened to share the name Abimelech. In other words, we again have a single incident which was differently reported in two independent sources. Which of these two accounts comes closer to the factual core? With so little to go by, the point could be argued either way. But if Abimelech was actually host to Isaac and Rebekah at Gerar, it would have to be Isaac and not Abraham who was the other party to the Treaty of Beer-sheba—assuming, of course, that tradition was still fairly close to the truth.

35. ISAAC DECEIVED
(xxvii 1–45: *J*)

XXVII ¹ When Isaac was so old that his eyesight had faded away, he called his older son Esau and said to him, "Son!" "At once," he answered. ² And he said, "As you see, I am so old that ᵃthere is no tellingᵃ when I may die. ³ So take your gear—your quiver and bow—and go out to the country to hunt some venison for me. ⁴ Then prepare it as a festive dish, the way I like, and bring it to me to eat, so that I may give you my very own blessing before I die."

⁵ Rebekah had been listening as Isaac spoke to his son Esau. So when Esau had gone off to the country to hunt venison for his father,ᵇ ⁶ Rebekah said to her son Jacob: "I just overheard your father speaking with your brother Esau, thus, ⁷ 'Bring me venison and prepare it for me as a festive dish that I may eat it and bless you with Yahweh's approval before I die.' ⁸ Now, my son, listen carefully to my instructions. ⁹ Go to the flock and fetch me from there two choice kids. I will prepare them as a festive dish for your father, the way he likes. ¹⁰ Then take it to your father to eat that he may bless you before he dies."

¹¹ "But my brother Esau," Jacob said to his mother, "is a hairy man, and I am smooth-skinned! ¹² Suppose my father feels me? He will think me frivolous, and I shall bring on myself a curse instead of a blessing." ¹³ His mother replied to him, "Let any curse against you, my son, be my concern! Just do as I say. Go and fetch them."

¹⁴ So he went and got them and brought them to his mother; and his mother prepared the festive dish, the way his father

---

ᵃ⁻ᵃ Literally "I do not know the day of my death"; cf. NOTE.
ᵇ Heb. "to bring"; see NOTE.

liked. 15 Rebekah then got the best clothes of her older son Esau which she had in the house, and put them on her youngest son Jacob; 16 and with the skins of the kids she covered up his hands and the hairless parts of his neck. 17 She then handed to her son Jacob the festive dish and the bread that she had prepared.

18 He went to his father and said, "Father!" "Yes?" he answered, "Which one of my sons are you?" 19 Jacob said to his father, "I am Esau, your first-born. I did as you told me. Pray sit up and eat of my venison, that you may give me your very own blessing." 20 Isaac asked his son, "How is it that you succeeded so quickly, my son?" He answered, "Because Yahweh your God made things go well for me." 21 But Isaac said to Jacob, "Come closer, that I may learn by feeling you whether you really are my son Esau or not. 22 Jacob moved up to his father Isaac, who felt him and said, "The voice is the voice of Jacob, yet the hands are the hands of Esau." 23 He had not identified him, because his hands were hairy, like those of his brother Esau. Still, as he was about to bless him, 24 he asked again, "You are my son Esau?" "Of course," he replied. 25 So he said, "Serve it to me, and let me eat of my son's venison, that I may give you my very own blessing." He served it to him, and he ate; then he brought him wine, and he drank. 26 Then his father Isaac said to him, "Come closer my son, and kiss me." 27 As he went up and kissed him, [Isaac] sniffed the smell of his clothes. Then, at last, he blessed him, saying,

> "Ah, my son's smell
> Is like the smell of a field*c*
> Which Yahweh has blessed.
> 28 May God give you
> Of the heaven's dew
> And of the earth's riches—
> Abundance of new grain and wine.
> 29 Let peoples serve you,
> And nations may homage to you.

c Sam., LXX, Vulg. add "full (rich)."

> You shall be your brothers' master
> And your mother's sons shall bow to you.
> Cursed be they who curse you,
> And blessed they who bless you."

30 Jacob had no sooner left his father Isaac, right after Isaac had finished blessing Jacob, than his brother Esau came back from his hunt. 31 He too prepared a festive dish, which he took to his father. Said he to his father, "Let my father please*d* eat of his son's venison, that he may then give me his very own blessing." 32 "Who are you?" his father Isaac asked him. "Why," he answered him, "your son Easau, your first-born!"

33 Isaac was seized with a violent fit of trembling. "Who was it, then, that hunted the game and brought it to me? I finished eating it just before you came, and I blessed him; and now he must remain blessed!" 34 On hearing his father's words, Esau burst into sobbing of the most violent and bitter kind. "Bless me too, Father," he begged. 35 But the other answered, "Your brother came here by a ruse, and he carried off your blessing. 36 He replied, "Did they name him Jacob so that he should cheat*e* me twice? First he took away my birthright,*f* and now he has gotten away with my blessing!*f* Haven't you saved a blessing for me?" he pleaded. 37 But Isaac answered Esau, "I have already made him master over you; I have made all his kinsmen his slaves, and have braced him with new grain and wine. What, then, is there that I could do for you now, my son?" 38 Esau pleaded with his father, "Have you just that one blessing, my father? Bless me too, Father!" [Isaac said nothing]*g*; and Esau wept. 39 Then Isaac spoke up and said to him,

> "Your home shall be far*h* from the earth's riches
> And the dew of heaven above.
> 40 By your sword you shall live,

d Literally "rise."
e "Be at my heel," play on Jacob.
f Heb. cons. *bkrty* : *brkty*.
g So LXX; MT omits.
h See NOTE.

And your brother you shall serve.
But as you grow restive,[4]
You shall throw off his yoke from your neck."

[41] Esau harbored a grudge against his brother Jacob on account of the blessing that his father had given him. And Esau
said to himself, "As soon as the time to mourn for my father is
at hand, I will kill my brother Jacob." [42] When these words of
her older son Esau were reported to Rebekah, she called her
younger son Jacob and said to him, "Your brother Esau is
hoping for redress by killing you. [43] Now, then, my son, listen
to my request: flee at once to my brother Laban in Haran,
[44] and stay with him a while, until your brother's anger has
subsided—[45] until your brother's wrath turns away from you
and he has forgotten what you did to him. I will then send
for you to bring you back. Let me not be bereft of both of you
in a single day!"

[4] Meaning of Heb. verb uncertain.

Notes

xxvii 1. *his eyesight had faded away*. Literally "his eyes were too dim
to see (with)."

At once. Literally "Here I am," which must be varied in translation
according to the context; cf. "Yes?" in vs. 18, and see xxii 1, Note.

2. The literal "I know not the day of my death," would be meaningless, since nobody could be said to know that; cf. JBL 74 (1955), 252.

3. *country*. Literally "field," the outdoors; see xxv 27.

4. *festive dish*. The traditional tasty, savory dish is a slavish rendering
of Heb. All dishes were presumably meant to be tasty. Moreover, the
plural ending of the Heb. noun suggests something more or less abstract,
not unlike our "delicacy." The qualifying phrase means either "the way
I like (it)" or "the kind I like."

that I may give you my very own blessing. Literally "that my being
may bless you"; but this is not "that I may bless you myself." That the
added term carries some technical nuance is suggested by the fact that
it is used no less than four times in this narrative; cf. 19, 25, 31. But
what that connotation may be is difficult to decide. Conceivably, how-

ever, the emphasis is thus put on the special circumstances of a deathbed declaration.

5. *for his father.* So LXX, which reflects *l'byh/w* for the *lhby'* of MT. The latter might be forced to yield "to take home," yet such a phrase without indirect object would violate Heb. usage.

7. *with Yahweh's approval.* Another inescapable instance of the idiomatic use of *lipnē,* for which see vi 11, NOTE. Incidentally, this particular phrase was added by Rebekah; it is missing in Isaac's own statement, vs. 4.

13. Not "your curse," which would be ambiguous; for a significant analogue of the entire phrase, cf. xii 3.

18. *He went.* LXX, Syr., Vulg. offer "he brought (them)," which implies a slight revocalization of the cons. text. The change is no improvement.

Which one of my sons are you? This is the idiomatic force of Heb. "Who are you, my son?" which conveys nothing when rendered literally.

20. *you succeeded so quickly.* Not the traditional "you found," which would be suspect in any case without a pertinent object. The basic sense of the verb is "to reach, attain."

made things go well for me. The idiom is identical with the one used in xxiv 12 ("grant me a propitious sign"), for which see NOTE *ad loc.*

21. *learn by feeling you.* Literally "feel you . . . (whether . . .)".

23. *identified him.* The verb (*nkr*) is in this instance not so much "knew, recognized" as "discovered, unmasked."

Still, as he was about to bless him. Not "and he blessed him," as a sequel to the preceding clause, which would mean that Isaac blessed "Esau" twice—an event that would completely vitiate the inner logic of the context and destroy the relentlessly increasing tension; but a necessary prelude to the next in the series of tests. This verbal aspect is one of the many denotations of the Heb. imperfect.

24. *Of course.* Literally "I am"; for the mode of reply to a question in Heb., cf. xviii 15, NOTE.

27. The reading "[full, lush] field" in some of the versions adds little to the impact of the passage, while impairing its metric structure; yet to the combined authority of Sam., LXX, and Vulg. cannot be minimized; perhaps an authentic, though inferior, variant.

28. *new grain and wine.* Unlike the everyday terms for "grain, wine (and oil)," the words employed here are specialized for ritual and poetic purposes, notably so in Deuteronomy. In similar contexts, Akk. employs *ašnan* for the prosaic *še'um* "barley." The qualifying "new" in the translation may help to make the necessary distinction.

31. *please.* Heb. employs the verb "to rise" as an auxiliary element,

here to express courtesy rather than urgency; cf. the parallel "pray sit up" in vs. 19.

33. *I finished eating it*. MT *w'kl mkl*, literally "I ate of everything," perhaps a scribal slip for the infinitive absolute *w'kl 'kl*, for which cf. xxxi 15. The above translation can do justice to either reading.

he must remain blessed. A blessing given in such circumstances cannot be revoked; cf. vs. 7.

36. In addition to the play *y'qb : wy'qbny*, the verse also juxtaposes most skillfully the pair *bkrty* "my birthright" and *brkty* "my blessing."

38. [*Isaac said nothing*]. This clause is missing in MT but given in LXX; note Lev x 3, where a similar crisis is at issue. Although LXX is not supported in this instance by other versions, it is improbable that this highly effective remark was made up by the translators. It is brief enough to have been skipped accidentally by a scribe.

39. *far from*. Heb. employs here the preposition *mi(n)*, the same as in the corresponding portion of vs. 28, in a partitive sense, which is but another nuance of the common "from, away from." To treat both passages on a par, implying that Esau too was promised agricultural wealth, would undermine the whole tenor of the context. But to understand the particle as "without . . . ," with many older translators and most moderns, is not sanctioned by established Heb. usage. To be sure, the style remains awkward, quite aside from the preposition. Yet some such meaning as the one here reflected is clearly indicated: Edom is doomed to privations, yet his day will come.

40. *as you grow restive*. Cf. Jer ii 31; Ps lv 3. But the ancient versions differ widely in their understanding of the verb, which need mean no more than that the precise force would no longer be determined. The other occurrences are similarly inconclusive. An old textual error is by no means improbable.

42. *is hoping for redress*. Literally "is consoling himself (with the thought of)." On the basis of Isa i 24, Heb. *mtnḥm* could be a variant for *mtnqm* "is seeking vengeance," without the outright emendation that many have proposed. But the present text yields excellent sense as it is.

44. *a while*. Literally "some days/years."

45. *bereft of both of you*. Killing Jacob would expose Esau to the death penalty, through blood vengeance or otherwise.

COMMENT

The subject matter of this narrative is clearly related to the account in xxv 27–35; and the link is expressly underscored in vs. 36, above. Both stories feature the rivalry between Jacob and Esau, a rivalry that focuses on birthright in the one instance, and the father's blessing in the other. In both episodes, moreover, allusions to the name Jacob play an incidental part. Yet there is also a profound difference between the two narratives, even though both are the work of the same author (*J*). In the earlier episode Esau was presented as a virtual caricature of the uncouth hunter, who had only himself to blame for what happened; here, however, he is a deeply moving figure, an innocent victim of a heartless plot.

In evaluating the content of the present account, it is essential that we dismiss at the outset the various value judgments with which the story has been encumbered through the ages. For it goes without saying that the task of the interpreter is not to justify or sit in judgment, to condone or condemn, but only to inquire what the given source means in terms of its own context and background. To be sure, the background has been clarified only in relatively recent times, thanks to modern discoveries. The fact remains, however, that even the foreground has not always been kept in proper focus, with the inevitable result that the picture has suffered from needless distortion.

That the story before us poses a moral problem, among many others, was already clear in biblical times—although this point has been suppressed by many of the later moralizers. Both Hosea (xii 4) and Jer (ix 3) allude to Jacob's treatment of Esau with manifest disapproval. What is more, the author himself, by dealing so sensitively with the hapless plight in which Isaac and Esau find themselves through no fault of their own (cf. especially vss. 33–38), demonstrates beyond any doubt that his personal sympathies are with the victims. It is, furthermore, a fact that Jacob himself did not think up the scheme; he acted, though not without remonstrance and uneasiness, under pressure from his strong-willed mother; and he had to pay for his misdeed with twenty years of exile!

How, then, did the author view the situation as a whole? This is not made explicit in the narrative; yet a conclusion may be hazarded from the overtones of the story and, more especially, from the general tenor of *J*'s work. The fate of individuals caught up in the mainstream of history will often seem incomprehensible; for history is but the gradual unfolding of a divine master plan, many details of which must forever remain a mystery to mortals. It so happened that Abraham's family was singled out to serve God's ultimate purpose (von Rad); that is all we know. In short, *J* did not edit his data. He only retold, in his own matchless way, what

tradition had handed down to him. To be sure, much of this matter
has been immensely enriched by the depth of his own understanding. Yet *J* also recorded, with scrupulous impartiality, some things
that he did not comprehend, convinced no doubt, that there must
be a higher purpose behind it all.

The ultimate historical kernel of the story is problematic in itself.
There is here some hint, obviously, of earlier relations between
Israel and Edom—or Seir in the role of Edom's predecessor. But
there is no way of ascertaining the nature of those contacts. We
cannot draw for this purpose on the known facts from the age of
David and Solomon; for *J* himself was a product of that age, and
by *J*'s time the material had already passed into the domain of
popular tradition. The actual starting point would have to be
sought considerably earlier. Now according to Deut ii 12—a source,
incidentally, that had access to much antiquarian lore—combined
with Gen xxxvi 20, protohistoric Edom was dominated by Horites.
Thus Jacob and Esau, as eponymous figures, would symbolize early
interrelations between Israelites and an older strain: cf. also Gen
xxxiv.

The possibility just adduced—with all necessary circumspection—
is enhanced to some extent by the background detail of the present narrative. On this point we now have pertinent illustrations in
the Hurrian sources from Nuzi, which in turn mirror social conditions and customs in the patriarchal center at Haran. Birthright
in Hurrian society was often a matter of the father's discretion
rather than chronological priority. Moreover, of all the paternal
dispositions, the one that took the form of a deathbed declaration
carried the greatest weight. One such recorded statement (AASOR
16 [1936], No. 56) actually safeguards the rights of the youngest son
against possible claims by his older brothers. Another is introduced
by the formula "I have now grown old," which leads up to an oral
allocation of the testator's property or, in other words, a deathbed
"blessing." (See my detailed discussion in JBL 74 [1955], 252 ff.)

Isaac's opening words in the present instance reflect thus an old
and authentic usage. The background is Hurrian, which accords
with the fact that Haran, where the patriarchs had their roots,
was old Hurrian territory. On the socio-legal level, therefore, the
account is a correct measure of early relations between Hebrews and
Hurrians. With Seir—a synonym of Esau—assigned in Deut ii 12
to the Horites (even though not all of them can be equated with

Hurrians), it would not be surprising if the same account should also echo remote historical rivalries between the same two groups.

At any rate, tradition succeeded in preserving the accurate setting of this narrative precisely because the subject matter was deemed to be of great consequence. In essence, this matter was the continuity of the biblical process itself, a process traced through a line that did not always hold the upper hand. Legally, the older son was entitled to a double and preferential share of the inheritance, especially in Hurrian society. But since the status of older son (Akk. *māru rabū,* cf. vs. 1 and xxv 23, Note) could be regulated by a father's pronouncement, irrespective of chronological precedence, and since the legacy in this instance had been established by divine covenant, the emphasis of tradition on transfer of the birthright in a deathbed blessing—with Yahweh's approval (cf. vs. 7) —can be readily appreciated. With the passage of time, however, the background of a practice no longer in common use was gradually forgotten. The lost detail was dubbed in, out of context and with confusing results, as we have seen. *J* was not free to choose his incidents or slant their motivation; yet an artist of *J*'s caliber and integrity could not ignore altogether the human side of the issue.

The purely literary aspects of this vivid account require little comment. Tension mounts constantly as Isaac, sightless and never altogether convinced by the evidence of his other senses, resorts to one test after another: his visitor sounds like Jacob, but says he is Esau, yet the hunt took much less time than expected; the skin feels like Esau's and the food tastes right; the lips betray nothing, but the clothes smell of the chase; so it has to be Esau after all! The reader is all but won over by the drama of Jacob's ordeal, when Esau's return restores the proper perspective. The scene between Isaac and Esau, both so shaken and helpless, could scarcely be surpassed for pathos. Most poignant of all is the stark fact that the deed cannot be undone. For all the actors in this piece are but tools of fate which—purposeful though it must be—can itself be neither deciphered nor side-stepped by man.

36. JACOB IS SENT TO LABAN
(xxvii 46–xxviii 9: *P*)

XXVII ⁴⁶ Rebekah said to Isaac, "I am disgusted with life on account of the Hittite women. If Jacob should also marry a Hittite woman like these, another native, what good would life be to me?"

XXVIII ¹ So Isaac sent for Jacob, greeted him, and enjoined him, saying, "You are not to marry a Canaanite woman! ² Go at once to Paddan-aram, to the house of your mother's father Bethuel, and choose there a wife for yourself from among the daughters of your uncle Laban. ³ And may El Shaddai bless you, make you fertile and numerous, so that you may become an assembly of tribes. ⁴ May he extend to you the blessing of Abraham, and to your offspring along with you, so that you may take over the land in which you are sojourning, and which God gave to Abraham." ⁵ Then Isaac sent Jacob off, and he went to Paddan-aram, to Laban son of Bethuel the Aramaean, brother of Rebekah, the mother of Jacob and Esau.

⁶ When Esau saw that Isaac had blessed Jacob when he sent him to Paddan-aram to take a wife from there, enjoining him as he blessed him, "You shall not marry a Canaanite woman," ⁷ and that Jacob had obeyed his father and mother and gone to Paddan-aram—⁸ Esau realized how much the Canaanite women displeased his father Isaac. ⁹ So Esau went to Ishmael, son of Abraham, and took to wife, in addition to the wives he had, Mahalath daughter of Abraham's son Ishmael, the sister of Nebaioth.

NOTES

xxvii 45. This is a direct sequel to xxvi 34–35. For the last clause cf. xxv 22.

xxviii 1. *greeted him.* Heb. *bĕrēk,* though normally "to bless," is also used for greeting and parting; cf. NOTE on xxvi 31. In this instance, no blessing is recorded until vs. 3. The intervening passage deals, instead, with strictly mundane matters. It is not improbable that *P* had a particular purpose in mind in employing the stem *brk* repeatedly in this context (cf. 4, 6—*bis*), namely, to emphasize that Isaac had nothing but the friendliest feelings toward Jacob; see especially xlvii 7, 10.

3. *El Shaddai.* See xvii 1.

tribes. Heb. *'ammīm,* often "peoples," but also "kinsfolk," cf. xxv 8. The present terminology is not political (which would require *gōy*), the promised increase alluding not to peoples but people.

4. *the blessing of Abraham.* Cf. xii 7.

9. *Nebaioth.* Ishmael's first-born; cf. xxv 13.

COMMENT

The section differs sharply from the preceding narrative in style, phraseology, motivation, and timetable. To start with the last, the Isaac of this context should still have close to 80 years of life ahead of him: he was 60 when the twins were born (xxv 26), and Esau was 40 when he married (xxvi 34) and thus precipitated Rebekah's countermove; and Isaac lived to be 180 (xxxv 28). In the previous account, however, Isaac's days were numbered; he was blind and barely able to function a short time before Jacob's departure. It follows that the present source—which is *P* throughout—had no knowledge, or took no notice, of *J*'s version wherein Isaac was the victim of a cruel ruse, and in no mood to plan for Jacob's future.

The chronological chasm between the two versions is matched by the wide gap in the motives that each gives for Jacob's departure. In *J*'s version, it was fear of Esau's revenge; but in *P*'s account before us, the motive is Rebekah's aversion to Hittite women and her insistence that Jacob choose a wife from among her own Aramaean relatives. Nor is there in *P*'s version the slightest hint of Isaac's anguish and resentment, which *J* described so movingly just a few verses before (xxvii 33); Isaac is here the solicitous—and still alert—father who gives his son advice and blessing.

The section is typical of *P*'s style and vocabulary. In addition to El Shaddai, we find here also the land of the "sojourning(s)" (cf. xvii 8, xxxvi 7), the place Paddan-aram, and the term *qāhāl* for "congregation, assembly." The tradition or theory behind *P*'s chronological system is still obscure. But the interest of this source in purity of lineage is a factor that is both transparent and constant. *J* and *P* moved indeed in different worlds, yet somehow both sources were equally devoted to the same way of life.

37. JACOB'S DREAM AT BETHEL
(xxviii 10–22: J,/E/ᵃ)

XXVIII 10 Jacob left Beer-sheba and set out for Haran. 11 He
came upon a certain place and stopped there for the night, since
the sun had set. /Taking one of the stones of that place, he put
it under his head and lay down on that spot. 12 He had a dream:
a stairway was set on the ground, with its top reaching to the
sky; and angels of God were going up and down on it./ 13 And
there was Yahweh standing beside him and saying, "I Yahweh
am the God of your forefather Abraham and the God of Isaac;
the ground on which you are resting I will give to you and to
your offspring. 14 Your offspring shall be (as plentiful) as the
dust on the ground, and you shall spread out west and east,
north and south; and all the communities of the earth shall bless
themselves by you and your offspring. 15 Remember,ᵇ I am with
you; I will protect you wherever you go, and bring you back to
this land; nor will I leave you until I have done what I promised
you."

16 Jacob awoke from his sleep and said, "Truly, Yahweh
abides in this site, but I was not aware! /17 Shaken, he exclaimed, "How awesome is this place! This is none other than
the abode of God, and that is the gateway to heaven!" 18 Early
next morning, Jacob took the stone that he had put under his
head, set it up as a pillar, and poured oil on its top./ 19 He
named that site Bethel,ᶜ whereas the former name of that town
had been Luz.

/20 Jacob then made a vow, saying, "If God remains with

ᵃ Some of the "joins" remain doubtful.
ᵇ Literally "behold."
ᶜ Heb. "house of El," linked to "house of Elohim" in vs. 17.

me, protecting me on this journey that I am taking, and giving me bread to eat and clothing to wear, 21 and I come back safe to my father's house—/Yahweh shall be my God. /22 This stone that I have set up as a pillar shall be God's abode; and of all that you may grant me, I will always set aside a tenth for you."/

NOTES

xxviii 11. *a certain place.* The attribute is implicit in the definite article of Heb. The noun, Heb. *māqōm,* has several connotations, including "spot" (here in vs. 11) and "(religious) site" (in vss. 16, 19).

stopped . . . for the night. Not "spent the night," since his sleep was to be interrupted. The imperfect of Heb. often has an inchoative connotation.

12. *a stairway.* The traditional "ladder" is such an old favorite that it is a pity to have to dislodge it. Yet it goes without saying that a picture of angels going up and down in a steady stream is hard to reconcile with an ordinary ladder. Etymologically, the term (stem *sll* "to heap up, raise") suggests a ramp or a solid stairway. And archaeologically, the Mesopotamian ziggurats were equipped with flights of stairs leading up to the summit; a good illustration is the excavated ziggurat of Ur (Third Dynasty). Only such stairway can account for Jacob's later description of it as a "gateway to heaven" (17).

set. Literally "was stationed, planted."

13. *standing beside him.* This is the established meaning of the Heb. phrase, cf. xviii 2. The preposition, literally "upon," is a matter of idiomatic usage (cf. especially xxix 2), and should not be strained unduly.

I Yahweh am the God. . . . Not "I am Yahweh, the God. . . ." The description applies not to the name but to the deeds; cf. especially the introduction to the Decalogue, Exod xx 2, Deut v 6.

17. *Shaken.* Literally "terrified."

this . . . that. Heb. uses the same demonstrative pronoun both times, but the repetition makes it distributive.

20. *bread . . . clothing.* These two items were regularly issued to slaves, servants, and seasonal workers, and are often listed together in business documents. The sense here is equivalent to "just enough to subsist on."

21b. A manifest insert from *J. E*'s version read "If . . . house—(22) [then] this stone. . . ."

COMMENT

The narrative connects directly with xxvii 45. In compliance with his mother's request, Jacob lost no time in starting out on his journey. Normally, the narrator does not linger over a trip, no matter how long and strenuous (cf. xxiv 10). This time, however, an exception is made. The reason is soon apparent.

To the individuals concerned, Jacob's abrupt departure was a matter of personal safety (xxvii 41 ff.). But in the history of the patriarchs, especially as seen by *J*, the individual is a free agent only on the surface. Fundamentally, he is part of a larger pattern over which he has no control, and in which he functions as the unwitting tool of destiny. At this stage, Jacob's security and future are important because both bear on the continuity of the biblical process. The time has now come for the fugitive to be given a glimpse of the deeper truth.

That this broader meaning of the Bethel episode was sensed very early is evident from the fact that both narrative sources already have this tradition. They differ mostly as to detail, possibly also as regards the exact chronology (cf. Sec. 46); but Bethel stands out either way as a spiritual milestone. The upshot is that instead of parallel accounts separately presented, as is usually the case, we have this time a composite version intricately blended. Yet the fusion is unmistakable as soon as one pauses for a second look. Elohim and Yahweh alternate in consecutive verses (12:13; 16:17). God communicates with Jacob in a dream (12), as is customary in *E* (cf. xx 3, xxxi 10); whereas *J* speaks of Yahweh as standing beside Jacob and addressing him directly (13). The successive exclamations in vss. 16 and 17 would be redundant in an account by the same writer, but are natural enough when traced back to separate sources.

One particular detail of the narrative merits special attention. In his dream Jacob sees a stairway (not "ladder," cf. NOTE on vs. 12) whose base is on the ground but whose top reaches to the sky. The description evokes inevitably both the image and the concept of the Mesopotamian temple tower or ziggurat, especially when read in conjunction with vs. 17 (which immediately followed vs. 12 in the *E* version): "This is none other than the abode of God, and that is the gateway to heaven!" For a ziggurat rose hard by the main temple on the ground (the so-called *Tieftempel*), to provide on its summit a place for the deity to visit (*Hochtempel*) and communicate there with mortals: a spiritual symbol, in short, of man's efforts to reach out to heaven. The phraseology is much too typical of the temple tower to be merely coincidental, and the underlying imagery cannot be mistaken; the allusion is all the more suggestive when viewed in connection with Jacob's journey to Mesopotamia. The tradition that E reflects at this point is thus authentic in more ways than one.

The link with Bethel carries its own symbolism as well. The theophany made Jacob realize that this was an abode of the Deity, hence the new name replaced the older Luz, as this aetiology sees it. Actually, Bethel was an old center (cf. xii 8, xiii 3 f.), which managed to retain its religious influence until late in the seventh century, when the holy place was destroyed by Josiah (II Kings xxiii 15). The etymology seeks to fix the locale of Jacob's spiritual experience, but does not otherwise circumscribe its significance.

38. JACOB'S ARRIVAL IN HARAN
(xxix 1–14a: *J*)

XXIX 1 Jacob resumed his journey and made his way to the
land of the Easterners. 2 There before his eyes was a well out in
the open, and three droves of sheep huddled beside it, for the
droves were watered from that well. The stone over the mouth
of that well was large: 3 only when all the shepherds[a] had as-
sembled there together, could they roll the stone from the
mouth of the well and water the flocks; then they would put
back the stone over the mouth of the well.

4 Jacob said to them, "My friends, where are you from?"
They answered, "We are from Haran." 5 He asked them, "Do
you know Laban son of Nahor?" They said, "We do." 6 "Is he
well?" he asked them. "He is," they replied, "and there is his
daughter Rachel arriving with the flock." 7 He said, "It is still
broad daylight, hardly the time to round up the animals. Why
don't you water them and go on grazing?" 8 "We can't," they
answered, "until all the shepherds[a] are gathered together to roll
the stone from the mouth of the well, so that we can water the
droves."

9 While he was still talking with them, Rachel arrived with
her father's sheep; for she was a shepherdess. 10 As soon as Jacob
saw Rachel, the daughter of his mother's brother Laban, [b]with
the sheep of his mother's brother Laban,[b] Jacob went up, rolled
the stone away from the mouth of the well, and watered the
sheep of his mother's brother Laban. 11 He then kissed Rachel
and burst into tears. 12 Jacob told Rachel that he was her father's
kinsman, being Rebekah's son; and she ran to tell her father.

[a] So Sam., some MSS of LXX (see NOTE), reading *r'ym* for MT *'drym*
"droves."
[b–b] LXX omits.

13 When Laban heard the news about his sister's son Jacob, he rushed out to greet him; he embraced him, and kissed him, and took him to his house. The other than recounted to Laban everything that had happened; 14 and Laban said to him, "You are truly my *flesh and blood."*

– Literally "bone and flesh."

NOTES

xxix 1. *resumed his journey.* See NOTE on xxi 16, and cf. vs. 11. In all such instances, the verb *nś'*, literally "to lift," is only used to emphasize the particular activity.

the Easterners. See xxv 6, and cf. Judg vi 3, 33; Isa xi 14; Jer xlix 28, etc.

2. *beside it.* Clearly not "upon it"; cf. xxviii 13.

was large. The construction is predicative, not attributive ("a large stone").

3. *shepherds.* This is the reading of Sam. and some MSS of LXX; in vs. 8, the same reading is given by LXX A and B, as well as Sam. MT "droves" (cons. *'drym* for *r'ym*) may have been influenced by the preceding verse. The change supplies the necessary subject both here and in vs. 8; and it also furnishes an antecedent for the third masculine plural pronouns in vss. 4–8 to "they" at the beginning of vs. 8, which MT lacks.

5. *We do.* Since biblical Heb. lacks a word for "yes," it can only express affirmation by restating the question in positive terms: Do you know?—We know; Is he well? (vs. 6)—Well. Cf. xviii 15, NOTE.

7. *Why don't you.* Heb. uses imperatives, but these should not be construed as commands. Once again, it is a question of Heb. idiom, evidently the vernacular in the present context.

COMMENT

The narrative has much in common, necessarily, with the account in xxiv; for even though the principal characters represent another generation, the subject matter is much the same. This fact may be the reason why the author—who is *J* in both instances—uses here so much less space than he required on the earlier occasion. That he manages, nevertheless, to accomplish so much, is further proof of his consummate artistry.

The encounter between Jacob and the local shepherds is a model of effective characterization. The traveler is excited and talkative after his long journey, whereas the herdsmen are composed, almost taciturn; they act as if each word were just too much trouble. True to an ageless pattern, the prospective suitor is inspired to a display of superhuman prowess at the very first sight of Rachel. He also appears to be more affectionate than one would think proper under the circumstances. Yet Jacob's impulsive kiss—a detail that Calvin attributed to a redactional slip on the part of Moses (cf. von Rad)—need not have been out of tune with the mores of the times. We know from the Nuzi records, which so often mirror conditions in the Har(r)an area—and hence also in the patriarchal circle— that women were subject to fewer formal restraints than was to be the norm later on in the Near East as a whole.

39. JACOB'S MARRIAGES WITH LEAH AND RACHEL
(xxix 14b–30: *J*)

XXIX ¹⁴ᵇ After Jacobᵃ had stayed with him a month's time, ¹⁵ Laban said to him, "Just because you are my kinsman, should you serve me for nothing? Tell me what your wages shall be "

¹⁶ Now Laban had two daughters: the name of the older was Leah, and the name of the younger was Rachel. ¹⁷ Leah had tender eyes, but Rachel was shapely and beautiful. ¹⁸ Jacob loved Rachel, so he answered, "I will serve you seven years for your younger daughter Rachel." ¹⁹ "It is better," Laban replied, "that I give her to you than that I should give her to an outsider Remain with me." ²⁰ So Jacob served seven years for Rachel, yet they seemed to him but a few days because of his love for her.

²¹ Then Jacob said to Laban, "Give me my wife that I may unite with her, for my term is completed." ²² Laban gathered all the local inhabitants and gave a feast. ²³ And when evening came, he took his daughter Leah and brought her to Jacob; and he cohabited with her.— ²⁴ Laban had assigned his maidservant Zilpah as maid to his daughter Leah.— ²⁵ Came morning, and it was Leah! "Why did you do this to me?" Jacobᵇ demanded of Laban. "Was it not for Rachel that I have served you? Why did you trick me?" ²⁶ "It is not the practice in our place," Laban replied, "to marry off the younger daughter before the older. ²⁷ Wait until the bridal week of this one is over, and we will give you that one too—in exchange for your remaining in my service another seven years."

²⁸ Jacob agreed. He waited until the first bride's week was

ᵃ Moved up from next clause for clarity.
ᵇ So LXX; pronoun in Heb.

ended, whereupon Laban*c* gave him his daughter Rachel in marriage.— 29 Laban had assigned his maidservant Bilhah as maid to
his daughter Rachel.— 30 Jacob*d* cohabited with her also; in fact,
he loved her more than Leah. And so he stayed in service with
Laban*d* seven more years.

c So LXX, reading *lbn* for the extra *lw* "to him" in Heb.
d Personal pronoun in Heb.

NOTES

xxix 17. *tender*. Not necessarily "weak," for the basic sense of Heb. *rak*
is "dainty, delicate"; cf. xxxiii 13. The traditional translation has been
influenced by the popular etymology of the name Leah as "weak." What
the narrative appears to be saying is that Leah had lovely eyes, but
Rachel was an outstanding beauty.

19. *Remain with me*. The prepositional phrase *'immādī* stresses "under
my authority," for which cf. vs. 27, below; cf. also NOTE on xxiii 4.

21. *unite with*. For the Heb. idiom cf. NOTE on vi 4. In vss. 23 and 30,
the imperfect has been translated "cohabited."

23. Starting with the wedding festivities and until the marriage was
consummated, the bride is assumed to have been veiled; cf. xxiv 65.

24. See COMMENT; also vs. 29.

27. *Wait until the bridal week . . . is over*. The verb means literally
"fulfill" (imperative); cf. next verse. The bridal week is expressly defined
as "seven days of festivities"; cf. Judg xiv 12.

28. *Jacob agreed*. Cf. xlii 20; hardly "he did so," because what is expected in this context is some form of direct reply rather than long-term
compliance alone. Cf. Akk. *anna/anna kīna*, with *nadānu, šakānu, apālu*
"to give an affirmative response" (*kī/enu* is, of course, a cognate of Heb.
kēn "thus, right").

COMMENT

The older school of documentary criticism assigned this section,
or rather vss. 15 ff., to *E*, with the exception of vss. 24 and 29,
which were unanimously ascribed to *P* (cf. Dr.). The result was an
artificial fragmentation which ran counter to the logical unity of
the content. The more recent critics, on the other hand, no
longer find here any trace of either *E* or *P* (cf. Noth, *Über-*

lieferungsgeschichte . . . , p. 30). According to this view, all of ch. xxix (Secs. 38, 39 and part of 40) as well as all but the last verse of ch. xxvii (Sec. 35) constitute an integrated and virtually consecutive part in the total story of Jacob. The latter analysis accords admirably with the internal evidence of the narratives. It can be confirmed, moreover, by further arguments which should put the whole matter beyond any possibility of dispute. Two of these additional points are sufficiently important to deserve mention even in this non-technical context.

There never was any direct basis for attributing this section to *E.* No reference is made to Elohim, dreams, or angels. The supposed parallels in phraseology between vss. 25–26 and xx 9 are by no means complete; certain idioms, moreover, are bound to be the common property of all speakers—and writers. Where, then, did the older critics pick up the false scent? The spot happens to be vs. 14. Its second half appears to say, when mechanically interpreted, "and [Jacob] stayed with him a month's time." Since the author thus far has been *J,* and since vss. 15 ff. go on to describe the circumstances that caused Jacob's visit to be drawn out for twenty years (xxxi 41), it follows, so the argument ran, that the overextended stay was unknown to *J,* and had to be debited to *E.* Nevertheless, the alleged boundary is an optical illusion induced by erroneous verse division, of which there are many other instances (notably in ii 4). If the ancient Masoretic divider had been placed before 14b, that is, in other words, if vs. 15 had begun with the clause under discussion, the chances are that *E* would never have been injected into this particular narrative. For in that case, the natural reading of the text would be "After [Jacob] had stayed with him a month's time, [15]Laban said to Jacob," etc., which is the interpretation that has here been adopted. This way there is no striking chronological discrepancy, indeed no inconsistency whatever. On the contrary, the host waited no longer than convention prescribed, before embarking on a scheme calculated to exploit his guest.

Turning now to vss. 24 and 29, it must be admitted that they appear at first glance to be the type of statistical detail that is customary with *P.* Nevertheless, it is precisely these two verses that are most likely to constitute direct transcripts from some old and authentic document. The proof comes again from the Nuzi tablets; more specifically, from a document (HSS V [1929], No. 67) which was already

discussed at some length, though in a different connection, in the
COMMENT on Sec. 19. The text deals in part with a marriage involving a young woman of high standing in the local community. When
all the pertinent details have been set forth, the text adds parenthet-
ically: "Moreover, Yalampa (a slave girl) is herewith assigned to
Gilimninu (the bride) as her maid" (lines 35–36). This notation is
just as abrupt and marginal as are the present notices about Zilpah
and Bilhah. Evidently, it was the norm in the upper stratum of Hurrian society to treat the bride to a personal slave girl. If our author
had copied the two verses from an original contract from Harran, he
could not have come any closer to the cuneiform parallel just cited.
These particular notices bear thus authentic witness to conditions
that prevailed in Hurrian centers such as Harran during the patriarchal period, which is also true, of course, of the context as a whole.
Significantly enough, Lev xviii 18 expressly forbids marriage to two
sisters. The practice would probably not have been sanctioned in the
days of the narrator himself. As was the case with negotiable birthright (xxv 27 ff.), the subject matter of this section was similarly a
custom of a distant age and land, recorded only because tradition
insisted on citing it.

   With the documentary obstacles safely out of the way, the present
narative falls into its rightful place. It is a logical sequel to Sec. 38,
which analysis has never denied to *J;* and it leads up to Sec. 40,
which speaks of Yahweh in the very first clause (vs. 31). The continuity is now faultless. Laban's elaborate pretense of politeness and
family solidarity is maintained for just one month. Immediately
thereafter he puts into operation a scheme of singular cunning and
duplicity. But the schemer is himself the unwitting tool of destiny,
the means whereby Jacob is repaid for his part in the mistreatment of
Esau, through an ironic turn of fortune. The ultimate background,
therefore, has to be sought in ch. xxvii, an account necessarily from
the same hand as the present, in an over-all presentation to which
only a writer of *J*'s caliber could do full justice.

40. THE BIRTH OF JACOB'S CHILDREN
(xxix 31–xxx 24: *J*, with ╱*E*╱ᵃ)

XXIX 31 When Yahweh saw that Leah was unloved, he unclosed her womb, while Rachel remained barren. 32 Leah conceived and bore a son, whom she named Reuben; for she declared, "It means 'Yahweh has seen my distress,' and also, 'Now my husband will love me.' "ᵇ 33 She conceived again and bore a son, declaring, "It means, 'Yahweh heardᶜ that I was unloved,' and so he has given me this one also." Hence she named him Simeon. 34 Again she conceived and bore a son, declaring, "Now my husband will become attachedᵈ to me, for I have borne him three sons"; which is why sheᵉ called him Levi. 35 Once more she conceived and bore a son, declaring, "This time let me praiseᶠ Yahweh"; which is why she named him Judah. Then she stopped bearing.

XXX ╱1ᵃ When Rachel saw that she had failed to bear Jacob children, she became envious of her sister. Said Rachel to Jacob, "Give me children, or I shall die!" 2 Jacob became angry with Rachel, and he retorted, "Am I in the position of God, who has denied you fruit of the womb?"╱ 3 She said, "Here is my maid Bilhah. Cohabit with her, and let her give birth on my knees, so that I may reproduce through her!" 4 So she gave him her maid Bilhah as concubine, and Jacob cohabited with her; 5 and Bilhah conceived and bore Jacob a son. ╱6 Said Rachel, "God

---

ᵃ The borderline between *J* and *E* is sometimes uncertain in this section.
ᵇ For the explanations of the name Reuben see NOTE.
ᶜ Heb. *šāmaʿ* "heard," explaining *Šimʿōn*.
ᵈ Heb. *yillāwê*, explaining *Lēwī*.
ᵉ Sam., LXX; MT "he called him/was called."
ᶠ Heb. *'ōdê*, explaining *Yᵉhūdā*.

has vindicated[g] me: indeed, he has heeded my plea by giving me a son"; hence she named him Dan./ 7 Rachel's maid Bilhah conceived again and bore Jacob a second son. 8 Said Rachel, "A fateful[h] [i]contest waged I[i] with my sister: moreover, I have prevailed." So she named him Naphtali.

9 When Leah saw that she had stopped bearing, she took her maid Zilpah and gave her to Jacob as concubine.[j] 10 Leah's maid Zilpah bore Jacob a son. 11 Said Leah, "How propitious!"[k] So she named him Gad. 12 Then Leah's maid Zilpah bore Jacob a second son. 13 Said Leah, "How fortunate![l] It means that the women will consider me fortunate." So she named him Asher.

14 One day, at the time of the wheat harvest, Reuben came upon some mandrakes in the field and brought them home to his mother Leah. Rachel asked Leah, "Please give me some of your son's mandrakes." 15 Leah[m] answered, "Was it not enough for you to take away my husband, that you should also take my son's mandrakes?" Rachel replied, "Then let him lie with you tonight, in return for your son's mandrakes." 16 So when Jacob came home from the fields that evening, Leah went out to meet him. "You stay with me," she announced, "for I have paid[n] for you with my son's mandrakes." So he lay with her that night. /17 God heeded Leah, and she conceived and bore Jacob a fifth son. 18 Said Leah, "God has granted me my reward[o] for having given my maid to my husband." So she named him Issachar. 19 Leah conceived again and bore Jacob a sixth son. 20 Said Leah, "God has given me a precious gift.[p]/ This time my husband [q]will bring me presents,[q] for I have borne him six sons." So

---

[g] Heb. *dān*, cf. the name Dan.
[h] See NOTE.
[i-i] Heb. *naptūlẹ . . . niptaltī*, to explain Naphtali.
[j] LXX adds "Jacob went in to her and she conceived."
[k] So MT cons., but pointed to read *bā' gād* "luck has come," both forms explaining Gad.
[l] Heb. *be'ošrī*, for Asher.
[m] So with LXX, reading *l'h* for MT *lh*.
[n] Heb. *śākōr śekartīkā*, literally "I have hired you," for Issachar.
[o] Heb. *śekārī*, another explanation for Issachar.
[p] Heb. *zᵉbādanī zebed.* in assonance with Zebulun.
[q-q] Heb. *yizbᵉlẹnī*, another explanation for Zebulun.

she named him Zebulun. /21 Lastly, she bore a daughter, and named her Dinah.

22 God remembered Rachel: God heeded her and unclosed her womb. 23 She conceived and bore a son, declaring, God has removed[r] my disgrace./ 24 She named him Joseph, meaning, "May Yahweh add[s] another son for me!"

[r] Heb. *'āsap*, in assonance with *Yōsēp* "Joseph."
[s] Heb. *yōsēp*.

NOTES

xxix 31. *unloved*. Not so much "hated" (with tradition), as "rejected, unloved"; cf. xxvi 27, and especially Deut xxi 15. Akkadian presents an exact semantic counterpart in *zāru(m)*, which has the additional nuance of "renounce"; cf. Gilg., Tablet XI, line 26.

32. *Reuben*. The name, literally "Look, a son!" is given a composite symbolic explanation (from two sources): *rā'ā bᵉ*- "he saw, looked at," and (*yeᵉʰā*) *banī* "he will love me." The plain connotation is of course the real one; cf. the Akk. name *Awīlumma* "it's a man/male," and cf. Job iii 3.

It means. Heb. *kī* in its explicative sense (twice); see also xxx 13, and iv 25; note also the other use of the particle in the present verse, i.e., "for, because."

xxx 3. *on my knees*. To place a child on one's knees is to acknowledge it as one's own; cf. the Hurro-Hittite tale of Appu, ZA 49 (1956), 220, line 5. This act is normally performed by the father. Here, however, it is of primary interest to the adoptive mother who is intent on establishing her legal right to the child. For the pertinent verb *'ibbānᵉ* cf. xvi 2, in a closely related context (*J*); both passages stem undoubtedly from the same author.

4. *concubine*. For this usage of Heb. *'iššā*, normally "woman, wife," cf. xvi 3. The emphasis is manifestly on "connubium."

8. *fateful*. Literally "of/before God," with the adjectival use of Elohim to describe something extraordinary or numinous (cf. i 2) rather than "mighty"; see D. W. Thomas, VT 3 (1953), 209 ff. There is, furthermore, the inherent likelihood that the combination *naptūlē 'ᵉlōhīm* designates something more specific than is immediately apparent. Elsewhere, *'ᵉlōhīm* occurs not only in the specialized sense of "housegods," cf. xxxi 30, Exod xxi 6, but also as the instrument of divination by ordeal when data for a routine legal decision are lacking; cf. A. Draffkorn, JBL 76

(1957), 216 ff. The latter usage is frequent with *ilāni*, the Akk. cognate of *'elōhīm*, when an ordeal is involved. In the present instance, a metaphorical allusion to an ordeal is entirely plausible. What Rachel would thus be saying is approximately as follows: I have been entangled in a contest with my sister, which only celestial powers could resolve, and I have emerged victorious from the ordeal. It would be a figure of speech, of course, but one for which there must have been ample basis in everyday life; a less nebulous allusion, at any rate, than the traditional "wrestlings with God," or even the attenuated—and untenable—"mighty wrestlings." The above "fateful contest" leaves the issue open, without undue strain on sense or usage. (Incidentally, such use of Elohim as an appellative or attribute is not unusual with *J;* see also xxxii 10.)

13. *the women*. Literally "daughters, girls."

14. *mandrakes*. Heb. *dūdā'īm*, which has an erotic connotation; and the fruit of the plant is still considered in the East to have aphrodisiac properties (Dr.).

20. As is the case with Reuben, Issachar, and Joseph, the name Zebulun is given a double aetiology: (a) "a precious gift," Heb stem *zbd,* which is more commonly used in Aramaic (*E*); and (b) Heb. stem *zbl* (*J*). The latter has traditionally been interpreted as "to dwell," which lacks etymological justification, and cannot be forced in any case to yield "will dwell with me" on syntactical grounds. Others have proposed "uphold, support," partly in view of Heb. *zᵉbūl* "eminence," and Ugaritic *zbl* "prince," or the like. But the required link is supplied by Akk. *zubullû* "bridegroom's gift," which is construed with the cognate verb *zabālu;* for the specific technical application, cf. Assyrian Laws A 30.29, 31.2. The connection is self-evident: it supplies a natural semantic basis; it automatically accounts for the form (*zubullû   Zᵉbūlūn*); and it accords with the alternate interpretation based on *zbd.*

21. *Dinah*. Cf. xxxiv. No explanation of the name is given, which has caused critics to question the originality of the notice.

22 ff. Another double aetiology· Joseph is traced back to (a) *'sp* (*E*), and (b) *ysp* (*J*), with Yahweh adduced in the latter instance.

COMMENT

The section lists the births and names of eleven of Jacob's sons. The notice about the birth of the one daughter, Dinah, is given at the end, and it is the only instance in which no explanation is linked with the name; the notation may thus be a later gloss On the whole, the naming of a child was never a casual matter: cf M. Noth, *Die israelitischen Personennamen*, 1929, and J. J. Stamm,

Die akkadische Namengebung, 1939. And because name and person were viewed as interrelated, the explanations are symbolical; a correct, or even plausible, linguistic derivation would be purely coincidental, since the play on the name was the significant thing—aetiology rather than etymology.

Each of Jacob's sons came to be celebrated as the eponymous ancestor of a tribe. Yet all the allusions in the present account are personal, not tribal, in marked contrast with the analogous poetic passages in xlix and Deut xxxiii. This implies a distinctive tradition. Moreover, we find here a hint of agricultural pursuits (vs. 14), as opposed to the prevailing pastoral background in other sections; this would accord with the indicated locale in Central Mesopotamia, since the Har(r)an district was part of a thickly populated area (cf. the Mari records), with a long cultural and political history behind it. To be sure, the only positive link with that region is the name Zebulun, for which see the NOTE on 20. Nevertheless, the tradition as a whole presupposes a long process of transmission, since it reached *J* and *E* through separate channels which had time to develop considerable variations of detail.

The two documentary sources have been fused more intricately in this section than anywhere else in Genesis, more so even than in Sections 37 and 49. The eventual compiler did such a thorough job that redistribution at this time poses a delicate problem. The boundaries between *J* and *E* are sometimes indistinct; in a passage like xxix 32, they have been left unmarked in the translation for practical reasons. In general, it may be assumed that the section goes back basically to *J,* with *E* contributing specific additions and variants. One reliable criterion for separating the two sources is the alternation of the divine names (see, however, the NOTE on vs. 8, end); another criterion is furnished by duplicate aetiologies, which can then be safely allocated to *J* and *E* respectively. Thus *E* traces the name Issachar to Leah's reward for providing her husband with a concubine (vs. 18, note the occurrence of Elohim); the divergent explanation in vs. 16—namely, as repayment for Reuben's mandrakes—*J*'s. Similarly, *E* connects the name Zebulun with God's gift of a son to Leah (20), while *J* makes it a general acknowledgment for all six of her sons (*ibid.*); and whereas *J* derives "Joseph" from *ysp* "to add" (vs. 24, note "Yahweh"), *E* connects the name with *'sp* "to gather, remove" (23, note "Elohim"). Accordingly, since the first interpretation of Reuben is manifestly *J*'s, the second has to be ascribed to *E* (xxix 32).

The significant thing about this complex patchwork is not that it got put together, but that the compiler who did the work refrained from arbitrary leveling and harmonizing. However inconsistent the respective traditions might appear to be, they were not to be tampered with by later custodians.

41. JACOB'S BARGAIN WITH LABAN
(xxx 25–43: *J*)

XXX 25 After Rachel had borne Joseph, Jacob said to Laban, "Give me leave to go to my own homeland. 26 Give me my wives, for whom I have served you, and my children, that I may depart; surely, you know how much my service has done for you."

27 Laban answered him, "If you will permit me, I have learned through divination that Yahweh*a* has blessed me on account of you. 28 Therefore," he continued, "name any wages you want from me, and I will pay." 29 He replied, "You know what my service has meant to you, and how your livestock has fared in my care. 30 For the little that you had before I came has grown into very much, since Yahweh has blessed you for my actions. It is high time that I do something for my own household as well."

31 "What should I pay you?" he asked. And Jacob answered, "You need not pay me anything outright. If you do this one thing for me, I will again pasture and tend your flock: 32 Go*b* through your entire flock today and remove from it every animal*c* among the sheep that is dark-colored, and every one among the goats that is spotted or speckled; they alone shall be my wages. 33 And next time, when you check these wages, let your own view of my honesty be used as an argument against me: any goat in my possession that is not speckled or spotted, or any sheep that is not dark-colored, got there by theft!" 34 "Very well," said Laban, "let it be as you say."

a LXX, Old Latin, Syr., Vulg. read "God."
b MT "I will go," see NOTE.
c For the additional clause in MT see NOTE.

35 But that same day he removed the streaked and spotted he-goats and all the speckled and spotted she-goats—every one with white on it—as well as the fully dark-colored sheep, and left them in the charge of his sons. 36 And he put a distance of three days' journey between himself and Jacob, while Jacob went about pasturing the rest of Laban's flock.

37 Jacob then got fresh shoots of poplar, and of almond and plane, and peeled white stripes in them, laying bare the white of the shoots. 38 The rods that he had peeled he set up in front of the flocks in troughs—the water receptacles that the flocks came to drink from. Since they mated as they came to drink, 39 the goats*d* mated thus by the rods, and so the goats*d* brought forth streaked, speckled, and spotted young. 40 The ewes, on the other hand, Jacob kept apart and made these animals*d* face the streaked and the fully dark-colored animals*d* of Laban. Thus he produced special flocks for himself, which he did not put with Laban's flocks. 41 Moreover, when the sturdier animals*d* were mating, Jacob would place the rods in the troughs in full view of the animals,*d* so that they mated by the rods; 42 but with the feebler animals*d* he would not place them there. And so the feeble ones went to Laban and the sturdy ones to Jacob.

43 Thus the man grew exceedingly prosperous, and came to own large flocks, maidservants and menservants, camels and asses.

d Literally "flock."

NOTES

xxx 25. *Give me leave to go.* A self-evident nuance of the Piel stem; the identical idiom is used in Arabic.

my own homeland. Literally "my place and my land"; for an analogous hendiadys cf. xii 1.

26. *and my children.* In the case of slaves, children remained the property of the master; cf. Exod xxi 4 ff.; the same was true of the offspring (*šerru*) of slaves according to cun., and specifically Nuzian, law, which is particularly relevant in this context. The status of Jacob and his household was, of course, not of the same order, at least tech-

nically. Yet the narrative would seem to intimate that Jacob's treatment at the hands of Laban was not much better than that of slaves; cf. xxxi 43.

27. *I have learned through divination.* The same Heb. verb is found also in xliv 5, 15. In a Mesopotamian context, such as the present, the term refers undoubtedly to inquiries by means of omens; cf. Ezek xxi 26.

Yahweh. Many versions read Elohim, see textual note *a*; that variant may well be the superior reading, since the more general term for the deity is expected from Laban, in contrast to Jacob's mode of reference (vs. 30).

30. *for my actions.* Heb. *lᵉraglī,* literally "according to my foot, step," in the sense of either "in my wake, train," as here assumed, or perhaps "since I have set foot here"; cf. also xxxiii 14.

It is high time that. Literally "Now, when will I . . . ?"

31. *again.* Literally "I will come back and."

32. This verse and the next abound in problems of text and interpretation, partly no doubt because of the idiomatic language and the specialized character of the context, which made transmission that much more difficult.

Go. So Vulg. MT has "I will go," but this cannot be co-ordinated grammatically with a following imperative *hāsēr* "remove"; and a gerund would require *wᵉhāsēr.* Logically, too, MT is suspect, since Laban would scarcely agree to let Jacob make the division; what is more, vs 35 says explicitly that Laban did the removing.

animal. Heb. *śê,* which is not only "sheep" but also "goat"; cf. Exod xii 5; Deut xiv 4.

At this point, the Heb. text reads redundantly "speckled and spotted, and every sheep," evidently added through conflation with the following verse; LXX omits.

dark-colored. Heb. *ḥūm,* a different term from the common Heb. adjective for "black." Sheep were normally white, while goats were dark-brown or black all over; cf. "fully dark-colored," vss. 35, 40.

33. *when you check these wages.* Evidently a technical use of the phrase *bō' 'al* literally "to come over/upon." Uncertainty about the interpretation has led to different readings of the pronominal prefix: alongside the second person in the Heb. text, we find the first person in TP, and the third person in Sam. ("when [it] comes to my wages"). The above translation has the advantage of dispensing with an emendation and, what is more, it provides a logical premise for what follows.

your own view of my honesty. Literally "my honesty" (*ṣidqātī*), construed with "before you" (*lᵉpānēkā*), that is, as you yourself judge it.

let . . . be used as an argument against me. Literally "let it testify against me." For this force of the preposition *bī* with the verb in

question, see especially Num xxxv 30; II Sam i 16 (and I Sam xii 3);
"for me" would probably have been *lī*. The concluding clause (it got
there by theft") clearly presupposes adverse testimony.

in my possession. Heb. *'ittī,* at the end of the verse.

35. *every one with white on it.* Heb. *lābān* in this phrase is probably an
incidental wordplay on the name Laban.

36. At the end of this verse Sam. inserts the text of xxxi 11–13, perhaps in an endeavor to bring the two narratives into harmony. The three
days' distance applies only to this particular juncture in the narrative. The
events described in the rest of the account required more than one sea-
son; cf. NOTE on 43.

37. *shoots.* Literally "rods," cf. next verse; but the descriptive "fresh"
(Heb. *laḥ*) shows that the noun was also used of branches before they
were made into rods.

39. *goats.* Here Heb. *ṣō'n,* normally "flock." But just as the singular *śê*
(cf. NOTE on 32) is either "sheep" or "goat," so may its collective counterpart *ṣō'n* stand not only for sheep *and* goats, but also sheep *or* goats.
(Similarly, *bāqār* may be collective for "cattle," or discrete for "oxen"
alone; see Num vii 6 as contrasted with vii 3.) The present context shows
conclusively that only goats are involved, since the same markings are restricted to goats according to 32, 35. In Heb. the necessary identification
is conveyed automatically, as is true also of our "animals" (cf. 40, 41) in
given contexts. A translation, however, needs to be more specific at times.
The above interpretation, for which cf. R. P. de Vaux in SB, note,
removes an old crux; see the COMMENT below.

40. *The ewes, on the other hand.* This nuance is assured by the prominent inversion in Heb. These animals are thus sharply contrasted with the
"flock," i.e., goats of the preceding verse.

41. *when.* For this sense of Heb. *kol* (=every time that) followed by
an infinitive, cf. Ehrl.

sturdier. TO, Symmachus, and Vulg. offer "early-bearing/born," and
similarly "late" for "feebler." The end result is the same, since the
stronger ewes are known to lamb in winter, and the weaker ones in spring
(Dr.). But the alternative rendering is a paraphrase, nonetheless: Heb. *'ṭp*
"to be faint" is well attested, and *qšr* in this particular sense corresponds
to Akk. *gašrum* "sturdy, robust," an adjective applied to animals, among
others.

43. This progress was obviously a matter of years, not just days; cf.
xxxi 41, at least according to one of the sources.

COMMENT

Having first tricked Jacob into a double bride-payment, Laban now seeks to extend the profitable arrangement beyond the stipulated total of fourteen years of service. This time, however, he is due to be repaid in kind for his machinations. It is a theme that is made to order for vivid presentation. Yet the treatment in this instance is not just another variation on a popular literary motif. The indicated Mesopotamian locale is borne out by authentic background detail. The subject matter, moreover, is later treated anew by an independent narrative source (xxxi 5 ff.). The underlying tradition, in short, is of long standing, and it would seem to point back to patriarchal Mesopotamia.

The present account may safely be ascribed to *J,* not only because of the use of the name Yahweh (especially in vs. 30), but also because it differs significantly from a parallel account (xxxi 5 ff.) which is clearly *E*'s. Jacob consents to remain in Laban's service, in return for all such increase in Laban's flock as may prove to have abnormal coloring—black or dark-brown lambs and parti-colored kids. Laban is delighted with the terms, and promptly proceeds to violate the spirit of the bargain by removing to a safe distance all the grown animals that would be likely to produce the specified sports. Nevertheless, Jacob finds a way to outwit his father-in-law, through prenatal conditioning of the flock by means of visual aids— in conformance with universal folk beliefs.

In *E*'s version, on the other hand (see especially xxxi 8 ff.), Jacob does not act at all on his own initiative: he merely follows God's advice as conveyed to him in a dream. The difference is significant, and may be due to later ethical reflections: Jacob himself is blameless, whereas Laban must be taught a lesson. Yet the background of *E*'s narrative is itself authentic in its detail (see COMMENT on next section). Thus each narrative source rested on sound traditional data.

The bargain between Jacob and Laban is limited to new births among Laban's droves, and specifically to lambs and kids with rare markings and pigmentation. Mesopotamian economy always paid very close attention to distinctive breeds of sheep and goats, as is amply attested in countless business and lexical documents. More significant still is that country's preoccupation with biological sports among those species, to judge from the omen texts. Many such abnormalities, both real and theoretical, are minutely described. Of particular relevance to the present context is the following entry: "If a sheep has the appearance of a goat, its wool being black, the position of the country will be secure" (CT 31, plate 31, line 19). In other words, not only does the omen make note of this particular coloring, but it regards its occurrence as a favorable sign. Such local beliefs and practices could have been reason enough for Jacob's seemingly peculiar request—if it is granted that Laban was temporarily thrown off by his own greed. What matters, however, is not so much the application of the scheme as the reasoning behind it.

The biblical writers, however, operating as they did in a different cultural environment, may well have been puzzled by some of the transmitted detail. Yet they managed to put down the involved details that tradition had handed down in a form that still lends itself to plausible reconstruction. The subsequent difficulties have been largely translational, arising from the flexibility of the term *ṣō'n*, which is generally "flock," but can stand also for either sheep or goats, as the case may be; see NOTE on vs. 39. To obtain appropriately pigmented kids, Jacob resorted to the visual stimulus of rods with chevron markings whittled onto them. The sheep, on the other hand, needed only to face the goats, which came naturally by the dark color required. These were the goats of Laban (40), who had thought it safe to leave them with Jacob, while he was removing the parti-colored specimens out of Jacob's reach; he had not figured on crossbreeding between the two kinds on so occult a basis.

Lastly, the use of the phrase "that same day" in vs. 35 should not be taken to imply that the whole operation was a matter of hours or, at most, days. Actually, vss. 41–42 are frequentative. Moreover, the results described in vs. 43 presuppose a number of seasons. We know from xxxi 38 that Jacob's total length of service with Laban added up to twenty years, which leaves six years over and above the fourteen stipulated as payment for Jacob's two wives. And six years would be about the minimum to permit the kind of natural increase that the concluding verse seeks to stress.

42. JACOB'S FLIGHT FROM HARAN
(xxxi 1–18a: *J* and *E*ᵃ; 18b: */P/*; 19–54: *J* and *E*ᵃ)

XXXI ¹ Now Jacobᵇ learned of the things that Laban's sons were saying: "Jacob has taken everything that belonged to our father, and he has built up all this wealth out of what should be our father's." ² Jacob also noticed that Laban's manner toward him was not as it had been in the past. ³ Then Yahweh said to Jacob, "Return to the land of your fathers, where you were born, and I will be with you."

⁴ So Jacob sent for Rachel and Leah to meet him in the field where his flock was, ⁵ and he said to them, "I have noticed that your father's manner toward me is not the same as in the past; but the God of my father has been with me. ⁶ You know that I have put all my effort into serving your father. ⁷ Yet your father has cheated me, and has changed my wages time and again. But God would not allow him to do me harm. ⁸ If he should state, 'Speckled animals shall be your wages,' then the whole flock would drop speckled ones; and if he should announce, 'Streaked animals shall be your wages,' then the whole flock would drop streaked ones. ⁹ Thus had God reclaimed your father's livestock and given it to me.

¹⁰ "Once, at the mating time of the flocks, I suddenly saw in a dream that the he-goats in the flock, as they mated, were streaked, speckled, and mottled. ¹¹ And in the dream an angel of God called to me, 'Jacob!' 'At once!' I answered. ¹² He said, 'Note well that all the he-goats in the flock, as they mate, are streaked, speckled, and mottled—for I too have noted all the

ᵃ Documentary distribution unclear at times; see COMMENT and NOTES.
ᵇ LXX; Heb. "he."

things that Laban has been doing to you, 13 I the God ᶜwho appeared to youᶜ in Bethel, where you anointed a stele and made a vow to me. Up, then, leave this land and return to the land of your birth.' "

14 Rachel and Leah answered him, saying, "Have we still an heir's portion in our father's estate? 15 Are we not considered by him as outsiders? Not only did he sell us, but he has used up the money he got for us! 16 All this wealth that God has reclaimed from our father is really ours and our children's. Do just as God has told you."

17 Thereupon Jacob put his children and his wives on camels, 18 and he drove off with all his livestock, /and all the possessions that he had acquired—the property in his possession that he had acquired in Paddan-aram—to go to his father Isaac in the land of Canaan./

19 Laban was away at the time to shear his sheep. Rachel meanwhile had appropriated her father's household images; 20 and Jacob had lulled the mind of Laban the Aramaean, so that he would not be forewarned of his flight. 21 He thus got away with all that he had. Soon he was across the Euphrates, heading toward the hill country of Gilead.

22 On the third day, Laban got word that Jacob had fled. 23 Having rallied his kinsmen, he pursued him a distance of seven days, until he caught up with him in the hill country of Gilead. 24 But God appeared to Laban the Aramaean in a dream that night and warned him, "Take care not to press matters with Jacob for good or bad!"

25 When Laban overtook Jacob, Jacob's tents were pitched on the Height; and Laban pitched his tentsᵈ on Mount Gilead. 26 "What did you mean," Laban demanded of Jacob, "by lulling my mind and carrying off my daughters like captives of the sword? 27 Why did you flee so furtively, and dupe me, and not tell me? I would have sent you off with festive music, with timbrel and lyre. 28 You didn't permit me so much as a parting kiss for my grandchildren and daughters! It was certainly a sense-

ᶜ⁻ᶜ So LXX, "T"; MT omits.
ᵈ MT literally "his brothers"; see NOTE.

less thing for you to do. 29 I have it in my power to harm all of
you; but the God of your father said to me last night, 'Take care
not to press matters with Jacob for good or bad!' 30 Very well,
then: you had to leave because you were homesick for your
father's house; but why did you steal my gods?"

31 "I was frightened," Jacob replied to Laban, "at the thought
that you might take your daughters away from me by force.
32 But as for your gods, you find them with anybody, and he
shall not live! In the presence of all this company, if you discover here anything that belongs to you, take it!" Jacob, of
course, did not know that Rachel had appropriated them.

33 Laban went through Jacob's tent, and Leah's tent, and the
tents of the two maidservants, but did not find them. He came
out of Leah's tent and went into the tent of Rachel. 34 Meanwhile, Rachel had taken the idols, put them inside a camel cush-
ion, and sat on top of them. When Laban had combed through
the rest of the tent, to no avail, 35 Rachel*ᵉ* said to her father,
"Let not my lord take it amiss that I cannot rise before you, for
a woman's period is upon me." And so, though he searched, he
did not find the idols.

36 Aroused now, Jacob took up his grievance with Laban. He
spoke up to Laban, and said, "What is my crime, what is my
guilt, that you should have hounded me? 37 Although you have
rummaged through all my things, have you found a single object
from your household? If so, produce it, before your companions
and mine, that they may decide between us two.

38 "In the twenty years that I was under you, your ewes and
your she-goats never miscarried, nor did I ever feast on rams
from your flock. 39 I never brought to you the prey of beasts: I
myself made good the loss; you exacted it from me, whether
snatched by day or snatched by night. 40 Often, scorching heat
ravaged me by day and frost at night; and sleep drifted from my
eyes. 41 Of the twenty years that I spent in your household, I
slaved fourteen years for your two daughters, and six years for
your flock, since you changed my wages time and again. 42 If my

ᵉ *MT* "she."

ancestral God, the God of Abraham and the Awesome One of Isaac, had not been on my side, you would have sent me away empty-handed. But God saw my plight and my labors, and he gave judgment last night."

43 "The daughters are mine," Laban replied to Jacob, "and the children are mine; so too is the flock. Everything you see belongs to me. Yet what can I do now about these my daughters, or about the children they have borne? 44 So come, let us conclude a pact, you and I, that there^f may be a witness between you and me." 45 Jacob then took a stone and set it up as a stele.

46 Jacob said to his companions, "Gather stones." They got stones and made a mound, and they broke bread there over the mound. 47 Laban named it Yegar-sahadutha,^g but Jacob called it Galeed.^h 48 Said Laban, "This mound shall be witness, as of this day, between you and me." That is why it was named Galeed— 49 also Mizpah, for he said, "May Yahweh keep watchⁱ between you and me when we are out of sight of each other: 50 if you ill-treat my daughters, or take other wives besides my daughters— though no one else be about, know that God will be witness between you and me."

51 And Laban said to Jacob, "Here is this mound, and here the stele which I have erected between you and me: 52 this mound shall be witness, and this stele shall be witness, that I am not to cross to you past this mound, and that you are not to cross to me past this mound, or this stele, with hostile intent. 53 May the God of Abraham and the god of Nahor (their respective ancestral deities)^j maintain order between us." And Jacob took the oath by the Awesome One of Isaac his father.

54 Jacob offered a sacrifice on the Height, and invited his companions to partake of the meal. After the meal, they passed the night on the Height.

^f See NOTE.
^g Aramaic for "mound of testimony."
^h "Mound of witness."
ⁱ MT cons. ysp, in assonance with mṣph "Mizpah."
^j An obvious marginal gloss; omitted in LXX.

NOTES

xxxi 1. *Laban's sons.* The relationship need not be taken literally. In vs. 28, e.g., the same Heb. term stands for "grandchildren." Here it could refer to any prospective heirs, such as adopted sons, or the like. At any rate, nothing was said about any sons of Laban in ch. xxix, where such a reference would surely have been in order; and vs. 23, below, speaks only of "brothers," i.e., kinsmen, but no sons.

Verse 1 connects directly with the preceding chapter, and is followed by vs. 3, the whole stemming from *J*'s account: note "Yahweh" in vs. 3.

2. In this verse, it is Laban's altered attitude toward Jacob that is cited as the reason for Jacob's flight, thus reflecting a variant tradition (*E*).

as . . . in the past. Literally "as yesterday, day before yesterday"; same phrase in 5.

4. *E*'s account is resumed and continues in the main through 44; note the use of Elohim for the Deity in 7, 9, 11, 16, 24, 29.

7. *time and again.* Literally "ten times," also in vs. 41; cf. especially Num xiv 22, and see NOTE on xxiv 10.

9. *reclaimed.* Cf. 16 (the approximate sense is that of "salvaged").

10. *I suddenly saw in a dream.* Literally "I lifted up my eyes and saw, and there ('behold') in a dream. . . ." The dream is in *E* the usual medium of communication between God and man. In the parallel account by *J* (xxx 32), no such suggestion from above is either mentioned or implied.

the he-goats in the flock, as they mated. Literally "the he-goats that mounted on the flock"; similarly in 12.

12. *Note well.* Heb. "Lift up your eyes and see."

13. *I the God.* For the appositional construction, cf. xxviii 13: see *ibid.* for the theophany, vs. 18 for the anointing of the stele, and vss. 20–22 for the vow.

The Heb. text is obviously defective, not because "God Bethel" would be an improbable title (for one just like it, cf. *Ilu-Bayti-ilī,* in an Assyro-Tyrian treaty, AFO 9 [1933/34], 109, line 6), but because the phrase is syntactically untenable; the missing words, which automatically right the syntax, are supplied by two of the ancient versions.

14–16. On this passage, see M. Burrows, "The Complaint of Laban's Daughters," JAOS 57 (1937), 259–76.

14. *an heir's portion.* Literally "portion and inheritance" (hendiadys).

15. *outsiders.* Literally "foreign women." The Nuzi texts furnish new evidence on the favored status of native women compared with that

of outsiders; see ZA 41 (1933), 16. Under certain conditions, moreover, transfer of property to such "foreign women" is expressly forbidden.

used up. Literally "eaten up" (infinitive absolute). The terminology ("sell" in marriage, "eat" the monies received) is again in complete harmony with cun. technical usage. The point in this instance, as elucidated by tablets from Hurrian centers, is that part of the bride payment was normally reserved for the woman as her inalienable dowry. Rachel and Leah accuse their father of violating the family laws of their country. Significantly enough, the pertinent records antedate Moses by centuries.

17. *Thereupon*. Literally "he rose (and)," another instance of the auxiliary use of *wyqm;* cf. xxii 7, NOTE. In vs. 21 the same term is translated "soon."

18b. A transparent insert from *P*.

19. The initial clause is circumstantial, as shown by both the tense and the inverted construction; cf. i 2.

appropriated. Also vs. 32. Heb. stem *gnb*, which usually means "to steal." But it also has other shadings in idiomatic usage. Thus the very next clause employs the same verb, no doubt deliberately and with telling effect, in the phrase "lulling the mind," i.e., stealing the heart; the phrase is repeated in 26; in 27, with Laban speaking, the verb is used by itself in the sense of "to dupe." Finally, in vs. 29, the passive participle occurs (twice) to designate animals snatched by wild beasts. The range of *gnb* is thus much broader, in Heb. in general, and in the present narrative in particular, than our "to steal" would indicate.

A reasonably precise translation is especially important in this instance. The issue is bound up with the purpose of Rachel's act. If it was inspired by no more than a whim, or resentment, or greed, then Rachel stole the images. But if she meant thereby to undo what she regarded as a wrong (cf. COMMENT), and thus took the law, as she saw it, into her own hands, the translation "stole" would be not only inadequate but misleading. On the other hand, when Laban refers to the same act further down (vs. 30), he clearly meant "steal."

household images. Heb. *t^erāpīm*. They were figurines, sometimes at least in human shape (I Sam xix 13, 16), which were in popular use for purposes of divination (Ezek xxi 26; Zech x 2; cf. also Judg xvii 5, xviii 14 ff.; Hos iii 4). The etymology is obscure, but derivation from (cons.) *rph* "to be limp" is not improbable; hence perhaps "inert things, idols." The usage in the present narrative suggests a pejorative connotation; for when the author speaks for himself, he refers to these objects as *t^erāpīm* (also vss. 34 f.); Laban, on the other hand, calls them "gods" (vs. 30; when Jacob does the same in vs. 32, he is only quoting Laban).

20. *the Aramaean*. The term is troublesome for chronological reasons.

It is used in patriarchal contexts by *E* (here and in vs. 24, if these passages have been correctly attributed to *E*), by *P* (xxv 20, again with Laban; xxviii 5, with Bethuel), and in Deut xxvi 5 (referring to Jacob). Moreover, the analogous "Chaldeans" would seem to have the endorsement of *J* in xi 28 and xv 7. Yet Aramaeans as such are not independently attested until the late centuries of the second millennium; cf. R. T. O'Callaghan, *Aram Naharaim*, 1949.

Ordinarily, one might dismiss this usage as the product of later geographic terminology. Laban and the other Nahorides were settled in an area which came to be known as Paddan-aram (cf. vs. 18; see also xxv 20, xxviii 2, 5 ff., xxxiii 18, xxxv 9, 26, xlvi 15), or Aram-naharaim (xxiv 5). On this basis, all the inhabitants could have been identified as Aramaeans by retrojection. The Mari material, however, which comes close to the patriarchal age in date, shows that the Semitic population of the Nahor area itself was Amorite, not Aramaean. An analogous example of telescoping would be the use of the term Philistines by *J;* see NOTE on xxvi 1.

The problem is complicated, however, by vs. 47 (*J*), which shows Laban as speaking Aramaic. The identification, therefore, was not only geographic but also linguistic. Accordingly, we must either attribute the confusion to the relatively early period of *J*, if not earlier still, or else we must entertain the notion that actual Aramaeans were on the scene a good deal earlier than is generally assumed. At all events, the problem should not be minimized.

23. *a distance of seven days.* This is meant as a general figure indicating a distance of considerable length; cf. II Kings iii 9. Actually, Gilead could scarcely have been reached from Har(r)an in seven days, especially at the pace of Jacob's livestock.

24. *to press matters.* Literally "to speak (with)," in the juridical sense which *dbr* often carries. Yet even "to dispute, argue," or the like, would not suit the context, since Laban proceeds to argue bitterly, even though he claims to heed God's warning (29). The phrase requires, therefore, some such translation as the above.

25. *tents* (twice). Heb. uses the singular, but obviously in a collective sense, in view of vs. 33.

the Height. It has been conjectured that the text originally gave the name of the mountain, perhaps Mizpah, for which cf. vs. 49. But the text repeats the present reading in vs. 54 (*bis*), which lessens the likelihood of accidental omission; nor is the context of vs. 49 a close enough parallel. The translation assumes, on strictly methodological grounds, but without undue confidence, that the noun was used here as a place name for one of the elevations in the Gilead range; cf. "the River" for the Euphrates in vs. 21.

and Laban pitched his tents. The present Heb. text is contrary to established usage; and the literal "he pitched his kinsmen" is hopeless. The translation accepts the long-favored change of cons. *'ḥyw* "his kinsmen" to *'hlw* "his tent," as in the immediately preceding clause. The intrusive *'ḥyw* is apparently a misreading influenced by vs. 23.

27. *dupe.* See remarks on *gnb*, vs. 19.

29. *all of you.* To reflect thus the plural form of the Heb. pronoun.

31 f. Jacob's rejoinder is in two parts, corresponding to the two-point complaint by Laban (vs. 30). The reply embodies Laban's phraseology, hence "your gods."

32. *this company.* Literally "our brothers, companions."

that belongs to you. The translation follows LXX; MT has a slightly different arrangement of the words.

of course. This nuance is implied by the prominent inversion in Heb.

38. *under you.* Cf. xxiii 4, NOTE. For this legal connotation of Heb. *'im* "with," cf. Akk. *itti* "with," short for *ina bīt N* "in the household of X," i.e., dependent. Actually, in the present context we find the exact duplicate of the latter phrase in vs. 41 "in your household," in parallelism with "under you."

30. The pertinent law in the Code of Hammurabi (par. 266) reads: "If there occurs in the fold an act of god, or a lion takes a life, the shepherd shall clear himself before the deity; the owner of the fold must then accept the loss incurred." Thus Laban is accused of disregarding the explicit legal provision for such contingencies; cf. also Exod xxii 12.

40. *Often.* Heb. literally "I was" in absolute usage: the verb imparts here a durative or iterative denotation to the rest of the clause; cf. xxxviii 21 f., xlvi 34 for a similar extension into the past.

42. *the Awesome One of Isaac.* The appellative (Heb. *paḥad*) remains obscure. It may have here its customary sense of "fear," in which case some reference to the Ordeal of Isaac (xxii) may be implicit; or it might be an altogether different term; cf. A. Alt, *Der Gott der Väter*, 1929, pp. 27 ff.

labors. Not so much the effort expended as (with Ehrl.) the returns from it, analogous to Akk. *mānaḫātu* "earnings" (literally "the fruit of strain").

44. *that there may be a witness.* The clause as it now reads in MT cannot be right. The implied subject is not the pact, because (1) Heb. *berīt* is feminine whereas the verb before us is masculine; (2) it is not the treaty but the deity invoked that is really the witness (cf. vs. 50). Some critics assume accidental loss of "Yahweh" following the verbal form, cons. *whyh* (haplography); yet this simple textual remedy is not favored by the context, since the expected divine term should be Elohim (as in vs. 50). The LXX version probably points to the correct solution. It adds just before the clause in question, "though no man be with us,

know that God (will be witness between you and me)," that is, the same clause as 50b. Two such passages in the original, only a few lines apart, could readily lead to the loss of one of them in the course of repeated copying (so-called homoioteleuton). The translation given above is neutral.

46 ff. Here we get two versions of the mutual friendship and non-aggression pact between Jacob and Laban, one from *J* (46–50), and the other from *E* (51–54). In all likelihood, the mound of stones (*gal*) served as the symbol of the treaty in *J*'s version, and the stele or stone slab (*maṣṣēbā*) in *E*'s. In course of time, however, a certain amount of cross-harmonization took place. Thus *gl'd* (Galeed, Gilead), which is appropriate only to *J*'s *gal*, was joined by *mṣph* (Mizpah), evidently a symbolic echo of *E*'s *mṣbh;* and conversely, vss. 51 ff. were eventually filled out with balancing references to the mound from the earlier source.

50. The stipulation against taking other wives is basic to many cuneiform marriage documents.

53. The phrase enclosed between parentheses is immediately betrayed as redactional by its use of the third person ("their"), as opposed to the direct address in the preceding verses. Apparently, a marginal notation in an early copy sought to explain how the god of Nahor had come into the picture. But such marginal comments have found their way more than once into the body of the text with the passage of time.

COMMENT

This narrative has long been celebrated in its own right. In the light of recent discoveries, moreover, it has become a key witness on the subject of patriarchal traditions in general. But before we consider the extra-biblical connections, the traditional data need to be surveyed in brief.

The documentary distribution appears to be clear-cut at first glance. The hand of *J* is manifest in vss. 1 and 3, and then toward the end, in 46–50. Verse 18 contains a typical summation of *P*. The rest of this long chapter would thus seem to belong to *E,* and the assumption has strong evidence in its favor, both external and internal. Nevertheless, sporadic echoes of *J* would seem to be present here and there, notably in 38–40. As was the case with ch. xxii, where one source appears to have colored another, we may have here instance where the hand is mainly *E*'s, yet the voice is sometimes *J*'s. At any rate, the problem is too complex to be discussed here in detail. It did not seem advisable, however, to mark the documentary boundaries in the translation, except for the transparent intrusion by *P;* the salient points have been touched upon instead in the NOTES.

The subject matter of the narrative subdivides into two parts. The first, and much the longer of the two, tells of Jacob's increasing difficulties with Laban, the flight and pursuit, and the dramatic encounter in Gilead. The other portion takes up the treaty between Jacob and Laban (46–54).

That the account of the flight is essentially the work of *E* is immediately apparent from the frequent mention of Elohim and the repeated stress on dreams (10 f., 24). Even more significant, however, is the internal evidence of the contents, as compared with the pertinent passages from the hand of *J*. According to *J*, Jacob's flight was precipitated by agitation on the part of Laban's prospective heirs (vs. 1). On the other hand, *E* ascribes Jacob's abrupt departure to Laban's menacing moods (vs. 2). We have, moreover, conflicting explanations of Jacob's prosperity itself: *J* describes it as the result of Jacob's own ingenious countermoves to Laban's schemes (xxx 27–42), whereas in *E* (xxxi 10 ff.) the initiative is God's.

The two sources differ likewise in their interpretation of the treaty between Jacob and Laban. To *J*, the ostensible, if not the actual reason for the pact is Laban's new-found solicitude for his daughters' future (50). In *E*'s formulation, the object is a mutual non-aggression pact (52), that is, a strictly political agreement. The outward symbols of the treaty are no less distinct. *J*'s version features a mound of stones, or cairn (Heb. *gal*), as a permanent witness (*ʿēd*), the two terms together supplying an explanation for the regional name Gilead. For his part, *E* concentrates on a stele or pillar (Heb. *maṣṣēbā*). Interestingly enough, the text also alludes to the respective deities of the contractual parties (53), in apparent compliance with treaty practices throughout the ancient Near East; nor does *E* omit to record the meal that was an important concluding feature of treaty ceremonies (vs. 54; cf. xxvi 30). Both reports, incidentally, have the authentic ring of legal and political documents; they thus appear to hark back to an actual agreement between early Israelite and Amorite/Aramaean elements; cf. the date formula in *Alalakh Tablets* 58 (Old Babylonian period).

There is, however, one particular feature in this chapter which is exclusive with *E*. It concerns the household images which Rachel removed from her father's house without his knowledge. The author handles the entire episode with outstanding skill. When he speaks of the figurines on his own (19, 34 f.), he uses the secular, and sometimes irreverent, term *t^erāpīm* (perhaps "inert things," cf. NOTE on vs. 19); but Laban refers to them as "my gods" (*'^elōhay,* vs. 30). The search is suspensefully depicted, as Laban combs through one tent after another until he gets to the tent of Rachel, where they have been hidden. Rachel's pretense of female incapacitation is a literary gem in itself. The crowning touch of drama and irony is Jacob's total unawareness of the truth—the grim danger implicit in his innocent assurance that the guilty party would be put to death.

But the basic significance of the incident now transcends all such considerations of human interest or literary presentation. It derives from underlying social practices as they bear on the nature of the patriarchal narratives in general. According to the Nuzi documents, which have been found to reflect time and again the social customs of Haran (see COMMENTS on Secs. 15, 25, 35, and the NOTE on xxv 23), possession of the house gods could signify legal title to a given estate, particularly in cases out of the ordinary, involving daughters, sons-in-law, or adopted sons (see Anne E. Draffkorn, *Ilāni/Elohim,* JBL 76 [1957], 219ff.).

This peculiar practice of Rachel's homeland supplies at last the motive, sought so long but in vain, for her seemingly incomprehensible conduct. Rachel was in a position to know, or at least to suspect, that in conformance with local law her husband was entitled to a specified share in Laban's estate. But she also had ample reason to doubt that her father would voluntarily transfer the images as formal proof of property release; the ultimate status of Laban's daughters and their maidservants could well have been involved as well. In other words, tradition remembered Rachel as a resolute woman who did not shrink from taking the law—or what she believed to be the law—into her own hands.

The above technical detail would help to explain why Laban was more concerned about the disappearance of the images than about anything else (vs. 30). For under Hurrian law, Jacob's status in Laban's household would normally be tantamount to self-enslavement. That position, however, would be altered if Jacob was recognized as an adopted son who married the master's daughter. Possession of the house gods might well have made the difference.

Laban knew that he did not have them, but chose to act as though he did, at least to save face. Thus his seeming magnanimity in the end (43 f.) would no longer be out of character. He keeps up the pretense that he is the legal owner of everything in Jacob's possession; yet he must have been aware that, with the images gone, he could not press such a claim in a court of law.

Was the author conscious of all these complex and to him alien details? Such intimate knowledge on his part is scarcely to be expected in the circumstances, after a lapse of centuries and under totally different conditions. In view of E's known tendency to present his heroes in the best possible light (cf. COMMENT on Sec. 25), his present failure to tone down Rachel's apparent misconduct can only mean that he had no basis for doing so. To put it differently, E did not invent this story any more than J made up the wife-sister motif (Sec. 15), since so much intricate background detail could not be improvised and still prove to be authentic by coincidence. Yet this material must have reached the writer (independently of J, it should be stressed!) after a long period of transmission, long enough for the meaning behind the incident to have been completely lost. On both these counts, the ultimate tradition points back to mid-second millennium Har(r)an or earlier, the period to which the story itself is dated. One such example by itself may not be dependable. But when it is joined by others like it, the cumulative evidence becomes increasingly impressive.

43. ENCOUNTERS
(xxxii 1–3: *E;* 4–33: /*J*/)

XXXII 1 Early next morning Laban kissed his daughters and grandchildren good-by; then Laban left on his homeward journey, 2 while Jacob went on his way. And angels of God encountered him. 3 When Jacob saw them, he said, "This must be God's encampment." So he named that site Mahanaim.*a*

/4 Jacob sent messengers ahead to his brother Esau in the land of Seir, the country of Edom 5 and gave them this message:

"To my lord Esau say as follows, 'Thus speaks your servant Jacob: I have been staying with Laban, and have been held up there until now. 6 I own cattle and asses and sheep, menservants and maidservants. I am sending this information to my lord in the hope of gaining your favor.' "

7 The messengers returned to Jacob to say, "We reached your brother Esau; he himself is on his way to meet you, accompanied by four hundred men." 8 Jacob was badly frightened. In his anxiety, he divided the people with him—as well as the flocks, the cattle, and the camels*b*—into two camps.*c* 9 For he reasoned, "If Esau should come upon the one camp and attack it, the other camp may still survive."

10 Then Jacob prayed, "O God of my father Abraham and God of my father Isaac, O Yahweh who told me, 'Go back to your native land and I will be good to you!' 11 I am unworthy of all the kindness that you have so steadfastly shown your servant: I crossed the Jordan with nothing but my staff, and now I have grown into two camps. 12 Deliver me, I pray, from the hand of my brother Esau! Else, I fear, he may come and

---

a Connected with Heb. for "camp."
b LXX omits, cf. NOTE.
c Cf. the name Mahanaim "Twin camps."

strike us[d] down, mothers and children alike. 13 For it was you who said, 'I will be very good to you, and I will make your off-spring like the sands of the sea which are too numerous to count.'"

14 After passing the night there, he selected from what was ready to hand the following present for his brother Esau: 15 200 she-goats and 20 he-goats; 200 ewes and 20 rams; 16 30 milch camels with their colts; 40 cows and 10 bulls; 20 she-asses and 10 he-asses. 17 He put them in the charge of his servants, each drove by itself, and told his servants, "Go on ahead of me, but keep a space between the droves." 18 He instructed the one in the lead, "When my brother Esau meets you and asks, 'Whose man are you? Where are you going? And who is the owner of all this in front of you?'— 19 you shall answer, 'Your brother Jacob's; it is a present dispatched for my lord Esau; and Jacob[e] himself is right behind us.'" 20 He gave similar instructions to the second one, and the third, and all the others who followed behind their droves, namely, "Thus and so shall you say to Esau when you reach him. 21 And be sure to add, 'Your servant Jacob is right behind us.'" For he reasoned, "If I first propitiate him with advance presents, and then face him, maybe he will forgive me." 22 And so the gifts went on ahead, while he remained in camp that night.

23 In the course of that night he got up and, taking his two wives, the two maidservants, and his eleven children, he crossed the ford of the Jabbok. 24 After he had taken them across the stream, he sent over all his possessions. 25 Jacob was left alone. Then some man wrestled with him until the break of dawn. 26 When he saw that he could not prevail over Jacob, he struck his hip at its socket, so that the hip socket was wrenched as they wrestled. 27 Then he said, "Let me go, for it is daybreak." Jacob[e] replied, "I will not let you go unless you bless me." 28 Said the other, "What is your name?" He answered, "Jacob." 29 Said he, "You shall no longer be spoken of as Jacob, but as

[d] Literally "me."
[e] Heb. "he."

Israel, for you have striven*f* with beings divine*g* and human, and have prevailed." 30 Then Jacob asked, "Please tell me your name." He replied, "You must not ask my name." With that, he bade him good-by there and then.

31 Jacob named the site Peniel,*h* meaning, "I have seen God face to face, yet my life has been preserved." 32 The sun rose upon him just as he passed Penuel,*i* limping on his hip.

33 That is why to this day the children of Israel do not eat the sciatic muscle that is on the hip socket, inasmuch as Jacob's hip socket was stricken at the sciatic muscle./

f Heb. *śārītā*, linked with first part of "Isra-el."
g Heb. *'elōhīm*, for second part of "Isra-el."
h Taken as "The face (*pny*) of El."
i Older form of the place name.

NOTES

The verse count follows the Hebrew text. In many English translations, ch. xxxii begins with the present vs. 2.

xxxii 1. *good-by.* Literally "and he blessed them"; cf. xxvi 31, and vs. 30, below.

2. *encountered him.* Heb. *pg'* construed with *b*ᵉ- conveys the idea of physical contact. On this basis, the present incident has an inner connection with the encounter at Peniel, vss. 23 ff.

3. *Mahanaim.* The name is formally a dual of the noun for "camp"; cf. the "two camps" of vss. 8, 11.

5. The correct syntax of this verse, as against the traditional accents, was recognized by Ehrl., although he was not aware of the conclusive outside evidence. A man who is about to pray to God for help against his brother is not likely to speak of him privately as "my lord"; this address is part of the message to be delivered. An exact parallel is provided by the routine epistolary formula of Akk.: *ana N bēliya qibima umma N waradkāma* "To my lord X say, Thus (speaks) your servant Y."

6. The size of the possessions is subtly left undefined through the use of singular nouns with the force of collectives.

in the hope of gaining your favor. Another nuance of the idiomatic phrase "to find favor in one's eyes."

8. *the camels.* This entry, which is lacking in LXX, is syntactically suspect in that it lacks the prepositional *'et*. No camels are mentioned in vs. 6, but they are included in the list of presents (vs. 16).

9. *he reasoned.* Literally "said (to himself)"; also in vs. 21.

10. *I will be good to you.* That is, "make it advantageous for you"; cf. Num x 32.

11. *all the kindness . . . steadfastly.* An extension of the principle of hendiadys.

12. *strike us down.* The pronoun in Heb. is in the singular, "me" referring to the master and all that is his.

14. *present.* Heb. *minḥā,* perhaps in intentional assonance with Mahanaim; also vss. 19, 21, 22 ("gifts").

21 f. Note the five occurrences of the stem *pny,* each with a different connotation, yet all leading up to *Peniel* in vs. 31.

21. *propitiate.* Literally "screen the face."

forgive. Literally "lift the face"; cf. xl 13.

26 f. The question about Jacob's name is rhetorical. The object is to contrast the old name with the new and thereby mark the change in Jacob's status.

Israel. The name is best explained etymologically as "May El persevere" (Dr.). But both Jacob and Israel are treated here symbolically, to indicate the transformation of a man once devious (Jacob) into a forthright and resolute fighter.

29. *beings divine.* Not specifically "God"; note the allusion to the present incident in Hos xii 5.

30. *he bade him good-by.* Cf. NOTE on vs. 1; no blessing can be involved at this point, since that was already represented in the change of the name.

31. *Peniel.* The spelling in this instance points back to the multiple aetiology, vss. 21 f. Elsewhere Penuel (as in 32). For this locality in Transjordan, cf. Judg viii 8 f.; I Kings xii 25.

COMMENT

In this section, an incident with overtones that are all too mundane (4–22) has been fitted between two frightening spiritual experiences. To be sure, the authorship is not uniform. The Mahanaim episode (1–3) is manifestly from *E* (note the occurrence of Elohim in vs. 2), whereas the rest of the chapter bears the stamp of *J* (cf. vs. 10). Nevertheless, Mahanaim would seem to have an inner relationship with Penuel (32), aside from an external connection with the "twin camps" of vs. 8. In all likelihood, therefore, the subject matter of the entire section was familiar to both sources.

In fact, the chapter as a whole is given over to encounters of one kind or another: actual and anticipated, sublime and trifling. Ironically enough, it is the incalculable that turns out to be real, while the carefully calculated never comes off. The contrast is significant, if not altogether deliberate. As has been stressed repeatedly in other sections, biblical history in general, and patriarchal history in particular, unfolds on two planes. At the one level, man is entangled in his ephemeral personal affairs; at the other level, there can be glimpsed a master plan wherein man is used as the unwitting tool of destiny.

On several occasions, Abraham was favored with an insight into the divine purpose: Promise and Covenant (Sec. 18: *J*); Abraham intercedes for Sodom (Sec. 22: *J*); the Ordeal of Isaac (Sec. 28: *JE*). The wonder is greater in the case of Jacob, who would not appear offhand to be marked as an agent of destiny. Yet Jacob is afforded a glimpse of a higher role through the medium of his vision at Bethel (Sec. 37: *JE*), on the eve of his long sojourn with Laban. Now that he is about to return to Canaan, he is given a forewarning at Mahanaim, and is later subjected to the supreme test at Penuel.

The general purpose of the Penuel episode should thus be sufficiently clear. (For various views on the subject, cf. F. Van Trigt, OTS 12 [1958], 280–309.) In the light of the instances just cited, such manifestations serve either as forecasts or as tests. Abraham's greatest trial came at Moriah (xxii). That the meaning of Mahanaim was similar in kind, though clearly not in degree, is indicated by the affective *pg' bᵉ-* (see NOTE on vs. 2). The real test, however, was reserved for Penuel—a desperate nocturnal struggle with a nameless adversary whose true nature does not dawn on Jacob until the physical darkness had begun to lift. The reader, of course, should not try to spell out details that the author himself glimpsed as if through a haze. But there can surely be no doubt as to the far-reaching implications of the encounter. Its outcome is ascribed to the opponent's lack of decisive superiority. Yet this explanation should not be pressed unduly. For one thing, Jacob's injury was grave enough to cost him the contest, if such a result had been desired. And for another thing, the description now embodies three distinct aetiologies: (1) The basis for the name Israel; the change of names is itself significant of an impending change in status (as with Abraham and Sarah; see Sec. 20); (2) The origin of the name Penuel, for which a basis is laid in vss. 21–22 by their fivefold use of the stem *pny* (von Rad). (3) The dietary taboo about the sciatic muscle. Any one of these motifs would suffice to color the whole account.

One may conclude, accordingly, that the encounter at Penuel was understood as a test of Jacob's fitness for the larger tasks that lay ahead. The results were encouraging. Though he was left alone to wrestle through the night with a mysterious assailant, Jacob did not falter. The effort left its mark—a permanent injury to remind Jacob of what had taken place, and to serve perhaps as a portent of things to come. Significantly enough, Jacob is henceforth a changed person. The man who could be a party to the cruel hoax that was played on his father and brother, and who fought Laban's treachery with crafty schemes of his own, will soon condemn the vengeful deed by Simeon and Levi (xxxiv) by invoking a higher concept of morality (xlix 5–7). It is noteworthy that this transformation is intimated by *J* who, unlike *E*, does not normally go out of his way to portray his protagonists as blameless heroes.

44. MEETING BETWEEN JACOB AND ESAU
(xxxiii 1–17: *Jᵃ;* 18a: |*P*|; 18b–20: /*E*/)

XXXIII 1 Looking up, Jacob saw Esau coming, accompanied by four hundred men. He divided his children among Leah, Rachel, and the two maidservants, 2 putting the maids and their children first, Leah and her children next, and Rachel and Joseph last. 3 He himself went on ahead, bowing to the ground seven times, until he was next to his brother.

4 Esau had rushed out to meet him. He hugged him, flung himself upon his neck and kissed him as he wept. 5 Looking about, he saw the women and the children. "Who," he asked, "are those with you?" "The children," he answered, "with whom God has favored your servant." 6 Then the maids came forward with their children, and bowed low; 7 next came Leah with her children, bowing low; lastly, Joseph and Rachel came forward, and bowed low.

8 Esauᵇ asked, "What did you want with all that train that I came across?" He answered, "To gain my lord's favor." 9 Esau replied, "I have enough, my brother; you should keep what you have." 10 But Jacob said, "No, I beg of you! If you will do me the favor, please accept this present from me; just to see your face is like seeing the face of God, now that you have received me so kindly. 11 Accept, then, from me, the bounty that ᶜis offeredᶜ you, inasmuch as God has favored me, and I have plenty." And since he urged him so, Esauᵇ accepted.

12 Esauᵇ said, "Let us start on our journey, and I will travel alongside you. 13 But he replied to him, "As my lord knows, the

ᵃ But cf. COMMENT.
ᵇ Heb. "he."
ᶜ⁻ᶜ Some of the versions read "that I offer" (same cons.).

children are frail. Besides, the flocks and herds are nursing, much to my encumbrance: if one should drive them hard just one day, all the flocks would die. 14 So let my lord go on ahead of your servant, while I travel slowly in the wake of the caravan before me, and of my children, until I join my lord in Seir."

15 Esau answered, "Let me at least put at your disposal some of the men who are with me." But he said, "What for? Please indulge me, my lord." 16 So Esau started back that day on his way to Seir. 17 And Jacob journeyed to Succoth, where he established quarters for himself and made stalls for his livestock. That is why the place came to be called Succoth.ᵈ

|18 Jacob arrived safe in the city of Shechem, which is in the land of Canaan—having come thus from Paddan-aram.| /He encamped within sight of the city; 19 the plot of ground where he pitched his tent he then bought from the sons of Hamor, the father of Shechem, for a hundred kesitahs.ᵉ 20 He erected there an altar and called it *El-elohe-Israel!*/

ᵈ "Huts."
ᵉ A monetary unit of unknown value.
ᶠ That is, "El, the God of Israel."

NOTES

xxxiii 2. *next.* MT has *'ḥrnym*, same form as for "last," evidently through erroneous duplication; the context calls for *'ḥryhm.*

3. *bowing to the ground seven times.* A gesture of submission common in the Amarna Letters.

4. *flung himself upon his neck and kissed him.* For the first verb (literally "fell"), cf. xiv 10, NOTE. The whole is duplicated in (and thus indirectly confirmed by) *Enūma eliš* I, ll. 53 f.: *ītedir kišassu . . . unaššaq šāšu* "he encircled his neck . . . and kissed him." The text is thus correct, even though the Masora indicates some doubt by placing dots over the second verb (evidently because of a Midrashic wordplay—*nšq* "kiss" : *nšk* "bite").

as he wept. MT gives the plural, but it is out of place; LXX has to supply "both of them" for clarity. The text is a simple case of dittography, since the form ends in *-w*, and the next word begins with the same letter.

8. *What.* Heb. literally "who?" which may be so employed under certain conditions; cf Judg xiii 17; Mic i 5.

train. Literally "camp," but the pertinent noun also has the sense of "marching company, division"; cf. Num ii 3 ff.

to gain my lord's favor. Cf. xxxii 6, and vss. 10, 15, below.

11. *bounty.* Literally "blessing."

12. *alongside you.* For Heb. *lngdk*, cf. *kngdw*, ii 18.

13. *much to my encumbrance.* Literally "upon/against me"; cf. xlviii 7.

14. *in the wake.* Cf. xxx 30 (equivalent to "in my footsteps").

caravan. Literally "expedition," from stem *l'k* "to send."

15. *men.* Literally "people."

17. *quarters.* Literally "house"; but this would not be appropriate in view of the short stay, and the normal "tents" elsewhere. The noun is used here solely in contrast with "huts," thus pointing up the aetiology of Succoth.

19. For the significance of such purchases, cf. COMMENT on xxiii; note also the approximate correspondence between "the children of Heth" in that passage and "the sons of Hamor" in the present instance.

COMMENT

The meeting between the two brothers turned out to be an affectionate reunion. Jacob's apprehensions had proved unfounded and his elaborate precautions altogether unnecessary. While the intervening twenty years could not erase Jacob's sense of guilt, Esau's resentment had long since vanished.

The sympathetic portrayal of Esau accords well with the picture that J drew of him in ch. xxvii. The present account of the meeting is largely from the same hand, perhaps even entirely. To be sure, vss. 5, 10, and 11 use the term Elohim, hence many critics would assign all or most of 4–11 to E. Actually, however, the argument is far from conclusive. The remarks are addressed to Esau, who would not necessarily be portrayed as a follower of Yahweh; in vs. 10, moreover, the term Elohim is plainly used in the sense of "superior, divine being," exactly as J used it in xxxii 29, and apparently also in 31; see also xxvii 28, and xxxi 50 (Laban speaking). For a reasonably safe division into sources we need not only external but also, and more especially, internal evidence. The entire account of the brothers' reunion is much too well integrated to be composite.

On the other hand, and as a good case in point, the appended notices about Succoth and Shechem are of a different order. Verse 18 contains a gloss from *P,* to judge from the phraseology and the abrupt syntax. And the naming of the altar as "El, the God of Israel" marks the rest as an apparent addition from *E.*

45. THE RAPE OF DINAH
(xxxiv 1–31: *J*)

XXXIV ¹ Dinah, the daughter whom Leah had borne to Jacob, went out to visit some*ᵃ* of the women of the land. ² Shechem son of Hamor the Hivite,*ᵇ* head of the region, saw her, seized her, and slept with her by force. ³ But being deeply*ᶜ* attracted by Dinah daughter of Jacob, and in love with the maiden, he then sought to win her affection. ⁴ Shechem also asked his father, "Get me this girl for a wife."

⁵ Jacob had learned that Shechem*ᵈ* had defiled his daughter Dinah. But his sons were out in the fields with his livestock, so Jacob took no action until they came home. ⁶ Meanwhile Hamor, father of Shechem, had gone to Jacob to make arrangements with him, ⁷ just as Jacob's sons were returning from the fields. When they heard the news, the men were shocked and seething with anger: what Shechem had done, by sleeping with Jacob's daughter, was an outrage in Israel; such things cannot be tolerated.

⁸ Hamor addressed them, saying, "My son Shechem has his heart*ᵉ* set on your daughter. Please give her to him in marriage. ⁹ Intermarry with us; give your daughters to us and take our daughters for yourselves. ¹⁰ You can thus live among us: the land shall be open to you to settle, move about freely, and acquire holdings in it." ¹¹ Then Shechem addressed himself to her father and brothers, "Do me this favor, and I will pay whatever

---

ᵃ Expressed in Heb. by *bi-*.
ᵇ LXX "Horite," see COMMENT.
ᶜ Literally "his soul, being."
ᵈ Heb. "he."
ᵉ Cf. textual note *ᶜ*.

you say. 12 Ask of me a bridal payment ever so high, and I will pay whatever you say; only give me the maiden in marriage!"

13 Jacob's sons replied to Shechem and his father Hamor with guile—speaking as they did because their sister Dinah had been defiled— 14 and said to them, "We could not do this thing, and give our sister to someone uncircumcised, for that would be a disgrace among us. 15 On one condition only will we give in to you: if you become like us by having all your males circumcised. 16 Then we can give our daughters to you and marry your daughters, settle among you, and be one kindred. 17 But if you do not agree to our terms as regards circumcision, we will take our daughter and go."

17 Their request seemed fair to Hamor and Shechem son of Hamor. 19 The youth lost no time in acting on the request, so strong was his desire for Jacob's daughter; and he was more respected than anyone else in his clan.

20 Hamor and his son Shechem went to their town council and addressed their fellow townsmen as follows: 21 "These men are our friends. Let them settle in the land and be free to move about in it; there is ample room in the country for them. We can take their daughters in marriage and give our daughters to them. 22 But the men will accede to our request that they live with us and become one kindred only on one condition: that all our males be circumcised as they themselves are circumcised. 23 Would not the livestock they have acquired—all their animals —then become ours? So let us give in to them, that they may settle among us."

24 All the ꞌable-bodied men in the communityꞌ agreed with Hamor and his son Shechem, and every male—every able-bodied man in the community—was circumcised.

25 On the third day, while they were still ailing, Dinah's brothers Simeon and Levi, two of Jacob's sons, took each his sword, advanced against the city unopposed, and massacred all the males. 26 They also put to the sword Hamor and his son Shechem, removed Dinah from Shechem's house, and left.

ꞌ–ꞌ Literally "all who go out at the gate of his city"; see NOTE.
ᵍ Initial *u-* omitted in MT through haplography, but attested in Sam., LXX, Syr.

²⁷ When⁹ the other sons of Jacob came upon the slain, they plundered the city in reprisal for the sister Dinah's defilement. ²⁸ They seized their flocks and herds and asses, everything that was inside the city and outside, ²⁹ and all their possessions; they took all their children and their wives as captives, and plundered everything that was in the homes.

³⁰ Jacob said to Simeon and Levi, "You have brought trouble upon me by making me obnoxious to the inhabitants of the land, the Canaanites and the Perizzites. With our ranks so meager, if they unite against me and attack me, I shall be wiped out with all my people." ³¹ But they retorted, "And should our sister have been treated like a whore?"

NOTES

xxxiv 1. Dinah. Cf. NOTE on xxx 21.

2. the Hivite. One of the terms that MT applies to the Hurrians, reserving "Horite" as a rule for the predecessors of Edom in Seir. LXX, however, still recognizes Horites in Palestine proper; cf. NOTE on x 15 and the COMMENT on Sec. 30.

head. That is, "chief," not "prince": cf. NOTE on xxiii 6. The non-authoritarian nature of his office is plainly indicated in vs. 20.

slept with her by force. Literally "lay with her and violated her" (hendiadys).

3. he then sought to win her affection. Literally "he spoke at/upon her heart," not so much to comfort her as to persuade her; see Judg xix 3; Hos ii 16 (Ehrl.).

5. were out in the fields. This could have been a considerable distance away, so that the men did not necessarily come home every night.

took no action. Literally "kept still"; cf. xxiv 21.

6. to make arrangements. Literally "to speak," i.e., enter into negotiations for the girl on behalf of his son.

7. an outrage in Israel. A deed regarded as moral anathema by the Israelites; cf. Judg xix 23; Deut xxii 21; Jer xxix 23.

cannot be tolerated. Literally "is/are not done."

10. You can thus live among us. Heb. inverts for special emphasis.

move about freely in it. The prevailing translation "trade therein" is against both syntax and context. The Heb. verb shr signified originally "to circle, follow an irregular course," and this range of meaning persists in Akkadian and Aramaic. The verb is construed with the accusative (also and xlii 34), which accords well with "to traverse," but could not possibly yield "to trade in" (i.e., *in* the land, not buy and sell land). The connotation "to trade" is a late secondary development in Heb. and Jewish Aramaic based on the noun *sōḥēr* "merchant" (cf. xxiii 16), i.e., "peddler, one who makes the rounds." The main point of Hamor's argument is that as relatives by marriage, the Israelites would be regarded as full-fledged citizens rather than as *gērīm;* in xlii 34, Joseph tells his brothers that, once they have established their innocence by producing Benjamin, they would be free to go about as they pleased instead of being detained as spy suspects. Moreover, the patriarchs are constantly described as pastoral folk (cf. xlvi 32, 34, xlvii 3), and not as merchants. For a full discussion, cf. my paper in BASOR 164 (1962), 23–28.

12. *a bridal payment.* Heb. *mohar umattān,* not as two separate items but as one payment of the amount due the family for release of the girl; for a similar hendiadys in Akkadian cf. *biltu u mandattu,* literally "tribute and payment," i.e., payment of tribute.

13. *speaking . . . because.* For the same use of *'ăšer* in this narrative, cf. vs. 27.

16. *one kindred.* Heb 'am as a consanguineous body; see JBL 79 (1960), 157 ff.

20. *their town council.* Literally "the gate of their town," the place where all public business was transacted and hence, by extension, "community," as in Ruth iii 11.

23. *the livestock they have acquired.* Heb. "their property/livestock and their possessions," clearly a hendiadys as proved by xxxi 18, where the same two nouns are in construct state, "the livestock/property in their possession"; this way the appended "their beasts" is explicative instead of redundant; see also xxxvi 6.

24. *All the able-bodied men in the community.* Literally "all those who go out at the gate of his city," with the verbal stem used in its technical sense of going to war; a phrase analogous to "all those who come in at the gate of his city," i.e., who participate in the city council; for the latter term, cf. NOTE on 20, above, and for the idiom, see xxiii 10, NOTE and reference. The whole point of the passage before us is that all the potential defenders were incapacitated (cf. next verse). Women and children were not involved directly (cf. 29), yet they too would be included in this description if the phrase were to be interpreted literally; for the original discussion on the subject see Ehrl.

25. *unopposed.* Heb. "in security," which describes not the confident mood of the city but the attackers' immunity from effective interference.

27. *the other sons of Jacob.* Heb. often expresses the sense of the "other" through mere juxtaposition. Simeon and Levi are obviously not

involved in this particular deed, having been responsible for the massacre in the first place, so that they could not be among the brothers who "came upon" the corpses by accident.

in reprisal for. Literally "because of"; cf. vs. 13.

29. Cf. Num xxxi 9.

30. *You have brought trouble.* The basic meaning of the stem is to muddy waters, hence to upset, and the like.

with all my people. The Heb. noun is literally "house," i.e., *bẹt* in the sense of *bẹt 'āb* "clan."

COMMENT

The narrative is unusual on more counts than one. For one thing, it is the only account to concern itself with Jacob's daughter Dinah, who is otherwise relegated to two statistical entries (xxx 21, xlvi 15). For another, Jacob himself has a minor part, while the spotlight rests throughout on the next generation. For still another, there is a pronounced chronological gap between this section and the one before. There, Jacob's children were still of tender age (xxxiii 14); here, they have attained adulthood.

Most important of all, the history of Jacob has hitherto been in the main a story of individuals. This time, to be sure, personalities are still very much in the forefront of the stage; but their experiences serve to recapitulate an all but lost page dealing with remote ethnic interrelations. The account, in other words, presents personalized history, that is, history novelistically interpreted. And since we have so little independent evidence about the early settlement of Israelites in Canaan, the slender thread that we find here assumes that much more importance. By the same token, extra caution is needed to protect the sparse data from undue abuse.

With such a stratified context before us, it is no wonder that the documentary analysis of the chapter has run into its share of snags. All critics are agreed that the core stems from *J;* many of them, however, have been bothered by various intrusions, obvious or imaginary, but have not been able to decide whether they are to be attributed to *P, E,* or to both. If *P* has received the majority vote, it is due largely to certain unmistakable connections between this chapter and ch. xxiii, notably the idiomatic reference to the "city gate" (vs. 24, *bis,* xxiii 10, 18). But the last-named chapter as a whole can no longer be credited to P (see *ad loc.*). What is more, the present section is no respecter of home talent. Jacob is presented in an unimpressive light, and his sons Simeon and Levi are all but condemned for their primitive impulses (cf. also xlix 5–7); on the other hand, the portrayal of Shechem and Hamor is certainly not lacking in sympathy. Such impartiality and forthrightness cannot be said to be typical of *E*, let alone *P*; but we have met with it in *J*, especially in ch. xxvii. All in all, therefore, and having regard also to the smooth flow of the narrative as a whole, there is no valid reason for assuming a conflate text. The whole may be attributed to *J* with moderate confidence, beyond such minor blemishes as are to be expected in the transmission of very old tales.

Now if the narrative rests somehow on a historical foundation, what is its ultimate background in fact? The actual events behind the story would have to go back far enough in time to allow for the transformation into the personalized version that was handed down to *J*. Fortunately, there still are a few scattered guideposts for a tentative, yet plausible, reconstruction. Shechem was inhabited at the time by Hurrian elements; the text (vs. 2) calls Hamor a Hivite, but the LXX identifies him as a Horite. This latter identification is supported by two independent details: (1) The Shechemites are as yet uncircumcised, a circumstance that supplies the key feature of the story; the contrary was presumably true of Semitic Canaanites. (2) Cuneiform records from the region of Central Palestine have shown that Hurrians were prominent there during the Amarna age (ca. 1400 B.C.); they must have arrived prior to that date.

There is, furthermore, the fact (as has already been mentioned) that Simeon and Levi are depicted here as headstrong and vengeful. In later sources, Simeon is a rudimentary tribe settled in the south of Judea, a long way from Shechem; and Levi has no territorial holdings whatsoever. Evidently, therefore, a pair of once vigorous tribes had suffered critical losses in their attempt to settle in Central Palestine, losses which they were never able to recoup. Standard tradition retained no memory of that remote event, except for the faint echo in the Testament of Jacob (xlix), where the blame is laid, significantly enough, on the two brother tribes themselves. The period in question should thus be dated before the Exodus, and very likely prior to Amarna times.

The story before us is a tale of sharp contrasts: pastoral simplicity and grim violence, love and revenge, candor and duplicity. There is also a marked difference between the generations. Hamor and Jacob are peace-loving and conciliatory; their sons are impetuous and heedless of the consequences that their acts must entail. The lovesick Shechem prevails on his father to extend to the Israelites the freedom of the land—with the requisite consent of his followers. But Dinah's brothers refuse to be that far-sighted. After tricking the Shechemites into circumcising their males, and thus stripping the place of its potential defenders, they put the inhabitants to the sword. Jacob is mournful and apprehensive. But his sons remain defiant and oblivious of the future.

XXXV ¹ God said to Jacob, "Proceedᵇ to Bethel, where you shall remain to build there an altar to the God who appeared to you when you were fleeing from your brother Esau." ² So Jacob told his household and all the others who were with him, "Rid yourselves of the alien gods in your midst, then cleanse yourselves and put on fresh garments. ³ We will proceedᵇ to Bethel, where I shall build an altar to the God who answered me when I was in distress, and who has been with me wherever I have gone." ⁴ They handed over to Jacob all the alien gods in their possession, and the rings that were in their ears; Jacob buried them under the terebinth near Shechem, ⁵ and they set out. And a terror from God fell on the settlements round about them, so that they did not pursue Jacob's men.

⁶ Thus Jacob arrived in Luz—that is, Bethel—in the land of Canaan, together with all the people who were with him. ⁷ There he built an altar and named it El-bethel, for it was there that God had revealed himself to him when he was fleeing from his brother.

⁸ Death came, meanwhile, to Deborah, Rebekah's nurse; she was buried under the oak below Bethel; hence it was named Allon-bacuth.ᶜ

/⁹ God appeared again to Jacob upon his arrival from Paddan-aram, and blessed him. ¹⁰ God said to him,

> "You whose name is Jacob,
> You shall be called Jacob no more,
> But Israel shall be your name."

ᵃ Basically.
ᵇ Literally "arise, go up."
ᶜ That is, "Oak of Weeping."

Thus he was named Israel. 11 And God said to him,

> "I am El Shaddai.
> Be fertile and increase;
> A nation, yea an assembly of nations,
> Shall descend from you,
> And kings shall issue from your loins.
> 12 The land that I gave to Abraham and Isaac
> I now give to you,
> And to your offspring to come
> Will I give this land."

13 Then God was gone from him—*at the spot where he had spoken with him.*/

14 On the site where he had spoken with him, Jacob set up a stele of stone, over which he offered a libation; and he poured oil upon it. /15 And Jacob named that site Bethel, because God had spoken there with him./

d–d Perhaps dittography from next verse; omitted in Vulg.

NOTES

xxxv 2. *alien gods.* That is, images which some of Jacob's people were bound to have brought along from Har(r)an; for the usage, cf. xxxi 19 in the light of xxxi 30.

the others. Implied through juxtaposition; cf. xxxiv 27, NOTE.

put on fresh garments Literally "change your garments," for the forthcoming occasion.

4. *the terebinth near Shechem.* See NOTE on xii 6.

5. *a terror from God.* On the numinous use of Elohim cf. i 2, xxx 8.

settlements. Heb. *'ir* designates settlements of various sizes.

6. This verse may well be from *P.*

7. On El-bethel, cf. NOTE on xxxi 13 (especially for the cun. reference).

God. According to xxxi 13, it was God who appeared to Jacob at Bethel; but xxviii 12 speaks of "angels of God." The present occurrence is construed with the verb in the plural, and should perhaps be rendered "divine beings."

8. *Rebekah's nurse.* Cf. xxiv 59, where no name, however, is given; this laconic notice may have been displaced (Dr.).

9. *again.* There has been so far no mention of an actual theophany

since Jacob's departure from Paddan-aram. The writer (*P*) may have had in mind the first visit to Bethel; or else, the adverb is intended as a general (and later) reference to the account given above.

10. For another version of the change of names (in a different source), see xxxii 28 f.

13. The second part of the verse is duplicated exactly in vs. 14, where the preposition *b-* (in/at) is in order, whereas here it is out of place; evidently, a dittographic error in the present instance.

14–15. Cf. xxviii 18–19. Between the two passages, all three sources, *J*, *E*, and *P*, are on record on this particular subject—with inevitable conflation and duplication.

COMMENT

Bethel marks two significant stages in Jacob's life: one on his flight from Esau (Sec. 37), and the other on his return trip home, many years later. Each received attention from more than one source. The first episode was duly noted by *E* as well as *J*. The present account is likewise composite. The main contribution comes from *E* (1–8); *J* is probably to be credited with vs. 14. But we now have also an unmistakable addition from *P* (vss. 9–13, and apparently 15), one of the few passages from this source to be woven into the Jacob story.

With three documents thus converging on the same site, a site that was the scene of two episodes, a certain amount of duplication and confusion is to be expected. In the previous narrative, it was *J* who recorded the aetiology of the name Bethel (xxviii 19), while *E* had Jacob set up a commemorative stele (xxviii 18). This time the naming is recorded by *P*, who also notes the change of Jacob into Israel; the latter event was traced back by *J* to Jacob's nocturnal contest at Penuel (xxxii 28 f.). Thus the one thing on which all three sources are in accord is the spiritual significance of the site in patriarchal times.

47. BRIEF NOTICES ABOUT JACOB'S FAMILY
(xxxv 16–20: *E;* 21–22a: ╱*J*╱; 22b–29: |*P*|)

XXXV 16 Then they set out from Bethel; but when they were still some distance away from Ephrath, Rachel was in child-birth; she had hard labor. 17 When her labor was at its hardest, her midwife said to her, "Have no anxiety, for you have another boy." 18 With her last gasp—for she was dying—she named him Ben-oni[a]; his father, however, called him Benjamin.[b] 19 Thus Rachel died; she was buried on the road to Ephrath—now Bethlehem. 20 On her grave Jacob set up a monument, the same monument that is at Rachel's grave to this day.

╱21 Israel journeyed on, and pitched his tent beyond Mig-dal-eder. 22 While Israel was encamped in that region, Reuben went and lay with Bilhah, his father's concubine; and Israel found out.╱

|The sons of Jacob were now twelve. 23 The sons of Leah: Jacob's first-born Reuben; and Simeon, Levi, Judah, Issachar, and Zebulun. 24 The sons of Rachel: Joseph and Benjamin. 25 The sons of Rachel's maid Bilhah: Dan and Naphtali. 26 And the sons of Leah's maid Zilpah: Gad and Asher. These are the sons of Jacob who were born to him in[c] Paddan-aram.

27 Jacob came home to his father Isaac at Mamre, in Kiriath-arba—now Hebron—where Abraham and Isaac had sojourned. 28 Isaac's age came to 180 years. 29 Then he breathed his last and died, old and in the fullness of years; and he was gathered to his kin. He was buried by his sons Esau and Jacob.|

[a] Understood as "son of misfortune," or "son of my vigor."
[b] Understood as "son of the right"; see COMMENT.
[c] See NOTE.

Notes

xxxv 16. *They were still some distance away from Ephrath.* Literally "there was still a stretch of land to go to Ephrath."

was in childbirth. Not "gave birth" because she was still in labor. The same inchoative aspect of the verb is found also in the next verse, "she was dying," not "she died."

17. *When her labor was at its hardest.* A parade example of the "elative" use of the Hiphil, for which see JCS 6 (1952), 81 ff., and cf. for other intransitive uses iii 6. Note the contrast between "she had hard labor" (Piel) and "her labor was at its hardest" (Hiphil). Failure to observe this idiomatic distinction has led to redundant translations and misjudgment of the text.

22. *was encamped.* For this connotation of the stem *škn* cf. xvi 12. This usage is characteristic of *J*.

26. *in Paddan-aram.* If the preposition was not loosely used, this statement would imply that Benjamin too was born in Mesopotamia. Very likely, we have here a difference in traditions. The preceding notice about the birth of Benjamin in Canaan stems from *E*, whereas the present summary is from *P*.

29. Cf. the similar notice (also by *P*) in xxv 8 (death of Abraham).

Comment

The section combines several notices, which deal with various topics: birth of Benjamin and death of Rachel (16–20); Reuben's transgression (22a); list of Jacob's sons (22b–26); and death of Isaac (27–29). All three sources have contributed. *P*'s hand in 22b ff. is immediately apparent. But the preceding segment is in itself not of a piece. The difference is marked externally by the alternation of the names Jacob (20) and Israel (21 f.), which becomes a consistent documentary criterion in the Joseph story, where Jacob is employed by *E* and Israel by *J*. Accordingly, vss. 16–20 are assigned to the former, and 21–22a to the latter.

The birth of Benjamin is specifically linked by *E* to the last stage of Jacob's long journey, when he was virtually within sight of home after many years of exile; for the possibility of a variant tradition in *P* cf. Note on vs. 26. The infant is given two names. One, Ben-oni, is attributed to the dying mother, but its meaning is obscure. The element 'ōnī may signify "my vigor" (cf. xlix 3), and this sense is supported by the orthography; the context, however, favors (at least symbolically) "misfortune, suffering" (from a different root), and this interpretation is preferred by tradition (cf. also Hos ix 4); it has furthermore good extra-biblical parallels (e.g., Akk. *Bilti-marṣat* "my burden is grievous"). The other name, Benjamin, is ascribed to the father. It means literally "son of the right (side, hand, or the like)," that is, one on whom the father expects to count heavily for support and comfort; or, alternatively, one who promises good fortune, a propitious turn of events. The analysis of the name has been complicated by the occurrence of the tribal term *DUMU* (plural) *-yamin* in the Mari documents; the first element is written logographically, so that the reading is uncertain, but it means "sons of." This designation is applied to southern Amorite elements, as opposed to their northern counterparts, the *DUMU* (plural) *-šim'āl*. The correspondence, however, could be coincidental; if it is not, the original meaning of the biblical name would have to be "Southerner."

The laconic notice about Reuben's immorality is echoed in xlix 3 f. and Deut xxxiii 6; the offense cost Reuben his birthright (I Chron v 1). In terms of history, these scattered hints suggest that the tribe of Reuben once enjoyed a pre-eminent position, only to fall upon evil days. In the Song of Deborah, Reuben is reproached and taunted for his failure to respond to the national emergency (Judg v 15 f.). Together with Simeon and Levi (cf. xxxiv), the two descendants next in order of seniority, Reuben became politically insignificant. But tangible evidence about the events in question is unfortunately lacking.

The list of Jacob's sons would be pointless if it stemmed from the same writers who have already introduced us to all twelve brothers in a far more vivid manner (xxix 31–xxx 24; and 16–18, above). But the present enumeration has come down not from J and E but from P, a fact that may account also for the apparent reference to Paddan-aram as the birthplace of Benjamin (vs. 26), along with that of his brothers.

There still remains the chronological discrepancy between the present notice of Isaac's death at the age of 180 (vs. 28), and the account in xxvii, according to which Isaac was all but dead before Jacob ever set out for Haran. Yet on the basis of xxv 26 and xxvi 34 (both from *P*), Isaac would have had to survive that deathbed scene by some 80 years (see COMMENT on Sec. 36). *P*'s chronology is self-consistent, but it cannot be integrated with the data of *J* and *E*. Moderate documentary analysis, by enhancing the credibility of each separate source, can only add to one's appreciation of the work as a whole.

48. EDOMITE LISTS
(xxxvi 1–xxxvii 2a: P*a*)

XXXVI 1 This is the line of Esau—that is, Edom.

2 Esau chose his wives from among Canaanite women: Adah, daughter of Elon the Hittite, Oholibamah, daughter of Anah-son*b*-of-Zibeon the Hivite,*c* 3 and Basemath, daughter of Ishmael and sister of Nebaioth.*d* 4 Adah bore Eliphaz to Esau; Basemath bore Reuel; 5 and Oholibamah bore Jeush, Jalam, and Korah. These are the sons of Esau who were born to him in the land of Canaan.

6 Esau took his wives and his sons and daughters, and all the members of his household, his livestock comprising various beasts, and all the property that he had acquired in the land of Canaan, and went to the land *of Seir,*e* away from his brother Jacob. 7 For their possessions had become too many for them to stay together; and the land in which they were sojourning could not support them on account of their livestock. 8 So Esau settled in the hill country of Seir—Esau being Edom.

9 This is the line of Esau, ancestor of Edom, in the hill country of Seir.

10 These are the names of Esau's sons: Eliphaz, son of Esau's wife Adah; Reuel, son of Esau's wife Basemath. 11 The sons of Eliphaz were: Teman, Omar, Zepho, Gatam, and Kenaz. 12 Eliphaz son of Esau also had a concubine Timna, who bore Amalek to Eliphaz. These are the descendants of Esau's wife Adah.

---

a In final compilation, see COMMENT.
b MT "daughter"; see NOTE.
c "Horite" in vs. 20; see NOTE.
d For conflicting lists of Esau's wives, see NOTE on vs. 3.
e–e Mt omits; see NOTE.

13 And these are the sons of Reuel: Nahath, Zerah, Shammah, and Mizzah; they were the sons of Esau's wife Basemath.
14 And these were the sons of Esau's wife Oholibamah, daughter
of Anah-son*b*-of-Zibeon, whom she bore to Esau: Jeush, Jalah,
and Korah.

15 These are the clans*f* of the children of Esau.

Descendants of Eliphaz, Esau's first-born: the clans of
Teman, Omar, Zepho, Kenaz, 16 Korah, Gatam, and Amalek.
These are the clans of Eliphaz in the land of Edom; they are de-
scended from Adah.

17 Descendants of Esau's son Reuel: the clans Nahath, Zerah,
Shammah, and Mizzah. These are the clans of Reuel in the land
of Edom; they are descended from Esau's wife Basemath.

18 Descendants of Esau's wife Oholibamah: the clans of
Jeush, Jalam, and Korah. These are the clans of Esau's wife
Oholibamah, daughter of Anah.

19 These are the sons of Esau—that is, Edom—with their
clans.

20 These are the sons of Seir the Horite,*g* occupants of the
land: Lotan, Shobal, Zibeon, Anah, 21 Dishon, Ezer, and Dishan; they are the Horite clans descended from Seir, in the land
of Edom.

22 Lotan's sons were Hori and Hemam; and Lotan's sister was
Timna. 23 These are the sons of Shobal: Alvan, Manahath, Ebal,
Shepho, and Onam. 4 These are the sons of Zibeon: Aiah and
Anah—he is the Anah who found water*h* in the wilderness while
he was pasturing the asses of his father Zibeon. 25 These are the
children of Anah: Dishon and Oholibamah daughter of Anah.
26 These are the sons of Dishon*i*: Hemdan, Eshban, Ithran,
and Cheran. 27 These are the sons of Ezer: Bilhan, Zaavan, and
Akan. 28 And these are the sons of Dishan: Uz and Aran.

29 These are the Horite clans: the clans Lotan, Shobal, Zib-

---

f Traditional "dukes, chiefs."
g "Hivite" in vs. 2.
h Syr.; trad. "hot springs."
i Cf. vss. 21, 30, and I Chron i 41; Heb. "Dishan."

eon, Anah, 30 Dishon, Ezer, and Dishan. These are the clans of the Horites, clan by clan, in the land of Seir.

31 These are the kings who reigned in the land of Edom before any king reigned over the Israelites. 32 Bela son of Beor became king of Edom, and the name of his city was Dinhabah. 33 When Bela died, he was succeeded as king by Jobab son of Zerah, from Bozra. 34 When Jobab died, he was succeeded by Husham from the land of the Temanites. 35 Upon the death of Husham, Hadad son of Bedad became king in his stead, the one who defeated the Midianites in the land of Moab; the name of his city was Avith. 36 When Hadad died, Samlah of Masrekah succeeded him as king. 37 Upon the death of Samlah, Shaul from Rehoboth-on-the-River became king in his stead. 38 When Shaul died, he was succeeded by Baal-hanan son of Achbor. 39 Upon the death of Baal-hanan son of Achbor, Hadad[j] became king in his stead; the name of his city was Pau, and his wife's name was Mehetabel daughter of Matred-son[k]-of-Mezahab.

40 And these are the names of the clans of Esau—each with its subdivisions and localities—by their names: the clans Timna, Alva, Jetheth, 41 Oholibamah, Elah, Pinon, 42 Kenaz, Teman, Mibzar, 43 Magdiel, and Iram.

These are the clans of Edom, as settled in territories which they hold—Edom's father being Esau.

XXXVII 1 Jacob, meanwhile, settled in the land where his father had sojourned, the land of Canaan.

2 Such, then, is the line of Jacob.

[j] Heb. "Hadar," but see I Chron i 50 f., and cf. Sam.
[k] MT "daughter"; cf. textual note[b].

NOTES

xxxvi 2. *Anah.* In MT "daughter of Zibeon" (same as in 14), but "son" in Sam., LXX, Syr. In vs. 24, however, Anah is a celebrated son of Zibeon. The error (*bt* for *bn*) was probably induced by the correct *bt* after Oholibamah. A better way to indicate the relationship in English would be "Oholibamah daughter of Anah-ben-Zibeon," or Anah "Zibeon-son."

Hivite. The analogue in vs. 20 uses "Horite"; the latter reading is undoubtedly correct. For while Hivite is a virtual synonym of Horite/Hurrian, it is not interchangeable with the homophonous "Horite" of Seir; See COMMENT.

3. The present list of Esau's wives agrees with vss. 9–14 below, but departs from xxvi 34 and xxviii 9. The other two jointly yield:

> Adah, daughter of Beeri the Hittite
> Basemath, daughter of Elon the Hittite
> Mahalath, daughter of Ishmael and sister of Nebaioth;

whereas the list before us gives

> Adah, daughter of Elon the Hittite
> Oholibamah, daughter of Anah the "Horite"
> Basemath, daughter of Ishmael and sister of Nebaioth.

Curiously enough, both notations (in the three passages in question) go back to P. This is not a matter of textual dislocation but rather one of conflicting compilations, evidently by different researchers in the "P" school.

6. *his livestock comprising various beasts.* Literally "his livestock, that is (explicative wᵉ-, cf. i 14), all his beasts." The trad. "and his cattle, and all his beasts" is obviously illogical; *miqnê* "livestock" alone covers all domestic animals; cf. xxxiv 23.

and went to the land of Seir. MT "and went to a/the land" is manifestly defective; hence the Targumim add "(to) another (land)," while LXX reads "from the land of Canaan"; the text here assumed is given by Syr. (where it is surely conjectural), and supported indirectly by vs. 8.

away from. Heb. *mippᵉnē* either "from the presence" or "on account of" (as in vs. 7).

7. *their livestock.* Note that this term is inclusive; cf. preceding verse.

11. *Teman.* Elsewhere, the name of a district in Edom; cf. Amos i 12; Jer xlix 7, 20, etc.

Kenaz. Cf. xv 19.

12. The notice about the concubine appears to be parenthetical; if it is not, then Timna's son was legally counted as Adah's.

Amalek. Cf. xiv 7; here probably a branch of that people (Dr.).

15. *clans.* See COMMENT.

20. *Seir the Horite.* According to Deut ii 12, the Horites of Seir were supplanted by descendants of Esau.

24. *water.* MT *hymm* (vocalized *hayyēmīm*) is variously reproduced by the ancient versions: Sam. "the Emim," cf. Deut ii 10; TO "the

giants"; Ar. "the mules." There is no warrant for the traditional "hot springs." The simplest solution is to assume (with Syr.) a mechanical transposition of an original *hmym*. The discovery of water in the desert would be sufficient cause for astonishment.

26. *Dishon.* MT mispoints to "Dishan." But the descendants of the latter are listed in 28; cf. also 30. I Chron i 41, in a passage which reproduces the list, spells out Dishon; see also LXX, Sam. (manuscripts).

32. *Bela.* Heb. cons. *bl'* calls to mind Balaam (cons. *bl'm*), likewise son of Beor, Num xxii 5; but the similarity appears to be coincidental.

37. *Rehoboth-on-the-River.* "The River," used absolutely, is normally the Euphrates. But an Edomite king of Mesopotamian origin cannot be posited without other evidence. A local river could conceivably have figured in such a place name, to distinguish it from other names with the same popular connotation; cf. x 11, and for a well by the same name, see xxvi 22.

39. *Hadad.* MT "Hadar" is an obvious slip (see textual note *j*), involving the frequent interchange of written *D/R*; cf. x 4: D/Rodanim.

Mehetabel. An Aramaic formation.

40. *each with its subdivisions and localities.* Traditional "according to their families, after their places."

xxxvii 2a. For the significance of this clause, see the discussion in the COMMENT.

COMMENT

The evaluation of this section depends to some extent on our understanding of xxxvii 2a. The clause in question reads, "These are the *tōleḏōt* of Jacob." The technical term can be taken in its usual sense of "line, genealogy," in which case it could not possibly refer to what follows, since no genealogy is given there; or it may be understood in its secondary sense of "history, story" (as in ii 4a), in which case it would definitely be a colophon. Either way, therefore, this particular occurrence of *tōleḏōt* must go with what precedes. If the term stands for genealogy, then ch. xxxvi is pertinent in that it deals with the descendants of Esau, who was a son of Isaac; the clause under discussion would then be tantamount to something like "This concludes the genealogies of Jacob." But if the secondary meaning is more appropriate, the clause marks the dividing line between the story of Jacob, whose generation must now yield to the next, and that of Joseph, which is just beginning. In that event, the notation need not have anything to do with ch.

xxxvi directly; indirectly, however, it would still point up the fact that the Edomite lists have to be traced back to Esau's father Isaac. The section itself, of course, is sufficient proof of a solid interest in Edom; the *tōlᵉdōt* clause seeks only to show why these lists were included in a composite history of patriarchal times.

Esau-Seir is the ancestor of the Edomites in the same way that Jacob-Israel is the eponym of the Israelites. As Israel's neighbor and close relative, Edom is no stranger to biblical tradition, even though it never loomed large in historical times. There must have been, however, a period in the formative stage of Israel when Edom's position had been of greater consequence. This is still reflected by Esau's status as the older of the twins. The surrender of his birthright to Jacob (xxv 29 ff.) is but a reminder of the eventual turn in political fortunes. The present section contains another such reminder—indeed, a far more impressive one in a historical sense—with its list of Edomite rulers who antedate any king of Israel (vs. 31; that this statement may be incompatible with the assumption that Moses wrote the Pentateuch was already an issue to Ibn Ezra). It is a bare skeletal framework, to be sure, which archaeology may yet articulate some day. But it has its interest and its value, nevertheless. Eduard Meyer was able to utilize the passage for immensely fruitful deductions—which were later confirmed—as early as 1906 (*Die Israeliten und ihre Nachbarstämme,* pp. 328 ff.). The material, in short, dry though it may seem, is significant in its own way, and it has retained its importance to this day precisely because the nameless researchers who compiled it in ancient times had great respect for such data. But by the time that the results had to be incorporated in the general framework of Genesis, the compilations had grown into several lists, based on much the same facts but arranged according to different principles; hence the various duplications in the composite account that has come down to us.

In these circumstances, the customary breakdown into documentary sources cannot be attempted with much hope of success. The material was based on independent files, so to speak, to be processed eventually, in whole or in large part, by *P*. The fact remains, however, that *P* exercised little if any editorial supervision. This is clearly demonstrated by the record of Esau's wives (vss. 2–4), which departs in detail from *P*'s other lists on the same subject (xxvi 34, xxviii 9; cf. NOTE on vs. 3). It was thus a question of incorporation rather than co-ordination; and it is only in this limited sense that *P* may be described as the "author" of the present section.

The section as a whole subdivides into several lists (cf. von Rad) which appear to be curiously interlocked and repetitious: (a) vss. 1–9; (b) 10–14; (c) 15–19; (d) 20–30; (e) 31–39; and (f) 40–43. List "b" combines the names cited in "a" and "c," while "f" duplicates in turn some of the names in "b." On further probing, however, a pattern begins to emerge. List "a" gives the names of Esau's three wives and their children; "b" starts out with the sons and goes on to the grandchildren; "c" treats the same individuals as heads of clans, and "f" deals outright with "the clans of Esau— each with its subdivisions and localities—by their names" (vs. 40). Some of these tribal elements are actually attested in independent contexts (e.g., Teman, Kenaz, Amalek). The pertinent technical term *'allūp,* trad. "chieftains, dukes" (the latter based on Vulg. *dux*), stands here for "clan, group" (cf. *'elep* "thousand"). This meaning is confirmed by the supplementary comment "in the land of Edom" (vss. 16, 17; cf. 20); individuals would not be so described (cf. also Exod xv 15).

The two remaining lists are substantially different from the above. List "d" records a number of clan-eponyms who are explicitly designated as Horite (29 f.); it also contains an incidental notice (vs. 24) that is in the style and spirit of narratives (cf. xxx 14). And list "e" gives a succession of Edomite kings, all of whom antedate the Israelite monarchy. Interestingly enough, none of these rulers was succeeded by his son; this feature is paralleled in Israel under the period of the Judges, but the institution of kingship presupposes a more developed system of government in ancient Edom. The same list "e" includes also an aside (vs. 35), which recalls the marginal notations in the Mesopotamian king lists. All in all, there is a marked difference between "d"–"e" and "a"–"c," "f"; but it would be going too far to attribute the first two to *J.*

The term Horite (vss. 20, 21, 29) calls for special comment. In vs. 20, one of the men so characterized is Zibeon son of Seir; but in vs. 2 the same person is designated as a Hivite. The assumption that "Hivite" is here a textual slip for "Horite" fails to take account of other aspects of the problem. The received Heb. text does not recognize any Horites in Palestine proper; the LXX, on the other hand, reads "Horite" for Heb. Hivite in xxxiv 2 and Josh ix 7. These Horites/Hivites may safely be equated with the extra-biblical Hurrians, whose personal names have turned up in the very areas where MT speaks of Hivites. The latter term was evidently a synonym for "Horite," which MT used consistently where Hurrians were involved.

But the Horites of Seir-Edom can no longer be equated with Hurrians. There is no archaeological or epigraphic trace of the Hurrians anywhere in Edomite territory. Moreover, the Horite personal names recorded in this section (20 ff.) are clearly Semitic in so far as they can be analyzed at all (so already Meyer, *op. cit.*). It follows that Heb. *Ḥōrī* (in common with Cush, see NOTE on x 6) designated two unrelated groups: the non-Semitic Hurrians, who had spread to Syria and North-Central Palestine; and the Semitic group that bore by coincidence the same name and was centered in Seir. Hebrew tradition evidently sought to differentiate between these homophones: for the Hurrian Shechemites and their relatives it adopted the synonymous term "Hivite" (as in xxxiv 2); but for the proto-Edomites Hebrew retained the other and unrelated term *Ḥōrī*, which was apparently of Semitic origin, perhaps even "cave dweller," as tradition has suspected all along. That the writer of vs. 2 should have called them Hivites can only indicate that he must have confused them with their non-Semitic namesakes. The variant in vs. 2 would thus be a "learned" but unsuccessful correction of vs. 20.

II. THE STORY OF THE PATRIARCHS

C. Joseph and His Brothers

49. JOSEPH SOLD INTO EGYPT
(xxxvii 2b–36: J, /E/ᵃ)

XXXVII 2b At seventeen years of age, Joseph tended flocks with his brothers. He was assisting the sons of his father's wives Bilhah and Zilpah; and Joseph brought his father bad reports about them.

3 Now Israel loved Joseph more than any of his other sons, for he was the child of his old age; and he made him an ornamentedᵇ tunic. 4 When his brothers saw that their father loved him more than any of his ᶜother sons,ᶜ they came to hate him so much that they could not say a kind word to him.

5 One time, Joseph had a dream, which he told to his brothers; and this made them hate him even more. 6 He said to them, "Listen to the dream I had! 7 In it,ᵈ we were binding sheaves in the field, when suddenlyᵈ my sheaf rose up and stood upright; and your sheaves formed a ring around my sheaf and bowed down to it!" 8 "Do you propose," his brothers asked him, "to rule over us? Are you to be our master?" And they hated him all the more for his talk about his dreams.

9 Then he had another dream, which he told to his brothers, saying, "Look, I had another dream! This time,ᵈ the sun and the moon and eleven stars were bowing down to me!" 10 When he recounted it to his father,ᵉ his father rebuked him. "What is the meaning," he asked him, "of this dream of yours? Shall I and your mother and your brothers come bowing to you to the

---

ᵃ For details cf. COMMENT and NOTES.
ᵇ Traditional "of many colors," or "with sleeves."
ᶜ–ᶜ So with several manuscripts, Sam., LXX; MT "brothers."
ᵈ Literally "here, behold."
ᵉ MT adds "and to his brothers"; LXX, Syr. omit.

ground?" 11 But while his brothers were wrought up at him, his father pondered the matter.

12 One day, when his brothers had gone off to pasture their father's flocks at Shechem, 13 Israel said to Joseph, "Look, your brothers are with the flocks at Shechem. Come, let me send you to them." "I am ready," he answered. 14 "Go then," he went on, "find out how your brothers and the flocks are faring, and bring back word." With that, he sent him off from the valley of Hebron, and he made his way to Shechem.

15 A man came upon him as he was wandering in the fields. "What are you looking for?" the man asked him. 16 "I am looking for my brothers," he replied. "Could you tell me where they are pasturing?" 17 The man answered, "They have moved on from here; in fact, I heard them say, 'Let us go on to Dothan.'" So Joseph followed his brothers and caught up with them in Dothan.

18 They noticed him from a distance; and before he got close to them they conspired to kill him. 19 They said to one another, "Here comes that dreamer! 20 Why don't we kill him now and throw him into one of the pits? We could say that a wild beast devoured him. We shall then see what came of his dreams!"

/21 When Reuben[f] heard this, he tried to save him from their hands. He said, "Let us not take his life! 22 Shed no blood!" Reuben told them. "Just throw him into that pit, out there in the desert, but don't do away with him yourselves"—his purpose being to deliver him from their hands and restore him to his father. 23 So when Joseph reached his brothers, they stripped Joseph of his tunic, the ornamented tunic that he was wearing, 24 and they seized him and threw him into the pit. The pit was empty; there was no water in it./

25 They sat down to their meal. Looking up, they saw a caravan of Ishmaelites coming from Gilead, their camels bearing gum, balm, and ladanum to be taken to Egypt. 26 Then Judah said to his brothers, "What would we gain by killing our brother and covering up his blood? 27 I say,[g] let us sell him to the Ish-

f So MT; for the proposed emendation to "Judah," see NOTE.
g Literally "come."

maelites, but let us not do away with him ourselves. After all, he is our brother, our own flesh!" His brothers agreed.

/28 Meanwhile, Midianite traders passed by, and they pulled Joseph up from the pit./ They sold Joseph to the Ishmaelites for twenty pieces of silver.   /Joseph was thus taken to Egypt. 29 When Reuben went back to the pit and saw that Joseph was missing, he rent his clothes 30 and returned to his brothers, exclaiming, "The boy is gone! What am I to do now?"

31 They took Joseph's tunic, slaughtered a kid, and dipped the tunic in its blood. 32 They had the ornamented tunic taken to their father, and they said, "We found this. Make sure whether it is your son's tunic or not." 33 He recognized it, and exclaimed, "My son's tunic! A wild beast devoured him! Joseph fell prey to beasts!"

34 Jacob rent his clothes, put sackcloth on his loins, and mourned his son many days. 35 All his sons and daughters tried to console him, but he refused to be consoled, saying, "No, I will go down to Sheol in mourning!" Thus did his father lament him.

36 The Midianites, meanwhile, sold Joseph^h in Egypt to Potiphar, a courtier of Pharaoh, his chief steward./

^h MT "him."

NOTES

xxxvii 2b. *He was assisting.* For this sense of Heb. *na'ar* "attendant," or the like, cf. Exod xxxiii 11.

bad reports. For the same phrase, cf. Num xiv 37.

3. *Israel.* As applied to Jacob (but not in the phrase "children of Israel"), an invariable indication of J's authorship; cf. xxxv 21, and COMMENT *ad loc.;* see also vs. 13.

and he made. Note the circumstantial aspect in Heb. (signified by the use of the perfect).

an ornamented tunic. The traditional "coat of many colors," and the variant "coat with sleeves" are sheer guesses from the context; nor is there anything remarkable about either colors or sleeves. The phrase, Heb. *k^etonet passīm,* occurs aside from this section (also vss. 23, 32) only in II Sam xiii 18 f., where it describes a garment worn by daughters of kings. Cuneiform inventories may shed light on the garment in question. Among various types of clothing listed in the texts, there is one called *kitû* (or *kutinnû*) *pišannu* (cf. JNES 8 [1949], 177). The important thing there, besides the close external correspondence with the Heb. phrase, is that the article so described was a ceremonial robe which could be draped about statues of goddesses, and had various gold ornaments sewed onto it. Some of these ornaments would occasionally come undone and need to be sent to the proper craftsman for repairs, hence the notation in the inventories. If the comparison is valid—and there are several things in its favor—the second element in the Heb. phrase, i.e., *passīm*, would be an adaptation of Akk. *pišannu*, a technical term denoting appliqué ornaments on costly vests and bodices.

The last clause is generally attributed to *E* on account of vss. 23, 32 (*E*).

4. *him*. The pronoun is emphasized in Heb. through inversion.

his other sons. So with Sam., LXX, and several Heb. manuscripts, ("other" is implicit in the juxtaposition), against "his brothers" in the text, which was probably copied inadvertently from the beginning of the clause.

5. *One time*. Implicit in the initial *wa-*.

and this made them hate him even more. Literally "and they proceeded to hate him more"; this clause is missing in LXX.

8. *his talk about his dreams*. Literally "his dreams and his words."

10. *to his father*. Heb. adds "and to his brothers," which LXX leaves out, no doubt justifiably, since Joseph had already described his dream to his brothers (vs. 9); by the same token, the added "and to his father" in the LXX version of vs. 9 is equally gratuitous. Joseph apparently reported first to his brothers (9) and then to his father, without realizing how invidious his words might seem; later copyists tried to fill in imaginary lacunae, to the detriment of the original account.

11. *pondered*. Literally "guarded" (i.e., in his mind). Jacob knew enough to realize, on second thought, that dreams should not be discounted offhand.

13. *Look*. Heb. *haḷō'* "is it not?" which is merely another way of saying *hinnē* "here, behold."

14. *I am ready*. Heb. *hinnēnī*, literally "here I am," for which cf. xxii 1, NOTE. A mechanical translation would be particularly pointless in this sequence.

17. *Dothan*. Modern Tell Dothan, about a day's journey north of Shechem.

18. *conspired*. Literally "sought/weighed clever schemes."

20. *Why don't we kill him*. Literally "come, let us kill him."

pits. Primarily, water holes or cisterns.

21. Most moderns would change Reuben in this verse to Judah, on the assumption that the next verse would otherwise be a duplicate; the change to Judah, would certify the present verse as J's, so that the redundancy would actually be due to two separate sources. The reasoning, however, is by no means cogent. It calls for an emendation for which there is no encouragement from any of the ancient versions. What is more, the alleged duplication vanishes once the Heb. imperfect is understood in a conative sense, i.e., "he tried, attempted to save him"; for the related inchoative aspect of the Heb. verb, cf. xxxv 16 f. On this basis, both vss. 21 and 22 go naturally together; accordingly, both may be attributed to the same source, in this case E. Judah's independent effort (according to J) is dealt with in vss. 26–27.

22. *his purpose being*. Literally "in order that," which introduces the author's comment.

25. *Ishmaelites*. The traders in question according to J; also vs. 27 f.; Joseph's protector is now Judah.

For a discussion of the goods which the Ishmaelites were transporting to Egypt, cf. the monograph by J. Vergote, *Joseph en Egypte*, 1959, pp. 10 ff.; this study will be cited henceforward as "Vergote"; see also J. M. A. Janssen, *Ex Oriente Lux* 14 (1955–56), 63–72.

27. *I say*. Literally "come," with the auxiliary connotation that this stem shares with the Heb. verb "to rise."

let us not do away with him. Literally "let us not lay (our) hands on him"; but such a translation would be misleading inasmuch as the brothers had to take Joseph by force in order to throw him down the cistern.

28. The first part of this verse is manifestly from another source (*E*) which knew nothing about the Ishmaelite traders. It speaks of Midianites who pulled the boy up from the pit, without being seen by the brothers, and then sold him in Egypt into slavery. This is why Reuben was so surprised to find that Joseph was gone. The sale to the Ishmaelites, on the other hand (28b: *J*), had been agreed upon by all the brothers (27: *J*), so that Reuben would have no reason to look for the boy in the pit, let alone be upset because he did not find him there. This single verse alone provides a good basis for a constructive documentary analysis of the Pentateuch; it goes a long way, moreover, to demonstrate that *E* was not just a supplement to *J*, but an independent and often conflicting source; cf. pp. xxii ff.

34. *Jacob*. A reliable witness of *E;* contrast vss. 3, 13.

36. *Potiphar*. An Egyptian personal name, "One whom (the god) Re has granted."

courtier. Literally "eunuch."

chief steward. Literally "chief/master of the cooks," a royal post which was probably as far removed from its original connotation as, say, "Lord Chamberlain." For a possible Eg. prototype, cf. Vergote, pp. 31 ff. The title, Heb. *šar haṭṭabbāḥīm*, should not be confused with the analogous *rab haṭṭabbāḥīm* (II Kings xxv 8 ff.; Jer xxxix 9 ff., etc.), approximately "captain of the guard," but reflecting a non-Egyptian office.

COMMENT

The last major division of Genesis concentrates with but a few exceptions (notably xxxviii) on the eventful story of Joseph. It is at once the most intricately constructed and the best integrated of all the patriarchal histories. For sustained dramatic effect the narrative is unsurpassed in the whole Pentateuch. The theme is essentially personal and secular. Other aspects, to be sure, are in evidence here and there, yet they are never allowed to distract attention from the central human drama.

In retrospect, of course, the story of Joseph was seen as a link in a divinely ordained course of human history. But while the writing is by no means oblivious of this approach, the theological component has been kept discreetly in the background. And the ultimate historical framework is understated to such a degree that the related data on the Sojourn in Egypt and the eventual Exodus are to this day beset by uncertainties. What has come down is a richly personal document, which accounts no doubt for its great appeal.

An achievement of such literary excellence should be, one would naturally expect, the work of a single author. Yet such is definitely not the case. While *P*'s part in the story of Joseph is secondary and marginal, *J* and *E* are prominently represented throughout, each in his own distinctive way. The casual reader is hardly aware that he has a composite story before him; and even the trained analyst is sometimes baffled when it comes to separating the parallel accounts. All of which points up the skillful and unobtrusive achievement of the compiler or redactor. For the most part he was content to take substantial portions from each source and arrange them consecutively. Only on rare occasions did he find it necessary to intertwine the two narratives. The present section is a case in point; it is also a parade example of the problems involved in documentary detection of this kind, as well as the benefits which may lie in store.

In this particular instance we lack the immediate external evidence from references to the Deity, since neither Yahweh nor Elohim happens to occur in the chapter before us. Nor can much be made of the motif of dreams, prominent though it is here. For while it is true that dreams play a significant part in the E narrative (cf. chs. xx, xxviii, xxxi), they help to identify the source only when used as a medium of contact between God and man. This time, however, no such message is as yet involved. Joseph's two dreams are a factor in the relations between him and his brothers; as such, they would not be ignored by any good writer, certainly not by J.

We do get, however, for a start, a valuable hint from another quarter. Joseph's father is called Israel in vss. 3 and 13, but Jacob in 34. Elsewhere in the Joseph story, Israel can be traced confidently to J (also in xxxv 21), and Jacob to E (and P). Thus J's hand is apparent in the first part of the chapter, and E's toward the end; but the middle portion is chaotic at first glance.

It goes without saying that external evidence from personal names or typical motifs is valid only to the extent to which it accords with the internal evidence of the content as a whole. The work of a competent writer surely presupposes an inner consistency of theme and details. Yet vss. 21–30, as they now read, are marked by inconsistency, duplication, and discrepancies. First Reuben, in the hope of saving Joseph later on, persuades his brothers not to kill him but throw him instead into an empty cistern, which they do (21–24). Then Judah, who is also intent on sparing Joseph's life, prevails on his brothers to sell the boy to a passing caravan of Ishmaelite traders, which they do likewise (25–27). Meanwhile, Midianite traders turn up who, unnoticed by the brothers, discover Joseph in the pit, pull him out, and take him with them to Egypt— where he is eventually sold to Potiphar; the discovery takes place at the same time that the same boy is bought by the Ishmaelites at the low slave rate of twenty shekels (28). Small wonder that Reuben, who knows nothing about the sale, is shocked at not finding his brother in the cistern (29–30).

All this confusion is dissipated automatically once the narrative is broken up into two originally independent versions. One of these (J) used the name Israel, featured Judah as Joseph's protector, and identified the Ishmaelites as the traders who bought Joseph from his brothers. The other (E) spoke of Jacob as the father and named Reuben as Joseph's friend; the slave traders in that version were Midianites who discovered Joseph by accident and sold him in Egypt to Potiphar. Each source is entirely self-consistent thus far, and goes on to build on its own set of data, which hold up meaningfully as the story unfolds. Indeed, each version gains in significance and impact when viewed as a unit unto itself.

For all the existing differences in detail, sight should not be lost of the prevailing similarities. In both versions Joseph is his father's favorite and is bitterly resented by his brothers; he can count on only one friend among them; eventually he falls into the hands of nomadic traders who sell him into slavery in Egypt. Without this common core there would be no story of Joseph in Egypt. The divergencies must be due to the fact that tradition had seized on the subject matter long before it was committed to writing, so that there was ample time for the details to develop differently, and to fall into slightly varying patterns during the process of oral transmission. Today, the documentary distribution may not be clear in every given instance (cf., for example, the NOTE on vs. 21). But the main contours would seem to be assured.

Lastly, it may be in order to return, in passing, to the question about the ultimate compiler's approach to his task. A verse like 28 could hardly have been regarded as satisfactory by a conscientious redactor. It was impossible to ignore the discrepancy between the Midianites and the Ishmaelites in two adjoining clauses. The omission of either one would have eased the problem considerably; yet the remedy was not applied. Undoubtedly it could not be because no such editorial license was permissible. R could still rearrange the material in J and E into a connected text, but he was not free to suppress any statement in either source. The remarkable thing is that the whole still appears to be deceptively smooth, after so much legitimate scrutiny by modern critics.

50. JUDAH AND TAMAR
(xxxviii 1–30: *J*)

XXXVIII ¹ At about that time, Judah parted from his brothers and put in with a certain Adullamite named Hirah. ² There Judah met the daughter of a Canaanite named Shua, and he married her and cohabited with her. ³ She conceived and bore a son, *ᵃwho was namedᵃ* Er. ⁴ She conceived again and bore a son, whom she named Onan. ⁵ Then she bore still another son, whom she named Shelah; they wereᵇ at Chezib when she bore him.

⁶ Judah got a wife for his first-born Er, and her name was Tamar. ⁷ But Er, Judah's first-born, displeased Yahweh, and Yahweh took his life. ⁸ Then Judah said to Onan, "Unite with your brother's widow,ᶜ fulfilling the duty of a brother-in-law, and thus maintain your brother's line." ⁹ But Onan, knowing that the seed would not count as his, let it go to waste on the ground every time that he cohabited with his brother's widow, so as not to contribute offspring for his brother. ¹⁰ What he did displeased Yahweh, and he took his life too. ¹¹ Whereupon Judah said to his daughter-in-law, "Stay as widow in your father's house until my son Shelah grows up"—for he feared that this one also might die like his brothers. So Tamar went to live in her father's house.

¹² A long time afterward, Judah's wife, the daughter of Shua, died. When the period of sorrow was over, Judah went to Timnah for the shearingᵈ of his sheep, in the company of his friend Hirah the Adullamite. ¹³ When Tamar was told, "Your father-in-law is on his way to Timnah for the sheep-shearing,"

ᵃ⁻ᵃ MT "he named him," but see NOTE.
ᵇ MT "he was"; LXX "she was"; cf. NOTE.
ᶜ Literally "wife."
ᵈ Literally "upon the shearers."

14 she took off her widow's garb, wrapped a veil about her to disguise herself, and sat down at the entrance to Enaim, which is on the way to Timnah; for she saw that, although Shelah was grown up, she had not been given to him in marriage. 15 When Judah saw her, he took her for a harlot, since she had covered her face. 16 So he turned aside to her by the roadside, and said, "See now, let me lie with you"—not realizing that she was his daughter-in-law. She answered, "What will you pay me for lying with me?" 17 He replied, "I will send you a kid from my flock." But she answered, "You will have to leave a pledge until such time as you send it." 18 He asked, "What pledge shall I leave you?" She answered, "Your seal-and-cord, and the staff you carry." So he gave them to her, and lay with her, and she conceived by him. 19 She left soon, took off her veil, and resumed her widow's garb.

20 Judah sent the kid by his friend the Adullamite to redeem the pledge from the woman, but he could not find her. 21 He inquired of the men of that place, "Where is the votary, the one by the Enaim road?" They answered, "There has never been here a votary!" 22 So he went back to Judah and said to him, "I couldn't find her. What is more, the townspeople told me, 'There has never been here a votary.' 23 And Judah replied, "Let her keep the things, or we shall become a laughingstock. I did my part in sending her the kid, but you never found her."

24 About three months later, Judah was told, "Your daughter-in-law has played the harlot; moreover, she is with child from harlotry." "Bring her out," Judah shouted, "and she shall be burned!" 25 As they were taking her out, she sent word to her father-in-law, "It is by the man to whom these things belong that I am with child. Please verify," she said, "to whom these things belong—the seal-and-cord and the staff!" 26 Judah recognized them, and said, "She is more in the right than I, inasmuch as I did not give her to my son Shelah." Nor was he intimate with her again.

27 When it was time for her to give birth, there were twins in her womb! 28 While she was being delivered, one put out his hand, and the midwife tied a crimson thread on his hand, to

signify: this one came out first. ²⁹ But just then he drew back his hand, and out came his brother; and she said, "What a breach*e* you have opened for yourself!" So he was named Perez. ³⁰ Then his brother came out, with the crimson thread on his hand. So they named him Zerah.*f*

e Heb. *pereṣ.*
f Perhaps "brightness," alluding to the crimson band.

NOTES

xxxviii 1. *At about that time.* Literally "at that time," which in this context would amount to "at the precise time that Joseph was being sold to Potiphar." But the Heb. phrase is formulaic and just as general as the corresponding Akk. *ina ūmišu* "on his/that day, then."
parted from. Heb. "went down from," namely, from the hill country.
put in with. Literally "turned aside next to."
2. *met.* Literally "saw."
3. *who was named.* The corresponding Heb. has masculine singular, which is often used impersonally (as in 29 f.). But Sam., TJ, and some Heb. manuscripts have the feminine, the same as Heb. in vss. 4 and 5, no doubt correctly. The translation is neutral.
5. *Chezib.* Probably the same as Achzib, Josh xv 44; Mic i 14.
7. *displeased.* Literally "was bad in the sight of." The nature of the offense is not specified here, unlike vs. 10.
8. *widow.* Heb. uses "wife," namely, "your (dead) brother's," but such ambiguity is less acceptable in translation; in vss. 14, 19 Heb. employs the abstract noun "widowhood," in speaking of a widow's garb.
fulfilling the duty of a brother-in-law. Heb. literally "levirate her." The institution of levirate, whereby a man married his brother's childless widow in order to provide continuity for the line of the deceased, is an alternative to adoption; cf. JBL 79 (1960), 161 f. The requirement was later relaxed, cf. Deut xxv 5 ff.
line. Literally "seed"; the same noun, Heb. *zera',* is used in the next verse both in its literal sense and in the secondary sense of "offspring."
11. *Stay.* The cons. text *šby* can be vocalized to yield either "return" (cf. Lev xxii 13) or with tradition, "stay, dwell"; but no repointing appears necessary in this instance.
12. *A long time afterward.* Literally "days/years multiplied, and."
When the period of sorrow was over. Literally "when he had been consoled," when the time for mourning and condolence was past.

for the shearing. The Heb. noun is vocalized as "shearers"; but cf. the infinitive in vs. 13. If the text is retained, the translation should read "to (supervise his) shearers," or the like; the original may have used an abstract plural.

14. *to disguise.* Literally "she covered up"; cf. vs. 15.

the entrance to Enaim. TO, Syr., and Vulg. understand this as the road juncture of/for Enaim. The place is probably the same as Enam in Josh xv 34 (in the Shephelah).

16. The circumlocution for sexual intercourse which Heb. employs here (literally "to go in to"; see NOTE on vi 4) was chosen no doubt as a matter of tact. The phrase has been shaded in the translation of the various passages, depending on the context.

17. *from my flock.* The definite article of Heb. often has the force of the personal pronoun in English, and vice versa; see vs. 21.

pledge. Heb. *ʿērābōn.* A loanword from Akkadian, which is also found in Greek.

18. *seal-and-cord.* The two nouns of Heb. must represent a hendiadys, something like "the seal on the cord" (cf. also the plural form of the second noun in vs. 25, approximately "cording"), for the following reasons. The items named by Tamar were not chosen for their intrinsic value but for purposes of personal identification, as is made clear by vs. 25; when produced in due time, they must allow of no doubt as to their owner. The cylinder seal was such an object above all else; it served as the religious and legal surrogate for the person who wore it, and its impression on a document signalized the wearer's readiness to accept all consequences in the event of non-compliance, through sympathetic magic among other things (like sticking pins in a doll). The possessor of such a seal was thereby marked as a responsible person; and, as Herodotus reminds us, no Babylonian of any standing would ever be seen without one. The use of the cylinder seal spread from Mesopotamia throughout the Near East, and even to Crete; and many specimens have turned up in Palestine. While the stamp seal fulfilled a similar function, its use was limited in time and space; moreover, the term for the latter would be *ṭabbaʿat* (xli 42), not *ḥōtām* as here. Now all cylinder seals were perforated vertically for suspension, so that the seal and the cord or chain on which it was worn became a unit. A cord by itself would be a worthless thing, and meaningless in the present context. Incidentally, the inclusion of the cord is further proof that no signet ring was involved.

the staff. Necessarily, another distinctive means of identification. Cuneiform records of the Old Babylonian period often mention the *bukānum,* an object which looked liked a pestle and which changed hands to symbolize the conclusion of certain types of transaction. Whether Judah's staff was comparable cannot be determined. In any case, Tamar knew exactly what she was doing in telling Judah what she wanted from him as a pledge.

19. *soon.* Literally "she arose," as an auxiliary verb; cf. xxxi 21.

21. *that place.* Literally "her place"; cf. vs. 17.

votary. Ancient Near Eastern society, notably in Mesopotamia, recognized various classes of temple women other than priestesses, who were employed for services connected with the cult. We know now that they had to be virgins in order to qualify (HSS XIV [1950], No. 106, line 31); any subsequent promiscuity was ritually conditioned. One of these classes was the *qadištu*, a cognate of Heb. *qᵉdēšā* (vs. 21). There is no indication that they were socially ostracized, although their status was inferior to that of married women. It is obvious that the *qᵉdēšā* was not the same as the *zōnā* (vss. 15, 24; cf. xxxiv 31).

25. *As they were taking her out.* Passive in Heb.

28. *a crimson thread.* Literally "some crimson" (indefinite).

29 f. For the clans of Perez and Zerah, cf. I Chron ii. The aetiologies are, as usual, symbolic retrojections in which the correct etymology is immaterial.

COMMENT

The narrative is a completely independent unit. It has no connection with the drama of Joseph, which it interrupts at the conclusion of Act I. Judah, we are informed, has left his kin and moved to Adullam, in the Canaanite lowlands to the west (cf. Josh xv 35). There he marries a Canaanite woman and has three sons by her, all of whom reach manhood in the course of that stay. Yet no such prolonged interval is indicated when the story of Joseph resumes. Judah is then still a member of Jacob's household (the genealogical notice in xlvi 12 is an insert from *P*).

It is especially interesting that this narrative should stem from *J* (cf. vss. 7, 10), precisely because *J* also has a substantial stake in the Joseph story. Once again it becomes self-evident that the narrators acted in the main as custodians of diverse traditions which they did not attempt to co-ordinate and harmonize when the respective data appeared to be in conflict. The history of Judah was significant in its own right, and it was not to be tampered with, let alone ignored. The place of the present account was chosen with keen literary sensitivity. To his family, Joseph had disappeared from view—forever, as far as they knew. From the viewpoint of the reader, moreover, the ill-treated boy is in temporary eclipse. What better place, then, to take up the slack with a different story, one that covers many years?

Because of the eventual pre-eminence of the tribe of Judah, the personalized history of that branch was of obvious interest to tradition. Through the period of Judges and down to the time of David, Judah expanded by absorbing various Canaanite elements. This beginning of that composite history is here intimated by Judah's settlement among Canaanites and his acquisition of a Canaanite wife. His line, however, is in danger of extinction; but a daughter-in-law by the name of Tamar, apparently another Canaanite, takes heroic measures and triumphs in the end. In resolutely following the intent of the law, by unorthodox and hazardous means, Tamar thus takes her place alongside Rachel (xxxi 19). She had the stuff, it was felt, to be the mother of a virile clan, which is clearly the main theme of the story.

What brings this theme into bold relief is the institution of the levirate marriage, that is, marriage with the wife of a deceased brother (or another relative in special circumstances). The objective was to maintain the family line in a society that set great store by blood ties, and consequently had little use for adoption (see JBL 79 [1960], 161 f.). Biblical law upholds this obligation and frowns on any attempt to circumvent it (cf. Deut xxv 5 ff.; Ruth iii f.).

Judah sought to live up to this practice, yet shrank from risking the life of his last surviving son. When Tamar became convinced that her father-in-law was temporizing, she tricked him into leaving her with child, by waylaying him in the disguise of a harlot. But she had the presence of mind to secure positive proof of her mate's identity (see NOTE on vs. 18). Here *J* adds a subtle human touch. Judah mistakes Tamar for a common harlot (Heb. *zōnā,* vs. 15), just as he was meant to do. But when his friend Hirah seeks to redeem the pledge, he asks for the local *qᵉdēšā* (votary, hierodule, cult prostitute), in order to place the affair on a higher social level.

At the critical moment, Judah finds out that Tamar was no wanton, and absolves her of any guilt in the matter. She rewards him for his candor and understanding by presenting him with twins. An aetiological notice about the boys' names brings the unique tale to a close.

51. THE TEMPTATION OF JOSEPH
(xxxix 1–23: *J*)

XXXIX ¹ When Joseph was taken to Egypt, a certain Egyptian—Potiphar, a courtier of Pharaoh and his chief steward—bought him from the Ishmaelites who had brought him there. ² But since Yahweh was with Joseph, he did very well, and was assigned to his Egyptian master's household. ³ And when his master saw that Yahweh was with him, and that Yahweh lent success to everything that he undertook, ⁴ he took a fancy to Joseph and made him his personal attendant; he also put him in charge of his household and entrusted to him all his possessions. ⁵ And from the moment that he had put him in charge of his household and all his possessions, Yahweh blessed the house of the Egyptian for Joseph's sake; indeed, Yahweh's blessing was on everything he owned, inside and outside. ⁶ And everything he owned was left in Joseph's charge; with him there, the other gave no thought to anything, except the food that he ate.

Now Joseph was handsome of figure and features. ⁷ After some time, his master's wife fixed her eye on Joseph, and said, "Sleep with me." ⁸ He refused. "Look," he told his master's wife, "with me here, my master gives no thought to anything in this house, having entrusted to me all his possessions. ⁹ He wields no more authority in this house than I, and he has withheld from me nothing except yourself, for you are his wife. How then could I commit so great a wrong, to stand condemned before God?" ¹⁰ And much as she cajoled him day after day, he would not agree to lie down beside her ᵃor stay with her.ᵃ

¹¹ One such day, when he came into the house to do his work,

ᵃ⁻ᵃ LXX omits.

and none of the house servants were there inside, 12 she caught hold of him by his coat and said, "Sleep with me!" He got away and escaped outside, leaving his coat in her hand. 13 When she saw that he had left his coat in her hand as he fled outside, 14 she called out to her house servants and said to them, "Look, he had to bring us a Hebrew fellow to make love to us! He broke in on me to sleep with me, but I screamed as loud as I could! 15 When he heard me screaming for help, he left his coat near me and fled outside."

16 She kept the coat by her until his master came home. 17 Then she told him the same story: "The Hebrew slave whom you brought to us only to make love to me broke in on me. 18 But when I screamed for help, he left his coat near me and fled outside."

19 When his master heard the story that his wife told him, namely, "Thus and so did your slave do to me," he was enraged. 20 So Joseph's master took him and threw him into the jail where the crown's prisoners were confined. But even while he was in that jail, 21 Yahweh remained with Joseph; he extended kindness to him and disposed the chief jailer favorably toward him. 22 The chief jailer put Joseph in charge of all the prisoners who were in that jail; and whatever had to be done there, was done through him. 23 Since Yahweh was with him, the chief jailer did not himself supervise anything in his charge whatsoever. And whatever he undertook, Yahweh made prosper.

NOTES

xxxix 1. The words between dashes are a redactorial gloss carried over from xxxvii 36 (E), the last previous verse in the Joseph narrative. Throughout the rest of the chapter, Joseph's master is never referred to by name, but only as "the Egyptian" or "the master."

2. *he did very well*. Literally "he was a man who succeeded." The Hiphil stem *hṣlḥ* is used in this narrative both as intransitive and as transitive (cf. vss. 3, 23).

was assigned to . . . his household. Literally "he was in the house," as opposed to having to toil in the fields.

4. *he took a fancy to Joseph.* Another variation on the theme of "to find favor in one's eyes."

made him his personal attendant. Literally "he ministered to him" (intransitive); the transitive rendering is required in English for clarity.

6. *except the food that he ate.* Possibly an allusion to Egyptian dietary taboos (von Rad); cf. xliii 32.

handsome of figure and features. Same phrase as in xxix 17, but differently translated there because it was used of a woman.

7. *fixed her eye on.* Literally "raised her eyes at/to." The identical idiom is used in Akkadian to describe Ishtar's designs on Gilgamesh (Gilg., Tablet VI, line 6). Yet a literal rendering would be misleading since the Heb. phrase can also denote trustfulness (Ezek xxxiii 25) or prayerful appeal (Ps cxxiii 1 f.).

9. *God.* Not Yahweh this time, because Joseph is speaking to an Egyptian.

10. *cajoled.* Literally "spoke to."

The last clause is not give in one MS of LXX, and may well be a late gloss.

14. *He had to bring us a Hebrew fellow.* The nuance "he had to" is dictated by the sarcastic purpose of the exclamation. Instead of 'îš "man, fellow," it is preferable to read 'îšî "my husband" (same cons.), because the sequel (vs. 17) speaks of a "Hebrew slave," which is far more suitable (Ehrl.). In that case, the translation would read "My husband had to import a Hebrew [slave] . . . !"

The term "Hebrew" (see Note on xiv 13) is applied to Israelites when they speak of themselves to outsiders, or when outsiders refer to them; cf. vs. 17, xl 15, xli 12, xliii 32. It was clearly the more general and widespread designation.

to make love. For this nuance, cf. xxvi 8 (also *J*, but with a different preposition); the possible alternative "to toy with us" is not favored by the context.

to us. That is, Egyptians, who looked down on foreigners such as Hebrews.

15. *screaming for help.* Literally "that I raised my voice and called"; also vs. 18.

20. *jail.* Heb. *bēt hassohar;* cf. Vergote, pp. 25 ff.

COMMENT

The story of Joseph is now resumed with a dramatic episode from J's version; note the mention of Yahweh in vss. 2, 3, 5, 21, 23, and the reference to Ishmaelites in vs. 1. After Judah had prevailed on his brothers to sell the boy to nomad traders rather than take his life (xxxvii 26–27, 28b), the Ishmaelites disposed of him in Egypt to one of Pharaoh's officials. Fortune smiled on the handsome youth until his master's wife became aware of his charms and tried to seduce him. Spurned, she got her revenge by accusing Joseph of attempted rape, offering as proof the coat that Joseph had left in her hand as he fled from the scene. The master had him jailed, but the jailer was soon won over by Joseph, as his owner had been before him.

The name of Joseph's master is given in vs. 1b as Potiphar. But this accords ill with the appended "a certain Egyptian." Besides, there is no mention of the name in the rest of the narrative, where the man is described anonymously as "the master" (vss. 3, 7, 19, 20). Potiphar, on the other hand, is cited in the "Midianite" or E's version (xxvii 36), only one verse above the intrusive episode about Tamar. There can thus be no doubt about the secondary origin of this particular clause.

The motif of a faithless wife who turned on the young man who had spurned her was well known to the Egyptians from "The Tale of the Two Brothers" (now available in J. A. Wilson's candid translation, ANET, pp. 23–25). Whether this circumstance can be invoked to explain the surprisingly mild punishment of Joseph—in that other such accusers were ultimately exposed and the accused vindicated—it is now impossible to decide. Speculations on this subject are natural—but inconclusive. Nor should one overlook the simple point that if Joseph had been subjected to the fate that the ancient Near East normally reserved for such moral offenses—real or presumed—the Joseph story itself would have died an untimely death.

52. JOSEPH INTERPRETS THE DREAMS OF
PHARAOH'S SERVANTS
(xl 1–23: *E*)

XL 1 Some time afterwards, the Cup-bearer and the Baker of the king of Egypt gave offense to their lord, the king of Egypt. 2 Pharaoh was angry with his two courtiers, the chief cup-bearer and the chief baker, 3 and he put them in custody in the house of the chief steward—the same jail where Joseph was confined. 4 The chief steward assigned Joseph to wait on them.

After they had been in custody for some time, 5 both the Cup-bearer and the Baker of the king of Egypt, who were confined in that jail, had dreams the same night, each dream having its own meaning. 6 When Joseph came to them in the morning, he noticed that they were dejected. 7 So he inquired of Pharaoh's courtiers, who were with him in custody in his master's house, "Why are you so downcast today?" 8 They answered him, "We had dreams, and there is nobody to interpret them." Joseph said to them, "Surely, interpretations come from God. Tell me about them."

9 Then the chief cup-bearer told his dream to Joseph. "In my dream," he said to Joseph, "there was a vine in front of me, 10 and on that vine were three branches. It had barely budded, when out came its blossoms, and its clusters ripened into grapes. 11 Pharaoh's cup was in my hand; so I took the grapes, pressed them into Pharaoh's cup, and placed the cup in Pharaoh's hand."

12 Joseph said to him, "This is what it means: The three branches are three days: 13 within three days, Pharaoh will pardon[a] you and restore you to your post, and you will be handing

----

[a] Literally "lift your head"; cf. vss. 19, 20, also xxxii 21, and see COMMENT.

the cup to Pharaoh as was your former practice when you were his Cup-bearer. 14 So if you still remember that I was here with you, when all is well with you again, please do me the kindness to mention me to Pharaoh and try to free me from this place. 15 For I was in fact kidnaped from the land of the Hebrews; nor have I done anything here that they should have put me in a dungeon."

16 When the chief baker saw how well he had interpreted, he said to Joseph, "As regards my dream, there were three wicker baskets on my head. 17 In the uppermost basket were all kinds of pastries that a baker makes; and birds were picking at them out of the basket over my head. 18 Joseph said to him in reply, "This is what it means: the three baskets are three days: 19 within three days Pharaoh will lift off your head and have you impaled on a pole, and birds will be picking off your flesh."

20 And indeed, on the third day, when Pharaoh gave a banquet for all servants—for it was his birthday—he *singled out*[b] the chief cup-bearer and the chief baker from among his servants. 21 He restored the chief cup-bearer to his cup-bearing, so that he again placed the cup in Pharaoh's hand; 22 but the chief baker he had impaled—just as Joseph had indicated to them.

23 Yet the chief cup-bearer gave no thought to Joseph; he had forgotten him.

b–b Literally, "lifted the head of."

Notes

xl 1. *Cup-bearer . . . Baker.* Since these are titles of Pharaoh's officials which alternate with "chief cup-bearer, chief baker," they have been marked by capital letters.

gave offense. Literally "proved to be at fault." Traditional "sinned" is inappropriate, particularly in a secular context.

3. *house.* There is no indication whether the building was private or public.

The second clause refers back to xxxix 20 (*J*). Actually Joseph was not Potiphar's prisoner but his duly acquired slave (xxxvii 36), and as such was assigned by his master to wait on the incarcerated courtiers.

In vs. 15 the noun translated "dungeon" is the same that was rendered "pit" in xxxvii 28a; the whole clause was apparently inspired by that passage, which also records the kidnaping by the Midianites. It is possible, therefore, that vss. 3b, 15b, and also xxxix 20b, are to be regarded as cross references inserted by the compiler.

5. On the general subject of dreams, see E. L. Ehrlich, *Der Traum im Alten Testament*, 1953, and A. Leo Oppenheim, *The Interpretation of Dreams in the Ancient Near East*, 1956.

14. This is an intricately construed sentence, but it yields good Hebrew and excellent sense. The apodosis begins with "please do me the kindness" (Ehrl.). In the protasis, Heb. has literally "if you remember me with you," that is, if you can still recall this occasion, when I was with you.

16. *wicker*. This interpretation of Heb. *ḥōrī* is favored by Arabic; see also Rashi and Ehrl. Such baskets would permit birds to peck at the pastries from the sides as well as the top.

19. *impaled*. Not "hanged"; aside from other evidence, a beheaded man is not for hanging; also vs. 22.

20. *singled out*. Cf. BASOR 149 (1958), 17 ff. On the triple use of *nś' r'š* in this chapter, see COMMENT.

COMMENT

The story of Joseph reached both *J* and *E* in essentially the same outline, but with marked variations in detail. This is why episodes that are really parallel could be construed by the compiler as separate and consecutive, since outward signs of duplications (as in xxxvii 28) are relatively infrequent. On closer probing, however, discrepancies become apparent at every stage, thus helping to distinguish the two separate strands in the narrative.

The whole of ch. xxxix (if one disregards an occasional cross reference) could be safely assigned to *J*. In the present section, on the other hand (as in much of the following), *E*'s authorship is equally assured. One cannot but be struck immediately by the sudden cessation of all references to Yahweh, as against seven such instances within the brief space of the preceding section alone. On the positive side, there is the mention of Elohim in vs. 8; what is more, the passage in question deals with dreams, not merely as a curious experience (such as in xxxvii) but as a prediction of imminent events. The emphasis on the kidnaping (vs. 15), moreover, points back to *E*'s statement about the Midianites who made off with Joseph and sold him to Potiphar (xxxvii 28a, 36). *J*, it will be recalled, had no record of any such thing; in his version, Joseph was sold by his brothers to itinerant Ishmaelites. Incidentally, the pertinent Heb. verb *gnb* is elsewhere used by *E* in a number of shadings and with telling effect (see NOTE on xxxi 19).

Since chs. xxxix and xl thus had different authors, it is not surprising that their accounts of Joseph as prisoner are at variance. *J*'s version had the Hebrew youth advance to the position of unofficial head of the jail (xxxix 22 f.). On the other hand, when we rejoin Joseph with *E* as our guide, he is a hapless stranger who was "kidnaped from the land of the Hebrews" and is now a servant of Egyptian prisoners. In other words, the present chapter is the direct sequel to xxxvii 36, and shows no awareness of *J*'s account in xxxix.

The central theme at this juncture is Joseph's way with dreams. As a gifted interpreter, he has the knack, shared by many oracular mediums, of couching his pronouncements in evocative terms. The key phrase this time is *nś' r'š*, literally "to lift the head." It has several widely deviating connotations, and Joseph—or *E*—plays on these with great skill. One of the meanings is to lift up the head of one who is depressed, mentally or socially, hence "to comfort, pardon"; this nuance is pressed into service in vs. 13. Another sense is grimly literal, namely, "to lift off the head, behead," and this is used in vs. 19. Still another idiomatic usage is "to poll, take the census of, give minute attention to," and the like, exactly as with the corresponding Akk. *rēšam našûm* (BASOR 149 [1958], 17 ff.); cf. Num i ff., where the repeated use of this idiom has supplied the very name of the Book of Numbers. Joseph takes full advantage of this aspect in vs. 20.

The author succeeds thus in making a single phrase symbolize an entire episode: Pharaoh will *review* the cases of his two disgraced appointees, *pardon* the Cup-bearer, but *behead* the Baker. Any one of these distinctive uses might apply to Joseph himself. But the writer is not ready as yet to tip his hand. Good storyteller that he is, *E* knows how to maintain suspense. Restored to grace, the cup-bearer promptly forgets the slave for whom he was to intercede with Pharaoh.

53. WHAT DREAMS DID FOR JOSEPH
(xli 1–57: *E*,ᵃ except 46a: /*P*/)

XLI ¹ After a lapse of two years, Pharaoh had a dream: He was standing beside the Nile, ² when out of the Nile came up seven cows, handsome and sturdy, and grazed in the reed grass. ³ But right behind them, seven other cows, ugly and gaunt, came up out of the Nile and stood on the bank of the Nile beside the others. ⁴ And the ugly gaunt cows ate up the seven handsome sturdy cows. Then Pharaoh awoke.

⁵ He went back to sleep and dreamed a second time: Seven ears of grain, solid and healthy, grew on a single stalk. ⁶ But close behind them sprouted seven other ears, thin and scorched by the east wind. ⁷ And the seven thin ears swallowed up the seven solid and full ears. Then Pharaoh woke up: it had been a dream!

⁸ Next morning, his spirit agitated, he sent for all the magicians of Egypt and all its wise men. Pharaoh recounted his dreams to them, but none could interpret them for Pharaoh. ⁹ Then the chief cup-bearer addressed Pharaoh; "I must make confession of my remissness at this time. ¹⁰ Once, when Pharaoh was angry with his servants, he placed me in custody in the house of the chief steward—me and the chief baker. ¹¹ We both had dreams the same night, he and I; each of us had a dream with a meaning of its own. ¹² A Hebrew youth was there with us, a servant of the chief steward; and when we told him our dreams, he interpreted them for us, telling each the meaning of his own dream. ¹³ And just as he told us, so it turned out: I was restored to my post, but the other was impaled."

ᵃ For a few suspected glosses see NOTES.

14 Pharaoh sent immediately for Joseph, who was rushed from the dungeon. He cut his hair, put on fresh clothes, and appeared before Pharaoh. 15 Pharaoh said to Joseph, "I had dreams that nobody can explain. But I have heard it said of you that you can interpret a dream the instant you hear it." 16 "Not I," Joseph replied to Pharaoh. "God will give Pharaoh the right answer "

17 Pharaoh then said to Joseph, "In my dream, I was standing on the bank of the Nile, 18 when out of the Nile came up seven sturdy and well-formed cows and grazed in the reed grass. 19 But right behind them followed seven other cows, scrawny, exceedingly ill-formed, and emaciated—never have I seen their likes for ugliness in all the land of Egypt! 20 And the seven lean and ugly cows ate up the first seven sturdy cows. 21 Yet when they consumed them, no one could tell that they had consumed them, for they looked just as bad as before. Then I awoke. 22 In my other dream, I saw seven ears of grain, solid and healthy, growing from a single stalk. 23 But close behind them sprouted seven other ears, shriveled and thin and scorched by the east wind. 24 And the thin ears swallowed up the seven healthy ears! I have spoken to the magicians, but none has given me the answer."

25 Joseph said to Pharaoh, "Pharaoh's dreams are one and the same: God has thus foretold to Pharaoh what he is about to do. 26 The seven healthy cows are seven years, and the seven healthy ears are seven years; it is the same dream. 27 The seven lean and ugly cows that followed are seven years also, as are the seven empty ears scorched by the east wind; they are seven years of famine. 28 It is just as I have told Pharaoh: God has revealed to Pharaoh what he is about to do. 29 Immediately ahead lie seven years of great abundance in all the land of Egypt 30 But these will be followed by seven years of famine, when all the abundance in the land of Egypt will be forgotten. As the land is ravaged by famine, 31 no trace will be left in it of the abundance because of the famine thereafter, for it will be most severe. 32 And as for Pharaoh having had the same dream twice, it means that the matter has been reaffirmed by God, and that God will soon bring it about.

33 "Let Pharaoh, therefore, seek out a man of discernment and wisdom, and place him in charge of the land of Egypt. 34 And let Pharaoh take steps to appoint overseers for the land so as to organize[b] the country of Egypt for the seven years of plenty. 35 They shall husband all the food of the good years that lie immediately ahead, and collect the grain by Pharaoh's authority, to be stored in the towns for food. 36 And let that food be a reserve for the country against the seven years of famine that are coming upon the land of Egypt, so that the land may not perish in the famine."

37 The whole thing pleased Pharaoh and all his officials. 38 Said Pharaoh to his officials, "Could we find another like him, one so endowed with the divine spirit?" 39 Then Pharaoh said to Joseph, "Since God has made all this known to you, there could be none so discerning and wise as you. 40 You shall be in charge of my palace, and all my people shall submit[c] to your orders; I shall outrank you only with respect to the throne. 41 See," said Pharaoh to Joseph, "I place you in charge of the whole land of Egypt." 42 With that, Pharaoh removed the signet ring from his hand and put it on Joseph's hand. He then had him dressed in robes of fine linen, and put a gold chain about his neck. 43 He also had him ride in the chariot of his second-in-command, and they shouted "Abrek"[d] before him. Thus was he installed over the land of Egypt.

44 Pharaoh told Joseph, "Although I am Pharaoh, no one in all the land of Egypt shall move hand or foot without your approval." 45 Pharaoh then gave Joseph the name of Zaphenath-paneah,[e] and he gave him as wife Asenath daughter of Potiphera, priest of On. And Joseph became known[f] throughout the land of Egypt.

/46 Joseph was 30 years old when he entered the service of Pharaoh king of Egypt./

b *See* NOTE.
c Meaning of Heb. uncertain.
d Perhaps Eg. "Attention!"
e Probably Eg. "God speaks: he lives."
f Precise meaning uncertain.

After Joseph left Pharaoh's presence, he traveled throughout the land of Egypt. ⁴⁷ During the seven years of plenty, when the land produced in overabundance, ⁴⁸ he husbanded the various crops⁹ of the seven years that the land of Egypt was enjoying, and stored the food in the cities, placing in each city the crops of the fields around it. ⁴⁹ Joseph gathered in grain in very large quantities, like the sands of the sea, until he stopped taking stock, for it was past computing.

⁵⁰ Before the years^h of famine set in, Joseph became the father of two sons, whom Asenath daughter of Poti-phera, priest of On, bore to him. ⁵¹ Joseph named the first-born Manasseh, meaning, "God ʰhas caused me to forgetⁱ entirely my hardships and my parental home." ⁵² And the second he named Ephraim, meaning, "God ʲhas made me fruitfulʲ in the land of my sorrow."

⁵³ The seven years of plenty that the land of Egypt enjoyed came to an end, ⁵⁴ and the seven years of famine set in, just as Joseph had predicted. There was famine in all the countries, but in the land of Egypt there was food. ⁵⁵ And when all of Egypt, too, came to feel the hunger and the people cried to Pharaoh for bread, Pharaoh would tell all the Egyptians, "Go to Joseph; do whatever he tells you."

⁵⁶ As the famine spread throughout the land, Joseph opened ᵏall the storesᵏ and rationed grainˡ to the Egyptians, since the famine in the land of Egypt was becoming severe. ⁵⁷ And all the world came to Joseph in Egypt to obtain rations, for famine had gripped the entire world.

ᵍ Literally "food."
ʰ Literally "year."
ⁱ⁻ⁱ Heb. naššanī, connected with Manasseh.
ʲ⁻ʲ Heb. hiprani, associated with Ephraim.
ᵏ⁻ᵏ Literally "what was in them."
ˡ Supplying br; see NOTE.

Notes

xli 1. *the Nile.* For the underlying Eg. term see T. O. Lambdin, JAOS 73 (1953), 151.

2. *sturdy.* Literally "healthy, robust of flesh."

3. *the others.* Heb. "the cows," i.e., the other cows by juxtaposition.

5. *healthy.* Literally "good(ly)."

8. *magicians.* See Vergote, pp. 80–94; cf. Exod vii 11, 22.

9. *remissness.* Heb. literally "omissions, 'sins,' failings," the plural being used in an abstract sense.

10. *Once.* Implicit in the word order and tense of Heb.

15. *dreams.* This time, singular with collective sense; cf. vs. 8 where the singular noun is construed with plural pronoun. In each instance (also vs. 25) more than one dream is manifestly involved.

27. *empty.* Heb. *rēqōt,* cons. *rqwt;* but Sam., LXX, TO, Syr. show "thin" (cons. *dqwt*), which involves the frequent graphic confusion of R/D. MT may have been influenced by *raqqōt* "lean" in first clause (same cons.). At all events, the sense remains the same.

31. *no trace will be left.* Literally "will not be known."

34. The overseers are regarded by some critics as contrary to the proposal of a single manager in vs. 33; hence they assign 34a to J (cf. Noth, *Überlieferungsgeschichte . . .* , p. 31). Yet the task clearly involved a large staff, so that all that the clause implies is that Joseph could pick his own assistants. Had J recorded the episode, or had his account been available to R, more of it would surely have come through than the few phrases and lines which are alleged to disrupt the flow of E's narrative.

to organize. Traditional "to take a fifth part of" (the land) or alternatively "to divide (the land) into five parts." But a denominative based on "five" is by no means the only possible solution of Heb. *wᵉhimmēš;* and xlvii 24 is not strictly parallel. The very next verse calls for state control over the whole crop. There is, however, a verbal stem *ḥmš,* the passive participle of which means "armed, equipped" in Josh i 14, iv 12; Judg vii 11; cf. also Exod xiii 18; and Arabic employs the identical cognate (Ehrl.). Accordingly, the present occurrence may be safely translated "to organize, regiment," or the like, in complete agreement with attested usage and etymology, not to mention the text.

40. *shall submit to.* Heb. cons. *yšq,* as now pointed (*yiššaq,* preceded by *'al pīkā*), can only mean "shall kiss you on the mouth." By re-pointing the verb to *yāšoq* (with Ehrl.), we obtain the sense here

indicated. For the same sense with *'al pī*, cf. especially Num xxvii 21. If, on the other hand, the meaning of the verb should be something like "be managed," there might be a connection with the noun *mešeq* in xv 2.

42. *signet ring.* Cf. JAOS 73 (1953), 151 and Vergote, pp. 116 ff.; this is not to be confused with the cylinder seal, for which a different noun is employed in xxxviii 18 (see NOTE *ad loc.*).

gold chain. On the royal chain in Egypt see Vergote, pp. 116 ff.

43. *his second-in-command.* For this sense cf. II Chron xxviii 7; not "the second best" (chariot). The Heb. term, like its Akk. analogue *terdennu* (cf. *tartān*, Isa xx 1), is used both as a title and an adjective. Here, however, the title is plainly indicated, for the reference is specifically to the Vizier, who was also the Royal Seal-bearer (42).

Abrek. For a probable Egyptian etymology, see JAOS 73 (1953), 146; contrast, however, Vergote, pp. 135 ff. The alleged "kneel down!" of Heb. origin is morphologically untenable and contrary to the Egyptian background of the episode.

45. *Zaphenath-paneah.* For the underlying Eg. form and meaning, cf. BASOR 140 (1955), 31 and Vergote, pp. 141 ff.

Asenath. Eg. "belonging to (the goddess) Neith"; see Vergote, pp. 148 ff.

Poti-phera. Eg. "he whom Re gave"; cf. Vergote, pp. 146 ff.; a fuller form of the same name as Potiphar (xxxvii 36), but referring to a different person. The name is of a type common to many languages and applicable to many individuals.

On. Cf. vs. 50 and xlvi 20; also Ezek xxx 17. Gr. Heliopolis, seven miles northeast of modern Cairo.

became known in. Heb. literally "rose over"; in this construction, the verb is attested in the sense of "to spread, become familiar" in Esther i 17, and perhaps Ps lxxxi 6. Accordingly, this clause is not a duplicate of 43c, and need not therefore indicate a different source.

46. The first part of the verse is an unmistakable insert from *P*. According to that source, therefore, Joseph's servitude lasted thirteen years (cf. xxxvii 2).

48. *of the seven years.* Sam. and LXX add "of plenty," which MT gives in vs. 53; the omission was caused by haplography ("seven" and "plenty" share the same letters).

51 f. The aetiological explanations of the names are, as usual, independent of correct etymology.

51. *meaning.* Both in vss. 51 and 52 Heb. *kī* takes the place of "saying"; this is clear proof, if such proof were needed, that the particle is not to be confused with the conjunction *kī* "that," in which case the direct address would be stylistically awkward; cf. iv 25, NOTE.

entirely. The repeated *kol* in vs. 51 is not "all" but comparable to our colloquial "all about"; note the use of the term with "parental home."

56. *all the stores.* Heb. literally "all that was in them" is unmanageable as it stands. Sam. reads an added *br* ("everything in which there was grain"; similarly LXX), and these conss. could have been lost through haplography, in view of the form *wyšbr* which follows. It is virtually certain that the same two conss. dropped out after *wyšbr*. The restored passage (with additions given in square brackets) would thus read: *'t kl 'šr bhm [br] wyšbr [br]*. The translation here offered presupposes some such text, since a slavish rendering would have been meaningless, and a neutral translation misleading.

rationed. The Heb. stem *šbr* (noun and verb) is used in the Joseph story specifically of countermeasures against hunger (note especially xlii 19). It is not to be confused, therefore, with "grain" (*br*), "bread" (*lḥm*), or "food" (*'kl*), but should be interpreted (with Ehrl.) as referring to "(emergency) supplies" and the sale or purchase of such; apparently based on the common verb *šbr* "to break (the fast)."

COMMENT

The section forms an organic unit with the preceding chapter. With all of Pharaoh's experts baffled by his two disquieting dreams, the cup-bearer recalls belatedly the lowly Hebrew youth who did so well by him in similar circumstances. Joseph is rushed to the palace, where he soon attains a position second only to that of Pharaoh himself. His subsequent rise to power exceeds even the extravagant promise of his boyhood visions.

The story that is thus artfully built up is in all essentials a secular account. Yet the very fact that the history of Joseph occupies such a prominent place in the patriarchal narratives is sufficient proof, as was indicated earlier, that the subject matter was viewed as part of a broader spiritual pattern. The factual background is now all but obliterated by the rich literary detail. Yet some intimation of a deeper purpose can be found fairly close to the surface. It is God, the author assures us through Joseph, who causes dreams to serve as guideposts to the future (vs. 16). Thus even the distractions of an unusually exciting story cannot crowd out entirely the recurrent refrain that human destiny is divinely ordained. By the same token, Joseph's career as a whole is ultimately but a link in a grander design.

Since the two consecutive sections are so closely interrelated, one expects them to derive from the same source; and they do. E's hand could be discerned throughout ch. xl, and the same holds true of the present chapter: it is Elohim, not Yahweh, whom Joseph invokes when he names his two sons, not to mention his address to Pharaoh; the dream motif is more prominent than ever before; and the cast of characters is basically the same as in ch. xl. To be sure, some apparent discrepancies and duplications have been pointed out toward the end of the chapter. But these are by no means as definite as is sometimes alleged. Indeed, in at least two instances (34a, 45c), the problem is one of interpretation rather than parallel documents (cf. NOTES *ad loc.*). Nor can the minor textual irregularities in vs. 56 be ascribed to an intrusive source. All in all, the case for fractional additions from *J* must be said to rest on very flimsy foundations. The statistical comment by *P* in 46a, on the other hand, is beyond serious dispute.

No appreciable progress has been made in the effort to establish the historical setting of the episode, and with it the identity of the Pharaoh "who knew Joseph." A faint hint, but no more than that, may be contained in vs. 39, which has Pharaoh refer to God with obvious reverence. An Egyptian ruler of good native stock would not be likely to do so, since he was himself regarded as a god. When the Pharaoh of the Oppression speaks of Yahweh in Exodus, he does so in defiance, or in extreme straits, but never in sincere submission. The attitude of the present Pharaoh, therefore (barring an oversight on the part of the author), might conceivably suggest that he was not a traditional Egyptian ruler; and such a description would fit best some member of the foreign Hyksos Dynasty (ca. 1730–1570). It has long been assumed on other grounds that the Hyksos age offered the best opportunity for the emergence of someone like Joseph. Nevertheless, the narrative before us furnishes too slender a basis for historical deductions.

On the other hand, the incidental detail is authentically Egyptian. Pharaoh elevates Joseph to the typically Egyptian post of Vizier (43). This is corroborated by the transfer to Joseph of the royal seal (42), inasmuch as the Vizier was known as the "Sealbearer of the King of Lower Egypt" as far back as the third millennium. (Cf. J. A. Wilson, *The Burden of Egypt*, 1951, pp. 81 f.; and for this and other details, see Vergote, pp. 96 ff.) The gift of the gold chain is another authentic touch. The three names in vs. 45 are Egyptian in type and components; so, too, in all probability, is the escorts' cry "Abrek" (43, see NOTE).

While the story is the main thing, the setting is thus demonstrably factual. And although the theme and the setting together cannot as yet be fitted into an established historical niche, the details are not out of keeping with that phase of Egyptian history which can be independently synchronized with the patriarchal period.

54. THE BROTHERS' FIRST TRIP TO EGYPT
(xlii 1–26, 29–38: *E*ᵃ; 27–28: /*J*/)

XLII ¹When Jacob saw that there were rations to be had in Egypt, heᵇ said to his sons, "Why do you keep staring at one another? ²I hear," he went on, "that there are rations in Egypt. Go down there and procure some for us, that we may survive and not die." ³So ten of Joseph's brothers went down to procure grain from Egypt; ⁴it was only Benjamin, Joseph's full-brother, that Jacob did not send with his brothers, for he feared that he might meet with disaster. ⁵Thus the sons of Israel were among the others who came to get rations, for there was famine in the land of Canaan.

⁶Joseph was the regent of the land; it was he who dispensed rations to the entire population. When Joseph's brothers came to him, they bowed low, face to the ground. ⁷Joseph recognized his brothers as soon as he saw them; but he kept his identity from them, and spoke to them sternly. Said he to them, "Where have you come from?" They answered, "From the land of Canaan, to procure food."

⁸Now when Joseph recognized his brothers, while they failed to recognize him, ⁹Joseph was reminded of the dreams that he had dreamed about them. So he said to them, "You are spies. You have only come to look at the land in its nakedness!" ¹⁰"But no, my lord," they said to him, "truly,ᶜ your servants have come to procure food! ¹¹All of us are sons of the same man; we are forthright men; your servants have never spied!"

ᵃ See Notes for details.
ᵇ Heb. "Jacob."
ᶜ Heb. *wa-*.

12 But he answered them, "Yes, you have come to look at the land in its nakedness."

13 They persisted, "We your servants were twelve brothers, sons of the same man in the land of Canaan; but the youngest is just now with our father, and another one is gone." 14 But Joseph answered them, "It is just as I told you: you are spies. 15 This is how you shall be put to the test: unless your youngest brother comes here, I swear by Pharaoh that you shall not go free from here! 16 So send one of you to fetch your brother, while the rest of you remain under arrest; thus shall your words be put to the test whether there is truth in you. Otherwise, by Pharaoh, you are nothing but spies!" 17 With that, he herded them into the guardhouse for three days.

18 On the third day Joseph said to them, "Do this, and you shall live, since I am a God-fearing man. 19 If you have been forthright, let but one of you brothers be detained in your place of custody, while the rest of you go and take home rations for your starving households. 20 But you must come back to me with your youngest brother; thus shall your words be verified, and you shall not die." They agreed. 21 To one another, however, they said, "Alas, we are being punished for our brother, since we looked on at his personal anguish, when he pleaded with us, but paid no heed. That is why this distress has come upon us." 22 Reuben retorted and said to them, "Did I not warn you to do no wrong to the boy? But you wouldn't listen! Now comes the accounting for his blood." 23 They did not know, of course, that Joseph understood, since there was an interpreter between them and him. 24 He turned away from them to cry. When he was able to speak to them again, he picked out Simeon from among them and had him bound before their eyes. 25 Then Joseph gave orders to fill their containers with grain, replace each one's money in his sack, and give them provisions for their journey; and it was so done for them. 26 Then they loaded their asses with their rations and departed.

/27 As one of them was opening his bag[d] at the night en-

d See NOTE.

campment to give his ass some fodder, he saw that his money was there at the mouth of his bag. 28 "Someone has returned my money," he called out to his brothers, "it is here in my bag!" Their hearts sank. They asked one another anxiously, "What is this that God has done to us?"/

29 When they got back to their father Jacob in the land of Canaan, they told him about all their adventures, saying, 30 "The man who is lord of the country spoke to us sternly and charged us with spying on the land. 31 We said to him, 'We are forthright; we have never spied! 32 There were twelve of us brothers, sons of the same father; but one is gone, and the youngest is just now with our father in the land of Canaan.' 33 But the man who is lord of the country replied to us, 'This is how I shall know that you are forthright: Leave one of your brothers with me while the rest of you go home with something^d for your starving households. 34 When you come back to me with your youngest brother, and I know that you are forthright, and not spies, I will restore your brother to you, and you shall be free to go about in the land.' "

35 As they were emptying their sacks, there in each one's sack was his money bag! On seeing their money bags, they and their father were dismayed. 36 Their father Jacob said to them, "I am the one you would leave bereft! Joseph is gone, and Simeon is gone, and now you would take away Benjamin! This always happens to me!" 37 But Reuben told his father, "You may kill my own two sons if I fail to bring him back to you! Leave him in my care, and I will get him back to you." 38 But he answered, "My son shall not go down with you, for his own brother is dead and he alone is left. If he should meet with disaster on the trip you take, you will send my white head down to Sheol in grief."

NOTES

xlii 3. *procure*. Here the verb *šbr* is combined with the noun *bār* "grain," yielding approximately "get us an emergency supply of grain"; also vs. 5, etc.

4. *it was only Benjamin*. Some such emphasis is indicated by the inversion in Heb.

full-brother. This nuance is self-evident from the specific construction with Joseph.

he feared that. Literally "he said: 'lest . . .' "; this is one of the methods that Heb. uses to express indirect discourse.

disaster. Comparison with Exod xxi 22 f. makes it clear that Heb. *'āsōn* is not just the traditional "harm" but a fatal misadventure; also vs. 38, below, and xliv 29.

5. *sons of Israel*. Whereas Joseph's father is called Israel by *J*, but Jacob by *E* (cf. xxxv 21), the same does not apply to the possessive compound "sons of Israel," as is definitely shown by xlvi 5 ("Jacob : sons of Israel"). Because of its prevailing ethnic connotation, the phrase "children of Israel" would occur automatically to any writer. The use of this compound as a documentary criterion is therefore fallacious.

were among the others who came. Lit. "came . . . among the comers."

7. *kept his identity from them*. Literally "made himself a stranger to them."

spoke to them sternly. Literally "spoke harsh things to them"; cf. the Akk. idiom *dannātim* (which is likewise a feminine plural) *šakānum* (same sense), which is common in the Mari texts.

8. Not necessarily, or even plausibly, a duplicate of 7a, and hence not to be credited mechanically to another source (*J*). This is the author's comment to explain Joseph's treatment of his brothers: Joseph was still very much aware of the past. Accordingly, this is a subordinate clause.

9. *to look at the land in its nakedness*. Heb. *'erwā* is not "nudity" (cf. ii 25) but "nakedness," in the sense of something that is unseemly (Deut xxiii 15), and improper to look at or expose (cf. ix 22 f.; Lev xviii 6 ff.); here metaphorically, things that are meant to be hidden from potential enemies.

10. *truly*. Or "on the contrary," Heb. *wa-* in the sense of Ar. *fa-*.

11. *sons of the same man*. A family unit as opposed to a reconnaissance task force.

forthright. Heb. *kēn*, cf. Akk. *kēnu* "right, legitimate"; here men who are what they appear to be, aboveboard, not undercover agents, in contrast with "spies."

12. *Yes.* See xviii 15, NOTE.

15. *by Pharaoh.* Literally "life of Pharaoh," with "life" having the technical sense of "oath," precisely as Akk. *nēšum.* In the translation, "I swear" is based on Heb. *'im* as used in oaths; in vs. 16, on the other hand, "by Pharoah" is a circumstantial expression.

20. *They agreed.* That is, "they made (the) Yes (sign)," cf. xxix 28; not "they did so" for no deed follows. Contrast vs. 25, where the same words are used with "to them" in a more general sense.

22. *Reuben.* Joseph's advocate throughout the *E* version; cf. vs. 37, and also xxxvii 22. In *J*, the same part is taken by Judah, cf. xxxvii 26, xliii 3, xliv 18.

the accounting for his blood. Cf. ix 6. In *E*'s version the brothers did not know what the Midianites had done (see xxxvii 29). For all they knew, Joseph was dead and they were responsible for his blood.

23. *of course.* Emphatic in Heb., cf. xxi 32.

between them and him. Heb. *bēnōtām* (not *bēnēhem*); cf. NOTE on xxvi 28.

24. *When he was able to speak to them again.* Literally "he returned to them and spoke to them." Some manuscripts of LXX omit the second half of the clause, probably because no speech is indicated. But with the first verb used adverbially, as it often is in hendiadys constructions, the whole has the force of "when he was able to face them again."

Simeon. Next in seniority to Reuben, who was spared because Joseph remembered him as his protector.

27 f. For this excerpt from *J*, cf. COMMENT.

27. *one of them.* The first one who happened to do so. We know from xliii 21 that the others followed suit.

his bag. MT has "his sack"; but LXX gives here the same term that is used to translate *'amtaḥat* "bag" at the end of this verse and in xliii 12, 18, 21 ff. The text apparently carried over the other term from vs. 25.

28. *God.* Heb. Elohim is not a stranger to *J* in the general sense of "Fate, Heaven, Providence"; cf. for example, xxvii 28. In this non-specific usage the term is not of itself a dependable documentary criterion. There is no call as yet for such an exclamation in *E*, where the discovery of the money does not take place until the brothers are back home.

33. *something.* MT appears to say "take home the starvation of your households," unless one ascribes to the noun the added meaning of remedy against starvation. In all likelihood, however, the phrase read originally "take home [rations for] . . . ," etc., just as in vs. 19; the supplemented text is found in LXX, TO, Syr.

34. *you shall be free to go about.* Cf. the discussion on xxxiv 10 (NOTE).

36. *make desolate.* Literally "bereave."

This always happens to me. Literally "all these things are against me."

37. *Reuben.* See above on vs. 22.

38. *you will send my white head down to Sheol in grief.* Trad. "you will bring down my gray hairs" etc. Actually, however, the Heb. noun in question is an abstract, either "grayness," or "whiteness," which applies, of course, to hair. But in very advanced age the hair is white rather than gray, and in an instance such as this it is not only the disembodied hair but the whole person that is involved; moreover, "white head" is a familiar figure of speech in English. For the converse image "happy old age," cf. xxv 8.

The verse as a whole is often attributed to *J* as the beginning of the long account that follows. The reason is Jacob's failure to say anything about the detention of Simeon, a detail of which *J* is apparently not aware (xliii 14, 23b are taken as cross references to *J*). Nevertheless, the present verse is concerned solely with Benjamin as Rachel's only surviving son, so that a reference to Simeon would not be expected at this point. Moreover, the next verse (xliii 1) is the logical starting point of a separate section, which cannot be said of the verse before us.

COMMENT

The leading theme of the Joseph story, as proclaimed at the outset, is the relationship between the protagonist and his brothers. Hence Joseph's rise from servitude to unprecedented authority, dramatic though this event may be in itself, is but one strand in a complex fabric. Before the dull design can be unfolded, therefore, the other main thread must be picked up and woven in with the first. In other words, Joseph's brothers need to be placed on the scene in Egypt.

The required impetus is provided by the catastrophic famine that grips all the countries, Canaan included. Egypt is still, for the time being, the traditional breadbasket of the region, but only so because of Joseph's foresight and his far-reaching countermeasures. When Joseph's brothers arrive thus in Egypt for emergency supplies (technical term *šeber*), they are brought face to face with their brother. They have, of course, no intimation of his true identity; to the best of their knowledge, Joseph perished long ago in the wilderness near

Dothan. The man who must approve their request for food rations is the Vizier of Egypt, to whom Pharaoh has ceded virtually unlimited powers. As for Joseph, the intervening years have left no outward sign of his origin. He is thoroughly Egyptian in rank, name (xli 45), and speech; he communicates with the petitioners through an interpreter (vs. 23). But there are no corresponding barriers to Joseph's recognition of his brothers. Joseph's private knowledge leaves him with mixed emotions, whereas his brothers go on unsuspecting, until events finally force to the surface their ever-present but hitherto unarticulated sense of guilt. All this is handled by the author with great subtlety and insight. The immediate personal drama overshadows, but is never allowed to drive out, the underlying moral issue.

The intimate structural connection between the present episode and Joseph's whole Egyptian career to date automatically presupposes a corresponding unity of authorship. It is natural, therefore, that all the incidental evidence should point once again to E. Indeed, the whole is so closely knit that any discordant note, any intrusive passage, is bound to stand out prominently. Such is the case with vss. 27–28. In that passage, the discovery of the money that Joseph caused to be replaced in his brothers' bags is made at a lodging place on their way home to Canaan (cf. also xliii 21). But a few verses farther down, in what is clearly an integral part of the present narrative, we find that the same disturbing discovery takes place while the brothers are unpacking upon their return home (vs. 35). Nor was there any need in the first place to open the bags on the way in order to feed the animals, since provisions for the purpose had been separately supplied (vs. 25). The brief conflicting statement is thus clearly marked as an excerpt from J, whose parallel account is given in xliii 1 ff. Significantly enough, the intrusive fragment uses 'amtaḥat "bag" (as opposed to E's śaq), the same term that J employs thirteen times in his own version.

On the other hand, there is no such manifold evidence to back up the claim of some critics that several other passages should be similarly ascribed to J, or at least denied to E; for details, cf. the NOTES on vss. 5, 8, 28c, and 38. It will be found that in each instance the point at issue can be logically accounted for and independently confirmed.

55. SECOND TRIP TO EGYPT
(xliii 1–34: J^a)

XLIII ¹ The famine in the land grew more severe. ² So when they used up the rations that they had brought from Egypt, their father said to them, "Go back and procure us some food." ³ But Judah told him, "The man warned us repeatedly, 'You may not come before me unless your brother is with you!' ⁴ If you are ready to let our brother go with us, we will go down and get you food. ⁵ But if you withhold permission, we cannot go down, for the man told us, "You may not come before me unless your brother is with you!" ' "

⁶ "Why did you make it so hard for me," Israel demanded, "by telling the man that you had another brother?" ⁷ They answered, "The man kept asking us about ourselves and our family: 'Is your father still living? Have you another brother?' We had to answer his questions! How were we to know that he would insist, 'Bring your brother here'?"

⁸ Judah then urged Israel his father, "Send the boy in my care, and let us be off and be on our way if any of us is to survive and not die—we and you and our children! ⁹ I will stand surety for him; you shall hold me accountable for him: if I fail to bring him back and produce him before you, I shall stand condemned before you forever. ¹⁰ As it is, had we not dillydallied, we could have been there and back twice!"

¹¹ Their father Israel replied to them, "If it must be so, do this: Put in your baggage the land's best products and take them to the man as a gift—some balm, and a little of the honey, gum, ladanum, pistachios, and almonds. ¹² Take also a double

ᵃ See Notes on vss. 14, 23.

amount of money, for you must return the sum that was put back in the mouths of your bags; it may have been an oversight. 13 Take your brother, too, and be off; go back to the man. 14 And may El Shaddai[b] dispose the man to mercy toward you, that he may let your other brother go, as well as Benjamin. As for me, if I am to suffer bereavement, I shall suffer it."

15 So the men took this gift, and double money they took in their hands, and Benjamin, and soon[c] made their way to Egypt, where they presented themselves to Joseph. 16 When Joseph saw them with Benjamin, he told his house steward, "Take these men into the house, and have an animal slaughtered and prepared, for the men are to dine with me at noon." 17 The steward[d] did as Joseph told him and took the men into the house. 18 But they became apprehensive on being taken into Joseph's house. They said, "It must be on account of the money which was put back in our bags the first time that we are being taken there—a pretext against us to attack us and seize us as slaves, with our animals." 19 So they went up to Joseph's house steward and talked to him at the entrance of the house.

20 "If you please, sir," they said, "we were here once before to procure food. 21 But when we got to a night encampment and opened our bags, there was each man's money at the mouth of his bag—our money in the exact amount! We have brought it back with us; 22 and we have brought other money to procure food with. We don't know who put the [e]first money[e] in our bags." 23 He replied, "All is well with you; have no fear. Your God and the God of your father must have put treasure in your bags for you. I got your payment." /With that, he brought Simeon out to them./

24 The steward[d] then brought the men inside Joseph's house. He gave them water to bathe their feet, and got feed for their asses. 25 They laid out their gifts to await Joseph's arrival at noon, for they had learned that they were to dine there.

[b] See NOTE.
[c] See xxxi 21 for a similar auxiliary use of the verb q-m.
[d] Literally "man."
[e-e] Literally "our money."

26 When Joseph came home, they presented to him the gifts that they had brought inside, and they bowed before him to the ground. 27 After inquiring how they were, he asked, "And how is your aged father of whom you spoke? Is he still ⌐in good health¹?" 28 They answered, "Your servant our father is well and still in good health." And they bowed respectfully.

29 As his eye fell on his brother Benjamin, his mother's son, he asked, "Is this the youngest brother of whom you spoke to me?" And he added, "God be gracious to you, my boy." 30 With that, Joseph hurried out, for he was overcome with feeling for his brother, and wanted to cry. He went into a room and wept there. 31 Then he washed his face, reappeared and—now in control of himself again—gave the order, "Serve the meal!" 32 They served him by himself, and them by themselves, and the Egyptians who partook of his board by themselves; for Egyptians could not eat with Hebrews, since that is loathsome to Egyptians. 33 And as the men took their seats ⌐at his direction,⌐ the oldest in the order of his seniority and the youngest in the order of his youth, they gazed at one another in astonishment. 34 Portions were served them from his table, but Benjamin's portion was several⌐ times as large as that of anyone else. And they feasted with him and drank freely.

ᶠ⁻ᶠ Literally "alive."
ᵍ⁻ᵍ Literally "before him"; see NOTE.
ʰ Literally "five."

NOTES

xliii 3. *warned us repeatedly.* Expressed in Heb. by the infinitive absolute. Verses 3 and 5 would thus seem to allude to a prior journey of the brothers to Egypt as told by *J* in a passage that is no longer extant. For according to *E*, Benjamin was to be produced as proof that the brothers were telling the truth (xlii 20, 34)—a motive that was apparently absent in *J*.

5. *if you withhold permission.* Literally "if you will not let go," without object. Cf. also vs. 14 in which the object is expressed.

9. *I will stand surety for him.* Technical sense of the verb '*rb*, partic-

ularly common in Akk. legal usage; cf. the cognate noun *ʿērābōn* "pledge," xxxviii 17 f.

stand condemned. Stem *ḥṭ'*, with the primary sense of "to fail, be guilty, at fault," hence also "to offend" (xl 1). The translation is complicated by the added "to you forever." The general force is that of "I shall be in chancery to you for the rest of my life" : "you can hold it over my head, I shall never be able to live it down," or the like.

12. *double the amount of money.* So certainly in vs. 15. Here, however, "extra money" is also possible; cf. "other money" in vs. 22. Heb. *mišnê* has these and many other nuances; cf. "second-in-command," xli 43.

14. *that he may let your other brother go.* Actually, Heb. has "that he may release your other brother to you," which can apply to Simeon, but cannot be referred at the same time to Benjamin, as the text does, since Benjamin has not been detained. This difficulty, however, is symptomatic of the marginal character of the verse as a whole. It is doubtful altogether whether *J* made any mention of Simeon's arrest; certainly nothing of this kind is apparent from the material before us; note the omission of any such allusion in the preceding verses (3 ff.). On these and other counts (note especially El Shaddai), the verse has long been regarded as conflate, and influenced mostly by the previous account from *E*.

18. The brothers became uneasy when they realized that they were going to Joseph's house. Heb. appears inconsistent at first glance, in that the men first go there, then they talk to the steward, and finally they go there again (24). Actually, however, the stem in question (causative of *b'*) is both ingressive (to conduct) and terminative (to bring); the first connotation is used in vs. 17 f.; the second in vs. 24. The talk with the steward takes place before the brothers got inside the house.

21. *in the exact amount.* Literally "in its weight." Until coins were introduced, toward the middle of the first millennium, all payments in metal were made by weight (stem *šql*, hence the monetary unit "shekel"). This mode of payment is still often practiced in the Near East.

22. *the first money.* Literally "our money," but it was no longer theirs; hence, in effect, the money we had paid, our payment.

23b. From *E;* cf. NOTE on vs. 14.

27. *in good health.* Literally "alive"; cf. I Kings xx 32 Akk. *balāṭu* "to live" carries the same two meanings.

28. *they bowed respectfully.* Literally, "they prostrated themselves and bowed" (hendiadys).

30. *he was overcome with feeling.* Literally "his emotions boiled over."

32. Joseph's eating by himself was evidently a matter of rank, since the cultic and social taboo ("abomination, anathema") against taking food

with Hebrews would scarcely include the Vizier who bore a pious
Egyptian name (xli 45).

33. *at his direction.* For this nuance of Heb. *lipnē,* see NOTE on vi 11.
It is possible, of course, that this term may have here its primary meaning
"before": Joseph's brothers were seated facing their host. In that case,
however, the seating of the men in the exact order of their ages—a
detail on which the text lays much stress—would have to be ascribed
to coincidence, or at most to prior instructions on the part of Joseph
which the author chose to pass over in silence. We have seen that the
same expression can signify "at the instance, behest, with the approval,
by the will of," and the like (cf. x 9, xvii 18, xxvii 7). Since the context favors some such meaning, this interpretation (with Ehrl.) has
been given preference.

34. *several.* For this non-specific sense of Heb. "five," see NOTE on
xxiv 10; cf. also xlv 22, and II Kings vii 13.

And they feasted with him and drank freely. Literally "and they
drank and became drunk with him"; cf. ix 21. Here, however, the
emphasis is not on the consequences of the carousal, but rather on
the contrast between the carefree banquet and the rude awakening that
awaits the brothers. The clause depicts thus a convivial, but not necessarily indecorous, occasion. The first verb, moreover, yields a noun
mištê, which means simply "feast"; cf. xxi 8.

COMMENT

As the story of Joseph progresses, the two parallel strands of
which it is composed stand out more and more sharply by reason
of their sustained and increasing differences in detail. According to
the *E* version so far, Joseph won a reprieve thanks to Reuben, only
to be kidnaped by Midianites, who sold him as slave to an Egyptian
official named Potiphar. Eventually, fate turns the tables on the
brothers by placing them at Joseph's mercy. They fail to recognize
him, having no reason to think that he is still alive, let alone that
he has become the all-powerful regent of mighty Egypt. But there
are no such obstacles to Joseph's immediate recognition of his
brothers. He charges them with spying against Egypt, demands
that they prove their innocence by producing Benjamin, and retains
Simeon as hostage. Upon their return home, the brothers are further
upset by the discovery of the money that Joseph had ordered to
be put in their grain bags. Reuben personally vouches to their father

for Benjamin's safe return from the unavoidable second trip to Egypt. The father is consistently referred to as Jacob.

In *J*'s account, on the other hand, it is Judah who prevails on his brothers to stop short of fratricide and instead dispose of Joseph to Ishmaelites, who sell him in turn to a high-ranking but unnamed Egyptian official. The official's faithless wife delays, but cannot cut off, Joseph's ultimate rise to great power. Eventually, there is a similar encounter in Egypt between the brothers and Joseph, but nothing is said apparently about Simeon's detention as hostage. The brothers discover the planted money a night encampment, long before their return home. Their anxious father is identified as Israel.

On the strength of these criteria, among others, the present narrative proves to be the work of *J*. The brothers' spokesman is not Reuben but Judah, and it is he who gives Israel his personal guarantee of Benjamin's return—with significant differences in language and specific detail. The replaced money has been discovered at a night encampment (21); and the term for "bag" is invariably *'amtaḥat*, not *śaq* as in *E*. Only two brief fragments, which refer to Simeon (14, 23b), appear to belie this uniformity; but these are precisely the kind of exceptions that point up the rule, and thus stand out as intrusive glosses, as does the use of El Shaddai in vs. 14.

Closer scrutiny, moreover, will reveal other characteristics that we have learned to associate with *J*. In dealing with his father, Judah does not hesitate to speak up forcefully, and even accuse Israel of dangerous indecision (10); in similar circumstances, *E*'s Reuben pleads, but does not reproach (xlii 37). A phrase or two at the proper time and place adds dimension to the portrayals of the steward (23) (whose use of *Elohim,* moreover, is natural in an Egyptian) and of Joseph himself (30 f.). Incidentally, the domestic is called simply "the man" in vs. 17, the same term that *J* applied to another trusted servant in the story of Rebekah (xxiv 21 ff.). And just as the long journey to Mesopotamia was summed up there in a few words (vs. 10), so too the trip to Egypt is here covered by a single phrase (vs. 15).

The ability to maintain suspense is common to both *J* and *E*. The episode ends on a merry note. But the reader knows, or will soon find out, that the very next morning will confront the brothers with their gravest crisis, just when their worst fears appear to have been allayed.

56. THE ULTIMATE TEST
(xliv 1–34: J[a])

XLIV [1] Then Joseph[b] instructed his house steward, as follows, "Fill the men's bags with all the food they can carry, and put each man's money in the mouth of his bag.[c] [2] Put also my goblet, the silver one, in the mouth of the youngest one's bag, with the money for his rations." He did as Joseph told him.

[3] With the first light of morning, the men were sent off, pack animals[d] and all. [4] They had gone but a short distance from the city, when Joseph said to his house steward, "Up, go after the men! When you overtake them, say to them, 'Why did you repay good with evil?[e] [5] It is the very one from which my master drinks and which he uses in divination. You have done a base thing!'"

[6] He overtook them and repeated those words to them. [7] They remonstrated with him, "How can my lord say such things? Far be it from your servants to act in such a way! [8] In fact,[f] we even brought back to you from the land of Canaan the money we had found in the mouths of our bags. Why then would we steal silver or gold from your master's house! [9] If any of your servants is found to have it, he shall die, and the rest of us, moreover, shall be slaves to my lord!" [10] He replied, "Even though what you propose is just, only he who is found to have it shall become my slave, and the rest of you will be exonerated."

[11] Each of them eagerly lowered his bag to the ground, and each opened his bag. [12] He searched, starting with the oldest and

[a] Except for glosses in vss. 1, 2; see NOTES.
[b] Literally "he."
[c] On this clause, see NOTE.
[d] Literally "they and their asses."
[e] LXX adds "and why have you stolen my silver goblet?"
[f] Literally "here, behold."

ending with the youngest. And the goblet turned up in Benjamin's bag.

13 At this, they rent their clothes. Each reloaded his animal, and they turned back toward the city.

14 As Judah and his brothers re-entered Joseph's house, he was still there. They flung themselves before him on the ground. 15 Joseph said to them, "What a thing for you to have done! Surely, you must know that a man like me resorts to divination!" 16 Judah answered, "What can we say to my lord? How can we plead, how try to prove our innocence? It is God who has uncovered your servants' misdeeds. Here we are, then, my lord's slaves, the rest of us no less than the one in whose possession the goblet turned up." 17 But he replied, "Far be it from me to act thus! Only he who was found to have the goblet shall be my slave; but the rest of you can go back to your father without hindrance."

18 Thereupon Judah stepped up to him and said, "I beg of you, my lord, may your servant speak earnestly[g] to my lord, and do not be impatient with your servant, you who are the equal of Pharaoh. 19 My lord asked your servants, 'Have you a father, or another brother?' 20 We said to my lord, 'We have a father, who is old, and there is a child of his old age, the youngest; his own brother died, and he is the only one by that mother who is left, so his father dotes on him.' 21 Then you told your servants, 'Bring him down to me that I may set my eye on him.' 22 We explained to my lord, 'The boy cannot leave his father; his father would die if he were to leave him.' 23 But you declared to your servants, 'Unless your youngest brother comes back with you, you shall not be admitted to my presence again!' 24 When we returned to your servant my father, we reported my lord's statement to him.

25 "In time, our father said to us, 'Go back and get us some food.' 26 We reminded him, 'We cannot go down; only if our youngest brother is with us, can we go, for we shall not be allowed to see the man if our youngest brother is not with us.' 27 Your servant my father said to us, 'As you well know, that

---

[g] Literally "in the ears/hearing of," cf. xxiii 10, 13, 16.

wife bore me two sons. 28 One, however, disappeared, and I had to conclude that he must have been torn by beasts; nor have I seen him again to this day. 29 If now you take from me this one, too, and he meets with disaster, you will send my white head down to Sheol in grief.'

30 "If I appear before your servant my father, and the boy—whose very life is so bound up with his—is not with us, 31 when he sees that the boy is missing, he will die; and your servants will thus send the white head of your servant, our father, down to Sheol in grief. 32 Besides, this servant got the boy from my father under the following pledge: 'If I do not restore him to you, I shall stand condemned before my father forever.' 33 Therefore, may your servant remain here as your slave instead of the boy, and let the boy go with his brothers. 34 For how can I go back to my father if the boy is not with me? Let me not be witness to the ill fate that would overtake my father!"

NOTES

xliv 1. *and put each man's money in the mouth of his bag.* This clause, and the phrase "with the money for his rations" in vs. 2, must both be out of place in view of vs. 12 where nothing is said about any money being replaced and the goblet alone is the object of the search. The insert appears to have been influenced by xlii 27 f., which in turn represents an excerpt from *J's* account of the brothers' first journey.

2. See the previous NOTE concerning the intrusive phrase.

4. LXX adds a direct question concerning the theft of the silver goblet, but the addition is not necessarily original. The text as it stands is effective by indirection: the steward pretends that the brothers know what he is talking about.

5. Divination by means of liquids is well attested, especially in Mesopotamia; cf. J. Hunger, *Becherwahrsagung bei den Babyloniern,* 1903 (see also Vergote, pp. 172 ff.). Oil or water was poured into a bowl or cup, and omens were then based on the appearance of the liquids inside the container; hence the importance of the receptacle was likely to exceed its intrinsic value.

uses in divination. Or "consults the omens"; also vs. 15, and cf. Num xxiv 1.

9. *the rest of us.* Heb. uses the pronoun alone, but the added nuance is apparent through juxtaposition; analogously in vss. 10, 16.

10. On the syntax and meaning of this verse, cf. Ehrl. The steward concedes that the suggested punishment would fit the crime, but pretends to be magnanimous: only the actual culprit is to be arrested, and his punishment shall be slavery, not death.

13. The brothers are too stunned to speak; but their actions are enough to show their abject resignation.

16. *God.* The choice of Elohim may have been for the Egyptian's benefit. But *J* is also known to use this appellation in the more general sense of "Heaven, Fate," or the like, e.g., xxvii 28; see xlii 28; the present translation does not, of course, preclude a broader meaning. Though innocent of the present charge, the brothers are now being punished for a past crime which cannot be covered up indefinitely. It would be Judah's way of saying that justice has finally caught up with them.

19. *My lord asked your servants.* It is worth stressing that in *E's* account the brothers volunteer this information; see xlii 13.

27. *that wife.* Literally "my wife," either in the sense of "my chosen/favorite wife," or "that particular wife"; cf. "that mother" vs. 20.

28. *disappeared.* Literally "is gone from me."
I had to conclude. Heb. "I said," followed by direct statement.

29. *white head.* See NOTE on xlii 38.

COMMENT

The episode links up intimately with the preceding section both in time and content. Only a few hours separate the two accounts—the short time between the end of the banquet and the onset of dawn; even this slight break is not entirely blank, since Joseph uses the interval to brief his steward about the part he wants him to play. The drama that will soon unfold depends, moreover, in some measure on the false sense of security into which the brothers have been lulled. In short, since the previous section was the work of *J*, the sequel must also stem from the same author. Other criteria, and especially the major part that Judah assumes, are fully in accord with this conclusion. Indeed, there is, for once, not the slightest trace of any other source throughout the chapter. The two discordant clauses in vss. 1–2, though intrusive, would still seem to derive from *J* in the final analysis (see NOTE on vs. 1).

Actually, the present narrative is not only an integral part of *J*'s account, but the real climax of that author's conception of the Joseph story. The events that now come to a head, reach back, beyond the carefree interlude of the preceding afternoon, to that fateful day far away and long ago when Joseph was surrendered by his brothers to Ishmaelite slave traders (xxxvii 28c). Nothing in the crowded period since then could drown out the memory of that deed. The brothers are haunted by a burden of guilt that is never far from the surface (vs. 16); and Joseph still harbors a feeling of resentment, which time and success may have helped to blunt, but could not altogether obliterate.

It is these deep-rooted and sharply contrasted personal issues that *J* makes into his principal theme. For the moment at least, everything else is underplayed and blended with the background detail. To be sure, the great famine and Joseph's spectacular rise to power are to *J* echoes of historical events, just as they are to *E*. Both *J* and *E*, moreover, see in these factors a higher design for vindicating Joseph and punishing his brothers. But Joseph is not interested in retribution. Still, he expects from his brothers something more than mere admission of their past guilt. As *J* has portrayed him, Joseph needs to find out whether the men have been morally regenerated (von Rad): if an emergency arose, would they now resist the temptation of saving themselves by sacrificing another of their number? To find the answer, Joseph offers them Benjamin as bait.

There is more to the choice of Benjamin than immediately meets the eye. Many years ago, his brothers had treated Joseph with incredible callousness and cruelty. Why? Was it because they had never forgiven their father for favoring Rachel over their own mothers, and then transferring his affections to Rachel's older son? If so, and if they were still much the same, they would be most likely to betray themselves now at the expense of Rachel's other boy.

Joseph's attachment to his full-brother is never left in doubt (xliii 29, 34). Benjamin was obviously in no danger of suffering personal harm. Joseph's choice of him was only meant to duplicate as closely as possible the other conditions. Would the brothers revert to type, and welcome the opportunity to leave without Benjamin, this time with a genuine excuse? This was the test.

Once again it is Judah who takes the initiative. This time, however, he rejects the course of least resistance. Instead, he offers his own person to the Vizier—who is still the forbidding stranger—as substitute for the boy for whose safe return he had vouched to his father.

The brothers had indeed changed. They passed the ultimate test. And Joseph had his answer.

57. THE DISCLOSURE
(xlv 1–28: *J, E*ᵃ)

XLV ¹ Joseph was no longer able to control himself in the presence of all his attendants. He cried out, "Have everyone withdraw from me!" Thus no one else was about when Joseph made himself known to his brothers. ² But his sobs were so loud that the Egyptians could hear, and so the news reached Pharaoh's palace.

³ Joseph said to his brothers, "I am Joseph! Is Father still in good health?" But his brothers were unable to reply, so dumfounded were they at him.

⁴ Joseph told his brothers, "Come closer to me." And when they had done so, he went on, "I am Joseph, your brother, whom you once sold down to Egypt. ⁵ But do not worry now or reproach yourselves for having sold me here. It was really God who sent me here in advance of you as an instrument of survival. ⁶ For it is now two years that there has been a famine in the land; and there are five more years to come in which there shall be no yield from tilling. ⁷ Therefore God sent me ahead of you to insure for you a remnant on earth and to save your lives in an extraordinary deliverance. ⁸ So it was really not you but God who sent me here; he has set me up as a father to Pharaoh, lord of all his household, and ruler over the whole land of Egypt.

⁹ "Hurry back, then, to my father and tell him, 'Thus says your son Joseph: God has made me lord of all Egypt; come to me without delay. ¹⁰ You will live in the region of Goshen, where you will be near me—you and your children and grandchildren, your flocks and herds, and everything you own.

ᵃ See COMMENT.

11 There I will provide for you—for there are still five years of famine ahead—so that you and your family and all that is yours may suffer no want.' 12 Surely, you can see for yourselves, and my brother Benjamin can see for himself, that it is I who am speaking to you. 13 Tell my father everything about my high station in Egypt and what you have seen here; but hurry and bring Father down here."

14 With that, he flung himself on the neck of his brother Benjamin and wept; and Benjamin wept on his neck. 15 Then he kissed all his brothers, crying upon them; only then were his brothers able to talk to him.

16 The news reached Pharaoh's palace, "Joseph's brothers have come." Pharaoh and his courtiers were pleased. 17 And Pharaoh said to Joseph, "Tell your brothers, 'This is what you shall do: Load up your beasts and go to the land of Canaan without delay. 18 Take your father and your households, and come back here. I will assign to you the best territory in Egypt, where you will live off the fat of the land. 19 You ᵇare further requested (to say),ᵇ 'Do the following: Take from the land of Egypt wagons for your children and your wives, and to transport your father, and come back. 20 And never mind your belongings, since the best in all the land of Egypt is to be yours."

21 The sons of Israel did accordingly. Joseph gave them wagons, as Pharaoh had ordered, and he supplied them with provisions for the journey. 22 To each of them, moreover, he gave fresh clothes; but to Benjamin he gave three hundred pieces of silver and severalᶜ changes of clothing. 23 And to his father he sent the following: ten asses loaded with Egypt's finest products, and ten she-asses loaded with grain, bread, and sustenance for his father on his journey. 24 And as he sent his brothers off on their way, he told them, "Don't be fretful on the way."

25 They left Egypt and made their way to their father Jacob in the land of Canaan. 26 When they told him, "Joseph is still alive, and it is he who is ruler over the whole land of Egypt," his

ᵇ–ᵇ So MT, but see NOTE.
ᶜ See xliii 34.

heart went numb, for he could not believe them. 27 But when they repeated to him all that Joseph had told them, and when he saw the wagons that Joseph had sent for his transport, the spirit of their father Jacob revived. 28 "Enough," said Israel, "my son Joseph is still alive! I must go and see him before I die."

NOTES

xlv 2. *his sobs were so loud that.* Literally "he gave/put his voice/sound in weeping."

3. *Is Father still in good health.* Literally "is my father still alive?" Cf. xliii 27. (*J*). If the present passage goes back to *E*, no actual redundancy is involved. But even if *J* was the author, the question may have been asked for reassurance: tell me the truth, is he really all right? As for the noun, Heb. actually says "my father," whenever Joseph refers to Jacob; but the noun without possessive pronoun would be unidiomatic. This time, at any rate, the pronoun may be advantageously left out in translation.

5. *God.* Here, and in vss. 8, 9, Elohim has distinctly the more general sense of "Heaven, Providence," so that the term cannot be an automatic indicator of *E*'s authorship; cf. xliv 16.

6. *there shall be no yield from tilling.* Nowhere is the special force of hendiadys—the use of two co-ordinated terms to express a single modified concept—better demonstrated than in the instance before us. The literal and traditional "there shall be neither plowing nor harvest" is out of the question. No farmer could be expected to stop tilling the soil because somebody had predicted five more years of famine, least of all in Egypt, where good crops depend on irrigation and not on rainfall. Quite the contrary, after two years of famine, the farmers would work that much harder instead of remaining idle. As a hendiadys, however, the phrase "tilling-and-reaping" describes cultivation which leads to harvesting, as opposed to whatever the earth might produce without man's efforts. This self-evident interpretation is independently supported by the syntax of Heb. The alleged "neither . . . nor" would call in the original for repetition of the negative particle *ʾēn* (Ehrl.). Note that when the same two nouns are separately employed, the pertinent particle is repeated: "both at plowing time and at harvest time" (Exod xxxiv 21).

7. *extraordinary.* Heb. *gādōl* "great" with reference to something supernatural.

8. *father to Pharaoh.* This phrase is applied to Viziers as far back as the third millennium.

9. The message from Joseph to his father is couched in epistolary style with the standard introductory formula; cf. xxxii 5. For letters reflect only the spoken word, which is why they begin with the imperative "speak," a term that is all the more appropriate in an oral message. The invitation to Jacob is sent in Joseph's own name, as opposed to Pharaoh's invitation in vss. 16–20. Yet, according to xlvi 31 ff. Jacob's arrival comes as news to Pharaoh. The inconsistency disappears once the present passage is assigned to J (on the independent evidence of sale into slavery, vss. 4 f.), and the other to E.

10. *the region of Goshen.* Identified with the Wādi Tumilāt, the eastern part of the Nile Delta. Since this is a part of Egypt, the traditional "land of Goshen" is misleading.

12. The original says "your eyes and Benjamin's see that it is my mouth which is speaking to you," to underscore the directness of the evidence.

14. *flung himself.* Literally "fell"; for this idiom see xiv 10, NOTE. If "neck" sounds somewhat strange in this context, it is mainly because the respective Heb. noun (and its Sem. analogues) designates not only neck but also the shoulder blades (note the plural, or rather dual, construct and possessive in this verse).

17. *go . . . without delay.* Literally "go . . . arrive," lose no time in getting there.

19. *You are further requested (to say).* Literally "you have been commanded," followed by the content of the command. In all probability, however, the present cons. text *ṣwyth* represents an original *ṣw 'tm*, or the like, that is "instruct them," cf. LXX, Vulg.

20. *never mind.* Literally "let not your eye grudge"; cf. Deut vii 16, xiii 9, xix 13, etc.

24. The Heb. stem *rgz* may describe excitement, anger, impatience, and the like. The proposed translation seeks to leave the choice open. Very likely, the general sense is, "let there be no recriminations."

25. *Jacob.* In the Joseph story, a direct sign of E's authorship; also vs. 27.

28. *Israel.* See COMMENT below.

COMMENT

After the strain and tension of the last episode, the present narrative is bound to appear as an anticlimax. Joseph's brothers had passed the critical test, which was all the more revealing since they did not know that they were being tested. Joseph's disclosure of his real identity brings relief at long last to himself, his brothers, and—a fact that should not be overlooked—the reader as well. Indeed, so welcome is this happy ending that one is not likely to realize right away that the account is no longer of a piece, but a blend of more than one source.

This is the point in the story at which the often separate paths of *J* and *E* must draw together. Both sources had to highlight Joseph's self-revelation and the receipt of the good news by Jacob. Such episodes could not be lifted bodily from the two parallel accounts and then arranged consecutively, as was done with the others (xxxix–xliv), without irreparable damage to the story as a whole. Hence the present chapter is no less composite and fused than was the start of the story in ch. xxxvii; but this time the component parts are much more difficult to separate and identify.

The beginning of the section is the obvious sequel to Judah's moving recapitulation immediately before it; therefore *J* must still be the author. Thereafter, however, the reflective reader runs into trouble. Do vss. 3 and 4 indicate that Joseph revealed himself to his brothers twice? If so, does such duplication betray the presence of *E*, alongside *J*? The critics who subscribe to the latter assumption find a measure of support in the use of the term Elohim in vss. 5, 7, 8, and 9. Yet the solution is not that simple. While *E* does not speak of Yahweh in Genesis, so that the use of this personal name becomes a direct witness of *J*, the converse does not apply; *J* employs the term Elohim on various occasions as a general term of reference to a superior power, and the present passage is especially well suited to just this kind of usage. To be conclusive, the external criterion of terms for the Deity should be corroborated by the internal evidence of the given context.

Now on such internal grounds, there can be no doubt that vss. 4 and 5a go back to *J;* for both say that Joseph was sold into slavery by his brothers, yet that detail was unknown to *E*, the Midianites having picked up the boy without his brothers' knowledge. The passage, moreover, which consists of vss. 9–13, must also stem from *J*. In it Joseph invites his father in his own name to come to Egypt; this accords well with xlvi 31 ff. (*J*), where the news of Jacob's arrival comes as a surprise to Pharaoh. Yet, significantly enough, this message too cites Elohim in vs. 9. Thus far, therefore, there is no sure sign of *E*'s contributions to the narrative; the repeated statement "I am Joseph" is entirely natural in the given circumstances.

For cogent proof of *E*'s participation we have to wait until vss. 16–20. There a separate invitation to Jacob is issued by Pharaoh himself; since he is unaware of this step in the episode in xlvi 31 ff., which is traceable to *J*, the author in the present instance must be *E*. Farther down, the name Jacob occurs twice (25, 27), and that is an independent witness of *E*. The last sentence, however, substitutes Israel (28), which points in turn to *J* (cf. xxxv 21 f., COMMENT on Sec. 47, and NOTE on xlii 5). There is thus at least a fair presumption that vss. 16–27 are to be attributed to *E,* and the rest to *J;* but since we cannot put it more definitely, it has seemed best to omit the usual source markers in the translation.

Because of the involved nature of the composition, which may have caused omissions from the originally separate and independent documents, a few loose ends remain that can no longer be tied together. As *J* tells the story, it was Judah's forthright confession that finally made Joseph reveal himself to his brothers. But no such motive is explicit in the extant material from *E*. Furthermore, it goes without saying that when the brothers brought the startling news to their father, they could not but make a clean breast of their previous crime and lies. This detail is passed over in silence, very likely by design rather than through accidental loss in the text. Good writers are not given to spelling things out; the reader, too, has his part to play. In this case, the joy of recovering a son who had long been given up for dead, coupled with the fact that the brothers' schemes had not only been frustrated but turned to good purpose, may have been reason enough for Jacob to forgive and forget. Such at least is the inference that the narrative would seem to favor.

58. JACOB'S MIGRATION TO EGYPT
(xlvi 1–34: *J*, ⁄*E*⁄, |*P*|)ᵃ

XLVI ¹ So Israel set out with all that was his, and arrived in Beer-sheba, where he offered sacrifices to the God of his father Isaac.

⁄² God spoke to Israel in a vision by night, and called, "Jacob! Jacob!" "At once," he answered. ³ He said, "I am El, the God of your father. Be not afraid to go down to Egypt, for I will make you there into a great nation. ⁴ I will go down with you to Egypt, and I myself will bring you back; and Joseph's hand shall close your eyes."

⁵ So Jacob left Beer-sheba, and the sons of Israel put their father Jacob, and their little ones and their wives, aboard the wagons that Pharaoh had sent to transport him. ⁄ |⁶ They took their livestock and the possessions that they had acquired in the land of Canaan, and arrived in Egypt—Jacob and all his offspring. ⁷ He brought with him his sons and grandsons, his daughters and granddaughters—all his offspring.

⁸ These are the names of the Israelites, Jacob and his descendants, who migrated to Egypt.ᵇ

Jacob's first-born Reuben; ⁹ Reuben's sons: Hanoch,ᶜ Pallu, Hezron, and Carmi. ¹⁰ Simeon's sons: Jemuel, Jamin, Ohad, Jachin, Zohar, and Shaulᵈ son of a Canaanite woman. ¹¹ Levi's sons: Gershon, Kohath, and Merari. ¹² Judah's sons: Er, Onan, Shelah, Perez, and Zerah—but Er and Onan had died in the land of Canaan; and the sons of Perez were Hezron and Hamul.

ᵃ For details, see COMMENT and NOTES.
ᵇ For parallels and variants, cf. Num xxvi and I Chron ii 1 ff.
ᶜ Same as Enoch.
ᵈ Same as Saul.

13 Issachar's sons: Tola, Puvah, Jashub,ᵉ and Shimron. 14 Zebulun's sons: Sered, Elon, and Jahleel. 15 These were the sons that Leah bore to Jacob in Paddan-aram, aside from his daughter Dinah. Persons in all, male and female—33.

16 Gad's sons: Ziphion,ᶠ Haggi, Shuni, Ezbon, Eri, Arodi, and Areli. 17 Asher's sons: Imnah, Ishvah, Ishvi, and Beriah, with Serah their sister; and Beriah's sons: Heber and Malchiel. 18 These were the descendants of Zilpah, whom Laban had given to his daughter Leah, that she bore to Jacob—16 persons.

19 The sons of Jacob's wife Rachel: Joseph and Benjamin. 20 Joseph became the father of two sons, Manasseh and Ephraim, whom Asenath daughter of Poti-phera, priest of On, bore to him in the land of Egypt. 21 Benjamin's sons: Bela, Becher, Ashbel, Gera, Naaman, ᵍEhi, Rosh, Muppim, Huppim,ᵍ and Ard. 22 These were the descendants of Rachel, who were born to Jacob—14 persons in all.

23 Dan's son:ʰ Hushim. 24 Naphtali's sons: Jahzeel, Guni, Jezer, and Shillem. 25 These were the descendants of Bilhah, whom Laban had given to his daughter Rachel, that she bore to Jacob—7 persons in all.

26 Altogether, Jacob's people who migrated to Egypt—his own issue, not counting the wives of Jacob's sons—numbered 66 in all. 27 Together with Joseph's sons who were born to him in Egypt—two persons—all the people comprising Jacob's family who came to Egypt came to 70 persons.|

28 Israelⁱ had sent Judah ahead to Joseph, ʲto precede himʲ to Goshen. When they reached the region of Goshen, 29 Joseph orderedᵏ his chariot and went up to Goshen to meet his father Israel. As soon as he appeared before him, he flung himself on his neck and wept upon it a long time. 30 And Israel said

---

ᵉ So Sam., LXX, Num xxvi 24; MT cons. *ywb* (Iob), textual error for *yšwb*.
ᶠ Sam., LXX, Num xxvi 15 *Zephon.*
ᵍ–ᵍ To be corrected to *Ahiram, Shephupham, Hupham,* for which see Num xxvi 39 f.; cf. I Chron viii 4 f.
ʰ Heb. "sons" in formulaic use.
ⁱ Cf. vs. 30; MT "he."
ʲ–ʲ See NOTE.
ᵏ Literally "tied, hitched up."

to Joseph, "Now I can die, having seen 'in person' that you are
still alive."

³¹ Then Joseph said to his brothers and his father's house-
hold, "I will go and inform Pharaoh, and say to him, 'My
brothers and my father's household, who were formerly in the
land of Canaan, have come to me. ³² The men are shepherds,
having long been keepers of livestock; and they have brought
with them their flocks and herds and everything they own.' ³³ So
when Pharaoh summons you and asks about your occupation,
³⁴ you shall answer, 'Your servants have been keepers of live-
stock from the beginning^m down to the present—we and our fathers too'—in order that you may stay in the region of Goshen.
For every shepherd is abhorrent to Egyptians."

^{l-l} Literally "face to face."
^m Literally "from our youth."

NOTES

xlvi 1. *Beer-sheba*. A logical stop on the way from Canaan (presumably Hebron) to Egypt.

2. *a vision by night*. For this indirect mode of communication, which is
characteristic of the *E* source, cf. xx 3, 6, xxxi 11, 24.

3. *a great nation*. Note that *E* uses here *gōy*, not *'am*, precisely as *J* did
in xii 2, see NOTE *ad loc*.

5. *the sons of Israel*. In this combination, the use of the name Israel is
not limited to *J*; cf. NOTE on xlii 5.

10. *Jemuel*. Num xxvi 12 and I Chron iv 24 give *Nemuel*. The present
reading is inferior because (1) Num xxvi has proved dependable on
many counts, and (2) Heb. *n* will be mistaken for *y* more readily than
the other way about.

12. According to the data in xxxviii, Perez was born to Judah after
the latter's three older sons had reached adulthood. Here Perez is
recorded as having two sons of his own, who in terms of the total
elapsed time could have been Judah's great-grandchildren. Yet at the
time of Jacob's migration to Egypt, Judah's brother Joseph had been
there only 22 years (combining xxxvii 2, xli 46 f., and xlv 6: 13 years
in Egypt plus 7 years of plenty and 2 years of famine). The chronological
discrepancy disappears, however, once it is established that the present

list had originally nothing to do with the record of the migration to Egypt.

13. *Jashub*. See textual note ᵉ. The dropping of a cons. (š) is easy enough to explain, whereas its addition in the parallel passages could not be accounted for.

15. *aside from his daughter Dinah*. This is believed to be a harmonizing insert, caused by the need to bring the total number of migrants up to 70.

19. *Jacob's wife Rachel*. The appositional "wife" is not found with Leah, let alone the two concubines. The same apparent partiality to Rachel is reflected in xliv 27 (*J*). Evidently, Heb. *'iššā* could carry the specialized meaning of "principle, favorite wife."

21. The list of Benjamin's sons has been badly mangled in the present version. Aside from mechanical textual corruptions, which can be corrected on the basis of parallel passages (cf. textual note ᵍ⁻ᵍ), Num xxvi 38–40 credits Benjamin with only five sons, as opposed to ten in the present instance; the others become grandchildren (cf. also LXX, which credits Benjamin with three sons and seven grandchildren). All of which serves to point up the secondary character of the list before us; see next NOTE.

26 f. The figure 66 would seem to be a later correction by someone who deducted from the total of 70 the two sons of Judah (Er and Onan) who died in Canaan, and Joseph and his two sons who were already in Egypt, but counted Dinah; cf. Dr.

28. *to precede him*. Little can be done with Heb. *lhwrt*, which would require an object if interpreted as "to show, point." LXX suggests that the original may have read *lhr'wt* "to present (himself)"; but even then the syntax would not be smooth. In any event, Joseph does not start for Goshen until he has been informed of his family's arrival (29). The translation here adopted is in the nature of a compromise, close enough to the admittedly defective Heb. and also to the not altogether convincing LXX.

34. *from the beginning*. The literal "from our youth" is ruled out by the following "and our fathers," since the ancestors' childhood could not be so described.

all shepherds are abhorrent to Egyptians. The taboo cannot apply to shepherds as such; cf. xlvii 6. In all likelihood, the term shepherds is here a play on the popular interpretation of the Hyksos as "shepherd kings" (SB), whose temporary domination of Egypt dealt a severe blow to national pride.

COMMENT

The section is made up of excerpts from all three major sources. But the component parts have been left more or less intact, so that each has retained its individuality and can be identified without much difficulty. The narrative portions comprise vss. 1–5 and 28–34. The break between them is filled by a long insert from P, which betrays itself as intrusive in more ways than one.

The first verse finds Israel on his way to Egypt, with his entire family and their possessions. The name Israel points directly to J, the same source from which the last verse of the preceding section was also derived. This version is resumed in vss. 28 ff.; note the two occurrences of the name Israel in 29 f., and the prominent role of Judah (as is customary with J) in 28. One needs only to read xlv 28 – xlvi 1 + 28–34 consecutively to see how well these passages fit together as a unit. It will be recalled, moreover, that in 31 ff. Pharaoh is shown to know nothing about Israel's arrival until Joseph's family had crossed into Egypt. This is why Joseph has to maneuver Pharaoh into assigning to the visitors a part of the Goshen district—an area good for grazing and close to the Asiatic border. The detail accords well with xlv 9–13 (J), where it is Joseph himself who issues the invitation to his family, but is in marked contrast with xlv 16 ff. (E), where the invitation originates with Pharaoh.

Verses 2–5, on the other hand, are manifestly from E. Not only does the divine name appear as El, but God communicates with Jacob (vs. 2) by means of a night vision, as is customary in this source. The patriarch is reassured that his departure from Canaan is not contrary to the divine plan but, in fact, in keeping with it; the isolated "Israel" in vs. 2 is an accidental carry-over from the preceding verse. The transportation, finally, is furnished by Pharaoh (vs. 5).

The extensive insert from P can be identified at a glance by its content and phraseology. The genealogical interest is dominant throughout. A record of Jacob's family was deemed necessary on the eve of the sojourn in Egypt, and this seemed to be the best place to give it. A similar record of the Israelites as they are about to return to Canaan is furnished by the same source in Num xxvi.

Indeed, the names of the principals are essentially the same in both instances, except for textual changes: the future clan-heads of Joseph's time become populous clans in the Mosaic period. On closer examination, however, the present list turns out to be a summary of the data in Num xxvi, compiled without reference to the Egyptian interlude and only later readjusted to the requirements of the present context (Dr.). Since Er and Onan died in Canaan (12), they could not be part of a record devoted expressly to "Jacob and his descendants who migrated to Egypt" (8). The two sons of Perez (12), who are in effect two generations removed from Judah (xxxviii), can scarcely be synchronized with a Joseph who is still a relatively young man. The traditional, and originally round, number of 70 male descendants (27) can be eked out only by adding Jacob himself and Dinah. And lastly, where the present list departs from that in Num xxvi (as, for example, in the case of ten sons of Benjamin, vs. 21, as against five in Num), it proves to be a distortion of the other. On all these counts, the list before us is not only intrusive in the present narrative but also secondary within the *P* source itself.

59. JACOB BEFORE PHARAOH.
JOSEPH'S LAND POLICY
(xlvii 1–26: J, /P/^a)

XLVII 1 Joseph then went and reported to Pharaoh, saying, "My father and brothers have come from the land of Canaan, with their flocks and herds and everything they own; they are at present in the region of Goshen." 2 He had picked several^b of his brothers and presented them to Pharaoh. 3 Pharaoh asked his brothers, "What is your occupation?" "We your servants," they replied to Pharaoh, "are shepherds, the same as our fathers were. 4 We have come," they said to Pharaoh, "to seek sojourn in this country, for there is no pasture for your servants' flocks in the land of Canaan, so severe has been the famine. Pray, then, let your servants stay in the region of Goshen." 5a Pharaoh turned to Joseph, saying,^c 6b "They may stay in the region of Goshen. And if you know any of them to be suitable, you may put them in charge of my own livestock."

/^d[Thus, when Jacob and his sons came to Joseph in Egypt, and Pharaoh king of Egypt heard about it, Pharaoh said to Joseph,]^d 5b "Your father and brothers have come to you; 6a the country of Egypt is at your disposal: settle your father and brothers on the pick of the land." 7 Then Joseph brought his father Jacob and presented him to Pharaoh. Jacob paid respects to Pharaoh. 8 Pharaoh then asked Jacob, "How many are the years you have lived?" 9 Jacob said to Pharaoh, "The years I have been granted^e add up to 130. Few and hard have been these years of my life; nor do they compare with the life-spans that my

---

^a See COMMENT.
^b Literally "five," cf. xliii 34.
^c From here through vs. 6, see LXX and NOTE.
^{d–d} Supplied from LXX.
^e Literally "of my sojournings"; see NOTE.

fathers were granted." 10 Then Jacob took his leave from Pharaoh and left his presence. 11 And so Joseph settled his father and brothers and gave them land holdings in Egypt, on the pick of the land—the region of Rameses—as Pharaoh had commanded. 12 And Joseph sustained his father and brothers, and his father's entire household, with food, down to the youngest./

13 There was, however, no food in any country, for the famine was very severe; and the lands of Egypt and Canaan languished from hunger. 14 Joseph gathered in all the money that was to be found in the land of Egypt and in the land of Canaan, as payment for the rations that were being dispensed, and he put the money in Pharaoh's palace. 15 And when the money in the land of Egypt and in the land of Canaan was spent, all Egypt came to Joseph, pleading, "Give us bread, or we shall perish under your eyes, for the money is gone." 16 Joseph replied, "Give me your livestock, and I will make distribution in return for your livestock, since your money is gone." 17 So they brought their livestock to Joseph, and he sold food to them in return for horses, for their stocks of sheep and cattle, and for asses. Thus he saw them through that year with bread in exchange for all their livestock. 18 And when that year was ended, they came to him the next year and said to him, "We cannot hide from my lord that, with the money and the animal stocks made over to my lord, there is nothing left at my lord's disposal except our persons and our farm-land. 19 Why should we perish before your very eyes, both we and our land? Take us and our land in exchange for bread, and we shall become serfs to Pharaoh, with our land; only give us seed, that we may survive and not perish, and that the land not turn into a waste."

20 So Joseph acquired for Pharaoh all the farm-land in Egypt; for every Egyptian sold his field, since the famine was too much for them; thus did the land pass over to Pharaoh. 21 As for the people, Joseph[f] [g]reduced them to serfs[g] from one end of Egypt's territory to the other. 22 Only the priests' land he did not take

[f] MT "he."
[g-g] So Sam., LXX; MT "transferred to the cities" (change of D/R), see NOTE.

over; for it was the priests' allotment from Pharaoh, and they lived off the allotment that Pharaoh had made them, which is why their land was not sold.

23 Joseph told the people, "Now that I have acquired you and your land for Pharaoh, here is seed for you to sow the land. 24 But when the harvest is in, you must give a fifth to Pharaoh, keeping four-fifths as seed of/for the field, as food for yourselves and members of your households, ʰand to feed the children.ʰ" 25 They answered, "You have saved our lives! We are thankful to my lord that we can be serfs to Pharaoh." 26 And Joseph made it a land law in Egypt, which is still valid, that a fifth should go to Pharaoh. Only the land of the priests did not pass over to Pharaoh.

ʰ⁻ʰ LXX omits.

Notes

xlvii 2. *He had picked.* Literally "he took from the edge/fringe" (Heb. *miqṣē*) in a context made emphatic through inversion. This strongly suggests something like "he took the outstanding ones" (cf. Ehrl.); Joseph evidently selected those brothers who were most likely to make a good impression. On "several" for "five," cf. NOTE on xliii 34.

3. *the same as our fathers were.* Literally "both we and our fathers," which is standard Heb. but unacceptable in translation since only one ancestor was still alive.

4. *to seek sojourn.* That is, permission for temporary residence; not "to sojourn" without modification, since the necessary permission should not be taken for granted.

in this country. Literally "in the land." Heb. *'ereṣ* appears in this narrative in three related connotations: (1) "country" as a political entity; (2) "land" in general (cf. vs. 1); and (3) "region," as with Goshen (*passim*) or Rameses (11), which are merely districts within a country.

5 f. The translation follows LXX both in the order of clauses and in supplying a sentence which is now missing in MT. The fact that LXX is self-explanatory indicates that the disturbance in MT is relatively late. The authenticity of the Greek version should be clear from the context; note especially the logical transition from 4b (Please, may we stay in Goshen) to 6b (Yes, they may stay in Goshen). Above all, the sentence

which LXX supplies will readily account for the difficulties in the received text: the added part ends with "Pharaoh turned (spoke) to Joseph, saying," the identical clause that both MT and LXX read in 5a. Such endings (a feature known as homoioteleuton) often cause copyists to confuse the first occurrence with the second, and hence skip the intervening part; for a parade example, cf. I Sam xiv 41, where LXX comes again to the rescue in a context of unusual importance. The upshot in the present instance has been the loss of a sentence and the consequent dislocation of 5b–6a.

6a. *at your disposal.* Literally "(open) to/before you"; cf. vs. 18.

7. *paid respects.* Cf. vs. 10.

8. *How many are the years you have lived.* The natural translation would be simply "how old are you?" But the question has to contain "the years," since the answer goes on from this very word.

9. *The years I have been granted.* The literal "the years of my sojournings" would be misleading. Jacob cannot be alluding to his ancestors' actual wanderings, inasmuch as Abraham's total time outside Mesopotamia was exactly 100 years, whereas the present verse goes on to say that Jacob cannot match his forefathers in this respect; this point gains in significance when *P* is found to be the author of all the relevant passages. The alternative, therefore, is to interpret the noun *megūrīm* in some other sense. But "pilgrimage," which has often been proposed, is unsatisfactory; such an allusion to wandering through life has rightly been suspect as unduly sophisticated. But the attested range of the stem *g-r* includes "to live on sufferance" (see especially xix 9), and this suits the present context admirably: any time that man is allowed to stay on earth is but borrowed time.

10. *took his leave.* For Heb. *bērēk* in the sense of either "to greet on arrival" (vs. 7) or "to bid farewell," cf. NOTE on xxviii 1.

11. *region of Rameses.* Used as a synonym for Goshen (which *is* J's term). It is, however, an anachronism, since the royal name became popular only under the Nineteenth Dynasty (not before the end of the thirteenth century).

2. *down to the youngest.* Literally "according to the little ones," which is obscure; perhaps, including the least significant members of the household, or the like; cf. vs. 24.

13. *in any country.* Literally "on all the earth," but hardly "in all the land (of Egypt)."

16. *I will make distribution.* Literally "I will give/sell," without direct object.

17. *he saw them through.* Literally "he guided them."

The question may be raised at this point why it was necessary for the Egyptians to exchange their livestock for bread when it would have been simpler, and more provident, to kill off their animals gradually as a means of feeding themselves. No plausible answer is immediately apparent. A possible reason may be sought in the existing animal taboo; another would be the exigencies of storytelling.

18. *our persons.* Literally "our bodies, carcasses," perhaps in the sense of "our bodily shells."

our farm-land. Heb. *'ᵃdāmā*, as distinct from *'ereṣ;* the emphasis is on arable land.

21. *reduced them to serfs.* Aside from the evidence of Sam. and LXX, and the mechanical nature of the slight chance that is involved (*h'byd . . . l'bdym* for MT *h'byr . . . l'rym,* primarily *D/R*), the reading here adopted is strongly favored by the context. The people had offered themselves for servitude, according to vs. 19. Nor would the transfer of the entire rural population—the overwhelming majority of the people—be practicable or serve any conceivable purpose.

24. *and to feed the children.* This is obviously related to the last phrase in 12, which is obscure (see above). The omission of the present passage in LXX hints at trouble of some sort, without betraying, however, its nature and significance.

COMMENT

Joseph presents his father to Pharaoh, along with several of his hand-picked brothers who have been specially briefed for the occasion (xlvi 31–34). The audience comes off according to plan. The brothers answer Pharaoh's friendly question with all due deference, stressing their pastoral pursuits as instructed. Pharaoh invites them to settle in Goshen. The end of the preceding chapter and the beginning of the present section are thus clearly from the same hand, in this case *J*. It will be remembered that *E* had Pharaoh issue an invitation to Jacob while the latter was still in Canaan (xlv 17 ff.).

The meeting of Jacob and Pharaoh is also recorded by another source. Some critics (cf. Noth, *Überlieferungsgeschichte* . . . , p. 38) would attribute this parallel to *E*. The majority, however, ascribe is to *P* with ample show of reason. The phraseology is distinctly *P*'s; note especially the literal "the days of the years" (f.) and the use of the term *mᵉgūrīm* (9). More important perhaps is the nature of the context. The subject matter is not primarily statistical as is so often the case with *P*. Neither is it, however, narrative in the sense that the story is materially advanced; what happens is that the two men meet, at which time polite comments are exchanged in the spirit of "Wisdom" literature. Such an unworldly approach, which totally ignores the essence of the story, is precisely what one is accustomed to in P. When Pharaoh shows a courteous interest in his visitor's venerable age, Jacob counters with a modest disclaimer: his stay on earth, on borrowed time, may appear to have been impressive in length, but it has really been brief and insubstantial. These are sentiments that are well known from many wisdom compositions of the ancient Near East.

The rest of the section (13–26) reverts to J. It dwells on the increasingly acute effects of the prolonged famine, and thereby highlights the importance of Joseph's precautionary measures. More than one modern writer has found in this report of the enslavement of the Egyptian peasant shocking proof of Joseph's inhumanity. But, as has been stressed repeatedly by more objective students, such censorious comments show little understanding of either history or literature. The Egyptian concept of state, whereby the king was viewed as a god, made the pharaoh an absolute ruler from the start, and hence the owner of all he surveyed, at least in theory (cf. Vergote, pp. 190 ff.). In practice, private ownership of land appears to have been sanctioned in the Middle Kingdom. But the pharaohs would seem to have reasserted their titular rights with the beginning of the New Kingdom, following the expulsion of the Hyksos. The need for a stronger government, which the Hyksos experience was bound to accentuate, may have brought with it corresponding curtailment of individual privileges.

To that extent, therefore, the agrarian changes that are here described may reflect actual socio-economic developments. There is no evidence that Egyptian society would have found such changes to be anything other than constructive. That they should be credited in this narrative to Joseph is part and parcel of his idealized historical image. Pharaonic Egypt followed its own due course, regardless of ancient visitors or modern moralizers.

60. THE BLESSING OF EPHRAIM AND MANASSEH
(xlvii 27–xlviii 22: *J, E,ª /P/*)

XLVII 27 Thus Israel settled in the land of Egypt, in the region of Goshen. /They acquired holdings in it, were fertile, and increased greatly. 28 Jacob lived in the land of Egypt 17 years; thus the span of Jacob's life came to 147 years./

29 When the time approached for Israel to die, he called his son Joseph and said to him, "If you really wish to please me, put your hand under my thigh as a pledge of your steadfast loyalty to me: do not let me be buried in Egypt! 30 When I lie down with my fathers, have me moved from Egypt and bury me in their burial place." He answered, "I will do as you have said." 31 "Swear it to me," he demanded; and he swore to him. Then Israel bowed at the head of the bed.

XLVIII 1 Some time later, Joseph was informed, "Your father is failing."

He took along with him his two sons, Manasseh and Ephraim. 2 When Jacob was told, "Your son Joseph has come to you," heᵇ summoned his strength and sat up in bed.

/3 Jacob said to Joseph, "El Shaddai appeared to me at Luz, in the land of Canaan, and blessed me 4 and said to me, 'I will make you fertile and numerous, and raise you into an assembly of tribes; and I will give this land to your offspring to come as an everlasting holding.' 5 Now your two sons who were born to you in the land of Egypt before I joined you in Egypt shall be mine: Ephraim and Manasseh shall be mine, no less so than Reuben or Simeon. 6 But progeny born to you after them shall

ª On the parts from *J* and *E*, see COMMENT.
ᵇ MT "Israel"; see NOTE.

remain yours; they shall succeed[c] their brothers in their inheritance. 7 [d]I want this because,[d] when I was returning from Paddan, [e]your mother[e] Rachel died, to my sorrow, as we were traveling in Canaan, only a short distance from Ephrath; and I buried
her there on the way to Ephrath—now Bethlehem."/

8 Noticing Joseph's sons, Israel asked, "Who are these?"
9 "They are my sons," said Joseph to his father, "whom God has
granted me here." He said, "Bring them to me that I may bless
them." 10 —Now Israel's eyes had faded from age; he could not
see. —So Joseph[f] brought them close to him, and he kissed them
and embraced them. 11 Said Israel to Joseph, "I never expected
to see your face again, and here God has let me see your progeny
as well!"

12 Joseph removed them from Israel's[g] knees, and bowed, face
to the ground. 13 Then Joseph took both of them, Ephraim with
his right hand, to Israel's left, and Manasseh with his left hand,
to Israel's right, and led them to him. 14 But Israel put out his
right hand and laid it on the head of Ephraim, who was the
younger, and his left hand on the head of Manasseh, although
Manasseh was the first-born—thus crossing his hands: 15 and he
blessed them,[h] saying,

"The God in whose ways walked my fathers, Abraham and
     Isaac,
The God who has been my shepherd from my birth to this
     day,
16 The Angel who has delivered me from all harm—bless the
     boys,
That in them be recalled my name, and the names of Abra-
     ham and Isaac, my fathers,
And that they may become teeming multitudes upon the
     earth!"

c Literally "shall be called by the names of."
d–d Heb. "I" in emphatic construction.
e–e Reading with Sam. and LXX. MT omits.
f Heb. "he."
g Heb. "his."
h So with LXX; MT "Joseph" (cons. *'t-ywsp for 'wtm*).

17 When Joseph saw that his father had laid his right hand on Ephraim's head, he deemed it wrong; so he grasped his father's hand in order to move it from Ephraim's head to Manasseh's. 18 Said Joseph to his father, "Not so, Father, for the other one is the first-born; lay your right hand on his head!" 19 But his father resisted, saying, "I know it, my son, I know. That one too shall become a tribe, and he too shall be great. But his younger brother shall surpass him, and his offspring shall suffice for nations." 20 And he blessed them then╱ on that day, saying,

"Through youⁱ shall Israel bless itself,ʲ thus:
May God cause you to be like Ephraim and Manasseh,"

putting Ephraim ahead of Manasseh.

21 Thereupon Israel said to Joseph, "I am about to die, but God will be with you and restore you to the land of your fathers. 22 As for me, I give you,ᵏ as the one above your brothers, Shechem, which I captured from the Amorites with my sword and bow."

ⁱ Singular in Heb.
ʲ Active form in Heb.
ᵏ Rest of the clause obscure; see NOTE.

NOTES

xlvii 29. *If you really wish to please me.* Literally "Please, if I have found favor in your eyes"; yet another variation on a versatile idiom.

put your hand under my thigh. For the same phrase, followed by an oath, cf. xxiv 2 (*J*).

as a pledge of your steadfast loyalty. Here the substance of the oath is expressed indirectly, literally "that you will act toward me with steadfast loyalty," followed by the heart of the matter (burial in Canaan). On the hendiadys describing "steadfast loyalty/kindness," see xxiv 27.

31. Joseph's promise (30) was not enough. Israel demanded an explicit oath.

Israel bowed at the head of the bed. So MT; but the text has given trouble to interpreters all the way back to LXX. The difficulty appears to be due to the verb; the literal "prostrated himself, bowed low" is hard to visualize in the circumstances, hence LXX read the pertinent conss.

mṭh as *maṭṭê* "staff," and not *miṭṭā* "bed," an interpretation which is echoed in Heb xi 21. But the picture of Jacob leaning here on his staff is equally implausible. The trouble derives in all probability from taking the Heb. stem too literally. The term "to bow low" need not signify here anything more than a gesture of mute appreciation on the part of a bedridden man on the point of death. The bow or nod would come naturally from the head of the bed.

xlviii 1–2. The passage would be abrupt and redundant if the author were still *J*. But the transition to "Jacob" suggests immediately that we have here a duplicate account by *E*, who had similar material before him (note "bed" in vs. 2). The ultimate joining of the two statements left its mark in the use of "Israel" and "Jacob" in the same verse.

4. *and raise you into an assembly of tribes.* For virtually the same statement, cf. xxviii 3 (also from *P*).

5b. In consequence of their adoption by Jacob, Joseph's two sons acquire the status of Jacob's sons, on a par with that of Reuben and Simeon (Jacob's oldest).

6. Concurrently, Joseph's younger sons will move up, in terms of inheritance, to the senior spots left vacant by their older brothers; see above, textual note *e*.

7. *to my sorrow.* For this "adversative" sense of Heb. *'alay*, cf. xxxiii 13.

8 ff. Direct sequel to vs. 2 (*E*); but the combination of Elohim and the repeated Israel indicates that this passage now represents a fusion of both narrative sources.

10. *had faded.* Literally "had grown heavy"; for the use of the same stem (*kbd*) with one of the other parts of the face (=mouth), cf. Exod iv 10 (impaired speech).

11. *I never expected.* Heb. *pll* has the basic sense of "to estimate"; cf. *pelīlīm*, which in Exod xxi 23 means "assessment" (by the husband of the age of the embryo), and in Deut xxxii 31 "(even in) the estimation (of our enemies)."

12. The act of placing a child on the father's knees signifies acceptance of the child as legitimate; the same act also serves to formalize adoption.

14. *crossing his hands.* The verbal form appears to denote "plaiting," if the generally cited Ar. cognate is pertinent. In any case, the context speaks for itself.

15. *he blessed them.* Heb. "he blessed Joseph" is obviously in disorder. Either the *ywsp* of the text is a mechanical slip for *'wtm* "them" (with LXX), or the word "sons of" dropped out in Heb.

in whose ways walked. Cf. xvii 1.

19. *a tribe.* Clearly not "a people" in this instance; see Note on xxviii 3.

shall suffice for nations. Literally "shall become a quantity of (=sufficient for) nations," i.e., sufficient in numbers to constitute nations (Ehrl.).

20. *Through you.* In place of the singular pronoun LXX and TP read plural, referring to both boys; but MT is acceptable in the sense of "each of you."

shall Israel bless itself. Pointing the conss. *ybrk* of MT as passive (Pual), with LXX, Syr. The trad. vocalization is due to the interpretation of Israel as a person (hence active singular) rather than a people.

22. A laconic and obscure allusion. Part of the difficulty arises from the fact that Heb. *šᵉkem* may stand either for the city of Shechem or the common noun "shoulder." In the latter case, we would have here a reference to a mountain side or slope, specifically Mount Gerizim, which dominates Shechem. The common noun, however, should be feminine, whereas the numeral that follows in the present text is masculine; the Sam. version makes it feminine ('*ḥt*), understandably enough, as a welcome allusion to Mount Gerizim. The translation here adopted construes the numeral (actually adjective) '*ḥd* with Joseph, who is thus described as "the one who is above/unique among" his brothers. To be sure, we have no independent notice of a conquest of Shechem by Joseph; nor does xxxiv state that the brothers who massacred the inhabitants actually retained the city itself. But the alternative interpretation runs up against the same difficulty, inasmuch as "mountain slope" would likewise presuppose possession of Shechem. For the present, at any rate, no plausible solution is in sight.

COMMENT

Joseph's eventful career is now drawing to a close. At such major junctures, the main concern is for the proper link with the next generation, to maintain the continuity of patriarchal traditions. Significantly enough, there appears to be a need to emphasize this continuity in both directions, the past as well as the future—in retrospect as much as in prospect. We have seen that the shift in emphasis from Jacob's generation to the next was marked both by the birth of Benjamin (xxxv 16 ff.: *J*) and the death of Isaac (xxxv 28 f.: *P*). This time, Jacob is on his deathbed, and so he makes far-reaching provisions for two of Joseph's sons. The theme is of sufficient consequence to have found its way into all three sources.

The portions from *P* (xlvii 27b–28, xlviii 3–7) are, as usual, easy enough to identify: note the characteristic remarks about fertility and increase (xlvii 27b, xlviii 4), El Shaddai (xlviii 3), "assembly of tribes" (xlviii 4) and the geographic term Paddan (xlviii 7)—short for the familiar Paddan-aram. Indeed, the whole of xlviii 4 is but a restatement of xxxv 11 f. (likewise *P*). What is new now is the adoption of Ephraim and Manasseh as Jacob's own sons. The genealogical reason for this extraordinary fact might be traced to the circumstance that the boys' mother was an Egyptian. Another reason, of course, is aetiological, in that Ephraim and Manasseh became eponyms of tribes and thus the equals of Jacob's natural sons. Verse 7 would seem to be irrelevant at first glance. On closer probing, however, its pertinence is easily vindicated. Death had robbed Jacob of his beloved Rachel (cf. the Akk. personal name *Išlul-ilum* "god has taken away," to designate a replacement). Hence Jacob feels justified in substituting two of Rachel's grandsons for such other sons as fate may have prevented her from bearing.

As for the remainder of the section, however, the source analysis is a task of a different order. *J* is plainly the author of xlvii 29–31. This is shown not only by the use of the name Israel (29, 31), but also by the "hand under thigh" form of oath, which is known elsewhere from only one passage (xxiv 2) in a celebrated account by *J*. The burden of this statement, made especially solemn by its deathbed setting (cf. xxvii), is that Jacob is to be buried in Canaan and not in Egypt's alien soil.

In xlviii 1–2, on the other hand, *E*'s hand is unmistakable. The name of the patriarch is now given as Jacob (see NOTE loc. cit.). The fragment, moreover, parallels the antecedent notice about Israel's impending death.

Verses 8 ff. constitute an obvious sequel to vs. 3, as is immediately apparent when the two passages are read consecutively. Joseph takes his two sons to be blessed by their grandfather, who raises himself to a sitting position (2), whereupon he notices the boys (8). The author, therefore, is once more *E*, so that the repeated mention of Elohim (9, 11, 15 *bis*) comes as no surprise. Yet the patriarch is now called Israel (10 ff.) instead of Jacob; and the blessing in vs. 20 would seem to be repetitive. It appears probable, therefore, that *E* and *J* are now so fused that they can no longer be pried apart.

A deathbed blessing is irrevocable, as we know from xxvii 33. Joseph tries to make sure that the hands of his unseeing father would not be misdirected. But Jacob crosses his hands, thus reversing the order of seniority, as though guided by an inner light. Thus the story anticipates history: Manasseh, originally the more prominent of the two tribes in question (cf. the order in Num xxvi 28, 34–35), was eventually outstripped by Ephraim, the ultimate leader of the Israelite group. For the enigmatic last verse, see the NOTE *ad loc.*

61. THE TESTAMENT OF JACOB
(xlix 1–27: X)

XLIX ¹ Jacob called his sons and said, "Gather round that I may tell you what is in store for you in days to come:

² Assemble and listen, O sons of Jacob,
  Listen to Israel your father.

³ You Reuben, my first-born,
  My strength and first fruit of my vigor,
  Exceeding in rank and exceeding in honor!
⁴ Unruly like water, you shall excel no more;
  For you climbed into your father's bed,
  Thus defiling my couch ᵃto my sorrow.ᵃ

⁵ Simeon and Levi are a pair;
  Their waresᵇ are the tools of lawlessness.
⁶ My person must not enter their council,
  Or my being be joined with their company!
  For they killed men in their fury,
  And maimed oxen at their whim.
⁷ Cursed be their fury so fierce,
  And their wrath so relentless!
  I will disperse them in Jacob,
  Scatter them throughout Israel.

⁸ Your brothers shall praise you, O Judah,
  Your hand ever on the nape of the enemy—
  The sons of your father shall bow to you.

ᵃ⁻ᵃ Assuming conss. '*ly*, in the sense of xlviii 7; MT '*lh* "he climbed"; LXX, TO "you climbed."
ᵇ MT obscure; see NOTE.

9 A lion's whelp is Judah;
　　You have battened on prey, my son.
　　He crouches like a lion recumbent,
　　A lion's breed—who would dare rouse him?
10 The scepter shall not move from Judah,
　　Or the mace from between his feet,
　　ᵒTo the end that tribute be brought him,ᵒ
　　And to him go the peoples' homage.
11 He tethers his ass to a vine,
　　His purebred to the choicest stem;
　　In wine he washes his garments,
　　His robes in the blood of grapes.
12 His eyes are darker than wine,
　　And his teeth are whiter than milk.

13 Zebulun shall dwell by the seashore,
　　Which shall be a haven for ships;
　　And his flank shall be based on Sidon.

14 Issachar is a rawboned ass,
　　Crouched amidst saddlebags.
15 When he saw how good was the homestead,
　　And how very pleasant the country,
　　He bent his shoulder to burdens
　　And became a willing serf.

16 Dan shall governᵈ his kindred
　　Like other tribes in Israel.
17 May Dan be a serpent by the roadside,
　　A horned snake by the path,
　　That bites the horse's heel,
　　So that backward is tossed the rider.

18 I long for your deliverance, O Yahweh!

ᵒ–ᵒ Obscure; see NOTE.
ᵈ Heb. *ydyn*, play on Dan.

19 Gad shall be raided*e* by raiders,
   And he shall raid at their *f*heels.

20 Rich shall be the yield*g* of Asher,
   And he shall furnish dainties for kings.

21 Naphtali is a hind let loose
   That brings forth lovely fawns.

22 Joseph is a wild colt,*h*
   A wild colt by a spring,
   Wild asses on a hillside.
23 Archers in their hostility
   Harried and attacked*i* him.
24 Yet each one's bow stayed rigid,*j*
   And their arms were unsteady,
   By dint of the Champion of Jacob,
   *k*The Shepherd, Rock of Israel,
25 The God of your father who aids you,
   Shaddai who grants you his blessings—
   Blessings of heaven above,
   Of the deep that couches below,
   Blessings of breast and womb,
26 *l*Blessings of grain stalk and blossom,
   Blessings of mountains eternal,*l*
   The delights of hills everlasting.
   May they rest upon the head of Joseph,
   The crown of one set apart from his brothers!

---

e Heb. *ygwdnw*, along with *gdwd* and *ygd*, all plays on Gad.
f So LXX, Syr., Vulg., reading *'qbm* for MT *'qb*, where the final *m* has been erroneously moved to the next line.
g Literally "bread, food."
h Relating the whole verse to fauna and not, with tradition, to flora.
i MT obscure.
j Trad. "strong," with reference to Joseph; LXX has "strong/with strength," *metà krátous*.
k Preceded in Heb. by *miššām* "from there," misread for *miššęm* "on account of," for which see TO, Syr. Omitted in the translation as redundant.
l–l See Deut xxxiii 13 ff., and cf. NOTE *ad loc.* for details.

27 Benjamin is a wolf on the prowl:
Mornings he devours the prey,
And evenings he distributes the spoils."

NOTES

xlix 1. *Superscription*, whereby the poem is attributed to Jacob. The name of the patriarch betrays a hand other than J's; but the heading does not necessarily stem from the compiler of the poetic sayings.

in days to come. Not "in the end of days," with tradition, but in the days to follow; cf. the analogous Akk. *ina arkāt ūmī* "in the future."

3. *You Reuben, my first-born.* The pronoun is appositional (you Reuben), not predicative (Reuben, you are); cf. vs. 8. The first three lines constitute the address. Such a statement as "you are my first-born" would be banal in this context.

exceeding in. Heb. *yeter* (twice), used as a construct adjective; cf. the cognate Akk. (*w*)*atar*, notably in the familiar *Atar-ḫasīs* "exceeding wise."

4. *you shall excel no more.* The verb (*tōtar*) is correctly pointed as Hiphil. The suggested repointing to a Niphal (intransitive/passive) following LXX, to yield "you shall remain, survive," would destroy the subtle literary effect (you were, but shall no longer be *yeter*), aside from contradicting the historical data (Reuben did survive, after all). This is yet another example of the "elative" Hiphil; cf. JCS 6 (1952), 81 ff., and see NOTE on iii 6.

Thus defiling my couch to my sorrow. MT literally "then *you* defiled; my couch *he* climbed." But the first verb requires an object; what is more, in the corresponding passage I Chron v 1, we actually find "he [Reuben] defiled his father's couch." The source of the difficulty lies in the last word, Heb. cons. *'lh*, which in this form had to be interpreted as "he went up." Yet TO and LXX give here the second person, which helps very little, except to indicate that the problem is of long standing. The very slight change of *'lh* to *'ly* (*h* and *y* are not unlike in the old script) yields an adverbial phrase, which we know from xxxiii 13 and xlviii 7, instead of a discordant and disruptive verb. To be sure, this is an emendation (accepted by SB); but the received text is unmanageable, contrary to usage, and acknowledged as a stumbling block by the oldest versions. That at least some portions of this old poem are demonstrably corrupt is shown most clearly by vs. 26.

For the offense that is alluded to here, see xxxv 22.

5. *a pair.* Literally "brothers," two of a kind.

wares. Heb. *mkrtyhm,* an old and stubborn puzzle. The form lends itself to a variety of derivations, none of which has proved convincing. Traditional "weapons" involves the anachronism of a Greek etymology. The ancient versions reflect little more than guesswork. Syr. and many moderns adduce the consonantally identical noun in Ezek xvi 3 and xxi 35, meaning "origins"; others operate with "schemes, plots, ruses," on flimsy linguistic grounds. The translation offered above hazards the possible, but unsubstantiated, derivation from *mkr* "to sell, trade"; it is intended as a neutral rendering and nothing else.

lawlessness. See xvi 5.

6. For the verb *b-'* used of participation in a council, cf. xxiii 10.

being. Tradition "glory," which is a frequent mistranslation of Heb. *kābōd.* Even when applied to the Deity, this noun usually has the meaning of "essence, being, presence"; and with mortals, "glory" is altogether out of place. LXX reads *kābēd* "liver, mood," which has been adopted by many moderns; but this is not a logical parallel to "self, soul."

For the pertinent incident and its setting, cf. COMMENT on xxxiv.

be joined with. Cf. Isa xiv 20; a suitable parallel to "enter" in the preceding phrase. Although the form appears to have caused trouble in more than one ancient version, the only problem is a grammatical one; the pronominal prefix is feminine, whereas *kābōd* is always (and *kābēd* usually) masculine; in fact, Sam. has here the masculine prefix. But the preceding parallel verb is feminine, which may have caused the error by attraction.

at their whim. Literally "at their pleasure, will," with the nuance of "willfulness."

8. *shall praise . . . Judah.* The verbal form (*yōdū-kā*) is in assonance with Judah; cf. xxix 35.

9. *You have battened.* Literally "you have risen, gone up" in the metaphorical rather than physical sense.

a lion's breed. Generally translated "a lioness"; for the latter, however, we would expect the feminine form of the noun, for which cf. Ezek xix 2. The several biblical synonyms for "lion" designate various breeds (e.g., the Asiatic as opposed to the African) or stages of growth. It so happens that no direct synonym is available in English.

10. *mace.* Etymologically, something pertaining to a legislator or one in authority; and from the context, an analogue of the scepter. When the dignitary was seated, the staff would rest between his feet.

To the end that tribute be brought him. Although this is one of the most widely discussed passages in the Bible, the clause continues to defy solution. Traditionally, the conss. are broken up into *'d ky yb' šylh.* The main stumbling block is the last group (variant *šylw*), which elsewhere stands for the sanctuary of Shiloh. On this basis, the phrase might be rendered either "until he [Judah] comes to Shiloh," or "until Shiloh comes." But the first runs into various difficulties, chronological as well as substantive, among them the decisive fact that Shiloh was an Ephraimite and not a Judaean shrine. The latter rendering involves faulty grammar, in that the verb should be feminine and not masculine; nor would the Heb. be idiomatic in such a case, and even if it were, the statement would remain incomprehensible. In these circumstances, it is methodologically precarious to construe the phrase, with rabbinical and later interpreters, as a Messianic allusion to David, who never had much to do with Shiloh. There is even less of an excuse to import for the same purpose the rare Akk. noun *šēlu* "counselor," when Hebrew (and Akkadian) had various direct terms for "ruler." Now is the situation improved if *šylh/w* is emended to *mšlh/w* "his ruler"; what would be the antecedent of "his"? Where the procedure is so forced, it tends to condemn itself. In a poem that is manifestly pre-Davidic on every apparent count, one does not strain for veiled references to David.

The older versions, notably LXX, TO, and manuscripts of Sam., appear to have read *šellō* "what is his, due him," with the general sense of "until he comes into his own." Perhaps more to the point is an old Midrashic interpretation, followed by some of the medieval Jewish authorities, which operates with *šay lō* "tribute to him," in agreement with the cons. text (cf. Ps xxvi 12, following Rashi); for the phrase and context cf. Isa xviii 7, where even the accompanying verb is analogous in meaning ("shall be brought"), and close enough in its written form (*ywbl : yb'*). The sequel would then be in perfect poetic parallelism (tribute is brought him: homage is his). The whole, then, would affirm that Judah is assured of a position of leadership. The above translation reflects this particular reading, without undue confidence, as the one that is least objectionable.

There is another possibility, however, which called for bolder remedies but is more plausible on the whole. The parallel Song of Moses, Deut xxxiii, contains in its concluding verse the phrase "your enemies shall come fawning to you" (29), the verb in that case being *ykḥšw*. If the same form was present here originally, the clause may have read **'dyw ykḥšw lh/w* "his foes shall come fawning to him," with a perfect sequel in "and the peoples' homage shall be his." The required change would be no more drastic than the well-supported alterations in vs. 26. At a minimum, the conjecture is worth noting in passing.

11. *purebred*. Literally "the young of (his) she-ass," for which see Zech ix 9, and cf. W. F. Albright, ANET, p. 482, n. 6. The identical phrase is now known from Mari, in the form of *mār atānim;* for the meaning "choice, purebred ass," as against the literal "ass foal," see Noth, *Gesammelte Studien*, 1957, pp. 144 f., n. 8.

12. *dark(er)*. Heb. *ḥaklīlī*, cognate of Akk. *ekēlu* "to be dark."

13. *a haven for ships.* Heb. uses the term *ḥōp* twice, the first time with seas and the second time with ships; there is, however, the possibility of textual corruption in the latter instance.

14. *saddlebags.* Against trad. "sheepfolds," cf. A. Saarisalo, *The Boundary between Issachar and Naphtali*, 1927, p. 92.

It is apparent that this pronouncement is caustic rather than complimentary.

15. *homestead.* Literally "place of repose, stability."

16. *Like other tribes.* Literally and trad. "one of," in the sense of "any other" (Ehrl.).

17. *is tossed.* Literally "falls"; cf. NOTE on xiv 10.

18. In all likelihood a marginal gloss or a misplaced general invocation; alternatively, the cry of a tumbling rider (Ehrl.).

19 f. On the erroneous verse division, see textual note *ᶠ*. All the other names, with the exception of Joseph, head their respective passages, and even the latter is without preposition.

21. The meaning of this distich depends entirely on the pointing of two words, cons. *'ylh* and *'mry*. The trad. reading of the first yields "hind"; but different pointing (*'ēlā*) would yield "terebinth," and this is what both LXX and TO appear to paraphrase; the accompanying article happens to be applicable to either form (a hind let loose; a branching tree). But the ambiguity is increased rather than resolved by the second word; for, depending on the vocalization, *'mry* may be "crowns, crests, tops" (*'ᵃmīrē*), "words" (*'imrē*), or "fawns" (*'immārē*="lambs" in Aramaic and Akkadian). Many of those who accept the received text and render "hind," still translate "words" in the next phrase; but the picture of an articulate animal, or an eloquent Naphtali (note the masculine form of the pertinent participle), gives rise to serious misgivings. It so happens, however, that the received *'imrē* is a permissible reduced form of *'immārē'*>*immᵉrē*, so that even the pointed text does not oblige us to separate the hinds from their young.

22. This verse, which introduces the long pronouncement about Joseph, leads to more problems than any other passage in the poem; but it also affords better prospects of a solution than, for example the "Shiloh" phrase in vs. 10.

a wild colt. The trad. "a fruitful bough" is vulnerable on various counts. Heb. *prt* could conceivably be connected with the stem for "to be fruitful" and "fruit," but that would still be a long way from an unspecified fruitful tree. Besides, the other such metaphors in this poem are taken from the animal world, not the flora: lion's whelp (9) rawboned ass (14), serpent (17), and wolf (27), not to dwell on the ambiguous allusion in vs. 21 which was discussed in the preceding NOTE. More important still, the present saying about Joseph is closely paralleled in Deut xxxiii, where the counterparts are an ox and a wild ox (vs. 17). Lastly, in the present passage, the next new term features animals once again, as we shall presently see, in apposition to *prt*. On this combined evidence, the phrase *bn prt*, in which *ben* designates a member of the given class, cannot but point to the animal world. Nor is the etymological basis far to seek; it is provided by the established term *pere'* "wild ass, equid," which is found in the poetical books and has already been met with in xvi 12; our *prt* (whatever the correct vocalization) would thus be the feminine form of *pr'*. The following phrase, then, depicts the same animal by a spring—recalling a common theme in Tablet I of the Gilgamesh Epic—and not a fruit tree, which would have to be transformed into a vine according to the prevailing interpretation.

wild asses. MT cons. *bnwt ṣ'dh*, whose first element, literally "daughters," is forced to serve as "shoots, branches," and the accompanying verbal stem is made to mean "to climb, run over." Yet Arabic dictionaries carry the term *banāt ṣa'dat* (the exact phonologic counterpart of the Heb. phrase before us) with the undisputed meaning of "wild ass(es)," as noted by Ehrl. The complete correspondence with our Heb. term cannot possibly be ascribed to mere coincidence. On this basis, Ehrl. viewed the preceding *prt* as a corruption of the common Heb. noun *pārā* "cow." There is no reason, however, to change species in the middle of a metaphor. Wild asses are logical literary companions of wild colts (of ass, horse, or onager); and the otherwise troublesome *ṣ'dh* turns out to be an integral component of the term.

hillside. Heb. *šūr* is a poetic term for "wall, terrace," cf. II Sam xxii 30; Ps xviii 30. The picture, then, is that of spirited young animals poised on some nearby elevation.

23. *in their hostility*. This represents the last of the three Heb. verbs in this clause; literally "and they opposed him."

and attacked him. MT cons. *wrbw*, which is generally derived from a questionable stem *rbb* "to shoot." Sam. and LXX read *wyrbhw* (from *rīb*) "and they contended with him," which the translation above reflects.

24. Here begins a long sentence which carries through 26a. In this regard, the present passage is paralleled by the pronouncement about Joseph in the Song of Moses, Deut xxxiii 13–16a. Both sayings, moreover, end with the identical distich (26b : 16b). The parallels are very helpful, precisely because they diverge in certain details.

Yet each one's bow stayed rigid. Traditional "But his bow abode in strength." The principal question is whose bow was involved. Heb. has the pronoun suffix "his," which is why tradition has made Joseph the subject. But we have just learned that the shooting came from the opposition; and singular forms can often be used collectively or distributively. LXX, moreover, read *wtšbr* (for Heb. *wtšb*) "it was broken," thus assigning the weapon to the hostile archers (and following up with "their bows"). The second Heb. word (*b'ytn*) normally describes something permanent. But if the text is right, and the bows belong to the enemy, the emphasis in this instance has to be on "rigid, inflexible." (For an illuminating parallel of a bow that failed, cf. the Akkadian myth of "Zu," ANET, p. 515, lines 16 ff.; and the military inventories from Nuzi often list bows that lost their resilience.)

their arms were unsteady. The pronominal suffix is again singular in Heb., and is to be interpreted the same way as with the bow. The predicate (Heb. *wypzw*) has an Ar. cognate (*fzz*) meaning "to tremble, shake."

By dint of. Literally "by the hands of"; the favorable result of the contest is traced to the intervention of Joseph's protector, the Champion (literally the "mighty one") of Jacob.

In the translation, "by dint of" carries over to the next phrase. MT gives *mšm*, vocalized *miššām* "from there," which is neither a co-ordinate of *mīdē* "by the hands of" nor appropriate to the context. TO, however, reads *miššēm*, "by the name," which can be a divine epithet ("Name," cf. SB), or can have the force of "because" (cf. Aram. *miššūm*, Akk. *aššum*).

Rock. Literally "stone"; if correctly transmitted, the epithet is an unusual one; cf. M. Dahood, *Biblica* 40 (1959), 1002 ff.

25. *who grants you his blessings.* The corresponding Heb. form governs the detailed list of blessings as given in 25b–26a.

26a. MT reads "the blessings of your father have been mightier than the blessings of my progenitors, unto the desire of the everlasting hills." This reading is hopeless on more counts than one: (1) the poetic meter is suddenly abandoned; (2) the prosaic content is even more disturbing; (3) emphasis shifts abruptly from boons to beneficiaries; (4) the term for "progenitors" (literally "conceivers") is without parallel in biblical Heb., the only form otherwise known being in the feminine singular (Hos ii 7; Song of Sol iii 4), and having the natural sense of "mother"; (5) the attested term for "parents" is *'ābōt;* (6) the connection with the next clause is disrupted; (7) above all, the parallel text in Deut xxxiii 15 gives *hrry qdm* "the ancient hills," which is paralleled in turn by *hrry 'd* (same meaning) Hab iii 6, the obvious prototype of the present *h(w)ry 'd.* The only difference is the graphically slight change of *r/w* (in the "square" script); but the misreading was sufficient to throw the rest of the verse completely out of balance.

It remains only to restore the beginning of the verse (26). With the "parents" (*hwry*) of the second hemistich gone in favor of "hills," the

text's "your father" is now all the more out of place. The received cons.
text is as follows:

   brkt 'abyk gbrw 'l—for which read (with SB)
   brkt 'abyb wgb'l

"blessings of grain-stalk and blossom." The whole sequence becomes at
once natural and cohesive—and an analogue to Deut xxxiii 13 ff. There
can be little doubt that this, or something very close to it, was the original
wording of the passage.

   one set apart from. In Heb., the same term that is used to designate the
"nazirite," one who is distinguished from his fellows and consecrated to a
specific task.

   27. *on the prowl.* Literally "who tears (the prey)."

   prey. Heb. *'ad,* a rare noun, the meaning of which is not definitely established; another possibility is "foe."

COMMENT

The traditional designation of this poem as the "Blessing of Jacob"
is a misnomer, since the pronouncements are not always favorable.
Indeed, the first three sons are sternly reproved, and the very word
"cursed" is employed in vs. 7. The misleading label is based no
doubt on vs. 28, where the stem *brk,* normally "to bless," is used;
but that passage is manifestly from a different source. To be sure, the
analogous composition which constitutes Deut xxxiii is described as
the Blessing of Moses in its superscription; but the tone of that poem
is uniformly benign. There are thus good reasons for renaming the
poem before us as the Testament of Jacob.

Aside from its poetic form, the Testament is notable also for its
approach to the subject matter. Elsewhere in Genesis, the descendants of Jacob are treated as individuals; here they are considered
as tribes, as is explicitly stated in the colophon (28a, see next section). This puts us immediately on guard as to the authorship of
the piece. We miss here the typical indications of the three familiar
sources. The occurrence of the name Yahweh in vs. 18 cannot be
viewed as a valid criterion, inasmuch as this term is part of a brief
ejaculation (three words in the original) that has little, if anything,
to do with the body of the poem, and could well be a displaced or
marginal gloss. In vs. 2, the names Jacob and Israel occur side by
side, yet it is obvious that the distich is not the joint effort of *E*
and *J*. The superscription cites Jacob, but this is not part of the

poem, and there is no way of deciding when it was added, or by whom. Most important of all, the body of the poem proves to be much earlier, on internal evidence, than even *J*, the oldest of the tangible sources. At best, *J* may have collected the tribal sketches before us and incorporated them at this point as a pertinent poetic retrospect and prospect.

The Testament of Jacob invites comparison with two other poems in which the Israelite tribes pass in review, i.e., Deut xxxiii and Judg v. The latter, the celebrated Song of Deborah, deals with one specific occasion—the critical war against a Canaanite coalition—in the early period of Judges, and cannot therefore be properly aligned with the present composition. The Blessing of Moses (Deut xxxiii), on the other hand, is a much closer analogue, as was indicated above. The pronouncements that are attributed to both Jacob and Moses cover an indeterminate period of time. Both are general in their characterization, and each abounds in poetic imagery and obscure allusions. And since each tribe is a subject unto itself, the reader is obliged to make his way without the guiding thread of a connected context.

The Blessing of Moses is the later of the two collections not only because of the titular author but also on internal grounds. Simeon had apparently ceased to exist as an independent tribe, while Levi is praised for his piety; the only significant feature that is common to both poems is their great respect for Joseph, which is expressed in similar terms. The Testament, for its part, still knows Simeon and Levi as impetuous and worldly; and the memory of Reuben's moral offense is fresh in the poet's mind. All of which points to an early stage in the Israelite settlement in Canaan, with some of the allusions resting perhaps on still earlier traditions. In no instance is there the slightest indication of a setting later than the end of the second millennium. Small wonder that the text is now uncertain at a number of points. Where the Blessing parallels the Testament, notably in the case of Joseph, the younger composition helps to correct obvious errors in the older poem, which was exposed to greater attrition in the long process of transmission.

For the most part, however, the interpretation of this poem is beset with extraordinary difficulties, as is to be expected from a work of such scope, complexity, and antiquity, and replete with unfamiliar expressions and allusions. It is indeed doubtful whether some of the problems here encountered can ever be resolved with any degree of confidence. On several points there is considerable disagreement among the oldest versions, and this lack of a firm tradition complicates still further the task of modern scholarship. At times, the attempted solutions are diametrically opposed to one another. Verses 21 and 22, for example, contain metaphors from the plant world according to some translators, and from the animal world according to others, even though each school operates with the same consonantal text.

In these circumstances, a comprehensive commentary on this poem would require a book in itself. Indeed, a summary of views about the four words in the "Shiloh" passage (10) would fill a good-sized monograph. Since such exhaustive detail would be neither suitable nor feasible within the present framework, the comment and notes have been held down to bare essentials. Having been warned about the problems and pitfalls of this particular section, and the tentative nature of some of the conclusions that are here embodied, the reader may be referred to more detailed works and special discussions. Among the recent articles on the subject are B. Vawter's "The Canaanite Background of Gen. 49," CBQ 17 (1955), 1–18, and J. Coppens' "La bénédiction de Jacob," VT 6 (1956), 97–115.

62. DEATH OF JACOB AND JOSEPH
(xlix 28–l 26: *P*, /*J*/, |*E*|)

XLIX   28 All these were tribes of Israel, twelve in number, and
this is what their father said about them as he bade them farewell, addressing to each an appropriate parting message.

29 Then he gave them instructions as he said to them, "I am
about to be gathered to my kin. Bury me with my fathers in the
cave which is in the field of Ephron the Hittite, 30 in the cave
that lies in the field of Machpelah, facing on Mamre, in the land
of Canaan—the field that Abraham bought from Ephron the
Hittite for a burial site. 31 There Abraham and his wife Sarah
were buried, and so were Isaac and his wife Rebekah; there, too, I
buried Leah— 32 the cave and the field in it having been bought
from the children of Heth."

33 When Jacob finished his instructions to his sons, he drew
his feet into the bed, breathed his last, and was gathered to his
kin.

L   /1 Joseph flung himself on his father's face and wept upon
him as he kissed him. 2 Then Joseph ordered the physicians in
his service to embalm his father, and the physicians embalmed
Israel. 3 It required forty days, for such is the full period of embalming; and the Egyptians bewailed him seventy days. 4 When
that wailing period was over, Joseph addressed Pharaoh's court
as follows, "Do me this kindness and convey to Pharaoh this appeal: 5 My father put me under oath, saying, 'When I die, be
sure to bury me in the grave that I made ready for myself in the
land of Canaan!' May I, therefore, go up now, bury my father,
and come back?" 6 Pharaoh replied, "Go and bury your father,
as he made you promise on oath."

7 So Joseph left to bury his father; and with him went up all

of Pharaoh's officials who were senior members of his court, and all of Egypt's dignitaries, 8 together with Joseph's household, his brothers, and his father's family; only their children, their flocks, and their herds were left in the region of Goshen. 9 Chariots, too, and horsemen went up with him; it was a very large train.

10 When they arrived at Goren-ha-Atad,ᵃ which is beyond the Jordan, they held there a very great and solemn memorial observance; and Josephᵇ observed a seven-day period of mourning for his father. 11 When the Canaanites who inhabited the land saw the mourning at Goren-ha-Atad, they remarked, "This is a solemn mourning by the Egyptians." This is why ᶜthe placeᶜ was named Abel-mizraimᵈ—which is beyond the Jordan./

12 Thus Jacob'sᵉ sons did for him as he had instructed them. 13 His sons bore him to the land of Canaan and buried him in the cave in the field of Machpelah, facing on Mamre, the field that Abraham had bought from Ephron the Hittite for a burial site.

/14 After burying his father, Joseph returned to Egypt, together with his brothers and all who had gone up with him to bury his father./

|15 When Joseph's brothers saw that their father was dead, they said, "Suppose Joseph is resentful toward us and tries to pay us back for all the wrong we did him!" 16 So they sent Joseph a message, as follows, "Before his death, your father left these instructions: 17 You shall say to Joseph, 'Forgive, I urge you, the crime and faults of your brothers who treated you so harshly.' So please, forgive the crime of the servants of your father's God!" Joseph broke into tears at this word from them.

18 Then the brothers went to him themselves, flung themselves before him, and said, "Let us be your slaves!" 19 But Joseph replied to them, "Have no fear. How could I act for God?"

ᵃ A place name, literally "threshing place of brambles."
ᵇ Heb. "he."
ᶜ⁻ᶜ Literally "it."
ᵈ Wordplay on "mourning"; see NOTE.
ᵉ Literally "his."

20 Besides, although you meant me harm, God meant it to good purpose, so as to attain the present end—the survival of many people. 21 So have no fear now. I will provide for you and your children." Thus he reassured them by speaking to them with affection.

22 Joseph stayed on in Egypt together with his father's family. Joseph lived 110 years; 23 he lived to see the third generation of Ephraim's line, and the children of Machir son of Manasseh were also born on Joseph's knees.

24 At length, Joseph said to his brothers, "I am about to die. God will surely take notice of you and take you up from this land to the land that he promised on oath to Abraham, Isaac, and Jacob." 25 Then Joseph put the sons of Israel under oath, saying, "When God has taken notice of you, be sure to take up my bones from here."

26 Joseph died at the age of 110 years. He was embalmed 'and laid to rest' in a coffin in Egypt.|

f–f Heb. impersonal; Sam. passive.

Notes

xlix 28. This verse could be placed just as readily at the end of the preceding section. The first half is a colophon, to go with the superscription in vs. 1, and it may be due to the compiler of the poem. The rest of the verse, at any rate, appears to stem from *P*, who is clearly the author of vss. 29–33.

about them. So rather than "to them," since the various sayings were primarily about the respective tribes, a term that is used here explicitly.

as he bade them farewell. For this connotation of *brk* see especially xlvii 10, and cf. NOTE on xxvi 31; accordingly, the corresponding noun is here "a parting message" rather than "blessing."

29. *my kin.* Heb. *'am* in the singular stands for "people, tribe," but in the plural the sense is normally that of "kin." In this verse, the term is pointed as singular, but in vs. 33 as plural, although the phrase is the same in both instances. It follows that either the form has been mispointed or the singular could also have the sense of "kin."

l 1. *flung himself upon.* Cf. xiv 10. Verses 1–11, 14 stem from *J*.

3. *forty days.* According to Diodorus Siculus I 91, the embalming proc-

ess lasted more than thirty days, while Herodotus speaks of as many as seventy (Dr.); Diodorus also states (I 72) that the Egyptians mourned their kings seventy-two days. Cf. also Vergote, pp. 197 ff.

4. *that wailing period.* Literally "his days of wailing."

5. *put me under oath.* Not "made me swear," for what follows is not the wording of the oath taken by Joseph but the content of the promise that Jacob exacted from his son. The Heb. stem in question can carry either of these meanings.

I made ready. For the pertinent verb, see Note on xxvi 18.

7. *senior members . . . dignitaries.* Heb. "elders" in both instances.

9. *train.* Literally "camp"; cf. xxxiii 8.

10. *Goren-ha-Atad.* A place name based evidently on some locally prominent threshing center. The customary translation "threshing floor of Atad" is not a suitable topographic designation. Analogously, Akk. *magrattu* (from **ma-gran-tu*), perhaps a cognate of Heb. *goren,* denotes in the Nuzi texts both private and communal threshing areas.

seven-day. The normal wailing period among the Hebrews; cf. I Sam xxxi 13.

11. *the place was named.* Literally "its name was called," the pronominal suffix (feminine) presupposing "the city's."

Abel-mizraim. This aetiology rests on the popular equation of *ʾēbel* "mourning" with *ʾābēl,* probably "watercourse, conduit"; cf. BASOR 89 (1943), 15, n. 44.

15–26. This account comes from E.

16. *they sent Joseph a message.* Literally "they ordered for Joseph," apparently elliptical for "they ordered someone to inform Joseph"; but LXX reads "they drew near to Joseph," suggesting an error in MT in anticipation of the same verb ("left instructions") in 16b.

17. *at this word from them.* Literally "as they spoke to him"; the brothers, however, have not as yet appeared in person.

19. *How could I act for God.* Same phrase as in xxx 2 (also E).

20. *you meant . . . God meant.* Cf. the proverbial "man proposes, God disposes."

21. *speaking to them with affection.* For the same Heb. idiom cf. xxxiv 3.

22. *110 years.* The Egyptians viewed this span as the ideal lifetime for a man; cf. Vergote, pp. 200 f.

23. *on Joseph's knees.* That is, in time for Joseph to accept them formally into his family; cf. xxx 3.

25. *put . . . under oath.* Cf. vs 5.

the sons of Israel. As previously noted (xxxvii 3), this phrase is not exclusive with J.

COMMENT

The Book of Genesis carries its account down to the end of the story of the patriarchs. This major milestone is now before us, and all three of our principal sources are on hand to witness it. As was to be expected, however, each author writes finis in his own characteristic fashion. Yet, while the differences of *J, E,* and *P* from one another are thus plainly in evidence, the three concluding passages have this feature in common: the stay in Egypt is but a passing phase, a sojourn; the focal point continues to be the Promised Land. Hence the physical remains of the main characters in the cast must not be left in alien soil; they are to be taken back to Canaan.

The verse that now constitutes xlix 28 is at once a colophon to the preceding section, the Testament of Jacob, and a transition to the epilogue of the book as a whole. It is probable that this verse has been pieced together from two different sources; in any event, vs. 28b comes from *P,* as do also 29–33 and l 12–13. *P* foreshadows the eventual shift back to Canaan no less than *J* or *E*. But *P*'s main concern remains formal and impersonal. Abraham's purchase of the cave of Machpelah (xxiii) gave Abraham a legally valid foothold in that land. And so it is there that Abraham's grandson must be buried, in conformance with patriarchal precedent.

J (vss. 1–11, 14) also ends the story of the forefathers with the death and interment of Jacob—who is again referred to as Israel (vs. 2). But it is the personal aspect of the story that this source emphasizes, here as elsewhere. Joseph is deeply moved by his father's death. Israel is embalmed, in accordance with the practices of the host country. The period of mourning that follows corresponds in round figures to the seventy-two days that were reserved for the pharaohs themselves (von Rad). Pharaoh is then petitioned to let Joseph accompany the funeral party to Canaan. The request is made through intermediaries, perhaps because of local taboos calculated to shield the Egyptian god-king from direct contact with persons who had been exposed to a corpse. After another period of solemn commemoration prior to the burial, Joseph and his people return to Egypt. This detail serves as a reminder that, although Jacob is gone, the Egyptian phase has barely begun for his descendants. But in the background there is always the main course of history, with all its twists and turns—and with occasional glimpses of an ultimate purpose.

E (vss. 15–26), for his part, brings his story down to the death of Joseph. Even in this brief passage, the author manages to assert himself again as a moralist. Joseph's brothers have never been able to rid themselves of the sense of guilt incurred when Joseph was still a boy. Now that the moderating influence of their father has been removed, the specter of reprisals comes up to plague them afresh. They fling themselves at Joseph's feet, as if to validate the dream recorded in xxxvii 7. In the end, Joseph succeeds in allaying their fears. It may be noted in passing that the problem of the brothers' guilt was no longer an issue with *J*. For him the matter had been resolved a long time ago, when his brothers met their severest test (xliv), which established them as morally regenerated.

Joseph's thoughts, too, turn in his dying moments to the Promised Land, as did Jacob's. Those at his bedside swear to see to it that his remains shall be removed to Canaan; and it is actually recorded that this promise was carried out in due time (Exod xiii 19). For the time being, however, the Sojourn is still unaccomplished, and it is to be followed by the extreme crisis of the Oppression. Significantly enough, the last Hebrew word in the book reads "in Egypt."

The interval between the death of Joseph and the emergence of Moses represents a dark age in two ways: (1) the Israelites in Egypt fell upon evil days; and (2) the available record is limited to a few meager references at the beginning of the Book of Exodus. Nevertheless, circumstantial evidence indicates that the quest which began with the patriarchs was never completely abandoned. It required, however, the challenge of the Oppression and the inspired leadership of Moses to reactivate that drive and give it new impetus and direction. The Genesis phase had served its purpose. In time, biblical history will enter upon its next stage, the Hebrew term for which (stem *yṣ'*) denotes not only physical departure but also spiritual liberation. It is in this dual sense that "Exodus" has to be evaluated.

KEY TO THE TEXT